AI-Driven Threat Intelligence Frameworks: Revolutionizing Enterprise Cybersecurity

Edited by

Pundru Chandra Shaker Reddy
Department of Computer Science and Engineering
Amity School of Engineering and Technology
Amity University, Noida
Uttar Pradesh, India

Yadala Sucharitha
Department of Computer Science and Engineering
Sharda School of Engineering and Technology
Sharda University, Greater Noida
Uttar Pradesh, India

&

Thillaiarasu N
School of Computing and Information Technology
REVA University, Bangalore
Karnataka, India

AI-Driven Threat Intelligence Frameworks: Revolutionizing Enterprise Cybersecurity

Editors: Pundru Chandra Shaker Reddy, Yadala Sucharitha & Thillaiarasu N

ISBN (Online): 979-8-89881-384-0

ISBN (Print): 979-8-89881-385-7

ISBN (Paperback): 979-8-89881-386-4

First published in 2026.

Bentham Science Publishers Pte. Ltd.
No. 9 Raffles Place
Office No. 26-01
Singapore 048619
Singapore
Email: subscriptions@benthamscience.net

BENTHAM SCIENCE

CONTENTS

FOREWORD

In today's hyperconnected digital era, the landscape of cybersecurity is evolving at an unprecedented pace. The exponential growth of data, the increasing sophistication of cyber threats, and the dynamic nature of enterprise IT infrastructures demand innovative and intelligent defense mechanisms. Amidst this rapid transformation, artificial intelligence (AI) has emerged as a pivotal force, capable of redefining how organizations perceive, predict, and prevent security breaches.

AI-DRIVEN THREAT INTELLIGENCE FRAMEWORKS:

Revolutionizing Enterprise Cybersecurity comes at a critical time when traditional cybersecurity approaches are proving insufficient against agile and adaptive threat actors. This timely volume presents a comprehensive exploration of AI-integrated threat intelligence systems, offering deep insights into how machine learning, natural language processing, and automated reasoning are being harnessed to fortify enterprise defenses.

The contributors to this book□?"comprising eminent researchers, cybersecurity experts, and industry practitioners□?"bring together theoretical foundations, cutting-edge frameworks, and practical applications that illuminate the transformative potential of AI in cybersecurity. From detecting zero-day attacks to automating incident response and enabling proactive threat hunting, the chapters collectively underscore the significance of intelligent systems in securing digital ecosystems.

What sets this book apart is not only its technical depth but also its forward-looking vision. It anticipates the challenges and opportunities that lie ahead, providing readers with both conceptual clarity and actionable strategies. Whether you are a cybersecurity professional, academician, student, or enterprise leader, this book offers invaluable knowledge that can empower your understanding and application of AI in protecting critical digital assets.

As we move toward an increasingly digital future, embracing AI-driven cybersecurity frameworks is not merely an option??"it is an imperative. I commend the editors and authors for their meticulous effort in compiling this insightful volume, which will undoubtedly serve as a cornerstone reference for years to come.

Dr. Vivekanand A
Department of Computer Science and Engineering
CMR College of Engineering and Technology
Hyderabad, India

PREFACE

The digital transformation of the modern enterprise landscape has ushered in an era of boundless opportunities-yet it also brings with it unprecedented challenges in cybersecurity. As organizations increasingly depend on interconnected systems, cloud platforms, and mobile infrastructures, the sophistication, scale, and frequency of cyber threats have risen alarmingly. In this context, the role of Artificial Intelligence (AI) has shifted from a futuristic concept to an indispensable asset in proactive threat detection and response.

This edited volume, ***AI-Driven Threat Intelligence Frameworks: Revolutionizing Enterprise Cybersecurity***, serves as a timely and comprehensive resource that explores how AI technologies are redefining threat intelligence and transforming cybersecurity operations across sectors. It brings together leading scholars, researchers, and practitioners who provide insights into the convergence of AI and cybersecurity, while also addressing the operational, ethical, and strategic considerations in deploying AI-driven frameworks.

The book is structured into twelve thought-provoking chapters, each contributing to a broader understanding of the evolving cybersecurity landscape:

- **Chapter 1** lays the foundation by discussing the broad spectrum of cybersecurity applications, current challenges, and forward-looking directions in the digital age.
- **Chapter 2** introduces fundamental AI concepts, tracing their historical evolution and relevance to modern applications.
- **Chapter 3** bridges the domains of AI and cybersecurity, highlighting synergies, overlaps, and practical implementations.
- **Chapter 4** presents an interdisciplinary perspective on how English language proficiency plays a role in AI-driven cybersecurity settings.
- **Chapter 5** delves into the dynamics of social networks, exploring how AI can be used for cyber threat intelligence and trend prediction, especially in platforms like X.
- **Chapter 6** offers a practical guide to Security Operations Centres (SOC), emphasizing their transformation in the AI era.
- **Chapter 7** focuses on endpoint security, showing the shift from traditional reactive approaches to intelligent, AI-enabled proactive strategies.
- **Chapter 8** explores sentiment analysis in cybersecurity contexts, including applications, datasets, challenges, and future outlooks.
- **Chapter 9** examines the convergence of AI and blockchain, investigating integration feasibility, research gaps, and emerging applications.
- **Chapter 10** introduces a novel framework for managing cybersecurity in Socially Responsible Investment (SRI) funds, balancing ethical compliance with threat mitigation.
- **Chapter 11** investigates security in smart cities, analyzing use cases, technological advancements, challenges, and evolving trends.
- **Chapter 12** concludes with a visionary chapter on the next generation of AI in cybersecurity, addressing upcoming trends and future research directions.

Together, these chapters offer a multidimensional perspective on AI-driven threat intelligence from foundational knowledge to advanced frameworks and practical use cases. The book aims to serve not only as a scholarly reference but also as a practical guide for professionals, decision-makers, and students navigating the complexities of modern cybersecurity ecosystems.

We extend our sincere gratitude to all the contributing authors and reviewers whose expertise and commitment have enriched this volume. We also acknowledge the support from Bentham Science, whose platform continues to foster meaningful contributions to emerging areas of science and technology.

We hope this book will inspire future research, encourage cross-disciplinary collaboration, and support enterprises in building resilient and intelligent cybersecurity strategies.

Dr. Pundru Chandra Shaker Reddy
Department of Computer Science and Engineering
Amity School of Engineering and Technology
Amity University, Noida
Uttar Pradesh, India

Dr. Yadala Sucharitha
Department of Computer Science and Engineering
Sharda School of Engineering and Technology
Sharda University, Greater Noida
Uttar Pradesh, India

Dr. Thillaiarasu N
School of Computing and Information Technology
REVA University, Bangalore
Karnataka, India

List of Contributors

Amdewar Godavari	Department of CSE (Networks), Kakatiya Institute of Technology and Science, Warangal, India
Ambati Suvarna	School of Business, SR University, Warangal, India
C Dastagiraiah	Department of CSE, Anurag University, Hyderabad, India
C Santhosh Kumar	Department of Electronics and Communication Engineering, Mailam Engineering College, Mailam, India
Diivyaam Shah	Department of Biochemistry and Forensic Science, Gujarat University, Ahmedabad, India
D Chitra	Department of MBA, Panimalar Engineering College, Chennai, India
Gousiya Begum	Department of CSE, Mahatma Gandhi Institute of Technology, Hyderabad, India
Goddumarri Suryanarayana	Symbiosis Institute of Technology, Hyderabad Campus, Symbiosis International University, Hyderabad, India
Kisara Rishitha	Department of CSE, BVRIT HYDERABAD College of Engineering for Women, Hyderabad, India
Kiran Dodiya	Department of Biochemistry and Forensic Science, Gujarat University, Ahmedabad, India
Kapil Kumar	Department of Biochemistry and Forensic Science, Gujarat University, Ahmedabad, India
Karibasappa Chatrapathi	School of Computing & Information Technology, REVA University, Bangalore, India
Kafila	School of Business, SR University, Warangal, India
K Venkatesh	Department of Engineering in Internetworking, Dalhousie University, Halifax, Canada
K Chatrapathy	School of Computing & Information Technology, REVA University Bangalore, Karnataka, India
LNC Prakash Koratamaddi	Department of Computer Science & Engineering-Data Science, CVR College of Engineering, Hyderabad, India
Lakshmi Hassan Nagaraja	Department of CSE (AI&ML), CVR College of Engineering, Hyderabad, India
Mudarakola Lakshmi Prasad	Computer Science and Engineering, Institute of Aeronautical Engineering, Dundigal, India
M Indrasenareddy	Computer Science and Engineering, BVRIT HYDERABAD College, of Engineering for Women, Hyderabad, India
M Lakshmi Prasad	Computer Science and Engineering, Institute of Aeronautical Engineering, Hyderabad, India
Medikonda Asha Kiran	Department of Information Technology, School of Engineering, Anurag University, Hyderabad, India

Manyam Thaile	Department of Information Technology, School of Engineering, Anurag University, Hyderabad, India
N Gurusamy	Department of Computer Science and Engineering, Dhanalakshmi Srinivasan University, Tamil Nadu, India
N Shanmugapriya	Department of Information Technology, St. Joseph's College of Engineering, Chennai, India
Nikita Gaur	School of Computer Science & AI, SR University, Warangal 506371, India
Niteesha Sharma	Department of Information Technology, School of Engineering, Anurag University, Hyderabad, India
Pundru Chandra Shaker Reddy	Amity School of Engineering and Technology Department of Computer Science and Engineering, Amity University, Noida, India
P Esaiarasi	Department of AI and DS, Sri Shanmugha College of Engineering and Technology, Sangakiri Salem, India
Peddada Nagamani	Department of Information Technology, School of Engineering, Anurag University, Hyderabad, India
Rafath Samrin	Department of Computer Science, College of Computer Science, King Khalid University, Asir-Abha, Saudi Arabia
Ranjit Kumar Elamadurthi	Department of English, Vardhaman College of Engineering, Hyderabad, India
Rayapati Venkata Sudhakar	Department of Computer Science and Engineering, Geethanjali College of Engineering and Technology, Hyderabad, India
Ramesh Babu Pittala	Department of Information Technology, School of Engineering, Anurag University, Hyderabad, India
Sudhanshu Kumar Jha	Department of Electronics and Communication, Faculty of Science, University of Allahabad, Uttar Pradesh, India
Seema Nagaraj	Department of MCA, Bangalore Institute of Technology, Bengaluru, India
Sri Rekha Uppuluri	School of Computer Science & AI, SR University, Warangal, India
Sasanko Sekhar Gantayat	School of Computer Science & AI, SR University, Warangal, India
S Nancy Lima Christy	Department of Computer Science and Engineering, SRM Institute of Science and Technology, Chennai, India
Sridhar Chintala	School of Computer Science & AI, SR University, Warangal 506371, India
Sridhar N Koka	Faculty of Business Administration, Panyapiwat Institute of Management, Pak Kret, Thailand
S Yuvalatha	Department of Computer Science and Business Systems, Bannari Amman Institute of Technology, Erode, India
Thinagaran Perumal	Department of Computer Science, University Putra Malaysia, Serdang, Malaysia
Vijay Bhanudas Gujar	Department of Computer Science and Engineering, Arvind Gavali College of Engineering, Satara, India

Vidyullatha Sukhavasi	Department of CSE, BVRIT HYDERABAD College of Engineering for Women, Hyderabad, India
Yadala Sucharitha	Sharda School of Computing Science and Engineering , Department of CSE, Sharda University, Greater Noida, India

CHAPTER 1

Cybersecurity in the Digital Age: Applications, Opportunities, Challenges, and Future Directions

Amdewar Godavari[1,*], **Gousiya Begum**[2], **Rafath Samrin**[3], **Vijay Bhanudas Gujar**[4], **C Dastagiraiah**[5] and **Sudhanshu Kumar Jha**[6]

[1] *Department of CSE (Networks), Kakatiya Institute of Technology and Science, Warangal, Telangana, India*

[2] *Department of CSE, Mahatma Gandhi Institute of Technology, Hyderabad, Telangana, India*

[3] *Department of Computer Science, College of Computer Science, King Khalid University, Asir-Abha, Saudi Arabia*

[4] *Department of Computer Science and Engineering, Arvind Gavali College of Engineering, Satara, Maharashtra, India*

[5] *Department of CSE, Anurag University, Hyderabad, Telangana, India*

[6] *Department of Electronics and Communication, Faculty of Science, University of Allahabad, Uttar Pradesh, India*

Abstract: Protecting people, businesses, and governments from the plethora of cyber dangers has made cybersecurity a top priority in today's highly linked digital world. In this research paper, we take a close look at cybersecurity in the modern day, analyzing potential risks and discussing ways to mitigate them. In this chapter, we'll take a look at cybersecurity from a high level, covering topics such as its significance, typical vulnerabilities and attacks, successful prevention techniques, and upcoming trends. Everything from private customer information to mission-critical company assets is abundant in today's digital age. With the proliferation of both data and connections, cybersecurity is now more important than ever. Data theft and loss, as well as the availability and integrity of digital systems, can be prevented with effective cybersecurity solutions. Legal responsibilities and regulatory fines may amplify the effects of cyberattacks, which already cause substantial financial losses, harm to reputations, and interruptions to operations. Standard cyber risks and Internet of Things security holes. We performed a comprehensive review to find out what the newest cybersecurity trends, problems, and opportunities are so we can stay ahead of the game. We also talk about where cybersecurity is going in the future, outlining potential tactics for dealing with the ever-changing landscape of cyber threats, new trends, and technological advancements like ML and AI for automated threat detection and response.

* **Corresponding Author Amdewar Godavari**: Department of CSE (Networks), Kakatiya Institute of Technology and Science, Warangal, Telangana, India; E-mail: godavariamdewar@gmail.com

Pundru Chandra Shaker Reddy, Yadala Sucharitha, & Thillaiarasu N (Eds.)

Keywords: Artificial intelligence, Cyber resilience, Cyber threats, Cyber-attacks, Cybersecurity, Defense strategies, Digital transformation, Machine learning.

INTRODUCTION

Cyberspace is expanding at a dizzying rate right now. There has been a growing consensus among academics that it is crucial to teach the next generation about cybersecurity principles in light of the ever-changing nature and prevalence of cyber threats. Negligence in cybersecurity and a lack of client knowledge lead to cybercrimes [1]. Recent studies have shown that the United States is the first country to implement threat intelligence frameworks. Nearly 70 countries have included cyber/information security strategies and major legislative measures in their military and national security plans to deal with this problem. Preparation for vulnerabilities, as outlined in the cyber network guide, involves exchanging information about potential dangers in a timely manner; this can help safeguard the environment, businesses, and infrastructure, as well as provide insight into current events. Recent research has used a broad definition of cybersecurity (ISO, 2018) [2]. In their draft, the International Telecommunications Union (ITU) also defines cybersecurity (ITU-T X.1205). Thus, cybersecurity, in its broadest sense, aids in risk management by preventing cyber assaults and data breaches [3].

More complex, targeted, and deadly cybercrimes and hostile actions have emerged in modern times, thanks to scientific progress. A ransomware attack was causing damage to the Atlanta City government and other previous cyber intrusions; this was discovered earlier in 2018. There is now an abundance of private data due to the way the digital revolution has altered our daily lives and the way we do business. Data types include sensitive personal information (such as SSNs and bank account details) and vital company information (such as proprietary systems and intellectual property) [4]. Cybersecurity has risen to the forefront of everyone's agenda due to the increased likelihood of cyber threats caused by the widespread use of digital technologies. Ensuring the availability and integrity of digital systems is an integral part of cybersecurity, which goes beyond simply preventing data theft or loss. The repercussions of a successful cyber assault can be devastating, including not only financial loss but also harm to one's reputation and the interruption of operations. Significant legal liabilities and regulatory fines can result from data breaches for corporations [5]. Both the stakes and the environment are dynamic and ever-changing. The sophistication of cyber-attacks is on the rise, as are the methods used by attackers to circumvent security measures. This means that cybersecurity is an ever-evolving discipline. This article explores the fundamentals of cybersecurity, including why it's important, what kinds of dangers are most prevalent, how to stay safe online, and what trends will shape digital security in the future [6].

Importance of Cybersecurity

Cyberattacks are becoming more common and more damaging, highlighting the need for better cybersecurity. Data privacy, operational continuity, and the protection of sensitive information all depend on robust cybersecurity measures. Having insufficient cybersecurity measures in place might have serious repercussions in this day and age of frequent data breaches and ransomware attacks. Not only can these breaches cause immediate damage, but they can also have long-term consequences, including lost business, legal expenditures, and regulatory fines, which can add up to a catastrophic financial impact [7].

For instance, consumer trust can be severely damaged by data breaches. Identity fraud, financial fraud, and other major consequences can result from the exposure of personal information. Businesses risk serious harm to their reputations when consumers lose faith in their data security measures after a data breach. Reduced consumer loyalty, lost business, and a weakened competitive edge are all possible outcomes of this trust erosion [8]. The increasing sophistication of phishing schemes—which employ misleading emails or websites to coerce consumers into divulging personal information—further emphasizes the importance of robust cybersecurity protocols. Significant financial losses and data breaches can arise because of phishing attempts, which take advantage of human vulnerabilities [9].

The expansion of the Internet of Things (IoT) and linked gadgets has also brought about new security holes. An attacker could potentially gain access to your system through any of your linked devices. If we care about keeping sensitive information safe and avoiding illegal access, we must make sure these devices and the networks they connect to are secure. With more and more of our daily lives taking place online, cybersecurity has become an essential part of contemporary existence [10]. To be effective, cybersecurity must focus on both the prevention of assaults and the development of resilient systems capable of withstanding and recovering from such attacks. Cybersecurity must be a top priority for all organizations and individuals who value their digital assets, privacy, and the security of their operations. Cybersecurity protects IoT devices by preventing unauthorized access, data breaches, and attacks that exploit device vulnerabilities. It ensures secure communication, device authentication, and data integrity, thereby maintaining the reliability and privacy of interconnected IoT systems.

AI-enabled Security Models

AI-enabled security models leverage artificial intelligence techniques such as machine learning, deep learning, and anomaly detection to enhance cybersecurity by identifying, predicting, and mitigating threats in real time. These models can analyze vast amounts of network data, detect unusual patterns, and adapt to emerging attack vectors more effectively than traditional rule-based systems. By continuously learning from new threats and behaviors, AI-driven security systems improve intrusion detection, fraud prevention, and malware analysis, thereby strengthening overall digital resilience across various sectors.

Enabling the Evolutionary Approach in Cybersecurity

An essential part of the evolutionary strategy for cybersecurity is adopting a mentality of capability growth and preventative protection measures [11]. This necessitates shifting from static security measures to more adaptive protection strategies in the face of cyber attacks [12]. A methodological strategy based on an evolutionary model can be employed to ward off cyber assaults. This model shows how cyber-physical systems in contemporary society can adapt to new threats by learning from previous security breaches. Consequently, firms can strengthen their defenses against cyber attacks by adopting an evolutionary approach to cybersecurity, which enables them to continuously adapt to new threats [13]. The capacity to foresee danger, plan reactions to attacks, and quickly restore operations after events is all part of these endeavors.

With this in mind, the evolutionary method serves to both mitigate and respond to cyber threats. The evolving strategy also facilitates cross-stakeholder and partner collaboration in the fight against cybercrime. Sharing knowledge on current cybersecurity dangers, effective techniques to address them, and new advancements in the sector is an important part of this. Organizations can better detect, assess, and resolve risks when they collaborate [14]. When it comes to cybersecurity, the evolutionary method offers a complete and adaptable framework that may help enterprises tackle the problems of the digital age. To better withstand cyber assaults and future threats, companies should adopt a mentality of capability growth and implement preventative protection measures [15]. Fig. (**1**) depicts our cybersecurity strategy for the modern digital age, which is based on the resilience paradigm. There are multiple stages to this method:

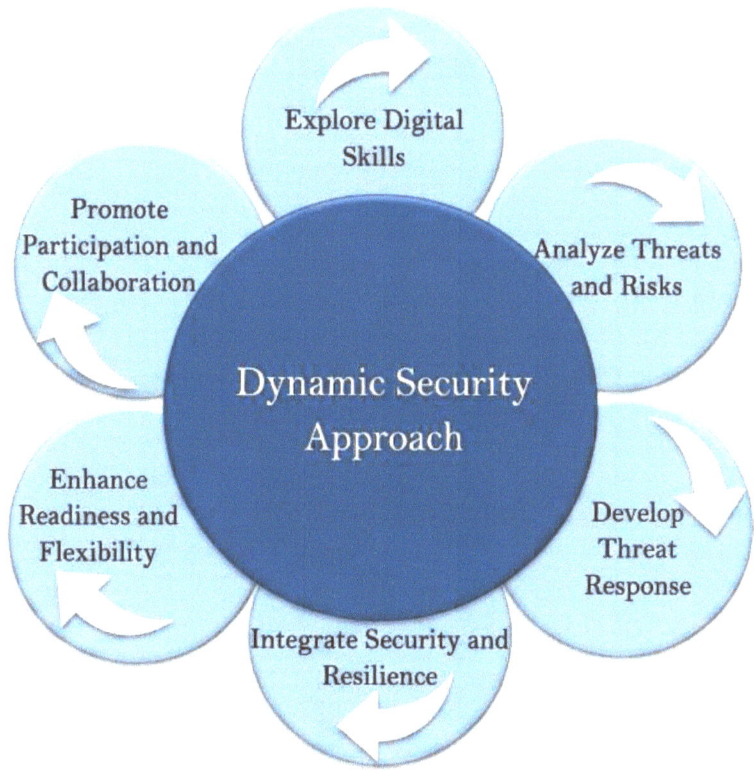

Fig. (1). Dynamic security approach.

1. Explore Digital Skills

First things first: figure out what kind of digital abilities are necessary to deal with cybersecurity risks. Collect data regarding technical skills, open procedures, and linked human elements to set up strong cybersecurity.

2. Evaluate Potential Dangers and Dangers

Evaluate potential dangers and risks in the cyber environment, such as malware, phishing, distributed denial of service attacks, and other complex threats. Analyze the dangers that these threats pose and how they could affect the organization's data security and operations.

3. Devise a Strategy for Responding to Threats.

This strategy should cover prevention, identification, and action. Plan ways to restore systems from incidents and counterattacks quickly and efficiently.

4. Build in Security and Resilience

Bring cybersecurity and resilience principles into your company's overall plan. To achieve attack resilience and adaptation, build a framework that integrates technology, processes, and human factors.

5. Strengthen Readiness and Flexibility

Make yourself more resilient to cyberattacks by strengthening your readiness and flexibility. Create and implement tried-and-true incident response plans; can quickly restore systems and data. Adjust to novel dangers by learning from past assaults.

6. Get Everyone Involved

Motivate everyone in the cybersecurity ecosystem to get involved and work together. In order to encourage organizations such as vendors, business partners, end-users, and others to take part in resilience and security projects, offer both monetary and non-monetary incentives.

An all-encompassing view of cybersecurity—one in which procedures, human factors, and technology all work together to build resilience against threats—forms the basis of this approach [16]. Organisations can improve their capacity to deal with changing cybersecurity risks by encouraging cooperation and concentrating on resilience and security integration. Ability monitoring and threat intelligence are essential components that enable evolving techniques. Having dependable technologies in place to continuously monitor system logs, network activities, and user behavior is essential for organizations [17]. Organizations can gain insight into emerging dangers, weak spots, and attack patterns through data collection and analysis. With this information in hand, proactive decision-making and adaptable defenses can be put into place [18].

While these activities have become easier to carry out because of advancements in information and communiqué knowledge, the necessity for rapid access to information has introduced significant security concerns that must be addressed by all parties involved, ranging from individuals to governments [19]. Threats to individuals, societies, and organizations from security breaches are becoming more common as a result of technological advancements. Individuals, groups, and communities frequently use cybersecurity measures, legislative frameworks, and awareness and education efforts to encourage ethical behavior and discourage evil intent in order to lessen the impact of these security threats. Cybersecurity refers to the practice of keeping information systems that belong to one company or are linked to another's network secure in terms of their secrecy, availability, and integrity [20]. As a result, ensuring secure inter-industry and societal contacts through cybersecurity has become the top method for preventing cybercrime and cyberattacks.

One of the most pressing global security concerns is the need to make the internet a safer place and to safeguard internet users [21]. A safe online environment has far-reaching consequences for people, companies, and countries to strengthen cyber defenses [22] as the digital landscape grows and permeates nearly every part of our lives. When creating new services, technology, or government policies, internet security is now a must. An all-encompassing and risk-free strategy is necessary to combat cybercrime. This suggests that technological safeguards are not sufficient to prevent cybercrime. Successful investigation and prosecution of cybercrime by law enforcement agencies is of the utmost importance [23]. As a precaution against data breaches, several nations have enacted stringent cybersecurity legislation, including Ethiopia.

The modern digital world is extremely dependent on technology for the upkeep of social and economic stability and security, making cybersecurity an essential component of this world. The healthcare and energy sectors, which rely on critical infrastructure, are particularly vulnerable to cyberattacks, which can cause enormous damage to their reputations and bottom lines as well as human casualties [24]. Businesses large and small, as well as government and military organizations, healthcare providers, schools, energy providers, and transportation networks all rely on cybersecurity to safeguard sensitive information, prevent unauthorized access, and secure critical infrastructures.

Machine learning and AI have several potential applications in the areas of threat detection, network vulnerability discovery, and IT workload reduction [25]. Also, many cybersecurity-related operations, including intrusion detection, malware analysis, and vulnerability assessment, can be automated with the use of ML and AI. Security personnel can then be free to concentrate on longer-term, more strategic projects. ML and AI are becoming increasingly important cybersecurity technologies for organizations as they face increasingly complex cyber threats. We look into how ML and AI are changing cyber defenses and the massive impact they are having on cybersecurity [26]. Nevertheless, there are assaults that target ML. In this chapter, we go over some of the problems with cybersecurity and where the field is headed in terms of research, touching on topics like AI, &ML, and other cutting-edge methods.

RELATED WORK

A Research [20] examines the pros and cons of employing AI in cybersecurity and gives a thorough review of the field's emerging use of the technology. Using examples such as anomaly detection, IDS, and malware analysis, the researcher delves into the field of AI and its applications in cybersecurity, exploring its potential to tackle cybersecurity difficulties. Next, it delves into the pros and cons of utilizing AI in cybersecurity, touching on topics including the importance of large data, the dangers posed by AI-powered attackers, and the necessity of human supervision [27]. Finally, the study delves into the potential applications of AI in cybersecurity and its future role in enhancing the field.

In a study [28], investigators discussed the growing complexity and volume of data, the scarcity of trained specialists, and the escalating costs of healthcare as part of a thorough review of artificial intelligence's role in cyber defense. The researcher delves into the possibilities of AI to tackle these cybersecurity issues in healthcare and explores ways to incorporate AI into Smart health and cyber defense. Implementing security measures and teaching personnel about cybersecurity threats and remedies are two of the potential options highlighted by the researcher. The goal of another study [29] was to find ways to use deep learning techniques to identify potential cyber hazards in IoT devices.

Cybersecurity authors highlight AI's usefulness in detecting, preventing, and mitigating cyber-attacks [30]. Using AI for malware detection, NIDS, vulnerability scanning, risk assessment, and security automation, the researcher outlines the current state-of-the-art, potential future directions, and responsibilities of AI in cyber threat mitigation. Utilizing AI in cybersecurity to automate processes, enhance decision-making, and detect threats more efficiently than traditional approaches is the focus of this paper, which is based on complete research [31]. The researcher suggests using a deep neural network (DNN) to learn the differences between legitimate and malicious apps on IoT devices after becoming dissatisfied with standard malware detection methods that have become ineffective due to the exponential proliferation of malware. When compared to more conventional signature-based approaches, the researcher found that the suggested model improved the accuracy of malware detection in IoT devices. Nevertheless, the author fails to address the issue of evasion techniques, which not only make malware harder to detect using traditional signature-based methods but also make the proposed DRNN models ineffective. It is necessary to test these approaches on various IoT devices [32].

The authors of a study present a new approach to evaluating the robustness of cyber-physical systems using bespoke criteria [33]. The researcher suggests a method that utilizes Systems-theoretic Process Analysis (STPA), a tool for top-down hazard analysis, and customized matrices to guarantee a more thorough inquiry into safety and security. By combining STPA with custom measurements, the researcher hopes to address STPA's shortcomings. Using STPA, one can identify potentially harmful control scenarios that could lead to unforeseen losses. Next, the custom matrices are used to check if these circumstances could be used by bad actors. The study's author explains how medical IoT might benefit from blockchain and AI to make it more secure online [34]. According to the authors, blockchain technology can provide a secure and unhackable way to store and share medical data, and Artificial Intelligence (AI) can detect and prevent cyberattacks by recognizing trends.

For the purpose of detecting abnormalities in IIoT data, the authors of a study [35] suggest an ensemble deep learning model that learns long-term data correlations; the AE model is employed to reduce data dimensionality and emphasize important features. Using two real-world industry IoT datasets, the researcher tests the model. A gas pipeline dataset and a water treatment dataset were both created by the same person. On the gas pipeline dataset, the model attained a precision of 99.3%, while on the water treatment dataset, it reached a precision of 99.7%. The usage of blockchain technology to safeguard electronic health records stored in the cloud was the subject of a study [36]. A distributed ledger that cannot be altered in any way is known as the blockchain. It follows that no one can add, edit, or delete an EHR from the blockchain without the consent of every other node in the network. To connect the blockchain to the EHR system, a smart contract is utilized. The blockchain stores smart contracts, which are contracts that can execute themselves. Electronic health records (EHRs) can have their access restricted and shared only with authorized individuals with the help of a smart contract.

Recent Developments and Emerging Trends in Cybersecurity

New algorithms, processes, and frameworks have contributed to numerous advancements in cybersecurity in recent times. Implicit mathematical equations, worked-out examples, flow diagrams, sophisticated attacks, weaknesses, and the many upgrades to established standards over the years are all covered in detail in this section.

The world is entering a new era of asymmetric security measures, which have the potential to alleviate current security issues. Polynomials are used to solve issues instead of the preset matrix attributes. Two cryptosystems that Marcin presented using the Chebyshev theorem demonstrate reduced space and temporal complexity [37]. Still, there are obstacles in the areas of performance analysis and security that need to be addressed. However, there are certain problems with this design that allow the criminal to find the private key directly from the public key; this was one of the concerns raised by Gomez's system, which was based on multivariate cryptography and used the idea of concealed irreducible polynomials.

Using data sets of varying sizes, a tweaked version of RSA (the public-key encryption technique) compares the two in terms of security and computational complexity. In order to make the system more stable, the author states that the algorithm operates with three prime numbers and two additional constraints [38]. The algorithm's efficiency improves as the security levels and key generation speed are increased. However, results show that RSA is still superior when considering total execution time and the speed of text encryption and decryption. An all-but-many encryption system is a public-key encryption method that uses a binary string of suitable length [39]. Based on this subject, the sender disclosed the secret key, which starts a forged cipher text, in order to decipher the message with stable haphazardness. Nobody can tell a false ciphertext from a real one or make one themselves unless they have the private key.

A lot of people in the research community use polynomials to steer security algorithms in new directions. Since these methods necessitate rendering the same secret for numerous given public keys, the author demonstrates that they are susceptible to a number of attacks. A safe combination of symmetric and asymmetric tactics was also one of their designs [40]. An innovative hybrid approach was presented, which combines weak symmetric and asymmetric strategies into a robust asymmetric scheme that is chosen ciphertext secure. Use the session key to decipher the message as quickly as possible while making the most efficient use of available resources by cutting down on the number of rounds and beefing up the security measures [41]. Nevertheless, the expense and difficulty of transmitting encrypted messages to the server grow. Additionally, security could be at risk if the third party is untrustworthy.

A state-of-the-art method of mutual authentication utilizing biometrics (key agreement). This method employs a small-key version of Elliptical Curve Cryptography, which is a public-key cryptography tool. The plan relies on the fact that each session key is guaranteed to be encapsulated in two randomly generated integers [42]. Even if an adversary manages to get their hands on the server's private key, deducing previous session keys would still require them to solve the seemingly intractable Elliptic Curve Discrete Logarithm Problem (ECDLP), which is no easy feat. We employed Burrows-Abadi-Needham (BAN) reasoning to prove the authenticity. The suggested method is safe and effective, although it might not work in a setting with multiple servers [43].

Despite widespread use, algorithms like RSA and AES are susceptible to a wide range of attacks due to recent developments in computational power. To ensure future communications are fully protected, researchers are actively trying to identify new forms of attack and develop effective countermeasures. We have covered some significant enhancements to new-generation security algorithms in this work. This section also provides an overview of the most essential algorithms covered earlier, along with the threats they can prevent. The advent of quantum computing has opened up a world of possibilities for creating cutting-edge algorithms for cyber defense [44]. Researchers are devoting a great deal of time and energy to uncovering the most promising avenues for developing smart cities. Here, we'll go over some of the benefits of quantum cryptography and the methods and schemes that use it in the modern quantum era.

In a study, the authors shed light on the greatest threat that quantum cryptography poses to the safety of the internet as it is now. The foundation of classical cryptosystems rests on a secret key; its fragility can lead to the system's collapse. Execute cryptographic operations by making use of characteristics of quantum mechanics. Quantum, which they also worked on, may be utilized to securely communicate between parties, compute privately, and share secret communications [45]. The author claims that in order to ensure the security of user-to-user communications over a network, quantum cryptography makes use of quantum mechanics.

One such method is the PKD, which employs a quantum channel for both message and arbitrary bit transmission between clients that do not initially disclose any secret data. The symmetric key in Quantum Key Distribution (QKD) is not derived from mathematical principles but rather from the laws of quantum physics [46]. Two parties communicate using both classical and quantum communication channels, as shown in Fig. (**2**), in the first real QKD protocol. Like the internet, a classical channel uses classical bits, which can be either 0 or 1, to allow the back-and-forth transmission of individual bits of information. A potential eavesdropper might just obtain the bits and transmit the fabricated data to a recipient, rendering privacy irrelevant. However, the quantum channel behaves in a different way. Instead of bits, it changes QUBITS, which stand for quantum bits [47]. A qubit's value can simultaneously be zero or one. The quantity of real-world entities that can serve as quantum bits, such as one electron or photon, is in the field of quantum mechanics.

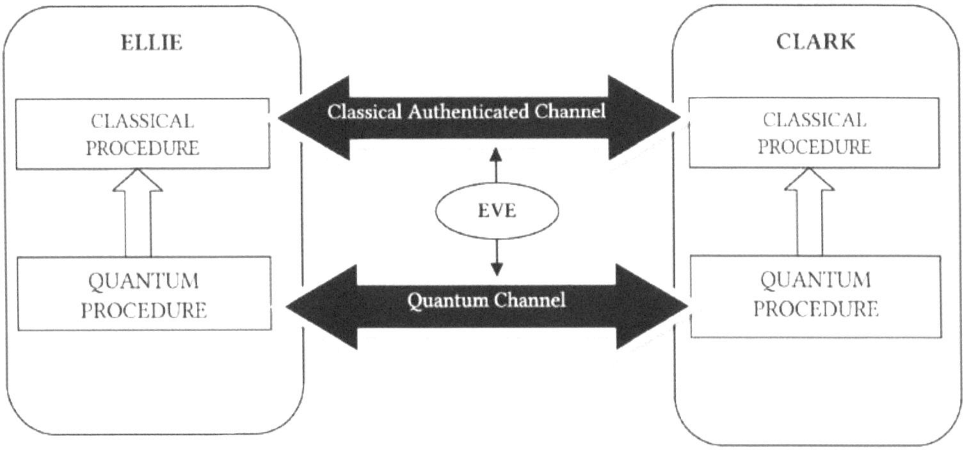

Fig. (2). Quantum communication channels.

Application Area of Cybersecurity

Defense, IDS, and encryption knowledge are all part of cybersecurity, which offers confidentiality, integrity, and reliability services to various areas [48]. It is primarily relevant to the subsequent domains due to the internet's centrality to both business and social interactions.

Cybersecurity in the Smart Grid

Power systems of the future are expected to be more efficient and reliable with the help of renewable energy sources, distributed intelligence, and demand response, thanks to the smart grid, which combines state-of-the-art processing and communication technology. Smart grids provide several advantages, including increased efficiency and dependability, because they optimize power generation, distribution, and consumption through the use of digital technologies [49]. Information interchange in energy infrastructure relies on mission-critical networks, and smart grid technology communication networks are no exception. As far as smart grid cybersecurity is concerned, trust, honesty, and secrecy are paramount [50]. Cybersecurity for smart grids guarantees dependable and timely data access and utilization. Protecting the smart grid system from threats, including advanced persistent threats (APTs), denial-of-service (DoS), and unauthorized access to data, is essential for keeping user data safe, private, and secure. In order to strengthen the online security of the Smart Grid, cybersecurity places an emphasis on the potential negative consequences of cyber-attacks, such as power outages, financial losses, and safety issues [51].

Not only should state-of-the-art authentication and encryption methods be implemented, but also better threat intelligence and sharing, regular security audits and assessments, and stakeholder education on cybersecurity awareness and best practices should be prioritized.

Cybersecurity in Vehicular Transmission

In order to improve road safety, traffic efficiency, and passenger comfort, cybersecurity is essential for vehicle-to-vehicle communication systems and infrastructures. Additionally, cybersecurity is necessary to protect the privacy and personal information of drivers and passengers, including their location, driving behavior, and health. Lastly, cybersecurity is essential for ensuring the continuity and availability of vehicle communication systems, particularly during emergencies when critical communications must take precedence over other forms of transportation [52]. This entails establishing redundancy and failover procedures in addition to doing routine system maintenance and testing. If we want to keep users' and stakeholders' trust in the system and make sure it's secure, private, and reliable, we need cybersecurity in-vehicle communications. So, everyone in the ecosystem—from users to regulators to infrastructure providers—needs to be involved in a comprehensive and proactive strategy.

Cybersecurity in a Smart City

To better serve its residents, a “smart city” integrates cutting-edge technological systems with well-developed communication networks. To protect residents' personal information and vital infrastructure from cyber threats, smart cities must handle the increasing dependence on interconnected systems and gadgets [53]. Cybersecurity applications in smart cities safeguard essential services like water, electricity, transportation, and communications; safeguard linked IoT devices like cameras and sensors; guarantee the privacy of citizens, including any personally identifiable information gathered; and safeguard disaster recovery systems.

Cybersecurity in Smart eHealth Systems

The collection of health-related data from a variety of sources, including medical devices and mobile apps, is essential to healthcare applications built on the IoT, such as remote patient monitoring and smart health. By linking together various medical equipment and the IoT, healthcare providers will be able to better monitor their patients in real time and report on their progress toward preventative measures [54]. More than ten million documents were compromised, including SSNs, medical histories, HIV test results, and personal details of healthcare professionals, as reported by the World Economic Forum. There have been occurrences where over 3M of these medical records from 33 nations were compromised, and the average number of records compromised is 155,000. The actual number of documents compromised could be greater [55]. Ensuring the safety of sensitive patient information, protecting healthcare services from cyber threats, and preventing unauthorized access to patient records all necessitate robust cyber defenses.

SECURITY THREATS AND CHALLENGES

In this part, we'll go over some of the dangers and difficulties that the majority of researchers have encountered. One side of the coin states that "quantum computing" is a new sort of computer device that uses quantum mechanical methods to "enable tremendous parallelism at the physical level" in calculations. In order to speed up classical algorithms, they provided the superposition rule for quantum states.

Security Threats

The WannaCry ransomware assault is another major concern in the field of cybersecurity. In their 2013 article, the authors detail the ransomware attack. New ransomware variant released; it encrypts client files and then requests payment to recover them. They go on to detail the various ransomware attacks and what they do. Another kind of ransomware infection, WannaCry, was the subject of a security warning in May 2017. In an effort to find a solution, numerous writers have investigated WannaCry's ideas, traits, exponential growth, and other metrics [56]. As an alternative to concentrating on the mathematical aspects of cryptography, such as the mapping between plaintext and ciphertext, some algorithms prioritize hardware implementation on interconnected physical devices. As a result of their actuation and inspection, these physical communications may yield data useful for cryptanalysis.

Physical channels require careful analysis since they are particularly vulnerable to attack. Both the data in question and the assaults that make use of it are known as Side-Channel Attacks (SCA). These attacks retrieve sensitive information from devices, such as time details, power usage, and traces of electromagnetic or even audible leakage, by taking advantage of different methodologies and evaluating non-functional activities [57]. Fig. (**3**) shows the attacker gaining or leaking the intermediate information by modeling the cryptographic procedure as a grey box. In this context, "side channels" refer to the system's unintended consequences. The authors of a study [58] revealed the key's abstract details through a leak. Still, it's important to note that there are scenarios where a targeted side-channel assault isn't a real concern.

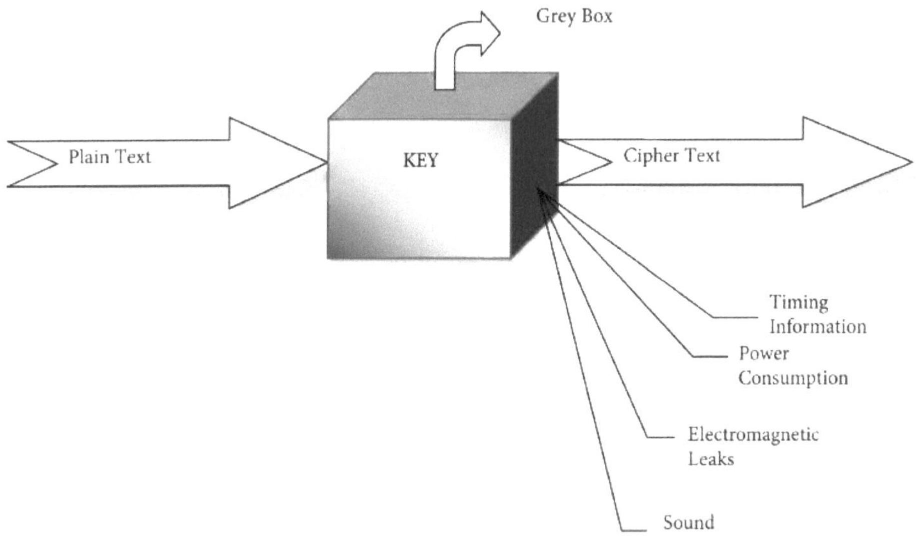

Fig. (3). Side channel attacks.

Challenges of Cybersecurity

Cybersecurity has become a significant issue for governments, businesses, and individuals in this digital age. It is more important than ever to protect electronic devices, networks, and data against unauthorized access, theft, or damage, especially considering the proliferation of digital devices. Keeping a company's data, personnel, and essential assets safe from cybercriminals has become more complicated as technology has progressed [59]. The cybersecurity industry is currently facing a number of problems, and this article will go over some of those problems and the ways forward that could assist in solving them.

Sophisticated Nature of Cyber-attacks

One of the biggest problems with cybersecurity is the complexity of cyber-attacks, which aim to gain illegal access to networks and computer systems [60]. Cybercriminals are masters of developing and implementing complex strategies to breach security and exploit weaknesses.

The diplomatic, IT, military, and chemical industries are among the most vulnerable to Advanced Persistent Threats (APTs), which are defined as "sophisticated, targeted, and organized attacks" [61]. APTs aim to filter confidential information and cause damage to the targeted industry or area by remaining persistent and employing various methods. Google, Adobe, Juniper Networks, and other computer organizations and IT industries were the targets of the "Aurora operation," a sophisticated cyberattack that occurred in 2009 and was one of the APT strikes. The assault was intricate and utilized cutting-edge methods to breach the networks of the targeted technology companies and organizations and steal their intellectual property.

Attacks known as "zero-day exploits" take advantage of security holes in software that have just been found. When hackers sell or exploit security holes before they are patched, organizations become vulnerable [62]. To find and stop zero-day vulnerabilities, you need behavior-based analysis, advanced threat intelligence, and software patches applied quickly. The five-stage life cycle of a zero-day exploit vulnerability attack:

- **Zero-Day Attack**: In the beginning, there are attacks that try to take advantage of security holes that neither the general public nor the software or hardware manufacturer is aware of. The bad guys, sometimes known as "black hat" hackers, usually find these security holes and don't tell anyone about them. Situation: - Specifically, the SCADA systems utilized by Iran's nuclear plants were the targets of the extremely advanced computer worm known as Stuxnet [63]. Centrifuges used for uranium enrichment were physically damaged as they took advantage of several zero-day vulnerabilities to access and control industrial systems.
- **Pseudo-Zero-Day Attacks**: When an exploit is still in the dark, but only a small group of malicious actors has found it, this is called a pseudo-zero-day attack. There has been some leakage about the vulnerability, but it is less of a secret now than it was in the beginning.
- **Potential for Pseudo-Zero-Day Attack**: At this point, a vulnerability may have been discovered, but it hasn't been extensively used. Unusual or unexpected behavior could lead security researchers or companies to suspect a vulnerability.
- **Potential for Zero-Day Attacks**: Disclosure of the vulnerability has taken place at this point. This could occur at any point after the vulnerability becomes known to the impacted party, such as when a security researcher or responsible disclosure mechanism notifies them [64]. Potentially more accessible to attackers might be the appearance of automated attack code or applications designed to exploit the vulnerability.
- **Passive**: The time that passes after a vendor finds, discloses, and patches or mitigates a vulnerability is known as the mitigation phase. Once this window has passed, the vulnerability is no longer considered a zero-day, and businesses must take action to secure their systems by implementing patches or countermeasures [65]. Since zero-day attacks aim for weaknesses that defenders are unaware of, they are essentially undetectable, much like invisible arrows. Proactive security measures, IDS, and a quick reaction to newly found

vulnerabilities are frequently necessary for detecting and protecting against such attacks.

IoT Security

A developing technology known as the IoT links billions of computing devices to the Internet. The IoT allows for the sharing and exchange of data by linking sensors and computing equipment using Internet protocols [66]. There are a lot of major cybersecurity issues with the IoT because of its weaknesses. Exposure of devices compromises the security of IoT devices since they are built with insufficient processing power and memory. Devices are susceptible to cyber-attacks due to insecure default settings, outdated software and firmware, and insufficient security updates.

AI-driven Attack

The exponential expansion of digitalization across all industries and the pervasiveness of new technologies have both contributed to the complexity and difficulty of cybersecurity threats. The use of ML and AI is one of the new trends in cyberattacks. These technologies are considered technological advances [67]. There is a negative aspect to Artificial Intelligence (AI) that is associated with cybersecurity, and that is AI-driven attacks. Artificial intelligence attacks fall into two categories:

Some of the threats posed by AI-driven attacks are: -

In order to deceive or impersonate persons or systems during social engineering attacks, deep fake assaults [68] use artificial intelligence and ML techniques to create realistic images, videos, audio, or text. False information dissemination, extortion, biometric authentication forgery, and other nefarious purposes are all within the realm of possibility when it comes to deep fakes. Cybersecurity systems rely on AI and ML for tasks such as malware detection, spam filtering, face recognition, and other biometric security mechanisms; however, AI-generated media such as images, videos, audio, and texts can be intentionally used to trick these models or systems.

Botnet attacks: Cybercriminals use these networks of networked devices, which are controlled from a central location, to launch various types of assaults against their targets. Botnets are responsible for a wide variety of malicious activities, including distributed denial of service assaults, spamming, data theft, and more. Botnet attacks employ AI and ML to automate and scale up assaults, discover targets, coordinate attacks, and elude detection, all while patching security flaws [69]. The agent is able to gain knowledge from its actions and the rewards it receives from its surroundings through reinforcement learning. As a result, RL machine learning technology aids autonomous AI-enabled cyberattacks, which automate the procedures of exploiting and patching vulnerabilities and adapt, learn, and refine their techniques based on feedback and response from the targeted system.

Cloud Computing

Organizations face new risks and weaknesses when they implement cloud security and rely more and more on cloud services [70]. Businesses that rely on cloud services face a host of cybersecurity issues, including data breaches, unauthorized access, insecure APIs, shared infrastructures that pose security risks, data loss, service disruption that causes critical services to go down, and other similar problems.

OPPORTUNITIES AND FUTURE RESEARCH DIRECTIONS

Academics and innovators face a number of challenges and opportunities in the ever-changing subject of cybersecurity. Cybersecurity companies are looking into a number of possible solutions to their problems, including the use of advanced AI and ML techniques to create defenses against cyber threats, enhance detection of cyber threats, automate security processes, and stop cyberattacks before they happen [71]. Automating the cyber defense mechanism through the use of AI and ML is necessary to strengthen cybersecurity in light of the increasing complexity and sophistication of cyber-attacks. Systems for detecting cyber threats are aided by real-time AI.

There are many different kinds of cyber attacks, and each one poses its own unique set of challenges. In order to create effective cybersecurity measures, it is crucial to understand these risks. To aid cyber professionals in responding to cyber-attacks more efficiently, the expert analyzes massive amounts of data, finds trends in cyber-attacks, identifies dangers and outliers, and automates security measures [72]. In order to protect the specified sectors, biometric authentication is second only to AI and ML in terms of effectiveness. One way to beef up safety is using biometric authentication, which uses a person's distinct biological traits, like fingerprints or face recognition, to verify their identity [73]. When used in conjunction with passwords and other traditional authentication methods, biometric authentication makes it far more difficult for hackers to get access to sensitive information and networks.

In today's interconnected world, safeguarding personal information and preventing unauthorized access is of paramount importance. Hence, it is necessary to enhance and reinforce privacy rules as well as data protection and privacy-preserving procedures. As a result, the study's emphasis should be on privacy-reserving methods that make use of homomorphic encryption and multi-party computation [74]. Also, improving an organization's cyber defenses should be a top priority, and blockchain technology's continued advancement is a key component in this. Several researchers have studied the potential applications of blockchain technology in several cybersecurity domains, including medical [75], supply chain [76], and transactions [77]. Distributed ledger systems and blockchain technology offer a fantastic answer for decentralized systems and security. Security concerns with blockchain technology include its reliance on external systems like oracles, the immutability of transactions, the susceptibility of smart contracts to attacks, and the weakness of consensus protocols like PoS and PoW. Despite blockchain technology's significant role in cybersecurity, there are still obstacles and challenges to overcome.

AI and machine learning enhance cybersecurity by automatically detecting threats, identifying anomalies, and predicting potential attacks through pattern analysis. They enable faster response to cyber incidents, adaptive defense mechanisms, and improved threat intelligence, strengthening overall security systems.

Developing a Future-ready Digital Organization

Digitization has brought new and complex cybersecurity concerns while also radically altering the way firms operate. In order to guarantee security in the long run, we have laid out a thorough procedure for creating a cybersecurity resilience architecture that uses the digital capabilities that were investigated in this study. Based on our study and analysis, we have determined that there are key digital capabilities that correspond to different stages of cybersecurity resilience [78]. In order to build cybersecurity resilience, our research shows that training and prevention must make use of a variety of tools. Business processes necessitate the use of digital solutions at different stages due to differences in information-sharing capabilities and process automation. Companies with improvisational skills are better able to react to unexpected and critical environmental occurrences because they are adept at making good use of digital information technology systems [79].

Cybersecurity evaluation and preventive processes must incorporate internet information capabilities. Securely sharing strategic and tactical information requires organizations to integrate their IT resources and procedures. Companies should keep an eye on how the digital environment is changing as they adapt in order to spot opportunities and comprehend major shifts in their digital ecosystem [80]. In order for businesses to react to different situations and incorporate innovations driven by consumer value, network activation skills are essential. These capabilities allow for the rapid reconfiguration of resources.

On the basis of previously established concepts, we have determined the main strengths impacting cybersecurity resilience in management processes. Utilizing a variety of resources and encouraging lifelong learning are the pillars upon which the training and preventive initiatives rest throughout the planning and preparation stages [81]. All three stages—planning, preparation, and adaptation—involve utilizing internet-based information capabilities to drive relevant evaluation and preventative measures. Impromptu skills power update processes, which are employed throughout the adaptation phase. One aspect of the adaptation phase is the ability to adjust to different situations. This is facilitated by computerized environmental scanning and the quick reconfiguration of resources [82]. To confirm and explore the connection between digital capabilities and cybersecurity resilience further, future empirical studies could use these findings as a foundation. Scholars and practitioners must prioritize understanding the reciprocal benefits of digital skills and cybersecurity resilience. For corporations, this collaboration marks a watershed moment in their digital transition [83]. Further research into cybersecurity resilience methodologies could uncover other digital capabilities that contribute to resilience and corporate strategies [84]. Understanding and utilizing the complex nature of digitization capabilities is crucial for firms to achieve cybersecurity resilience and thrive in their digital business transformation.

This study proved that the cybersecurity resilience architecture must incorporate digitization capabilities in order to attain long-term security. In this digital age, organizations can strengthen their ability to avoid, adjust to, and recover from cyber disasters by implementing digital practices, technologies, and tools [85]. To help businesses strengthen their cybersecurity, we have developed a framework and given some suggestions. To keep up with the ever-changing digital landscape and improve the framework, continual research and development are essential. Cybersecurity resilience should be a top priority for all businesses looking to succeed in the digital age and protect their operations, reputation, and client trust. This framework's ability to lessen cyber threats, protect business assets, and guarantee long-term security is its greatest strength [86]. To maximize cybersecurity resilience through the application of digitization capabilities, this framework offers firms a tactical approach. Given the dynamic nature of the digital ecosystem, it is critical to do additional research and development in this area in order to improve the framework and tackle emerging cybersecurity concerns. Cybersecurity resilience is essential for businesses to succeed in the digital age and safeguard their operations, reputation, and clients.

CONCLUSION

In order to keep information systems secure from cyber threats that could compromise their accessibility, integrity, or confidentiality, cybersecurity measures are put in place. Since people and businesses rely so heavily on digital technologies, cybersecurity is crucial to ensuring their safety. Numerous fields can benefit from cyber defense, including healthcare, banking, smart cities, power grids, government agencies, schools, and the armed forces. A wide variety of threats, including hackers, thieves, terrorists, state actors, and even insiders, pose unique difficulties to cybersecurity. Some of the problems that the cybersecurity sector has to deal with include advanced cyber-attacks, cyber-attacks that use reinforcement learning, malware that is enabled by AI, the susceptibility of IoT technology, cloud security concerns, and the use of cryptography. In any case, these problems may be amenable to future developments in cybersecurity, such as quantum computing (quantum-secure encryption), biometric authentication, sophisticated AI, and ML. Everyone, from individuals to governments, must keep pouring money into cybersecurity if we want our data, networks, and digital gadgets to be safe from cybercriminals.

LIST OF ABBREVIATIONS

ITU International Telecommunications Union

IoT The Internet-of-Things

AI Artificial Intelligence

ML Machine Learning

IDS Intrusion Detection System

DNN Deep Neural Network

DRNN Deep Recurrent Neural Networks

STPA Systems-Theoretic Process Analysis

EHRs Electronic Health Records

ECDLP Elliptic Curve Discrete Logarithm

BAN Burrows-Abadi-Needham

QKD Quantum Key Distribution

APTs Advanced Persistent Threats

DoS Denial-of-Service

SCA Side-Channel Attacks

REFERENCES

[1] W.S. Admass, Y.Y. Munaye, and A.A. Diro, "Cybersecurity: State of the art, challenges and future directions", *Cybersecurity and Applications,* vol. 2, p. 100031, 2023. [http://dx.doi.org/10.1016/j.csa.2023.100031]

[2] A.T. Somnathe, V.T. Selvi, N.G. Stepha, M.T. Kingslin, F.M. Inamdar, and P.C.S. Reddy, "An intelligent traffic conflict prediction using deep learning with long-term evolution access data", *In: Proc. 2025 3rd Int. Conf. Smart Syst. Eng. Solut. (ICSSES),* pp. 1-6, 2025.

[3] W. S. Admass, Y. Y. Munaye, and A. A. Diro, "Cyber security: State of the art, challenges and future directions", *Cyber Secur. Appl,* vol. 2, p. 100031, 2024. [http://dx.doi.org/10.1016/j.csa.2023.100031]

[4] P. Sharma, and H. Gupta, "Emerging cybersecurity threats and security applications in digital era", *in Proc. 2024 11th Int. Conf. Reliability, Infocom Technol. Optim. (Trends Future Directions) (ICRITO),* pp. 1-6, 2024. [http://dx.doi.org/10.1109/ICRITO61523.2024.10522135]

[5] N.M.A. Chisty, P.R. Baddam, and R. Amin, "Strategic approaches to safeguarding the digital future: insights into next-generation cybersecurity", *Eng. Int.,* vol. 10, no. 2, pp. 69-84, 2022. [http://dx.doi.org/10.18034/ei.v10i2.689]

[6] C. G. Rao, N. M. A. Chisty, S. K. Mishra, M. Sathe, S. Rizvi, and M. Soni, "Innovations, difficulties, and approaches for next-generation cybersecurity: Protecting the digital future," *in Proc. 2024 Int. Conf. Trends Quantum Comput. Emerg. Bus. Technol. (TQCEBT)*, Pune, India, 2024, pp. 1–6 [http://dx.doi.org/10.1109/TQCEBT59414.2024.10545178]

[7] A. Rayhan, "Cybersecurity in the digital age: Assessing threats and strengthening defenses", *in Proc. Cybersecurity Awareness Conf.,* pp. 1-26, 2024.

[8] L.P. Mudarakola, V.K. Bukkarayasamudram, S.D. Jadhav, S.S. Goviraboyina, S. Sharma, S. Mukherjee, and P.C.S. Reddy, "A deep learning framework for iot lightweight traffic multi-classification: Smart-cities", *Int. J. Sensors Wirel. Commun. Control,* vol. 14, no. 3, pp. 175-184, 2024. [http://dx.doi.org/10.2174/0122103279292479240226111739]

[9] V. Hiranandani, "Privacy and security in the digital age: contemporary challenges and future directions", *Int. J. Hum. Rights,* vol. 15, no. 7, pp. 1091-1106, 2011. [http://dx.doi.org/10.1080/13642987.2010.493360]

[10] P. Harshavardhanan, V. Muneeswaran, D. Saravanan, P. Vijayakarthik, R. Natchadalingam, and P.C.S. Reddy, "An adaptive intrusion detection system for iot networks using deep learning", *In: Proc. 2023 IEEE 5th Int. Conf. Adv. Electron. Comput. Commun. (ICAECC),* pp. 1-6, 2023. [http://dx.doi.org/10.1109/ICAECC59324.2023.10560150]

[11] N.G. Camacho, "The role of AI in cybersecurity: Addressing threats in the digital age", *Journal of Artificial Intelligence General science (JAIGS),* vol. 3, no. 1, pp. 143-154, 2024. [http://dx.doi.org/10.60087/jaigs.v3i1.75]

[12] R. Samrin, P. C. S. Reddy, K. A. Kumar, N. Deepthi, C. Mithra, S. B. Latha, G. Muralidhar, P. S. S. Prasad, P. B. Reddy, and G. K. Thakur, "A hybrid deep learning based framework for prediction of rice yield through integration of biophysical parameters and optical remote sensing data in India", *J. Atmos. Sol.-Terr. Phys.,* p. 106734, 2026. [http://dx.doi.org/10.1016/j.jastp.2026.106734]

[13] N. Shenare, and S. Moon, "Emerging trends, analytical tools, challenges and opportunities in cyber security: A steganography and digital forensics approach", *Int. J. Environ. Sci.,* pp. 1114-1125, 2025. [http://dx.doi.org/10.64252/tt797t90]

[14] M.M. Nair, A. Deshmukh, and A.K. Tyagi, "Artificial intelligence for cybersecurity: Current trends and future challenges," *in Automated Secure Computing for Next-Generation Systems*, A. K. Tyagi, Ed., Hoboken, NJ, USA: Wiley, 2024, pp. 83–114

[15] L. Albtosh, S. Gholami, G. L. P. K. Suryanarayana, and Y. Sucharitha, "Future directions in cybersecurity," *in Defense in Depth: Modern Cybersecurity Strategies and Evolving Threats*, A. K. Tyagi and S. Chahal, Eds., Hoboken, NJ, USA: Wiley, 2024, pp. 195–210 [http://dx.doi.org/10.1002/9781394340750.ch9]

[16] A. Sapiński, "The importance and challenges of information security in the digital age: analysis of the current situation and prospects for development", *Sci. J. Bielsko-Biala Sch. Finance Law,* vol. 27, no. 1, pp. 52-55, 2023.

[17] S. Yadala, S.R.P. Chandra, and V.K. Solanki, "A novel private encryption model in IoT under cloud computing domain", *in Intelligent Systems and Networks*, P. T. Nguyen, B. C. P. Singh, and M. P. C. J. Reddy, Eds., Singapore: Springer, 2023, pp. 261–267. [http://dx.doi.org/10.1007/978-981-99-4725-6_33]

[18] L. Sujihelen, R. Boddu, S. Murugaveni, Ms. Arnika, A. Haldorai, P. C. S. Reddy, S. Feng, and J. Qin, "Node replication attack detection in distributed wireless sensor networks", *Wirel. Commun. Mob. Comput.,* vol. 2022, p. 7252791, 2022. [http://dx.doi.org/10.1155/2022/7252791]

[19] A.I. Jony, and S.A. Hamim, "Navigating the cyber threat landscape: A comprehensive analysis of attacks and security in the digital age", *J. Inf. Technol. Cyber Secur.,* vol. 1, no. 2, pp. 53-67, 2023. [http://dx.doi.org/10.30996/jitcs.9715]

[20] F. Osasona, A. Atadoga, B.S. Ayinla, O.A. Farayola, and T.O. Abrahams, "Cybersecurity threats in the age of IoT: A review of protective measures", *Int. J. Sci. Res. Arch.,* vol. 11, no. 1, pp. 1304-1310, 2024. [http://dx.doi.org/10.30574/ijsra.2024.11.1.0217]

[21] A. Yadav, A. Kumar, and V. Singh, "Open-source intelligence: a comprehensive review of the current state, applications and future perspectives in cyber security", *Artif. Intell. Rev.,* vol. 56, no. 11, pp. 12407-12438, 2023. [http://dx.doi.org/10.1007/s10462-023-10454-y] [PMID: 37362900]

[22] E. Arjun, and P. Singh, "Future directions in digital forensics and cybersecurity," *in Securing the Digital Frontier: Threats and Advanced Techniques in Security and Forensics*, A. K. Tyagi, Ed., Hoboken, NJ, USA: Wiley, 2024, pp. 333–365. [http://dx.doi.org/10.1002/9781394268917.ch15]

[23] O.U. Khan, S.M. Abdullah, A.O. Olajide, A.I. Sani, M.W.F. Shah, A.A. Ogunola, and M.D. Lee, "The future of cybersecurity: leveraging artificial intelligence to combat evolving threats and enhance digital defense strategies", *J. Comput. Anal. Appl.,* vol. 33, p. 8, 2024.

[24] I.H. Sarker, "Machine learning for intelligent data analysis and automation in cybersecurity: current and future prospects", *Ann. Data Sci.,* vol. 10, no. 6, pp. 1473-1498, 2023. [http://dx.doi.org/10.1007/s40745-022-00444-2]

[25] P.C. Shaker Reddy, Y. Sucharitha, and Y. Sucharitha, "IoT-enabled energy-efficient multipath power control for underwater sensor networks", *Int. J. Sensors Wirel. Commun. Control,* vol. 12, no. 6, pp. 478-494, 2022. [http://dx.doi.org/10.2174/2210327912666220615103257]

[26] J. Yu, A.V. Shvetsov, and S. Hamood Alsamhi, "Leveraging machine learning for cybersecurity resilience in industry 4.0: Challenges and future directions", *IEEE Access,* vol. 12, pp. 159579-159596, 2024. [http://dx.doi.org/10.1109/ACCESS.2024.3482987]

[27] F. Jimmy, "Emerging threats: The latest cybersecurity risks and the role of artificial intelligence in enhancing cybersecurity defenses", *International Journal of Scientific Research and Management (IJSRM),* vol. 9, no. 2, pp. 564-574, 2021. [http://dx.doi.org/10.18535/ijsrm/v9i2.ec01]

[28] M. Al-Hawawreh, A. Aljuhani, and Y. Jararweh, "Chatgpt for cybersecurity: practical applications, challenges, and future directions", *Cluster Comput.,* vol. 26, no. 6, pp. 3421-3436, 2023. [http://dx.doi.org/10.1007/s10586-023-04124-5]

[29] Y. Sucharitha, and P.C. Shaker Reddy, "An autonomous adaptive enhancement method based on

learning to optimize heterogeneous network selection", *Int. J. Sensors Wirel. Commun. Control,* vol. 12, no. 7, pp. 495-509, 2022. [http://dx.doi.org/10.2174/2210327912666221012154428]

[30] M. Sharma, R.K. Kohli, and K. Sharma, "Tomorrow's shields: exploring future trends in cybersecurity and forensics," in *Securing the Digital Frontier: Threats and Advanced Techniques in Security and Forensics*, A. K. Tyagi, Ed., Hoboken, NJ, USA: Wiley, 2025, pp. 367–385. [http://dx.doi.org/10.1002/9781394268917.ch16]

[31] O. Layode, E. Johnson, T.T. Labake, G.S. Adeleke, E.O. Udeh, and E. Johnson, "Addressing cybersecurity challenges in sustainable supply chain management: A review of current practices and future directions", *Int. J. Manage. Entrep. Res.,,* vol. 6, no. 6, pp. 1954-1981, 2024. [http://dx.doi.org/10.51594/ijmer.v6i6.1208]

[32] M.D. Basith, P. Praveen, and P.C.S. Reddy, "Adaptive deep Q-GAN framework for enhanced breast cancer detection in medical imaging", *Biomed. Signal Process. Control,* vol. 112, p. 108638, 2026. [http://dx.doi.org/10.1016/j.bspc.2025.108638]

[33] A. Dehghantanha, A. Yazdinejad, and R.M. Parizi, "Autonomous cybersecurity: Evolving challenges, emerging opportunities, and future research trajectories", *in Proc. Workshop Auton. Cybersecur.,* pp. 1-6, 2023. [http://dx.doi.org/10.1145/3689933.3690832]

[34] M.A. Azer, and R. Samir, "Overview of the Complex Landscape and Future Directions of Ethics in Light of Emerging Technologies", *Int. J. Adv. Comput. Sci. Appl.,* vol. 15, no. 7, p. 7, 2024. [http://dx.doi.org/10.14569/IJACSA.2024.01507142]

[35] H. Rehan, "AI-driven cloud security: The future of safeguarding sensitive data in the digital age", *J. Artif. Intell. Gen. Sci.,* vol. 3, no. 1, pp. 113-128, 2024.

[36] A. Juneja, S.S. Goswami, and S. Mondal, "Cybersecurity and digital economy: opportunities, growth and challenges", *J. Technol. Innov. Energy,* vol. 3, no. 2, pp. 1-22, 2024.

[37] S. Baidya, V. Potdar, P. Pratim Ray, and C. Nandi, "Reviewing the opportunities, challenges, and future directions for the digitalization of energy", *Energy Res. Soc. Sci.,* vol. 81, p. 102243, 2021. [http://dx.doi.org/10.1016/j.erss.2021.102243]

[38] E. Altulaihan, M.A. Almaiah, and A. Aljughaiman, "Cybersecurity threats, countermeasures and mitigation techniques on the IoT: Future research directions", *Electronics,* vol. 11, no. 20, p. 3330, 2022. [http://dx.doi.org/10.3390/electronics11203330]

[39] M.L. Prasad, A. Kiran, and C.S.R. Pundru, "Chronic kidney disease risk prediction using machine learning techniques", *J. Inf. Technol. Manage.,* vol. 16, no. 1, pp. 118-134, 2024.

[40] S. Banaeian Far, A. Imani Rad, S.M. Hosseini Bamakan, and M. Rajabzadeh Asaar, "Toward Metaverse of everything: Opportunities, challenges, and future directions of the next generation of visual/virtual communications", *J. Netw. Comput. Appl.,* vol. 217, p. 103675, 2023. [http://dx.doi.org/10.1016/j.jnca.2023.103675]

[41] M. Roshanaei, M.R. Khan, and N.N. Sylvester, "Enhancing cybersecurity through AI and ML: Strategies, challenges, and future directions", *Journal of Information Security,* vol. 15, no. 3, pp. 320-339, 2024. [http://dx.doi.org/10.4236/jis.2024.153019]

[42] Y. Sucharitha, C.S.R. Pundru, and G. Suryanarayana, "Network intrusion detection of drones using recurrent neural networks," in *Drone Technology: Future Trends and Practical Applications*, S. L. Tripathi, O. Nyamwange, and R. Kipkoech, Eds. Hoboken, NJ, USA: Wiley, 2023, pp. 375–392. [http://dx.doi.org/10.1002/9781394168002.ch15]

[43] M. Adil, H. Song, S. Mastorakis, H. Abulkasim, A. Farouk, and Z. Jin, "UAV-assisted IoT applications, cybersecurity threats, AI-enabled solutions, open challenges with future research

directions", *IEEE Trans. Intell. Veh.,* vol. 9, no. 4, pp. 4583-4605, 2024. [http://dx.doi.org/10.1109/TIV.2023.3309548]

[44] N.K. Thawait, "Machine learning in cybersecurity: Applications, challenges and future directions", *Int. J. Sci. Res. Comput. Sci. Eng. Inf. Technol.,* vol. 10, no. 3, pp. 16-27, 2024. [http://dx.doi.org/10.32628/CSEIT24102125]

[45] H. Ullah, S. Manickam, M. Obaidat, S.U.A. Laghari, and M. Uddin, "Exploring the potential of metaverse technology in healthcare: Applications, challenges, and future directions", *IEEE Access,* vol. 11, pp. 69686-69707, 2023. [http://dx.doi.org/10.1109/ACCESS.2023.3286696]

[46] V.K. Bukkarayasamudram, P.C.S. Reddy, and K.A. Kumar, "Quantum computing revolution in healthcare: a systematic review of applications, issues and future directions", *Artif Intell Rev,* vol. 58, p. 389, 2025. [http://dx.doi.org/10.1007/s10462-025-11381-w]

[47] T. Zaid, and S. Garai, "Emerging trends in cybersecurity: a holistic view on current threats, assessing solutions, and pioneering new frontiers", *Blockchain Healthc. Today,* vol. 7, pp. 10-30953, 2024.

[48] M. Arsal, B. Saleem, S. Jalil, M. Ali, M. Zahra, A.U. Rehman, and Z. Muhammad, "Emerging cybersecurity and privacy threats of ChatGPT, Gemini, and Copilot: Current trends, challenges, and future directions", *Preprints,* p. 2024101909, 2024. [http://dx.doi.org/10.20944/preprints202410.1909.v1]

[49] Z. Wenhua, F. Qamar, T.-A.N. Abdali, R. Hassan, S.T.A. Jafri, and Q.N. Nguyen, "Blockchain technology: Security issues, healthcare applications, challenges and future trends", *Electronics,* vol. 12, p. 546, 2023.3 [http://dx.doi.org/10.3390/electronics12030546]

[50] T.R. Gadekallu, P.K.R. Maddikunta, P. Boopathy, N. Deepa, R. Chengoden, N. Victor, W. Wang, W. Wang, Y. Zhu, and K. Dev, "Xai for industry 5.0-concepts, opportunities, challenges and future directions", *IEEE Open J. Commun. Soc.,* vol. 6, pp. 2706-2729, 2024. [http://dx.doi.org/10.1109/OJCOMS.2024.3473891]

[51] A.V. Ramana, U. Bhoga, R.K. Dhulipalla, A. Kiran, B.D. Chary, and C.S.R. Pundru, "Abnormal Behavior Prediction in Elderly Persons Using Deep Learning", *in Proc. 2023 Int. Conf. Comput., Electron. Electr. Eng. their Appl. (IC2E3),* pp. 1-6, 2023. [http://dx.doi.org/10.1109/IC2E357697.2023.10262547]

[52] S. Kumar, and R.R. Mallipeddi, "Impact of cybersecurity on operations and supply chain management: Emerging trends and future research directions", *Prod. Oper. Manag.,* vol. 31, no. 12, pp. 4488-4500, 2022. [http://dx.doi.org/10.1111/poms.13859]

[53] S. Mehmood, T.M. Ghazal, M.A. Khan, M. Zubair, M.T. Naseem, T. Faiz, and M. Ahmad, "Malignancy detection in lung and colon histopathology images using transfer learning with class selective image processing", *IEEE Access,* vol. 10, pp. 25657-25668, 2022. [http://dx.doi.org/10.1109/ACCESS.2022.3150924]

[54] U. Son, and J.H. Huh, "A survey of cyber security for maritime autonomous surface ships: Opportunities, challenges, and future directions", *IEEE Trans. Intell. Transp. Syst.,* vol. 26, no. 6, pp. 7343-7361, 2025. [http://dx.doi.org/10.1109/TITS.2025.3560809]

[55] S.M. Alhidaifi, M.R. Asghar, and I.S. Ansari, "A survey on cyber resilience: Key strategies, research challenges, and future directions", *ACM Comput. Surv.,* vol. 56, no. 8, pp. 1-48, 2024. [http://dx.doi.org/10.1145/3649218]

[56] D. Baswaraj, R. Natchadalingam, R. S. Rekha, N. Sahni, V. Divya, and P. C. S. Reddy, "An Accurate Stock Prediction Using Ensemble Deep Learning Model", *in Proc. 2023 Int. Conf. Res. Methodologies Knowl. Manage., Artif. Intell. Telecommun. Eng. (RMKMATE),* 2023.

[57] V.K. Kanvaria, and A. Yadav, "Integrating and innovating: The role of ICT in education's evolution—an in-depth analysis of emerging technologies, current trends, challenges, and future directions in the digital age,", *Int. J. Multidimensional Res. Perspect.,* vol. 2, no. 2, pp. 33-48, 2024.

[58] C. Horan, and H. Saiedian, "Cyber crime investigation: Landscape, challenges, and future research directions", *Journal of Cybersecurity and Privacy,* vol. 1, no. 4, pp. 580-596, 2021. [http://dx.doi.org/10.3390/jcp1040029]

[59] P. Reddy, A. Sureshbabu, and A. Sureshbabu, "An Adaptive Model for Forecasting Seasonal Rainfall Using Predictive Analytics", *International Journal of Intelligent Engineering and Systems,* vol. 12, no. 5, pp. 22-32, 2019. [http://dx.doi.org/10.22266/ijies2019.1031.03]

[60] R. Chengoden, N. Victor, T. Huynh-The, G. Yenduri, R.H. Jhaveri, M. Alazab, S. Bhattacharya, P. Hegde, P.K.R. Maddikunta, and T.R. Gadekallu, "Metaverse for healthcare: a survey on potential applications, challenges and future directions", *IEEE Access,* vol. 11, pp. 12765-12795, 2023. [http://dx.doi.org/10.1109/ACCESS.2023.3241628]

[61] Z. Belkhamza, "Cybersecurity in digital transformation applications: analysis of past research and future directions", *ICCWS 2023 18th international conference on cyber warfare and security. Academic Conferences and publishing limited,* 2023. [http://dx.doi.org/10.34190/iccws.18.1.1005]

[62] C. Katsikeas, L. Leonidou, and A. Zeriti, "Revisiting international marketing strategy in a digital era", *Int. Mark. Rev.,* vol. 37, no. 3, pp. 405-424, 2019. [http://dx.doi.org/10.1108/IMR-02-2019-0080]

[63] D. Staheli, T. Yu, R.J. Crouser, S. Damodaran, K. Nam, D. O'Gwynn, S. McKenna, and L. Harrison, "Visualization evaluation for cybersecurity: Trends and future directions", *Proceedings of the Eleventh Workshop on Visualization for Cybersecurity,* pp. 49-56, 2014. [http://dx.doi.org/10.1145/2671491.2671492]

[64] M.M. Alani, "Big data in cybersecurity: a survey of applications and future trends", *J. Reliab. Intell. Environ.,* vol. 7, no. 2, pp. 85-114, 2021. [http://dx.doi.org/10.1007/s40860-020-00120-3]

[65] J. Pastor-Galindo, P. Nespoli, F. Gomez Marmol, and G. Martinez Perez, "The not yet exploited goldmine of OSINT: Opportunities, open challenges and future trends", *IEEE Access,* vol. 8, pp. 10282-10304, 2020. [http://dx.doi.org/10.1109/ACCESS.2020.2965257]

[66] P. Ravali, P.C. Reddy, and P. Pappula, "An efficient neuro-framework for brain tumor classification using a CNN-based self-supervised learning approach with genetic optimizations,", *Curr. Neuropharmacol.,* vol. 23, 2025. [http://dx.doi.org/10.2174/011570159X378103250806214613]

[67] L. Albshaier, S. Almarri, and M.M. Hafizur Rahman, "A review of blockchain's role in e-commerce transactions: Open challenges, and future research directions,", *Computers,* vol. 13, pp. 1-27, 2024. [http://dx.doi.org/10.3390/computers13010027]

[68] A.A. Khan, A.A. Shaikh, A.A. Laghari, M.A. Dootio, M.M. Rind, and S.A. Awan, "Digital forensics and cyber forensics investigation: security challenges, limitations, open issues, and future direction", *International Journal of Electronic Security and Digital Forensics,* vol. 14, no. 2, pp. 124-150, 2022. [http://dx.doi.org/10.1504/IJESDF.2022.121174]

[69] A.K. Bashir, N. Victor, S. Bhattacharya, T. Huynh-The, R. Chengoden, G. Yenduri, P.K.R. Maddikunta, Q.V. Pham, T.R. Gadekallu, and M. Liyanage, "Federated learning for the healthcare metaverse: Concepts, applications, challenges, and future directions", *IEEE Internet Things J.,* vol. 10, no. 24, pp. 21873-21891, 2023. [http://dx.doi.org/10.1109/JIOT.2023.3304790]

[70] A. Giannaros, A. Karras, L. Theodorakopoulos, C. Karras, P. Kranias, N. Schizas, G. Kalogeratos, and D. Tsolis, "Autonomous vehicles: Sophisticated attacks, safety issues, challenges, open topics, blockchain, and future directions", *Journal of Cybersecurity and Privacy,* vol. 3, no. 3, pp. 493-543, 2023.
[http://dx.doi.org/10.3390/jcp3030025]

[71] Y. He, D. Huang, L. Chen, Y. Ni, and X. Ma, "A survey on zero trust architecture: Challenges and future trends", *Wirel. Commun. Mob. Comput.,* vol. 2022, no. 1, p. 6476274, 2022.
[http://dx.doi.org/10.1155/2022/6476274]

[72] G. Arun, "Pundru Chandra Shaker Reddy, Nagaveni Budati, B. Rebecca, Subhadra Perumalla, and Vijay Bhanudas Gujar. "A Deep Learning Framework for Diabetes Prediction: PIMA Indian Dataset", *2024 International Conference on Innovative Computing, Intelligent Communication and Smart Electrical Systems (ICSES),* IEEE, pp. 1-6, 2024.

[73] Hany F. Atlam, Ndifon Ekuri, Muhammad Ajmal Azad, and Harjinder Singh Lallie, "Blockchain forensics: A systematic literature review of techniques, applications, challenges, and future directions", *Electronics 13.17,* p. 3568, 2024.
[http://dx.doi.org/10.3390/electronics13173568]

[74] H. Gull, D.A. Alabbad, M. Saqib, S.Z. Iqbal, T. Nasir, S. Saeed, and A.M. Almuhaide, "E-commerce and cybersecurity challenges: Recent advances and future trends", *Handbook of Research on Cybersecurity Issues and Challenges for Business and FinTech Applications,* pp. 91-111, 2023.

[75] J. Cook, S.U. Rehman, and M.A. Khan, "Security and privacy for low power iot devices on 5g and beyond networks: Challenges and future directions", *IEEE Access,* vol. 11, pp. 39295-39317, 2023.
[http://dx.doi.org/10.1109/ACCESS.2023.3268064]

[76] A.C. Dzuranin, and I. Mălăescu, "The current state and future direction of IT audit: Challenges and opportunities", *J. Inf. Syst.,* vol. 30, no. 1, pp. 7-20, 2016.
[http://dx.doi.org/10.2308/isys-51315]

[77] M. Ali, F. Naeem, G. Kaddoum, and E. Hossain, "Metaverse communications, networking, security, and applications: Research issues, state-of-the-art, and future directions", *IEEE Commun. Surv. Tutor.,* vol. 26, no. 2, pp. 1238-1278, 2024.
[http://dx.doi.org/10.1109/COMST.2023.3347172]

[78] D. Cevallos-Salas, J. Estrada-Jiménez, and D.S. Guamán, "Application layer security for Internet communications: A comprehensive review, challenges, and future trends", *Comput. Electr. Eng.,* vol. 119, p. 109498, 2024.
[http://dx.doi.org/10.1016/j.compeleceng.2024.109498]

[79] V. Saranya, "Leveraging artificial intelligence for cybersecurity: Implementation, challenges, and future directions," in *Machine learning and cryptographic solutions for data protection and network security*, J. A. Ruth, G. V. V. Mahesh, P. Visalakshi, R. Uma, and A. Meenakshi, Eds. Hershey, PA, USA: IGI Global, 2024, pp. 29–43

[80] Y. Chen, "Information security management: compliance challenges and new directions", *J. Inf. Technol. Case Appl. Res.,* vol. 24, no. 4, pp. 243-249, 2022.
[http://dx.doi.org/10.1080/15228053.2022.2148979]

[81] A. Rauniyar, D.H. Hagos, D. Jha, J.E. Håkegård, U. Bagci, D.B. Rawat, and V. Vlassov, "Federated learning for medical applications: A taxonomy, current trends, challenges, and future research directions", *IEEE Internet Things J.,* vol. 11, no. 5, pp. 7374-7398, 2024.
[http://dx.doi.org/10.1109/JIOT.2023.3329061]

[82] H.N. Alshareef, "Current development, challenges, and future trends in cloud computing: A survey", *Int. J. Adv. Comput. Sci. Appl.,* vol. 14, no. 3, 2023.

[83] D.S. Sarwatt, Y. Lin, J. Ding, Y. Sun, and H. Ning, "Metaverse for intelligent transportation systems (ITS): A comprehensive review of technologies, applications, implications, challenges and future

directions", *IEEE Trans. Intell. Transp. Syst.,* vol. 25, no. 7, pp. 6290-6308, 2024. [http://dx.doi.org/10.1109/TITS.2023.3347280]

[84] I.H. Sarker, "Deep learning: a comprehensive overview on techniques, taxonomy, applications and research directions", *SN Comput. Sci.,* vol. 2, no. 6, 2021. [http://dx.doi.org/10.1007/s42979-021-00815-1] [PMID: 34426802]

[85] K. Ofosu-Ampong, "Artificial intelligence research: A review on dominant themes, methods, frameworks and future research directions", *Telemat. Inform. Rep.,* vol. 14, p. 100127, 2024. [http://dx.doi.org/10.1016/j.teler.2024.100127]

[86] R.Y. Patil, Y.H. Patil, and A. Bannore, "Cybersecurity in medical Internet of Things: Issues, challenges, and future directions," *in Security Implementation in Internet of Medical Things*, L. Sapra, V. Sapra, and A. Bhardwaj, Eds. Boca Raton, FL, USA: CRC Press, 2023, pp. 87–110. [http://dx.doi.org/10.1201/9781003269168-5]

CHAPTER 2

Introduction to AI: Concepts, History, and Applications

Vidyullatha Sukhavasi[1], **Kisara Rishitha**[1] and **Yadala Sucharitha**[2,*]

[1] *Department of CSE, BVRIT HYDERABAD College of Engineering for Women, Hyderabad, Telangana, India*

[2] *Sharda School of Computing Science and Engineering , Department of CSE, Sharda University, Greater Noida, Uttar Pradesh, India*

Abstract: Artificial Intelligence (AI) is perhaps the most revolutionary technology today, driving innovation across sectors, transforming economies, and impacting daily life. This chapter gives an overview of AI, discussing its core concepts, historical development, and major applications. It starts by explaining AI and separating it from its associated disciplines, like machine learning and data science. The chapter further discusses the basic techniques and strategies in AI, such as rule-based systems, neural networks, and natural language processing. Through the exploration of how AI systems are constructed and trained to do things like speech recognition, image processing, and decision-making, the chapter illuminates the underlying mechanics of AI technology. This chapter gives readers a sound grasp of the fundamental principles of AI, what it can currently do, and what challenges and opportunities it is likely to offer. For business, healthcare, education, and security, AI will be instrumental in the future, and so it is vital to comprehend its changing landscape.

Keywords: Artificial Intelligence (AI), Autonomous Systems, Computer Vision, Deep Learning, Ethical AI, Explainable AI (XAI), Federated Learning, Intelligent Systems, Machine Learning (ML), Natural Language Processing, Neural Networks, Predictive Analytics, Quantum AI, Reinforcement Learning, Robotics, Smart Automation, Supervised Learning.

INTRODUCTION

The goal of Artificial Intelligence (AI), a revolutionary technology, is to create machines that can reason, learn, perceive, and make decisions in order to mimic human intelligence. This chapter's main goal is to give readers an understanding of Artificial Intelligence (AI), including its core concepts, scientific foundations,

* **Corresponding Author Yadala Sucharitha:** Sharda School of Computing Science and Engineering , Department of CSE, Sharda University, Greater Noida, Uttar Pradesh, India; E-mail: suchi.yadala@gmail.com

Pundru Chandra Shaker Reddy, Yadala Sucharitha, & Thillaiarasu N (Eds.)

practical applications, and societal consequences. The main focus is on how AI has developed from theoretical concepts to real-world applications in various industries. The chapter places Artificial Intelligence (AI) in the larger context of developing technologies and identifies both the advantages and disadvantages of its adoption by providing a well-organized analysis.

AI-Driven Threat Intelligence Frameworks: Revolutionizing Enterprise Cybersecurity

The recreation of human intelligence by machines, particularly computer systems, is known as Artificial Intelligence (AI). They are designed to perform functions including knowledge acquisition, problem-solving, perception, and understanding of languages that normally need human intellect [1], shown in Table **1**. AI systems are typically faster and more accurate than humans, can learn from information, and get better over time.

Table 1. Comparison of AI and human intelligence.

Aspect	Artificial Intelligence	Human Intelligence
Memory	Large storage capacity and speedy retrieval	restricted and prone to forgetting
Learning	Statistical models that are driven by data	Contextual and experience-based
Speed	Quick, simultaneous processing	Slow, step-by-step analysis
Emotional Intelligence	Absent or rudimentary	Relationships, feelings, and empathy
Adaptability	Constrained by context, retraining is necessary	Extremely adaptable and perceptive
Decision Making	Knowledge and reasoning based on rules	Knowledge, feeling, and perception
Creativity	Creativity based on patterns and rules	Innovative, Perceptive, and Creative

John McCarthy provided one of the first definitions of Artificial Intelligence, defining it as "the science and engineering of making intelligent machines" [2]. AI encompasses a wide range of methods and strategies, including deep learning, machine learning, and rule-based systems. Everyday applications of AI include voice recognition in smartphones, driverless cars, and digital platform content recommendations.

Why AI Matters in the Modern World?

AI is rapidly reshaping how we live, work, and interact. In the digital era, data is generated at an unprecedented scale. AI leverages this data to provide real-time insights, automate complex processes, enhance decision-making, and unlock new capabilities across industries. It powers self-driving cars, personalized medical diagnostics, financial fraud detection, virtual customer support, and smart city infrastructures [3].

AI's ability to handle repetitive tasks, process vast datasets, and operate continuously without fatigue makes it a transformative force. It not only boosts efficiency but also opens new avenues in fields like healthcare, education, agriculture, and environmental protection, as shown in Fig (**1**). As we increasingly rely on digital systems, the role of AI continues to expand, making its understanding critical for both technical and non-technical audiences.

Fig. (1). AI in everyday life.

In addition, the chapter discusses the benefits AI brings to society, the challenges it poses, and the ethical questions it raises. It concludes with a glimpse into the future of AI, including emerging trends and the potential societal impact. Whether you are new to AI or seeking a structured overview, this chapter sets the stage for a deeper exploration of this exciting and fast-evolving field.

AI and Its Broad Influence

A diverse field that incorporates elements of computer science, mathematics, cognitive science, linguistics, neurology, and even philosophy, Artificial Intelligence is not a single technology. Its methods—such as supply chain optimization, energy grid management, weather forecasting, and digital marketing campaign customization—are ingrained in both the visible and unseen layers of contemporary infrastructure. Many people engage with AI on a regular basis without even noticing it because of how deeply integrated it is [4].

AI can be divided into two categories based on its capabilities: general AI, which is a more theoretical idea that refers to robots that could comprehend and learn any intellectual work that a person can, and narrow AI, also known as weak AI, which is made for specialized tasks like language translation or facial recognition. Although research on broad AI and human-level cognition is still ongoing, all deployed AI systems today fall within narrow AI [5].

A Revolution in Society beyond Technology

AI is changing institutions and societies in addition to how businesses operate. AI helps with medication research and early detection in the healthcare industry [6]. It makes it possible for educational institutions to implement student-specific adaptive learning systems. AI helps with traffic control, urban planning, and predictive policing in public administration [7]. While efficiency and creativity are brought about by these changes, privacy, equity, transparency, and the possibility of job displacement are all brought up. AI's strength is increased when it converges with other technologies like big data, the Internet of Things (IoT), and 5G. Making sure AI systems are in line with human values and societal demands is vital as these systems grow more independent and have the ability to make decisions in real time. Therefore, comprehending AI is a civic duty as well as a technical imperative.

The Global Competition for Leadership in AI

AI research & development are receiving significant funding from both governments and businesses. The critical importance of AI for social welfare, economic competitiveness, and national security is acknowledged by governments worldwide. China's "Next Generation AI Development Plan," for example, seeks to lead the world in AI by 2030. The US and the EU have also published AI strategies to promote innovation and guarantee ethical development [8]. There are advantages and disadvantages to this worldwide competition for AI leadership. International cooperation can, on the one hand, promote creativity and enhance people's lives. On the other hand, control of vital AI technology and data ecosystems may give rise to geopolitical problems. As a result, in addition to being a technological area, Artificial Intelligence is also a forum for governance, policy, and ethical discussion.

This chapter proceeds by first introducing the history and evolution of AI, followed by foundational concepts such as learning paradigms and core technologies. It then explains how AI systems are built, trained, and deployed, and reviews their applications across various industries. The chapter also discusses the benefits and challenges of AI, ethical considerations, and concludes with future directions in AI research.

HISTORY AND EVOLUTION OF AI

The Origins of AI Theory

The concept of building sentient machines has been around since the time of ancient mythology and philosophy. Hephaestus created machines, which are artificial creatures that behave like real people, according to Greek mythology. In a similar vein, ancient Chinese and Indian literature mentioned devices that could imitate people. These early ideas demonstrate that the goal of creating Artificial Intelligence is based on humanity's desire to comprehend and reproduce intelligence rather than being solely a modern endeavor [9].

The intellectual foundation for Artificial Intelligence was laid in the 17th century by theorists, such as René Descartes and Gottfried Wilhelm Leibniz, who conjectured about automating reasoning. Modern computer science was made possible by the advancement of formal logic and the creation of programmable computing devices, including Charles Babbage's Analytical Engine, in the 19th and 20th centuries. The notion that robots could mimic human intellect was first presented by Alan Turing in his 1950 work, Computing Machinery and Intelligence, which also proposed the Turing Test [10].

The Turing Test, proposed by Alan Turing in 1950, is significant because it set the first benchmark for machine intelligence. It evaluates a machine's ability to exhibit human-like intelligence by determining whether its responses are indistinguishable from a human's, shaping the foundation for AI research and discussions on machine consciousness.

The Inception of AI as a Field (1950s-1970s)

Many people consider John McCarthy's 1956 Dartmouth Symposium, where he first used the phrase "Artificial Intelligence," to be the beginning of the academic discipline. Using logic and rules, early pioneers such as Herbert Simon, Allen Newell, and Marvin Minsky developed symbolic AI systems that imitated human problem-solving. Researchers thought that machines with human-level intelligence would be there in a few decades, hence there was a lot of optimism during this time [11].

The pioneers of AI include Alan Turing, who proposed machine intelligence; John McCarthy, who coined the term "AI"; Marvin Minsky, who advanced neural networks; and Herbert Simon and Allen Newell, who developed the first AI program, laying the foundation for modern AI systems.

Logic Theorist (1956) and General Problem Solver (1957), two early AI programs, were innovations in reasoning simulation. With advancements in robotics and natural language processing, Artificial Intelligence research took off in the 1960s and 1970s. Nevertheless, despite early achievements, outcomes declined due to a lack of processing power, systems governed by rules limited scalability, and their incapacity to manage the complexity of the real world. The first AI winter was the name given to this demoralizing time [12].

Slow Progress and AI Winters (1970s–1990s)

Funding and interest declined during the first AI winter, which lasted from the middle of the 1970s until the beginning of the 1980s, as expectations and real-world constraints collided. When expert systems like MYCIN (for medical diagnosis) and XCON (for computer configuration) emerged in the 1980s and encoded expert information into rule-based systems, enthusiasm was momentarily rekindled [13].

But these systems lacked learning capabilities, were fragile, and were expensive to maintain. In the late 1980s and early 1990s, a second AI winter resulted from their collapse. Around this time, a lot of attention moved from symbolic AI to data-driven methods, especially machine learning, which started to gain traction in academic circles in a quiet way [14].

Major milestones in AI include the creation of the first AI programs in the 1950s, the rise of expert systems in the 1980s, the introduction of machine learning and neural networks in the 1990s, the emergence of deep learning and big data analytics in the 2010s, and today's advancements in generative AI, autonomous systems, and natural language processing.

Modern AI's Ascent (1990s–2010s)

Significant advancements in computing power, storage, and algorithmic techniques during the 1990s signaled a sea change. An important turning point for AI occurred in 1997 when IBM's Deep Blue defeated world chess champion Garry Kasparov [15]. Statistical learning techniques, including decision trees, support vector machines, and ensemble approaches, emerged around this time, enabling machines to recognize patterns in data instead of depending just on pre-programmed rules.

The amount of data and processing power available increased exponentially in the 2000s. AI became widely used during the 2010s due to deep learning, a branch of machine learning that makes use of artificial neural networks. Systems like Google Translate, Siri, and Amazon Alexa showed off AI's powers in language processing and speech recognition, while innovations like AlexNet (2012) transformed computer vision [16].

The AI Revolution and Contemporary Events (2015–Present)

AI has advanced quickly in recent years in a number of fields. Due to the intricacy of the game, it was previously believed that it would take decades for Google DeepMind's AlphaGo to defeat the world champion Go player. Models based on transformers, such as GPT and BERT, have raised the bar for natural language creation and comprehension. These days, AI is incorporated into fraud detection systems, recommendation engines, driverless cars, and even artistic and musical fields. These days, the emphasis is shifting to Artificial General Intelligence (AGI), explainable AI, and ethical AI—systems that can learn and reason at the level of humans across a variety of tasks. Major breakthroughs in AI were shown in Table **2** below.

Table 2. Major breakthroughs in AI.

Year	Milestone	Significance
1950	Turing published "Computing Machinery and Intelligence."	The Turing test was introduced.
1956	Dartmouth conference	Birth of AI as a formal field
1966	ELIZA chatbot	Early Natural Language Processing
1972	SHRDLU	AI reasoning in a blocks world
1980	Rise in Expert Systems	Commercial adoption of AI enterprise
1997	Deep Blue beats Kasparov	AI major wins in board games
2012	AlexNet wins ImageNet	Revolution of Deep Learning
2016	AlphaGo defeats world champion	Major breakthrough in reinforcement learning and planning
2020+	GPT-3,DALL E,ChatGPT	Advancements in large language models and generative models

KEY CONCEPTS IN AI

Artificial Intelligence is an umbrella term encompassing several subfields and paradigms shown in Fig (**2**). Understanding its components is essential to grasping how it functions and where it is headed.

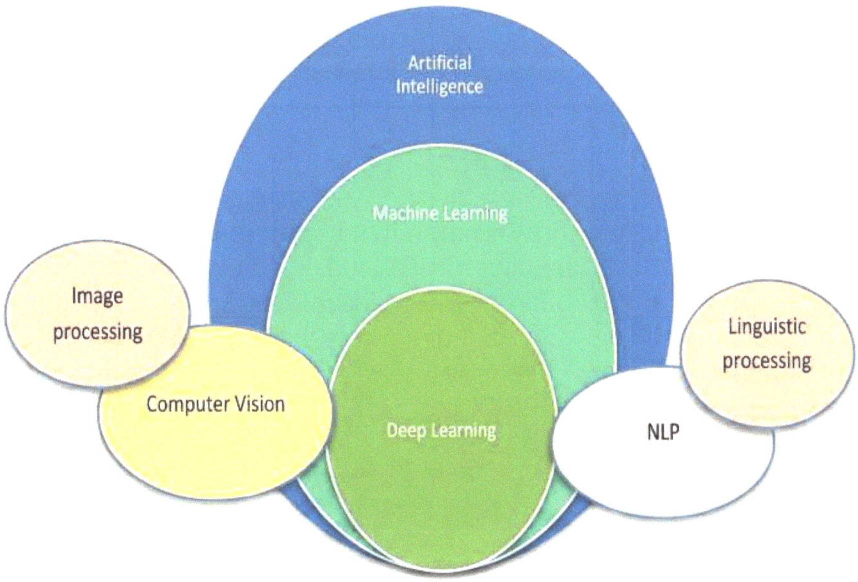

Fig. (2). Subfields of AI.

Narrow AI, General AI, and Super AI

- **Narrow AI:** Designed for specific tasks (*e.g.*, facial recognition, recommendation engines). This is the current state of most AI systems.
- **Artificial General Intelligence (AGI)**: Hypothetical AI with human-level cognitive ability across tasks.
- **Super AI:** A future stage where AI surpasses human intelligence in all respects.

Machine Learning (ML)

ML is a subset of AI that enables systems to learn from data rather than explicit programming. ML systems improve performance over time through training [17].

Types of Learning:

- **Supervised Learning:** Models learn from labeled datasets. Examples: image classification, email spam detection.
- **Unsupervised Learning:** Finds hidden patterns in unlabeled data. Examples: clustering, anomaly detection.
- **Reinforcement Learning:** Agents learn optimal behavior through reward-based interactions with an environment. Examples: robotics, game playing.

Deep Learning

A branch of ML that uses multi-layered neural networks (deep neural networks) to model complex patterns. It has achieved state-of-the-art performance in speech recognition, NLP, and image processing [18].

Natural Language Processing (NLP)

Machines can now meaningfully comprehend, interpret, and produce human language thanks to natural language processing, or NLP. It processes text and speech data by fusing machine learning, deep learning, and computational linguistics. Sentiment analysis, language translation, chatbot creation, and document summarizing are important uses. Recent developments such as Transformer models (*e.g.*, BERT and GPT) have greatly improved the performance of natural language processing (NLP) systems on tasks including conversational AI, text production, and question-answering [19].

Computer Vision

Similar to human vision, computer vision allows robots to perceive, interpret, and evaluate visual information from their surroundings. It includes tasks like medical imaging analysis, object detection, facial recognition, and picture categorization. Convolutional Neural Networks (CNNs) are one technique that has transformed computer vision capabilities. Applications span a variety of domains, including industrial automation, surveillance systems, healthcare diagnostics, and driverless cars. Real-time video processing and 3D scene reconstruction are recent developments [20].

Robotics and AI

By integrating cognitive decision-making into physical devices, robotics and Artificial Intelligence (AI) allow robots to carry out intricate, independent tasks. To adjust to changing conditions, these systems frequently include sensors, control schemes, machine learning algorithms, and real-time processing. Autonomous drones, industrial automation, surgical robots, and service robots for homes and workplaces are a few examples of applications. Robotic perception and navigation are frequently improved through the use of computer vision and reinforcement learning. The boundaries of AI-driven robotics are being expanded by new domains such as swarm robotics and human–robot collaboration [21].

HOW AI WORKS: COMPONENTS & WORKFLOW

AI development involves a systematic pipeline of stages from data acquisition to deployment, shown in Fig (**3**). These stages ensure that models are accurate, efficient, and adaptable to new inputs.

Fig. (3). AI development lifecycle.

Data Collection and Preprocessing

The quality of AI systems largely depends on the data they consume. Data preprocessing includes noise removal, normalization, and feature engineering to improve learning outcomes [22]. For instance, in healthcare, AI models trained on preprocessed imaging datasets have shown superior diagnostic accuracy.

Model Training and Evaluation

AI models learn patterns in data through training. The dataset is usually split into training, validation, and test subsets. Algorithms such as Gradient Descent are used to minimize error. Performance is evaluated using metrics such as accuracy, precision, recall, and F1-score. Recent work by Google Health shows that trained models can outperform radiologists in breast cancer detection [23].

Inference and Decision-Making

Once trained, AI models make predictions or classifications (inference) on unseen data. For example, a fraud detection system identifies anomalies in transactions in real-time [24].

Continuous Learning

In modern AI systems, models are often retrained with new data (online or continual learning) to remain effective. This dynamic adjustment enables applications like recommendation engines to adapt to user preferences over time [25]. The tools and frameworks used are shown in Table (**3**).

Table 3. Common AI Tools and Frameworks.

Tool/Framework	Developer	Use case
TensorFlow	Google	Deep learning, computer vision
PyTorch	Meta (Facebook)	Research-focused deep learning
Scikit-learn	Open source	Classical ML: classification, regression
Keras	Google	Simplified deep learning API
OpenCV	Open source	Image processing, computer vision tasks

APPLICATIONS OF AI

By automating processes, improving decision-making, streamlining operations, and revealing intricate patterns concealed in enormous datasets, Artificial Intelligence (AI) technologies are transforming a variety of sectors. AI is not just improving productivity in industries like healthcare and manufacturing, but it is also opening up previously unthinkable possibilities [26]. Table **4**. Summarizes recent studies that demonstrate the significant and expanding influence of AI in a number of important disciplines, as shown in Fig (**4**).

Table 4. Use cases of ai in key sectors.

Sector	Problem Solved	AI-Based Solution
Healthcare	Early disease detection	Deep learning in medical imaging
Finance	Fraudulent transactions	Real-time anomaly detection
Education	Student disengagement	Adaptive learning platforms
Surveillance	Privacy-preserving security	Federated learning with edge devices
Agriculture	Crop disease identification	Vision-based diagnostic models
Manufacturing	Equipment failure	Predictive maintenance with ML models
Autonomous	Human-free navigation	Deep RL in vehicles and drones
Entertainment	Content personalization	Collaborative filtering + NLP generation

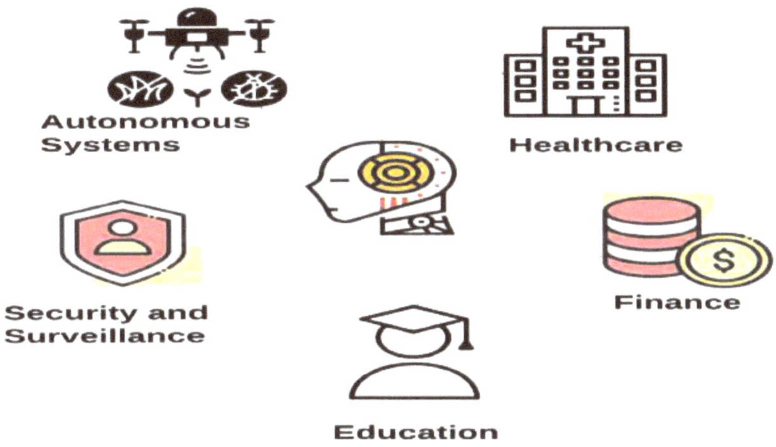

Fig. (4). Applications of AI.

Healthcare

AI-powered solutions have shown remarkable adeptness in drug development, treatment planning, and medical diagnostics. Multimodal AI models—those that integrate imaging data with patient histories—can read chest X-rays with an accuracy on par with qualified radiologists, according to a 2023 research published in Nature Medicine [27]. AI is revolutionizing drug discovery procedures beyond diagnostics. One ground-breaking accomplishment that is speeding up biomedical research is DeepMind's AlphaFold, which has predicted the three-dimensional structures of more than 200 million proteins [28]. Predictive analytics for disease outbreaks, wearable device patient monitoring, and tailored therapy suggestions are more examples of AI uses in healthcare.

Finance

AI has been quickly embraced by the financial services sector for a variety of uses, from algorithmic trading and fraud detection to individualized banking. Time-series forecasting has been significantly enhanced by AI models such as Transformer-based topologies and Long Short-Term Memory (LSTM) networks, which provide more accurate predictions of stock market activity [29]. AI-powered customer support chatbots effectively respond to common questions, increasing customer happiness and response times. Furthermore, increased transparency, equity, and regulatory compliance are being ensured by the incorporation of explainable AI (XAI) methods into lending and credit rating systems [30].

Education

By providing adaptive learning systems that tailor information according to each learner's unique profile, Artificial Intelligence is revolutionizing education. Reinforcement learning algorithms can dynamically modify the pace, level of difficulty, and nature of educational content to optimize student engagement and retention, according to a 2022 research published in Computers and Education: Artificial Intelligence [31]. Additional AI-based educational applications include virtual teaching assistants, essay scoring engines, automatic grading systems, and academic integrity monitoring using behavioral analytics and plagiarism detection algorithms.

Security and Surveillance

Artificial Intelligence (AI)-based technologies, including facial recognition, activity recognition, and anomaly detection, are increasingly enabling security and surveillance systems. Federated learning-based surveillance models were presented in 2023 by recent research, which preserves user privacy by enabling several camera networks to work together to increase detection accuracy without exchanging raw video data [32]. While AI raises significant ethical and privacy issues that need to be addressed, it also aids with real-time danger identification, predictive policing, crowd behavior monitoring, and critical infrastructure security.

Agriculture and Manufacturing

In order to increase agricultural productivity and decrease resource waste, AI-driven computer vision systems are used in agriculture to monitor crop health, identify plant illnesses early, and forecast the best periods for harvest. Large farmlands are also being effectively monitored by drone-based AI systems.

AI-powered predictive maintenance in manufacturing tracks the health of machines and anticipates problems before they arise, greatly cutting downtime and expenses [33]. Additionally, by reducing human error and improving overall production quality, vision-based robotic inspection systems guarantee high-precision quality control on manufacturing lines.

Autonomous Systems

Autonomous cars, drones, and robots rely on Artificial Intelligence (AI) to sense their surroundings, make judgments, and navigate on their own. Businesses such as Waymo (robotaxis), Boston Dynamics (autonomous robots), and Tesla (autopilot) have demonstrated practical uses of AI in path planning, obstacle avoidance, and navigation [34]. In order to teach these systems to adjust to changing settings and gradually enhance their performance, reinforcement learning is very important. AI is also a key component of delivery robots, drones for disaster response, and autonomous military systems.

Entertainment

Streaming platforms like Netflix and Spotify use AI for personalized recommendations. Generative AI is being applied in gaming, music creation, and scriptwriting. A recent example is the use of OpenAI's Codex to generate interactive game dialogues in real-time [35].

BENEFITS AND OPPORTUNITIES OF AI

Due to its revolutionary advantages, Artificial Intelligence (AI) is changing daily life, society, and industries. AI creates new opportunities for personalization, prediction, accessibility, innovation, and scientific discovery in addition to improving operational efficiency. It has an impact on a wide range of industries, including healthcare, finance, education, entertainment, and transportation, as shown in Table (**5**).

Table 5. Traditional *vs.* AI-powered systems.

Feature	Traditional System	AI-Powered System
Task Execution	Rule-based, static	Adaptive, data-driven
Scalability	Limited human-dependent	Scales easily with data and infrastructure
Personalization	Manual customization	Real-time user-specific optimization
Decision-making	Retrospective	Predictive and proactive
Accessibility Tools	Basic assistive technologies	Context-aware, AI-enhanced interfaces

Efficiency and Automation

The capacity of AI to automate labor-intensive, repetitive, and time-consuming jobs is one of its most obvious benefits. In addition to saving money and increasing production, this frees up human workers to concentrate on more complex problem-solving and creative endeavors. For example, Amazon has incorporated AI-powered robots into its warehouses to help with inventory management, sorting, and packing in the logistics industry. These robots have drastically decreased operating expenses and cut item picking time by more than 40% [36]. Customer service chatbots in the banking industry, such as Bank of America's "Erica," answer millions of questions every month, handling problems like bill payments and balance inquiries with excellent customer satisfaction and round-the-clock accessibility. In manufacturing, predictive maintenance powered by AI analyzes machine data in real-time, preventing costly downtime and extending equipment life.

Personalized Experiences

AI systems are able to customize goods, services, and user experiences based on past data, user behavior, and preferences. Customer loyalty, contentment, and engagement are all improved by this hyper-personalization. Stitch Fix, an online personal styling business that employs a hybrid AI-human approach, is a great example. While human stylists improve the choices, their AI models provide fashion recommendations based on consumer profiles, comments, and style preferences. Customer retention and purchase frequency have grown dramatically as a result of the synergy between AI insights and human intuition [37]. By tailoring content streams according to viewing or listening preferences, streaming services like Netflix and Spotify also utilize advanced AI recommendation algorithms to keep customers interested.

Predictive Insights

AI's capacity to find patterns in massive datasets provides strong predictive insights that promote quicker, more intelligent decision-making in a variety of businesses. Google's DeepMind and the UK's National Grid worked together to estimate wind power generation 36 hours ahead of time, attaining previously unfamiliar prediction accuracy in the energy industry [38]. This innovation lessens dependency on fossil fuels, facilitates improved grid integration of renewable energy, and advances environmental sustainability objectives. Predictive models help with hospital resource allocation, patient risk assessment, and early disease identification in the healthcare industry, which improves results and lowers expenses.

Accessibility Improvements

AI is also helping to promote independence and inclusion by making the world more accessible to those with impairments. For instance, Microsoft's Seeing AI software uses the smartphone's camera to narrate the environment for visually impaired users, recognizing objects, people, and text as well as explaining scenarios in real time [39]. This gives people the confidence they need to get through new situations. Similarly, AI-powered text-to-speech and speech-to-text technologies are improving communication for those with speech and hearing problems. Virtual sign language interpreters and AI-powered captioning systems are becoming more prevalent in professional and educational contexts.

CHALLENGES AND LIMITATIONS OF AI

Despite its transformative potential, AI poses numerous challenges that must be addressed to ensure safe, equitable, and sustainable deployment, as shown in Table **6**.

Table 6. Comparative analysis of key existing works in AI.

Reference	Focus Area	Strengths	Limitations
[13] LeCun *et al.*, 2015	Deep Learning	Groundbreaking conceptual foundation	Lacks application-specific coverage
[14] Silver *et al.*, 2016	Reinforcement Learning in Go	Breakthrough in planning/decision-making	Task-specific (Go)
[20] Shen *et al.*, 2017	Medical Image Analysis	Real-world diagnostic performance	Limited interpretability
[27] Zhang *et al.*, 2023	Multimodal Diagnosis	Combines image + patient data	Requires high data availability
[28] Jumper *et al.*, 2021	Protein Folding	Scientific accuracy	Not generalizable to all AI domains
[15] Zhang *et al.*, 2023	Multimodal Deep Learning	Effective cross-modal medical diagnosis	High data requirements
[32] Xu *et al.*, 2025	LLM Hallucination Benchmarking	Benchmark for evaluating LLM hallucinations	Lacks a mitigation strategy
[39] Koh *et al.*, 2024	Concept Bottleneck Models	Improves interpretability and trust	Limited generalization
[50] MIT, 2024	Green AI	Promotes sustainable AI lifecycle design	Early-stage implementations
[52] Google, 2025	Federated Learning in Healthcare	Privacy-preserving model training	Infrastructure complexity

Data Privacy and Security

Massive volumes of data, frequently containing private and sensitive information, are needed for AI systems. Poorly anonymized datasets may be re-identified by AI inference attacks, placing user privacy at serious risk, according to research published in IEEE Access [40]. As AI models themselves become more appealing targets for adversarial attacks, model inversion, and data poisoning, cybersecurity risks also increase. Maintaining trust and protecting users' digital identities now depend heavily on the security of AI pipelines, from data gathering to model deployment.

Bias and Discrimination

If machine learning models are trained on skewed, non-representative datasets, they may unintentionally reproduce and even magnify social prejudices. Even when retrained on purportedly balanced datasets, face recognition algorithms had noticeably worse performance for minority populations, according to a 2025 research by the AI Now Institute [41]. End-to-end openness in the phases of data selection, preparation, model training, validation, and deployment is necessary to address algorithmic bias. Furthermore, creating more egalitarian AI systems requires inclusive evaluation standards and diverse teams.

Explainability and Transparency

AI models, particularly deep learning networks, frequently act as "black boxes," making it challenging to understand the decision-making process. Adoption in crucial fields like healthcare, banking, and criminal justice is severely hampered by this opacity. Although tools for visualizing model reasoning are provided by Explainable AI (XAI) advancements such as SHAP (Shapley Additive exPlanations) and LIME (Local Interpretable Model-Agnostic Explanations), their use varies across sectors [42]. Transparency criteria are starting to be mandated by regulatory frameworks like the EU AI Act, although ethical and technological obstacles still exist.

Overreliance on Automation

An over-reliance on AI may result in automation bias, which reduces human oversight and causes serious mistakes to go overlooked. Delays in human intervention and overconfidence in autonomous car systems have resulted in deadly collisions. The necessity of "human-in-the-loop" methods was highlighted in a 2024 study of Waymo and Tesla collision data, especially in unanticipated or edge-case situations [43]. One of the top priorities of research is still developing systems that can intelligently rely on human judgment in ambiguous circumstances.

AI Hallucination in Generative Models

Large Language Models (LLMs) and picture creation systems are examples of generative AI technologies that can occasionally create information that is false, deceptive, or fabricated—a phenomenon referred to as "hallucination." According to a benchmarking study published in 2025 by Stanford's Center for Research on Foundation Models (CRFM), hallucination rates in high-stakes jobs such as financial forecasting, medical advice generation, and legal summary exceeded 20% [44]. Improving model topologies, honing training data, including retrieval-based techniques, and creating reliable fact-checking pipelines to guarantee output correctness are all necessary to reduce hallucinations.

ETHICS AND RESPONSIBLE AI

As AI becomes increasingly integrated into societal systems, ethical considerations and responsible governance have become paramount, as shown in Table 7. Ensuring fairness, accountability, transparency, and sustainability in AI systems is not only a technical challenge but also a socio-political imperative.

Table 7. Ethical concerns and real-world examples.

Challenge	Description	Real-World Example
Privacy Invasion	Re-identification from anonymized data	Health insurance data leaks *via* inference attacks
Algorithmic Bias	A Model that favors one group over another	Biased hiring platforms screen out qualified women
Lack of Explainability	Black-box decisions with no justification	AI-driven loan denials without rationale
Automation Dependence	Blind trust in AI outputs	Autonomous vehicle crashes from misclassified objects
Generative Hallucination	Outputting false or misleading info	AI-generated legal summaries containing fictitious laws

Fairness, Accountability, and Transparency (FAT)

FAT principles are core to responsible AI. Ensuring fairness requires diverse datasets and bias mitigation; accountability involves mechanisms for tracing responsibility when AI systems fail; and transparency ensures that AI decisions can be explained and understood [45]. Organizations like Google, Microsoft, and IBM have embedded FAT into their AI guidelines.

AI Governance and Guidelines

Various regulatory bodies have proposed ethical frameworks for AI:

- **EU AI Act (2024)**: Categorizes AI systems by risk (unacceptable, high, limited, and minimal) and enforces compliance for high-risk applications [46].
- **IEEE's Ethically Aligned Design**: Offers guidelines for embedding ethical considerations throughout AI system development [47].
- **OECD AI Principles**: Promote inclusive growth, sustainable development, and human-centric values in AI [48].

The Role of Humans in the Loop

Maintaining human oversight, particularly in high-stakes decision-making, is critical. A 2025 case study at Mayo Clinic demonstrated improved diagnostic reliability when radiologists used AI support tools in tandem with human judgment, rather than relying solely on algorithmic outputs [49].

Sustainable AI

AI has a growing carbon footprint due to large-scale model training. Initiatives like "Green AI" advocate for energy-efficient model design and sustainable infrastructure. A recent 2024 MIT study emphasized the importance of lifecycle assessments for AI tools deployed in environmental monitoring and climate forecasting [50].

THE FUTURE OF AI

AI is advancing rapidly, with emerging trends indicating that future systems will be more explainable, collaborative, decentralized, and powerful than ever before. These developments present both new opportunities and complex challenges for researchers, developers, and policymakers.

Explainable AI (XAI)

Explainability and transparency are more important than ever as AI systems are incorporated into more and more important decision-making processes, especially in high-stakes industries like healthcare, banking, law, and autonomous cars. Stakeholders, including physicians, attorneys, legislators, and end users, must be able to comprehend, have faith in, and successfully contest the judgments made by AI systems. Despite their great predicted accuracy, traditional deep learning models sometimes operate as "black boxes" that provide no explanation for their decision-making process. In addition to undermining user confidence, this opacity poses significant questions about responsibility, justice, and regulatory compliance. Recent advancements in XAI, such as Concept Bottleneck Models (CBMs), allow users to understand which high-level concepts influenced a model's prediction [51]. A 2024 study published in Nature Machine Intelligence demonstrated how XAI improved trust and compliance among clinical professionals using diagnostic AI.

Federated Learning

Federated learning allows for cooperative model training over dispersed devices while maintaining the privacy and locality of data. Models are trained locally on users' devices rather than uploading raw data to a centralized server; only the updated parameters are combined to create a better global model. This decentralized strategy encourages adherence to data protection laws like GDPR and HIPAA and dramatically lowers the danger of data breaches.

Federated learning is quickly becoming popular, particularly in industries like healthcare and finance, where privacy is a concern. Without ever exchanging sensitive patient data between institutions, Google's 2025 pilot program, which used federated learning across many hospitals, showed significant gains in the identification of diabetic retinopathy [52]. Similar applications are also starting to appear in insurance underwriting and mobile applications (such as predictive keyboards), where privacy and customization must coexist.

AI and Quantum Computing

By utilizing quantum mechanical qualities like superposition and entanglement, quantum computing promises to significantly speed up AI algorithms. This makes it especially well-suited for sophisticated simulations, optimization, and cryptography. The first quantum-enhanced Machine Learning (ML) pipeline was demonstrated by IBM's Qiskit team in 2025, marking a major advancement that allowed for the real-time analysis of massive, unstructured information, including genetic sequences and global weather patterns [53].

Although quantum AI is still in its early stages, scientists believe it will transform domains such as cybersecurity by developing new quantum-resistant encryption techniques and challenging established cryptographic protocols, and drug discovery by accurately simulating molecular interactions at the atomic level. To bridge the gap between today's capabilities and tomorrow's quantum improvements, companies like Google, IBM, and Rigetti are making significant investments in developing hybrid quantum-classical AI frameworks.

Human–AI Collaboration

The focus of AI in the future is shifting from replacing people to collaborative intelligence, in which robots and humans cooperate while utilizing their own advantages. Humans provide creativity, moral discernment, and emotional intelligence, while machines provide speed, scalability, and data-driven insights.

Designers, authors, and marketers are already utilizing AI-powered solutions such as Adobe Firefly and OpenAI's ChatGPT-5 to collaborate on textual and visual material in the creative professions [54]. For instance, visual artists use AI to rapidly prototype several iterations of design layouts, while writers utilize it to generate draft ideas or alternate wording. According to studies, these hybrid workflows greatly increase output, encourage variety in creativity, and allow people to do things that were not possible in the past. Furthermore, AI is a strong colleague rather than a substitute in domains like scientific research and medicine, helping experts with data analysis, diagnosis, and hypothesis formulation.

The Possibility of Artificial General Intelligence (AGI)

AGI is a type of Artificial Intelligence that can learn and carry out a wide range of activities without task-specific training. Its broad, generalized cognitive skills are equivalent to human intellect. Even though Artificial General Intelligence (AGI) is still mostly theoretical, top companies like OpenAI, DeepMind, and Anthropic are making huge investments and research efforts in this field. The Future of Life Institute's 2025 policy brief highlights the main moral, technological, and geopolitical issues surrounding the development of AGI [55]. Assuring value alignment (so AGI systems behave in accordance with human values), avoiding power concentration, and fostering international collaboration to responsibly manage risks are some of the main issues.

OPEN RESEARCH ISSUES AND FUTURE DIRECTIONS

Despite impressive progress, there are still a number of unresolved research issues in the field of Artificial Intelligence. Reducing hallucinations in generative models, producing energy-efficient AI systems, developing autonomous technologies that comply with the law, and making sure algorithmic development is ethical by design are important examples of these. AI for climate forecasting, continuous learning systems, hybrid quantum-classical models, and increasing human-AI collaborations in scientific and creative fields comprise a few future directions.

CONCLUSION

Artificial Intelligence (AI) is a defining technology of the 21st century, reshaping industries, enhancing decision-making, and introducing new paradigms of automation and human-machine collaboration. This chapter has provided a comprehensive overview of AI's evolution, key concepts, operational mechanisms, wide-ranging applications, and the ethical responsibilities tied to its development.

From the Turing Test to ChatGPT and beyond, AI has transitioned from theoretical exploration to a powerful enabler of real-world innovation. We explored foundational ideas in machine learning, deep learning, and natural language processing, examined the lifecycle of AI model development, and highlighted its applications in fields like healthcare, education, finance, and autonomous systems. However, with great capability comes great responsibility.

Challenges such as data privacy, algorithmic bias, explainability, and sustainability must be addressed with transparency and care. Ethical frameworks and global governance efforts are essential to ensure that AI development remains aligned with human values and societal well-being.

Looking forward, trends like Explainable AI, Federated Learning, Quantum AI, and human-AI collaboration point to a future where AI acts not only as a tool but also as a partner in solving the world's most pressing challenges. We encourage readers, researchers, students, and practitioners alike to explore specialized domains within AI, contribute to its responsible growth, and remain vigilant about the broader implications of its integration into society. Cybersecurity and the fundamentals of AI play a transformative role in creating intelligent, adaptive, and proactive defense systems. By leveraging machine learning, deep learning, and anomaly detection, AI enhances threat prediction, intrusion detection, and incident response. The integration of AI with cybersecurity ensures real-time protection against evolving digital threats, enabling secure data handling, user authentication, and network resilience—thereby bridging the gap between intelligent automation and digital safety in an increasingly connected world.

REFERENCES

[1] M. Indrasenareddy, N.S. Bohra, S. Mukherjee, Y. Sucharitha, M. Yesubabu, and M.L. Prasad, "Working toward a comprehensive approach for ensuring security and privacy in artificial intelligence," *in Leveraging Artificial Intelligence in Cloud, Edge, Fog and Mobile Computing*, Shrikaant Kulkarni, P. William, V. Prakash, and J. N. Dwivedi, Eds., Auerbach Publications, 2025, pp. 3–18
[http://dx.doi.org/10.1201/9781032703718]

[2] S.B. Latha, Y. Sucharitha, I.A. Tayubi, K. Shekar, D. Pandey, and R.V. Sudhakar, Virtual learning analysis using complex rule-based approach in the context of cloud computing," *in 2025 3rd International Conference on Communication, Security, and Artificial Intelligence (ICCSAI)*, Greater Noida, India, 04–06 Apr. 2025, vol. 3, pp. 1110–1115
[http://dx.doi.org/10.1109/ICCSAI64074.2025.11064645]

[3] M. Haenlein, and A. Kaplan, "A brief history of Artificial Intelligence: On the past, present, and future of Artificial Intelligence", *Calif. Manage. Rev.*, vol. 61, no. 4, pp. 5-14, 2019.
[http://dx.doi.org/10.1177/0008125619864925]

[4] V.K. Bukkarayasamudram, P.C.S. Reddy, and K. Arun Kumar, "Quantum computing revolution in healthcare: a systematic review of applications, issues and future directions", *Artif. Intell. ReV*, vol. 58, 20242025.
[http://dx.doi.org/10.1007/s10462-025-11381-w]

[5] K.N. DuBois, "Deep medicine: how Artificial Intelligence can make healthcare human again", *Perspect. Sci. Christ. Faith*, vol. 71, no. 3, pp. 199-201, 2019.

[6] E. Wong, "Media Review", *InnovAiT*, vol. 15, no. 10, pp. 611-611, 2022.
[http://dx.doi.org/10.1177/17557380211018237]

[7] E.D. Gennatas, and J.H. Chen, "Artificial intelligence in medicine: past, present, and future," in Artificial Intelligence in Medicine, L. Xing, M. L. Giger, and J. K. Min, Eds., Academic Press, 2021, pp. 3–18.
[http://dx.doi.org/10.1016/B978-0-12-821259-2.00001-6]

[8] B. Elov, A. Dauletov, Y. Sucharitha, F. Khalilova, M. Latipova, and M. Abdullayeva, "An intelligent traffic management of vehicles using deep learning approach in smart cities," *in 2025 3rd International Conference on Integrated Circuits and Communication Systems (ICICACS)*, Raichur, India, 21–22 Feb. 2025, pp. 1–5 [http://dx.doi.org/10.1109/ICICACS65178.2025.10967703]

[9] S. Yadala, C.S.R. Pundru, and V.K. Solanki, "A novel private encryption model in IoT under cloud computing domain," in Intelligent Systems and Networks: Proceedings of ICISN 2023, T. D. L. Nguyen, E. Verdú, A. N. Le, and M. Ganzha, Eds., Lecture Notes in Networks and Systems, vol. 752, Singapore: Springer, 2023, pp. 263–270.

[10] P. Ravali, P.C.S. Reddy, and P. Praveen, "Employing a deep learning approach for brain tumour detection using MR-images", *in 2024 4th International Conference on Mobile Networks and Wireless Communications (ICMNWC),* pp. 1-5, 2024. [http://dx.doi.org/10.1109/ICMNWC63764.2024.10872062]

[11] R. Samrin, K. A. Kumar, N. Deepthi, C. Mithra, Y. Sucharitha, and G. K. Thakur, "A hybrid deep learning based framework for prediction of rice yield through integration of biophysical parameters and optical remote sensing data in India,", *Journal of Atmospheric and Solar-Terrestrial Physics,* vol. 279, p. 106734, 2026. [http://dx.doi.org/10.1016/j.jastp.2026.106734]

[12] G.B. Madhavi, M. Sumithra, P.Y. Devi, U.S.B.K. Mahalaxmi, T. Saravanan, and P.C.S. Reddy, "Skin cancer classification of dermoscopic images using deep learning", *2024 4th International Conference on Advancement in Electronics & Communication Engineering (AECE),* pp. 1242-1247, 2024. [http://dx.doi.org/10.1109/AECE62803.2024.10911365]

[13] E.V.N. Jyothi, M. Kranthi, S. Sailaja, U. Sesadri, S.N. Koka, and P.C.S. Reddy, "An adaptive intrusion detection system in industrial internet of things (IIoT) using deep learning", *In: 2024 1st International Conference on Innovative Sustainable Technologies for Energy, Mechatronics, and Smart Systems (ISTEMS),* IEEE, pp. 1-6, 2024. [http://dx.doi.org/10.1109/ISTEMS60181.2024.10560245]

[14] Y.K. Duymaz, and Ş. Şahin, "From ancient mythology to modern technology: The historical evolution of Artificial Intelligence", *Eur. J. Ther.,* vol. 29, no. 4, pp. 964-965, 2023. [http://dx.doi.org/10.58600/eurjther1895]

[15] L.D. Jones, D. Golan, S.A. Hanna, and M. Ramachandran, "Artificial intelligence, machine learning and the evolution of healthcare", *Bone Joint Res.,* vol. 7, no. 3, pp. 223-225, 2018. [http://dx.doi.org/10.1302/2046-3758.73.BJR-2017-0147.R1] [PMID: 29922439]

[16] A. Toosi, A.G. Bottino, B. Saboury, E. Siegel, and A. Rahmim, "A brief history of AI: How to prevent another winter (a critical review)", *PET Clin.,* vol. 16, no. 4, pp. 449-469, 2021. [http://dx.doi.org/10.1016/j.cpet.2021.07.001] [PMID: 34537126]

[17] R. Krishnamoorthy, M. Gupta, G. Swathi, K. Tanaka, C. Raja, and J. V. N. Ramesh, "An intelligent IoT-based smart healthcare monitoring system using machine learning," in *5G-Based Smart Hospitals and Healthcare Systems*, CRC Press, 2023, pp. 230–247. [http://dx.doi.org/10.1201/9781003403678]

[18] P. Ravali, P.C.S. Reddy, and P Praveen, "An efficient neuro-framework for brain tumor classification using a CNN-based self-supervised learning approach with genetic optimizations", *Current Neuropharmacology,* vol. 24, no. 4, 2025. [http://dx.doi.org/10.2174/011570159X378103250806214613]

[19] D. Silver, A. Huang, C. J. Maddison, A. Guez, L. Sifre, G. van den Driessche, J. Schrittwieser, I. Antonoglou, V. Panneershelvam, M. Lanctot, S. Dieleman, D. Grewe, J. Nham, N. Kalchbrenner, I. Sutskever, T. Lillicrap, M. Leach, K. Kavukcuoglu, T. Graepel, and D. Hassabis, "Mastering the game of Go with deep neural networks and tree search", *Nature,* vol. 529, no. 7587, pp. 484-489, 2016. [http://dx.doi.org/10.1038/nature16961]

[20] A.T. Somnathe, V.T. Selvi, N.G. Stepha, M.T. Kingslin, F.M. Inamdar, and P.C.S. Reddy,, "An intelligent traffic conflict prediction using deep learning with long-term evolution access data", *In 2025 3rd International Conference on Smart Systems for applications in Electrical Sciences (ICSSES),* pp. 1-6, 2025. [http://dx.doi.org/10.1109/ICSSES64899.2025.11010032]

[21] G R Kumar, S B Latha, P C S Reddy Shaker, and Y Sucharitha, "Multi-agent IoT-based system for intelligent vehicle traffic management using wireless sensor networks", *Recent Advances in Electrical & Electronic Engineering,* vol. 17, no. 5, pp. 515-522, 2024. [http://dx.doi.org/10.2174/2352096516666230719114956]

[22] Godavari, A., Pattem, S., Marrikukkala, R. K., Yamsani, N., & Yuvalatha, S., "Deep ensemble 3d cnn framework for lung cancer detection using ct-images", *In 2025 International Conference on Intelligent Computing and Knowledge Extraction (ICICKE),* 2024. (pp. 1-5). IEEE, 2025, Bengaluru, India. [http://dx.doi.org/10.1109/ICICKE65317.2025.11136291]

[23] P. Rajpurkar, E. Chen, O. Banerjee, and E.J. Topol, "AI in health and medicine", *Nat. Med.,* vol. 28, no. 1, pp. 31-38, 2022. [http://dx.doi.org/10.1038/s41591-021-01614-0] [PMID: 35058619]

[24] S. Saidul Islam, H. Elmekki, and A. Elsebai, "A comprehensive survey on applications of transformers for deep learning tasks", *Mach. Learn. Knowl. Extr.,* vol. 6, no. 3, pp. 571-626, 2023.

[25] K.R. Rao, M.S. Kumari, R. Eklarker, P.C.S. Reddy, K. Muley, and V.K. Burugari, "An adaptive deep learning framework for prediction of agricultural yield", *2024 International Conference on Integrated Circuits and Communication Systems (ICICACS),* IEEE., pp. 1-6, 2024. [http://dx.doi.org/10.1109/ICICACS60521.2024.10498465]

[26] G.K. Thakur, S. Kulkarni, S. Khan, M.M.T. Ayyalasomayajula, and P.C.S. Reddy, "A bone metastatic cancer origin prediction using deep learning on digital pathological", *International Conference on Computer, Electronics, Electrical Engineering & their Applications (IC2E3),* pp. 1-6, 2024. IEEE [http://dx.doi.org/10.1109/IC2E362166.2024.10827171]

[27] G. Eysenbach, "The role of ChatGPT, generative language models, and Artificial Intelligence in medical education: a conversation with ChatGPT and a call for papers", *JMIR Med. Educ.,* vol. 9, no. 1, p. e46885, 2023. [http://dx.doi.org/10.2196/46885] [PMID: 36863937]

[28] M.D. Basith, P. Praveen, and P.C.S. Reddy, "Adaptive deep Q-GAN framework for enhanced breast cancer detection in medical imaging", *Biomedical Signal Processing and Control,* vol. 112, p. 108638, 2026. [http://dx.doi.org/10.1016/j.bspc.2025.108638]

[29] N. R. Reddy, P. Sudarsanam, N. Yathish, P. MJ, K. Kalyani, S. Asif, and P. C. S. Reddy, "A Hybrid Deep-Learning based Security Enhancement Framework for Intrusion Detection in WSNs", *International Journal of Sensors, Wireless Communications and Control,* vol. 15, no. 3, pp. 243-255, 2025.

[30] C.A. Gomez-Uribe, and N. Hunt, "The netflix recommender system: Algorithms, business value, and innovation", *ACM Trans. Manag. Inf. Syst.,* vol. 6, no. 4, pp. 1-19, 2016. [TMIS]. [http://dx.doi.org/10.1145/2843948]

[31] G. Arun, P.C.S. Reddy, N. Budati, B. Rebecca, S. Perumalla, and V.B. Gujar, "A Deep Learning Framework for Diabetes Prediction: PIMA Indian Dataset", In: *2024 International Conference on Innovative Computing, Intelligent Communication and Smart Electrical Systems (ICSES),* Chennai, India., 2024, pp. 1-6.

[32] P.C. Shaker Reddy, and Y. Sucharitha, "An energy-saving data transmission approach based on migrating virtual machine technology to cloud computing", *Recent Advances in Electrical & Electronic Engineering (Formerly Recent Patents on Electrical & Electronic Engineering),,* vol. 17, no. 6, pp. 573-581, 2024.

[http://dx.doi.org/10.2174/2352096516666230713163440]

[33] S.B. Shunmugavel, S.K. Nagarajan, K.D. Rangaswamy, and M. Muthiah, "A hybrid framework for fake news detection using explainability of artificial intelligence", *Recent Patents on Engineering,* vol. 19, no. 9, 2025.
[http://dx.doi.org/10.2174/0118722121313149240729044309]

[34] L. Su, X. Zuo, R. Li, X. Wang, H. Zhao, and B. Huang, "A systematic review for transformer-based long-term series forecasting", *Artif. Intell. Rev.,* vol. 58, no. 3, p. 80, 2025.
[http://dx.doi.org/10.1007/s10462-024-11044-2]

[35] N. Abdelshiheed, J.W. Hostetter, T. Barnes, and M. Chi, "Leveraging deep reinforcement learning for metacognitive interventions across intelligent tutoring systems", *IEEE Trans. Learn. Technol.,* vol. 17, no. 1, pp. 1-14, 2024.

[36] S. Shikalgar, R.K. Yadav, and P.N. Mahalle, "An AI federated system for anomalies detection in videos using convolutional neural network mechanism", *Int. J. Intell. Syst. Appl. Eng.,* vol. 11, no. 1, suppl. Suppl., pp. 218-227, 2023.

[37] J. Agrawal, and M.Y. Arafat, "Transforming farming: A review of AI-powered UAV technologies in precision agriculture", *Drones (Basel),* vol. 8, no. 11, p. 664, 2024.
[http://dx.doi.org/10.3390/drones8110664]

[38] S. Sai, A. Garg, K. Jhawar, V. Chamola, and B. Sikdar, "A comprehensive survey on Artificial Intelligence for unmanned aerial vehicles", *IEEE Open J. Veh. Technol.,* vol. 4, pp. 713-738, 2023.
[http://dx.doi.org/10.1109/OJVT.2023.3316181]

[39] K. Khandelwal, "Use of AI for personalized recommendations, streaming optimization, and original content production at Netflix", *International Journal of Scientific Research and Engineering Trends,* vol. 9, no. 6, pp. 1738-1743, 2023.
[http://dx.doi.org/10.61137/ijsret.vol.9.issue6.119]

[40] P.R. Wurman, R. D'Andrea, and M. Mountz, "Coordinating hundreds of cooperative, autonomous vehicles in warehouses", *AI Mag.,* vol. 29, no. 1, pp. 9-9, 2008.

[41] W. Gong, and L. Khalid, "Aesthetics, personalization and recommendation: A survey on deep learning in fashion", *IEEE Trans. Multimed.,* vol. 23, no. 5, pp. 1105-1120, 2021.

[42] C. Elkin, and S. Witherspoon, "Optimizing wind farm power output with neural networks: A DeepMind case study", *Wind Energy (Chichester Engl.),* vol. 27, no. 3, pp. 431-446, 2024.

[43] C. Carini, and A.A. Seyhan, "Tribulations and future opportunities for artificial intelligence in precision medicine", *J. Transl. Med.,* vol. 22, no. 1, p. 411, 2024.
[http://dx.doi.org/10.1186/s12967-024-05067-0] [PMID: 38702711]

[44] E. Kotter, and E. Ranschaert, "Challenges and solutions for introducing artificial intelligence (AI) in daily clinical workflow", *Eur. Radiol.,* vol. 31, no. 1, pp. 5-7, 2021.
[http://dx.doi.org/10.1007/s00330-020-07148-2] [PMID: 32797308]

[45] P. S. Muller, Y. Sucharitha, S. Kottapally, G. Ismoilova, L. Rakhimova, and P. C. S. Reddy, "A Novel Financial Market Prediction Framework Based on Deep Learning for Accurate Trend Forecasting", In: *Information Systems for Intelligent Systems*. ISBM 2025, A. Iglesias, J. Shin, N. Bhatt, A. Joshi, (eds) Information Systems for Intelligent Systems. ISBM 2025. Lecture Notes in Networks and Systems, vol 1748. Springer, Cham.
[http://dx.doi.org/10.1007/978-3-032-12990-1_5]

[46] A.B. Friedrich, J. Mason, and J.R. Malone, "Rethinking explainability: toward a postphenomenology of black-box artificial intelligence in medicine", *Ethics Inf. Technol.,* vol. 24, no. 1, p. 8, 2022.
[http://dx.doi.org/10.1007/s10676-022-09631-4]

[47] A. T. Somnathe, M. Parameshwari, S. Pattem, S. N. Koka, S. Abdurakhmanova, and P. C. S. Reddy, "An Attention-Based Deep Learning Framework for Gold Price Prediction Using Time Series Data", In: *Information Systems for Intelligent Systems*. ISBM 2025, A. Iglesias, J. Shin, N. Bhatt, A Joshi

(eds) Information Systems for Intelligent Systems. ISBM 2025. Lecture Notes in Networks and Systems, vol 1743. Springer, Cham. [http://dx.doi.org/10.1007/978-3-032-13006-8_6]

[48] S.M.T. Islam Tonmoy, S.M.M. Zaman, V. Jain, and A. Das, "A comprehensive survey of hallucination mitigation techniques in large language models", *ACM Comput. Surv.,* vol. 56, no. 4, p. 97, 2024.

[49] B.D. Mittelstadt, P. Allo, M. Taddeo, S. Wachter, and L. Floridi, "The ethics of algorithms: Mapping the debate", *Big Data Soc.,* vol. 3, no. 2, p. 2053951716679679, 2016. [http://dx.doi.org/10.1177/2053951716679679]

[50] V Alukapelly, M Vasudevarao, R Janagi, I. A. Tayubi, U. S. B. K. Mahalaxmi, and P. C. S. Reddy, "An Explainable AI—Driven Ensemble Model for Improved Heart Disease Diagnosis", In: *2025 International Conference on Advances in Next-Gen Computer Science (ICANCS).* IEEE, 2025, pp. 1-6. [http://dx.doi.org/10.1109/ICANCS65819.2025.11377960]

[51] M. DeCamp, and C. Lindvall, "Latent bias and the implementation of artificial intelligence in medicine", *J. Am. Med. Inform. Assoc.,* vol. 27, no. 12, pp. 2020-2023, 2020. [http://dx.doi.org/10.1093/jamia/ocaa094] [PMID: 32574353]

[52] M. Subramanian, J. K. Raguru, M. Yesubabu, V. V. Satyanarayana Paka, P. S. Rao, and C. Dastagiraiah, "Private blockchain-based efficient secure cloud data storage using federated learning framework", *Int. J. Sensors Wireless Commun. Control,* vol. 15, no. 1, pp. 2-13, 2025. [http://dx.doi.org/10.2174/0122103279311703240605075342]

[53] G. Anjaneyulu, P.C.S. Reddy, P. Praveen, S. Banoth, D. Pandey, and S.N. Koka, "A hybrid optimization deep learning frame work for efficient stock market forecasting", *2025 International Conference on Advanced Computing Technologies (ICoACT),* IEEE., pp. 1-6, 2025. [http://dx.doi.org/10.1109/ICoACT63339.2025.11004655]

[54] S. Surekha, R.V.S. Lalitha, M. Srikanya, S.J. Sri, R. Kinjagi, and D. Keerthana, "Deep Reinforcement Learning Approach for Autonomous Vehicles to Cross Junctions," *in Algorithms and Computational Theory for Engineering Applications: ICACTEA 2024*, S. Rama Sree and S. Kumar, Eds., Cham, Switzerland: Springer, 2025. [http://dx.doi.org/10.1007/978-3-031-72747-4_16]

[55] V. Sukhavasi, A. C. Mouli, D. V. Juneja, Y. Sucharitha, S. S. Joshi and S. Dey, "Establishing ensemble learning models for daily rainfall forecasting," in *2024 Int. Conf. Innov. Comput., Intell. Commun. Smart Electr. Syst. (ICSES)*, Chennai, India, 2024, pp. 1–6 [http://dx.doi.org/10.1109/ICSES63760.2024.10910429]

CHAPTER 3

Strategic Integration of AI in Modern Cybersecurity Frameworks

LNC Prakash Koratamaddi[1], **Goddumarri Suryanarayana**[2], **Lakshmi Hassan Nagaraja**[3], **Seema Nagaraj**[4] and **Pundru Chandra Shaker Reddy**[5,*]

[1] *Department of Computer Science & Engineering-Data Science, CVR College of Engineering, Hyderabad, Telangna, India*

[2] *Symbiosis Institute of Technology, Hyderabad Campus, Symbiosis International University, Hyderabad, Telangana, India*

[3] *Department of CSE (AI&ML), CVR College of Engineering, Hyderabad, Telangana, India*

[4] *Department of MCA, Bangalore Institute of Technology, Bengaluru, Karnataka, India*

[5] *Amity School of Engineering and Technology Department of Computer Science and Engineering Amity University, Noida Uttar Pradesh, India*

Abstract: The rapid advancements in Artificial Intelligence (AI) have significantly transformed the landscape of cybersecurity, providing both new opportunities and challenges. This chapter explores the dynamic interplay between AI and cybersecurity, focusing on how AI-driven solutions enhance threat detection, incident response, and risk mitigation while also examining the emerging threats posed by AI-powered cyberattacks. AI has revolutionized cybersecurity by enabling intelligent automation, real-time threat analysis, and predictive modelling. Machine learning algorithms can detect anomalies, identify malware patterns, and adapt to evolving attack strategies, making cybersecurity defences more proactive and efficient. Deep learning techniques further enhance Intrusion Detection Systems (IDS), enabling faster and more accurate identification of potential security breaches. Additionally, AI-powered security frameworks strengthen authentication mechanisms, fraud detection, and vulnerability management, reducing human errors and response time. However, AI itself is a double-edged sword in cybersecurity. While it strengthens defences, cybercriminals increasingly leverage AI to develop sophisticated attack methods, including adversarial AI, deepfake-based social engineering, and automated hacking tools. The rise of AI-driven cyber threats demands an equally robust AI-driven defence mechanism, necessitating the development of explainable AI (XAI) for transparent decision-making and ethical AI governance to prevent misuse. This chapter provides a comprehensive analysis of AI's role in cybersecurity, discussing real-world applications, challenges, and future trends. It also highlights the ethical and regulatory considerations in deploying AI-based security solutions. By addressing these aspects, this chapter aims to provide a balanced perspective on harnessing AI's potential to build a resilient cyber-

* **Corresponding Author Pundru Chandra Shaker Reddy**: Amity School of Engineering and Technology Department of Computer Science and Engineering Amity University, Noida Uttar Pradesh, India; E-mail: chandu.pundru@gmail.com

security framework while mitigating the risks associated with its adversarial applications.

Keywords: Artificial Intelligence, Cybersecurity, Explainable AI (XAI), Hacking, Intrusion Detection Systems (IDS), Machine learning, Social engineering, Vulnerability.

INTRODUCTION

In an increasingly interconnected digital world, cybersecurity has become a cornerstone of modern information infrastructure. As the volume, velocity, and variety of cyber threats continue to escalate, traditional approaches to securing digital assets are proving insufficient. The integration of Artificial Intelligence (AI) into cybersecurity offers a transformative approach to subdue these evolving threats. AI introduces a paradigm shift in how organizations detect, prevent, and respond to cyber incidents by leveraging data-driven insights, automation, and predictive capabilities [1]. The convergence of AI and cybersecurity represents a dual-use frontier. On one hand, AI empowers cybersecurity systems with enhanced pattern recognition, anomaly detection, and adaptive learning, helping security teams stay ahead of increasingly sophisticated threats [2]. On the other hand, adversaries are also adopting AI technologies to develop more complex and evasive attacks, such as adversarial machine learning and deepfake-based social engineering [3]. Traditionally, cybersecurity relied on signature-based systems and human expertise to identify threats and respond to breaches. These systems were effective against known threats but lacked the agility to detect zero-day exploits and novel malware variants. AI and machine Learning (ML) bridge this gap by enabling systems to learn from historical data, adapt to new threat signatures, and make intelligent decisions in real-time. One of the most impactful uses of AI in cybersecurity is in threat detection. Machine learning models, including supervised, unsupervised, and reinforcement learning, are employed to identify anomalous network behaviors, malware signatures, and phishing attempts [4]. Deep learning models further enhance intrusion detection systems by enabling faster, more accurate identification of malicious activity through pattern recognition across complex data [5]. AI also accelerates incident response by facilitating automation. Security Orchestration, Automation, and Response (SOAR) systems powered by AI can analyze logs, correlate threat intelligence, prioritize alerts, and initiate pre-defined mitigation protocols with minimal human intervention [6]. These capabilities drastically reduce response time and mitigate potential damage. In risk management and vulnerability assessment, AI tools scan vast codebases and network configurations to identify flaws, rank their severity, and recommend remediation strategies. Predictive analytics allow security teams to anticipate future threats and allocate resources efficiently [7]. Despite these benefits, AI in cybersecurity presents challenges. Deep learning models are often black boxes, offering little interpretability regarding their decisions. This lack of transparency complicates accountability, especially when false positives or negatives occur [8]. Hence, the need for Explainable AI (XAI) becomes crucial in high-stakes security environments.

The threat landscape is further complicated by adversarial AI, where attackers manipulate input data to deceive AI systems. This includes evading malware detectors or fooling biometric systems with deepfakes [9]. The growing use of generative AI, such as large language models and synthetic media generators, poses a new set of risks that current cybersecurity models must adapt to. In this context, robust AI governance and ethical guidelines are essential. Policies must address data privacy, model robustness, transparency, and the misuse of AI technologies [10]. Regulatory bodies such as the EU have begun drafting AI regulations to mitigate these risks, but international collaboration remains necessary. Human expertise continues to be vital. While AI enhances capabilities, it cannot replace human intuition and ethical judgment. The most effective cybersecurity strategies involve human-AI collaboration, where each complements the other's strengths [11]. This chapter provides a comprehensive exploration of AI's applications, opportunities, and challenges in cybersecurity. It addresses emerging trends, adversarial risks, ethical concerns, and future research directions. By understanding both the potential and pitfalls of AI in cybersecurity, we can work towards building resilient, transparent, and ethical digital defense systems. Cybercrime losses reached a staggering $12.8 billion in 2023. Experts project these losses to hit $23.84 trillion by 2027. Organizations now face an average of 1,308 cyber-attacks weekly in early 2024 - a 28% increase from the previous quarter. AI-powered cybersecurity has emerged as a critical defense strategy, with 90% of organizations implementing these security solutions. The relationship between AI and cybersecurity cuts both ways. Organizations embrace these technologies faster than ever, yet 75% of cybersecurity experts report more frequent attacks. Bad actors using generative AI account for 85% of this increase. The situation looks more challenging since 59% of cybersecurity teams lack adequate staffing. Less than half of these teams feel confident they can detect and respond to threats effectively. This piece dives into artificial intelligence and cybersecurity approaches that deliver results in 2025. You'll discover proven AI-powered threat detection systems and automated security responses that work. We'll also help you calculate the ground ROI of your AI security investments.

LITERATURE SURVEY

The integration of Artificial Intelligence (AI) and Machine Learning (ML) into cybersecurity has significantly enhanced the detection, prevention, and mitigation of cyber threats. With the rapid evolution of both cyberattacks and defensive technologies, AI-powered solutions have become crucial in addressing the growing complexity and sophistication of modern cybersecurity challenges. This literature review aims to provide a comprehensive overview of the key AI-driven techniques and methodologies used in cybersecurity, with a particular focus on threat detection, anomaly detection, malware classification, and the implications of adversarial attacks. By examining the latest advancements, the review highlights the opportunities that AI presents in strengthening security frameworks while also addressing the emerging risks associated with its use by cybercriminals. Each reference discussed in this review showcases the diversity of AI applications in cybersecurity, from deep learning models used for intrusion detection to novel approaches for enhancing privacy and resilience in dynamic network environments. A foundational study explores the integration of fuzzy data mining with genetic algorithms to enhance Intrusion Detection Systems (IDS) [12]. Fuzzy logic is employed to manage the uncertainty and imprecision often present in network traffic data. Genetic algorithms are used to evolve and optimize detection rules dynamically. The study demonstrates that combining these two AI techniques results in improved detection of both known and unknown attacks, as well as better adaptability to changing threat environments. Although early, the approach laid the groundwork for hybrid intelligent systems in cybersecurity. A research paper [13] presents HAST-IDS, a deep learning-based intrusion detection model that leverages hierarchical spatial-temporal features. The model combines convolutional neural networks (CNNs) for spatial feature extraction with recurrent neural networks (RNNs) to model temporal dependencies. It was tested on benchmark datasets and showed superior accuracy and reduced false positive rates compared to traditional IDS models. This work illustrates how combining different neural architectures enhances real-time threat detection and adaptation in dynamic environments.

The authors in [14] introduce the UNSW-NB15 dataset, which addresses the limitations of older IDS datasets like KDD99 by including more modern and realistic network traffic scenarios. It contains nine attack types and a variety of features useful for training and testing machine learning models in cybersecurity. The dataset has become a standard for evaluating AI-based IDS solutions, offering more relevant and diverse attack representations. It enables the development of models that are more robust in practical applications. A study [15] investigates the application of deep learning, specifically deep autoencoders, to network intrusion detection. The proposed model learns compressed representations of network traffic data and uses reconstruction error for anomaly detection. Compared to shallow learning models, the deep learning approach showed improved accuracy and reduced false positives. The research supports the growing consensus that deep learning can significantly enhance the capabilities of

IDS by capturing complex attack patterns. A comprehensive survey [16] examines recent advances in applying deep learning to cybersecurity tasks such as malware detection, phishing, and intrusion detection. It highlights the strengths of deep learning models in handling large-scale, high-dimensional data, but also discusses challenges related to explainability, adversarial robustness, and data privacy. The authors emphasize the need for interpretable models and reliable training data to ensure real-world effectiveness. This review serves as a guide for researchers and practitioners looking to develop trustworthy AI-driven cybersecurity systems. This critical paper [17] questions the overreliance on machine learning in Intrusion Detection Systems (IDS) without a proper understanding of operational challenges. It argues that many ML-based IDS fail in real-world settings due to issues like false positives, lack of labeled data, and changing attack vectors. The authors advocate for practical deployment strategies and for incorporating domain knowledge to improve ML model effectiveness. The work highlights the importance of evaluating ML systems not just by accuracy but by their usability and sustainability in production environments. A review article [18] categorizes and evaluates various AI applications in cybersecurity, including threat detection, malware classification, and behavior analysis. It emphasizes the role of supervised, unsupervised, and reinforcement learning across different cybersecurity domains. The paper also discusses AI's utility in automated vulnerability assessment, phishing detection, and botnet mitigation. This broad survey helps establish AI's impact on modern cybersecurity practices and research.

A paper [19] investigates adversarial examples—inputs crafted to mislead AI models—and their implications for cybersecurity. The authors examine how such attacks can compromise machine learning-based IDS and malware detectors. They also explore defensive strategies, including adversarial training and robust optimization techniques. The study underscores the vulnerability of AI systems to adversarial manipulations and the pressing need for defensive AI mechanisms. Another paper [20] presents a detailed overview of Explainable AI (XAI) methods applied in cybersecurity contexts. The authors explore techniques such as SHAP, LIME, and rule-based models to increase transparency in AI-driven IDS and malware detection systems. Challenges include balancing performance and interpretability, especially for deep learning models. The study makes a case for integrating XAI into cybersecurity governance frameworks to support trust and accountability. The authors of a study [21] analyze deep learning applications in processing IoT-generated big data, with special focus on cybersecurity use cases. They highlight the role of convolutional and recurrent architectures in detecting anomalous traffic patterns in IoT networks. This survey also touches on challenges such as data heterogeneity and latency. It is particularly relevant for security in smart environments and edge computing scenarios where real-time responses are critical. A study [22] investigates static detection of malicious JavaScript using machine learning models. By extracting n-gram features from JavaScript code, classifiers such as SVMs and decision trees are used to identify threats, including obfuscated code. The model significantly improves detection rates compared to signature-based techniques and highlights the effectiveness of ML in defending against evolving web-based threats. A paper [23] presents a hybrid approach using rough sets for feature selection and self-organizing maps (SOMs) for anomaly detection. The integration of these AI techniques offers both accuracy and computational efficiency in detecting malicious network behaviors. The model is particularly effective in minimizing false positives and handling high-dimensional cybersecurity data. The authors [24] propose a neural network-based system for detecting anomalies in time-dependent data streams, such as those in dynamic cybersecurity environments. The model adapts to evolving behavioral baselines and is effective in identifying stealthy intrusions and zero-day attacks. It exemplifies the importance of temporal learning in modern IDS design.

A comprehensive survey [25] examines the application of AI in financial fraud detection. It categorizes various ML and DL approaches, highlights challenges like class imbalance and adversarial manipulation, and suggests future research directions. The discussion is valuable to cybersecurity researchers, especially in areas with overlapping fraud and intrusion detection needs. Another study [26] leverages LSTM networks to detect domain names generated by malware using Domain Generation Algorithms (DGAs). The model identifies subtle patterns in domain structures that escape traditional DNS blacklisting. This contributes to real-time blocking of command-and-control traffic and enhances endpoint security. Another paper [27] introduces TCAV, an XAI method that evaluates how high-level human concepts influence predictions made by deep learning models. In cybersecurity, this aids in understanding how and why an AI system identifies a threat, making AI decisions more transparent and legally defensible, especially in high-stakes environments like digital forensics. Another study [28] provides an extensive overview of adversarial attacks on ML models, including poisoning, evasion, and model inversion. It presents countermeasures and design principles for securing AI systems used in cybersecurity. The authors emphasize the need for robustness testing and adversarial resilience in real-world deployment. A survey [29] outlines the unique security challenges of fog computing, which supports edge AI applications. Topics include secure data sharing, authentication, and attack mitigation in decentralized networks. The paper advocates for AI-enhanced defence strategies tailored to fog architectures, crucial for protecting IoT ecosystems. The authors of a study [30] convert binary malware files into grayscale images and apply convolutional neural networks for classification. This novel vision-based approach captures structural patterns not easily seen in traditional binary analysis. The model achieves high accuracy and provides a new perspective on leveraging AI for malware detection. A foundational article [31] addresses the security challenges in Cyber-Physical Systems (CPS), emphasizing real-time constraints and safety-critical applications. It discusses how machine learning and anomaly detection can monitor and protect CPS, such as smart grids and transportation systems. The work bridges AI, control systems, and cybersecurity in mission-critical domains. A systematic review [32] evaluates over 100 Intrusion Detection Systems (IDS) using machine learning techniques, focusing on datasets, evaluation metrics, and algorithms. It provides a comprehensive analysis of the effectiveness of supervised, unsupervised, and hybrid models. The authors emphasize the limitations in generalizability and dataset bias and propose guidelines for more standardized IDS research. This work serves as a benchmark for researchers developing next-generation intelligent IDS. A study [33] introduces a novel method to simulate realistic network traffic using Generative Adversarial Networks (GANs) for evaluating cybersecurity tools. By mimicking malicious and benign behaviors, GAN-generated data enhances IDS training, particularly for rare attacks. This technique is essential for improving detection accuracy without needing massive real-world labeled data.

A paper [34] provides an in-depth overview of XAI techniques in cybersecurity, mapping current methods to specific domains such as malware detection, IDS, and phishing. The authors discuss the interpretability–performance trade-off and propose hybrid models that balance accuracy and transparency. It's particularly useful for designing AI solutions that meet regulatory and ethical standards. A research [35] applies deep learning and NLP to detect phishing emails and other social engineering tactics. Using transformer models like BERT, it analyzes linguistic features to flag deceptive content. The model significantly outperforms traditional spam filters, marking a shift toward semantic-aware cybersecurity tools that understand language context. Biggio and Roli [36] revisit the evolution of adversarial machine learning, particularly in evasion and poisoning attacks. They provide a taxonomy of threats and defences, showing how adversarial AI undermines trust in ML-based security systems. Their work forms a foundation for developing robust, adversary-aware models in cybersecurity. A survey [37] covers traditional and AI-based approaches to network anomaly detection, including statistical, clustering, and classification-based techniques. It offers a historical view of how anomaly detection evolved toward intelligent, context-aware systems. The paper provides a solid grounding for comparing modern AI methods with classical techniques. Another study [38] investigates the use of Deep Belief Networks (DBNs) for identifying attacks on SCADA systems and other critical infrastructure. It shows that DL models outperform SVM and decision trees in recognizing stealthy and zero-day attacks. The paper emphasizes the role of AI in defending national security assets from cyber threats. Another paper [39] proposes a framework for integrating XAI into digital forensic investigations. By explaining AI-generated evidence, the framework helps investigators validate and trust machine outputs in court-admissible settings. It also highlights challenges such as data integrity and the need for traceable model decisions in legal contexts. This paper [40] explores deploying AI models on edge devices for real-time threat detection in IoT networks. The authors focus on lightweight neural networks optimized for constrained environments. It illustrates how local decision-making reduces latency and enhances security in decentralized architectures. The authors of a study [41] surveyed dynamic analysis techniques for detecting ransomware behaviour. They propose using AI to automate sandboxing, behavioural tracing, and feature extraction. The study underscores how intelligent automation can reduce analysis time and improve malware classification accuracy.

METHODOLOGY

Machine Learning (ML)

Machine Learning enables systems to learn from historical data and improve the detection and classification of threats. It is widely used to identify malware, phishing attacks, and suspicious behavior patterns without relying on predefined rules. Supervised learning classifies known attack types, while unsupervised learning helps discover new threats by clustering. Semi-supervised models combine the strengths of both. ML can adapt to changing cyber landscapes, offering dynamic and proactive defences. It is commonly integrated into antivirus software and Endpoint Detection and Response (EDR) systems. However, it requires large, high-quality datasets and proper feature engineering. False positives and adversarial attacks remain concerns.

Example: ML algorithms like Random Forests are used by Microsoft Defender to detect unknown malware by learning from labelled malware datasets.

Deep Learning

Deep Learning uses layered neural networks to process complex patterns in data, especially large-scale and unstructured inputs. It excels in areas like anomaly detection, intrusion detection, and malware analysis due to its ability to learn deep representations. Convolutional Neural Networks (CNNs) classify image-based malware, while RNNs analyze log data and command sequences. DL systems can detect polymorphic malware and zero-day threats with high accuracy. Though powerful, deep learning models are often opaque ("black boxes") and require high computational resources. They are also vulnerable to adversarial examples.

Example: Google uses deep learning in Gmail's spam filters and phishing detection, improving classification accuracy even for previously unseen attacks.

Natural Language Processing (NLP)

NLP empowers AI to process and understand human language, making it crucial for analyzing emails, social media, and chat logs. In cybersecurity, NLP helps detect phishing content, extract threat intelligence, and classify malicious text. It is used in automated threat intelligence platforms to scan the dark web or decode attacker forums. NLP models can identify social engineering attempts and malicious command instructions. With transformer-based architectures like BERT and GPT, the accuracy of text analysis has significantly improved. However, attackers use evolving language tactics to evade NLP filters.

Example: Security solutions like Proofpoint use NLP to detect phishing emails that contain deceptive language, even when they avoid known malicious URLs.

Anomaly Detection

Anomaly detection involves identifying behaviours that deviate from a baseline of normal activity. It is ideal for spotting insider threats, privilege abuse, or lateral movement during Advanced Persistent Threats (APTs). AI-based systems build profiles of normal behaviour for users, applications, and systems. When deviations are observed, such as logging in from an unusual location or accessing restricted files, alerts are generated. The approach is highly effective for detecting zero-day attacks or unknown threat vectors.

Example: Splunk's User Behaviour Analytics (UBA) tool uses machine learning-based anomaly detection to flag unusual employee activity that could indicate insider threats.

Reinforcement Learning (RL)

Reinforcement Learning allows AI agents to learn optimal actions through feedback from interactions with their environment. In cybersecurity, RL helps automate network defence, dynamically configure firewalls, or manage honeypots. The system rewards actions that reduce risk or detect attacks while penalizing ineffective ones. It's particularly useful for adaptive systems that evolve with threats. However, RL requires extensive training and simulations, and poor design may lead to unintended strategies.

Example: Researchers at IBM used reinforcement learning to train AI agents to detect and neutralize simulated attacks in a dynamic network defence game.

Support Vector Machines (SVM)

SVMs are powerful classifiers that find the optimal hyperplane separating classes of data, useful in binary classification tasks. In cybersecurity, they are used in Intrusion Detection Systems (IDS), spam filtering, and malware detection. SVMs perform well on small to medium datasets and are resistant to overfitting. They can handle both linear and non-linear decision boundaries using kernel tricks. However, they can be less efficient on very large datasets.

Example: An SVM classifier was used to detect DoS attacks in the KDD Cup 1999 dataset with high accuracy, forming the basis for academic IDS research models.

Decision Trees and Random Forests

Decision Trees are intuitive models that make decisions based on feature-based splits, while Random Forests aggregate multiple trees for more stable predictions. These models are easy to interpret and explain, making them useful in regulatory-compliant environments. They are commonly used to classify malware, predict system vulnerabilities, or prioritize alerts. They offer fast training and inference, though Random Forests can become computationally expensive.

Example: A cybersecurity startup used Random Forests to build a phishing URL detector by training on features such as URL length, domain age, and character distribution.

Clustering Algorithms (K-Means, DBSCAN)

Clustering groups data points without labels, allowing for the discovery of new or unknown threat patterns. K-Means is good for general grouping, while DBSCAN excels in identifying outliers and anomalies. These techniques are often used in exploratory data analysis and for detecting abnormal patterns in network traffic. They help segment users or IPs based on behavior and detect novel attack campaigns.

Example: Cisco Talos uses clustering to group similar malware variants and track how new malware families evolve over time in large-scale threat datasets.

Generative Adversarial Networks (GANs)

GANs consist of two neural networks—generator and discriminator—that compete to improve data realism. In cybersecurity, GANs are used to generate realistic-looking phishing emails, simulate malware behaviors, or create adversarial examples for testing detection robustness. They can also augment training data in rare-attack scenarios. However, attackers may also misuse GANs to generate polymorphic malware.

Example: Researchers developed a GAN-based system to generate synthetic malware samples, which helped improve the robustness of antivirus classifiers by expanding the training dataset.

Fuzzy Logic

Fuzzy logic deals with reasoning under uncertainty, making it ideal for ambiguous cybersecurity situations. Unlike binary logic, it allows degrees of truth, helping systems assess threat levels based on multiple imprecise indicators. It's used in intrusion detection systems, access control policies, and fuzzy rule-based firewalls. Its interpretability and flexibility are key strengths. Example: A fuzzy logic-based intrusion detection system was implemented to detect unauthorized access by evaluating factors such as login frequency, file access, and time of access with fuzzy thresholds.

AI enables real-time intrusion detection and response by continuously monitoring network activity, identifying anomalies, and recognizing unknown threats. It automates threat alerts, prioritizes risks, and initiates immediate counteractions like isolating compromised systems. This ensures faster, adaptive, and proactive defense against evolving cyberattacks.

ADVANTAGES AND DISADVANTAGES

Real-Time Threat Detection

AI systems can monitor network activity and user behavior continuously.
They can identify threats as they occur, without human delay. This enables faster mitigation of attacks before they cause harm. Machine learning models excel at spotting subtle anomalies in large data streams.

Automated Response and Remediation

AI can trigger automated actions in response to identified threats. For instance, it can block malicious IPs, isolate infected systems, or revoke access. This reduces dependence on human intervention during critical moments. Automation helps in scaling cybersecurity efforts without increasing manpower.

Predictive Threat Intelligence

Using historical data, AI can forecast potential threats or attack patterns. It allows organizations to prepare defences before an attack even happens. Predictive models help prioritize patching and resource allocation. This proactive approach shifts cybersecurity from reactive to preventive.

Enhanced Malware Detection

AI can analyse files, processes, and behaviors to detect unknown or zero-day malware. It doesn't rely only on known signatures like traditional antivirus software.
Deep learning can spot hidden malware features missed by human analysts.

This boosts the detection rate of polymorphic and advanced malware.

Adaptive Security Systems

AI-powered tools learn and evolve with time, adjusting to new threat landscapes.

They can retrain models or update rules based on new data. This continuous learning enables better handling of emerging threats. Such adaptability enhances long-term system resilience.

Reduced False Positives

Unlike rule-based systems, AI models can differentiate between benign and malicious activities more accurately. They reduce false alerts by analyzing patterns in context.
This improves analyst productivity and lowers alert fatigue. Security teams can focus on actual threats instead of noise.

Improved Identity and Access Management (IAM)

AI helps in analyzing login behavior, device data, and access patterns.

This enables dynamic access control and detection of identity theft or misuse. Unusual access attempts can be flagged or blocked in real time. This strengthens multi-factor authentication and reduces insider threats.

Fraud Detection and Prevention

AI models analyze financial transactions and user behavior for suspicious activity.

They can detect fraud in banking, e-commerce, and insurance sectors. Real-time fraud alerts help prevent losses and protect customers. AI continuously improves by learning from new fraud techniques.

Threat Hunting and Intelligence Gathering

AI helps in aggregating and analyzing threat intelligence from multiple sources. Natural Language Processing (NLP) enables AI to extract useful information from reports, logs, and dark web forums. This speeds up manual threat hunting processes. AI-powered tools can even suggest mitigation strategies.

Machine learning predicts and prevents cyberattacks by analyzing patterns in large datasets to detect anomalies and forecast potential threats. It learns from past attacks, adapts to new tactics, and enables real-time, proactive defense. This continuous learning helps identify zero-day vulnerabilities and strengthens overall cybersecurity resilience.

Scalability and Efficiency

AI allows organizations to scale their cybersecurity operations without needing a proportionate increase in staff. It can handle vast amounts of network traffic and user data efficiently. This is particularly useful for large enterprises and critical infrastructure.
AI makes cybersecurity both cost-effective and responsive at scale.

Ethical AI and Data Governance

It ensures that artificial intelligence systems operate responsibly, transparently, and fairly. Ethical AI focuses on preventing bias, ensuring accountability, and maintaining human oversight in automated decisions. Data governance establishes clear policies for data collection, storage, access, and usage while protecting privacy and compliance with legal standards. Together, they build trust in AI-driven systems, promote data integrity, and support responsible innovation. Effective implementation of these principles ensures that technology serves humanity ethically and sustainably.

CHALLENGES AND FUTURE TRENDS

Adversarial Attacks

AI models can be tricked using adversarial inputs—slightly modified data that looks normal to humans but deceives the model. This allows attackers to bypass malware detectors or intrusion detection systems. Such attacks undermine trust in AI predictions and require constant model hardening. These vulnerabilities are especially critical in deep learning-based systems.

Data Dependency

AI systems need large amounts of high-quality, labeled data to function accurately.

If training data is insufficient, outdated, or unbalanced, the model may misclassify inputs.

In cybersecurity, data labeling is difficult due to privacy and the rarity of certain attacks.

This limitation hinders the scalability and adaptability of AI models.

False Positives and Negatives

AI systems can produce false positives (flagging safe activity as malicious) or false negatives (missing actual threats). Frequent false alarms can lead to alert fatigue among security teams. Conversely, undetected attacks may go unnoticed and cause damage. Balancing precision and recall remains a major challenge.

Lack of Explainability

Many AI models, especially deep learning ones, are considered "black boxes" due to their complex internal logic. Security teams may not understand why a model flags or ignores a threat. This limits trust in automated systems and complicates decision-making.

Explainable AI (XAI) is still an emerging solution in cybersecurity.

High Computational Cost

AI, particularly deep learning, requires powerful CPUs/GPUs and vast storage.

Running real-time detection or training models can be expensive and time-consuming.

Cloud-based AI introduces additional operational costs and privacy risks.

This can be a barrier for small or resource-constrained organizations.

Model Drift

Cyber threats evolve constantly, but AI models trained on past data may not recognize new patterns. This leads to model drift, where accuracy degrades over time.

Without continuous retraining and updates, the model's effectiveness declines.

Automated systems require regular maintenance to stay current.

Bias in Algorithms

AI models can reflect and amplify biases in their training datasets. For example, a model trained on enterprise data might perform poorly in personal computing contexts. Bias can lead to unfair targeting or missing certain attack types. Ensuring fairness and generalization is an ongoing challenge in AI-based security.

Dual-Use by Attackers

AI tools are not limited to defenders—attackers also use them. They employ AI to automate attacks, generate deepfakes, and craft intelligent phishing campaigns. Generative models like GANs can create realistic malware variants. This arms race makes defensive AI more complex and urgent.

Ethical and Legal Issues

Automated security decisions, such as user blocking or surveillance, can raise privacy and ethical concerns. Improper use of AI may violate data protection regulations like GDPR.

Transparency and informed consent are often missing in AI deployment. Governance frameworks are still catching up with AI capabilities.

Integration Complexity

Deploying AI within existing cybersecurity infrastructure isn't always seamless.

It may require re-engineering systems, training staff, and aligning with workflows.

Some legacy environments cannot support AI-based tools easily. Misconfigurations during integration can even introduce new vulnerabilities.

AI enhances threat detection by learning from large volumes of data to identify anomalies and unknown threats that traditional rule-based systems often miss. It enables real-time monitoring, adaptive learning, and automated responses, improving accuracy and reducing false positives. Unlike static methods, AI continuously evolves with emerging attack patterns, providing faster and more intelligent threat identification.

APPLICATIONS OF AI IN CYBERSECURITY

Intrusion Detection Systems (IDS)

AI-powered IDS uses machine learning to monitor network traffic and identify abnormal patterns indicating possible intrusions. Unlike traditional rule-based systems, AI can detect novel attacks. Techniques like deep learning enhance accuracy and adaptability. Real-time detection minimizes breach response time. AI enables autonomous decision-making for threat mitigation.

Malware Detection and Classification

AI algorithms analyse file behaviour and characteristics to detect malware, even before execution. It helps classify various malware families using static and dynamic analysis. Deep learning models outperform traditional antivirus tools. AI adapts to polymorphic and metamorphic malware. This improves both endpoint and network protection.

Phishing Email Detection

Natural Language Processing (NLP) and AI detect phishing attempts in emails by analysing content, tone, and embedded URLs. These systems learn continuously from new attack data. AI identifies even well-crafted spear-phishing emails. It protects users from credential theft and data breaches. Integration with email servers ensures proactive defence.

Behavioural Biometrics for Authentication

AI analyses user behaviour such as typing speed, mouse movements, and swipe patterns. These behavioural traits are unique and hard to replicate. It adds an invisible layer of security during login or transactions. Machine learning enhances accuracy over time. Used in banking and enterprise systems for fraud prevention.

Network Traffic Analysis

AI inspects large volumes of network data in real-time to detect anomalies. It classifies benign *vs.* malicious traffic using predictive modelling. Helps identify threats like botnets, data exfiltration, or DDoS attacks. Reduces the load on human analysts. Essential in large-scale enterprise and cloud environments.

Spam and Bot Detection

AI distinguishes between legitimate and malicious user behaviour. Bots are detected by analysing request frequency, user-agent strings, and behavior. AI helps platforms reduce spam, fake accounts, and bot-driven abuse. Ensures the integrity of social media and online platforms. Adaptive systems evolve with changing bot tactics.

Threat Intelligence and Prediction

AI aggregates and analyzes threat data from multiple sources. It predicts future attacks based on trends and indicators. Enables security teams to take preventive action. Reduces dwell time and improves incident readiness. Enhances threat hunting capabilities through pattern recognition.

Anomaly Detection in User Behaviour

Machine learning monitors deviations from normal user behaviour. It flags unusual activity like logging in from unknown IPs or accessing abnormal data volumes. Useful for detecting insider threats. Models are tailored to user profiles. Real-time alerts prevent privilege abuse and data leaks.

Ransomware Detection and Prevention

AI can identify ransomware by analysing system behaviour, file access patterns, and encryption signatures. Early detection helps halt attacks before data encryption completes. It also aids in classifying ransomware strains. Behavioural analysis strengthens endpoint defences. Reduces damage and downtime from ransomware attacks.

Security Log Analysis

AI automates the analysis of vast system and security logs. It identifies critical events, unusual sequences, or signs of compromise. Saves time for Security Operations Center (SOC) teams by prioritizing alerts. NLP is used to parse unstructured logs. Enhances visibility across distributed systems.

Automated Incident Response

AI assists in automating triage, containment, and response workflows. It decides which alerts need human intervention. Reduces mean time to detect (MTTD) and respond (MTTR). Improves consistency in handling incidents. Enables 24/7 response without burnout.

Vulnerability Management

AI predicts which vulnerabilities are most likely to be exploited. It prioritizes patching based on risk, exploitability, and impact. Helps organizations avoid patching fatigue. Integrates with threat feeds and scanners. Supports efficient risk management in large environments.

Secure Access and Identity Management

AI enhances identity verification by learning from access patterns. Detects anomalies in authentication attempts. Supports adaptive access control and risk-based authentication. Integrates biometrics and contextual signals. Prevents unauthorized access even with stolen credentials.

Data Loss Prevention (DLP)

AI identifies and prevents sensitive data from leaving an organization. It classifies and monitors structured and unstructured data. Learns from data movement patterns and flags risky transfers. Reduces insider threats and accidental leaks. Key for compliance with data privacy regulations.

Endpoint Threat Detection

AI continuously monitors endpoint behaviour for signs of compromise. It detects fileless malware, abnormal process activity, or registry changes. Provides early alerts and forensics data. Integrates with EDR platforms for real-time protection. Essential for remote and BYOD environments.

Adversarial Attack Detection

AI systems are trained to recognize adversarial inputs crafted to fool models. These are important in detecting fake images, poisoned datasets, or obfuscated code. Improves model robustness. Vital in AI security applications like facial recognition or content moderation. Defends AI systems against AI-based attacks.

Cloud Security Monitoring

AI monitors cloud activity across services and regions. It detects misconfigurations, unusual access, and data exposure. Supports multi-cloud environments with scalability. AI adapts to changing cloud architectures. Ensures visibility and compliance in dynamic environments.

IoT Device Threat Detection

AI secures IoT networks by analysing device behaviour and communication. It detects compromised devices or unauthorized firmware changes. Uses lightweight models for low-power devices. Ensures safety in healthcare, smart homes, and industrial systems. Helps manage billions of connected devices securely.

Fake Content and Deepfake Detection

AI models are trained to detect synthetic media generated by other AI systems. These include deepfakes used in impersonation attacks or misinformation. Detection tools analyse artifacts, inconsistencies, and facial movements. Supports digital forensics and media integrity. Critical in preventing social engineering and fraud.

Explainable AI for Security Decision-Making

Explainable AI (XAI) helps cybersecurity analysts understand AI-generated decisions. This is vital for regulatory compliance and trust. XAI clarifies why a user was flagged or a threat classified. Aids in debugging and improving model performance. Ensures accountability in AI-driven security systems.

LIMITATIONS

Dependence on Quality Data

AI systems require large volumes of high-quality, well-labelled, and diverse datasets to train effectively. In cybersecurity, however, such data can be scarce due to privacy regulations, the proprietary nature of security logs, and the rarity of certain types of attacks. If the training data is biased, outdated, or incomplete, the model may produce inaccurate or misleading results. This data dependency makes AI vulnerable to performance degradation in real-world environments where threats are constantly evolving.

Inability to Handle Novel Threats Without Retraining

AI models often rely on historical data to make predictions and detect anomalies. While this allows them to recognize known patterns of malicious behaviour, it also limits their ability to identify new, never-before-seen threats such as zero-day vulnerabilities or novel malware. Without regular retraining or real-time learning capabilities, the AI system may fail to respond effectively to emerging threats, thereby compromising cybersecurity defences.

High False Positive Rates

Although AI excels at detecting anomalies, it can sometimes generate excessive false positives by misclassifying normal behaviour as suspicious. This can flood security teams with alerts, causing alert fatigue and diverting attention away from genuine threats. Tuning AI systems to balance precision and recall is a complex task, and even slight deviations in network behaviour can trigger unnecessary warnings. Consequently, these high false positive rates can reduce operational efficiency and trust in AI systems.

Lack of Transparency and Explainability

Many AI algorithms, especially deep learning models, operate as "black boxes," offering little insight into how decisions are made. In cybersecurity, where accountability and compliance are critical, this lack of transparency is a significant drawback. Analysts and stakeholders may find it difficult to understand or trust AI-generated alerts or actions. This can hinder adoption, complicate incident investigation, and raise challenges in legal and regulatory contexts.

Resource-Intensive Deployment

Implementing AI-based cybersecurity solutions requires significant computational power, especially when using deep learning or real-time processing. Training models demands high-performance GPUs and large memory capacities, which can be expensive and resource-intensive. Smaller organizations may struggle to afford the infrastructure or cloud services needed to deploy and maintain AI solutions. Additionally, ongoing maintenance, updates, and monitoring add to the operational cost.

Vulnerability to Adversarial Attacks

AI models can be exploited through adversarial attacks, where attackers deliberately manipulate input data in subtle ways that mislead the system. For example, a slightly altered malware signature may evade detection by an AI model. These attacks expose a fundamental weakness in many AI-based systems and highlight the need for improved robustness. In a cybersecurity context, such vulnerabilities can be catastrophic if not properly mitigated.

Complex Integration with Existing Systems

Integrating AI technologies into existing cybersecurity infrastructures is not always straightforward. Legacy systems may lack the flexibility or interoperability needed to accommodate AI tools. Organizations often need to overhaul their IT architectures, establish new data pipelines, and retrain personnel to fully leverage AI capabilities. This complexity can delay deployment, increase costs, and even introduce new security vulnerabilities during the transition.

Ethical and Legal Concerns

The use of AI in cybersecurity raises important ethical and legal issues, particularly around privacy, surveillance, and autonomy. Automated systems that make decisions about user behaviour can lead to false accusations or discriminatory practices. Furthermore, organizations must navigate data protection laws such as GDPR, which may limit the collection and use of personal data for training AI. Failure to address these concerns can result in reputational damage and legal penalties.

Limited Human Oversight

Over-reliance on AI can diminish human involvement in cybersecurity decision-making. While automation increases efficiency, it also reduces the capacity for contextual judgment and nuanced analysis. If AI systems make incorrect decisions—such as shutting down critical infrastructure or flagging innocent users—there may be no human intervention to override or review the action in time. Maintaining a balanced level of human oversight is essential for responsible AI deployment.

Cost and Skill Barrier

Deploying AI in cybersecurity is not just a technological challenge but also a financial and human resource issue. Skilled professionals with expertise in both AI and cybersecurity are in high demand but short supply. Training staff and maintaining AI systems can be prohibitively expensive for small to mid-sized enterprises. This cost and expertise barrier limits the democratization of AI and may widen the gap between organizations with advanced cyber defenses and those without.

AI-powered threat detection systems work much better than traditional security tools. Recent studies show detection rates have improved by 60% [42]. These systems can respond to incidents in seconds instead of the previous average of 168 hours. AI-driven behavioral analysis leads the charge in modern cybersecurity. These systems use sophisticated machine learning algorithms to learn about normal behavior patterns from network traffic, system logs, and user activities [43]. The system quickly alerts security teams when it spots anything unusual.

AI has made huge strides in cutting down false positives. Security teams used to waste time checking false alarms rather than dealing with real threats. The modern

AI systems have become fluent in spotting the difference between real suspicious activities and harmless changes through continuous learning [43]. Zero-day attack detection showcases AI's impressive capabilities in security. These attacks exploit unknown vulnerabilities and usually stay hidden for 312 days [44]. Machine learning models now spot these threats by analyzing complex statistical patterns before they cause major damage. Google's Project Zero shows new zero-day attacks pop up about every 17 days. Detection-as-Code (DaC) methodology improves SOC capabilities, especially when you have teams who need to program, control versions, and deploy detection logic precisely. This approach allows automated updates that match the latest threat intelligence [45].

Behavioral analytics serves as a powerful weapon in the AI security arsenal. The Ponemon Institute reports 70% of cybersecurity professionals say AI finds previously hidden threats. Deep Instinct's research shows AI-driven tools stop 92% of phishing attacks, while legacy systems only catch 60%. Fortune 500 companies have increased their use of advanced threat detection tools by 35%. Gartner predicts 70% of organizations will use AI-driven threat intelligence systems by 2025. These numbers show growing trust in AI's power to protect against sophisticated cyber threats [46].

Automated Security Response: From Theory to Practice

AI-powered automated incident response has transformed cybersecurity. Response times have dropped from 14 hours to just seconds [47]. Security teams now use sophisticated AI algorithms to automate routine tasks and can focus on making complex strategic decisions.

AI-driven automation makes the incident response process better by quickly spotting and isolating threats [48]. Companies that use automated response systems have cut their operational costs by 40% [49]. These systems handle high-volume, repetitive processes well and end up reducing potential damage and system downtime.

AI and human expertise work together smoothly in automated response systems. While AI powers the automated responses, human judgment plays a vital role in strategic decisions and solving complex problems [50]. This partnership lets AI handle immediate threats while security professionals develop sophisticated defense strategies.

Automated response systems work because they can assess threat severity and take predefined actions instantly [51]. Netflix's FIDO (Fully Integrated Defense Operation) system shows this in action. It analyzes security events and coordinates responses across its infrastructure automatically [51]. Their other tool,

Dispatch, handles incident data and resources by connecting with tools like Slack and GSuite [52]. Self-healing networks mark another breakthrough in automated security response. They detect, diagnose, and fix issues on their own - often before anyone notices problems. These networks use large language models and proactive systems to collect analytics, analyze data, and fix issues without human help [53].

Setting up automated response systems needs careful planning. Organizations should integrate them properly with existing security systems and keep detailed documentation. Regular updates to response playbooks are essential [54]. Teams should monitor performance continuously to spot areas for improvement and keep the system running effectively. The rise of automated security response shows no signs of slowing down. As AI gets smarter, these systems will predict and prevent threats more effectively while keeping the right balance between automation and human oversight.

Measuring ROI of AI Cybersecurity Investments

ROI calculations for artificial intelligence cybersecurity solutions require a different approach from traditional metrics. Organizations that implement AI-powered security solutions save an average of USD 2.20 million in breach costs [55]. These systems cut down containment time by over 100 days and reduce breach costs by 45% [56]. Organizations need specific Key Performance Indicators (KPIs) to measure AI cybersecurity ROI. The core metrics include mean time to detect (MTTD), mean time to respond (MTTR), threat intelligence accuracy, and compliance adherence rates [57]. These indicators help organizations learn about the effectiveness of their security investments. AI has brought a fundamental change to cybersecurity ROI calculations by introducing measurable metrics. Security teams can now track reductions in false positives, time saved on routine tasks, and improvements in incident response times [58]. Organizations that use AI-driven security automation reduce their incident investigation time by 60%.

The financial benefits go beyond direct cost savings. Companies that prioritize security retain twice as many customers. A security breach can affect stock value and revenue for more than five years. A full ROI assessment should include both short-term and long-term advantages. Data quality plays a crucial role in AI security investments, with 85% of leaders naming it their biggest challenge [4]. Most organizations spend 4-7% of their IT budget on cybersecurity, while AI implementations often need extra investment. The shortage of talent adds another factor to ROI calculations. The global cybersecurity workforce faces a gap of 3.4 million professionals. Organizations must include ongoing training and talent development costs in their calculations. About 60% of security teams now make use of AI tools to address staffing shortages. Small and medium-sized businesses (SMBs) can now access budget-friendly, expandable cybersecurity tools. SMBs that implement Zero Trust security models cut their breach risks by 50%. This shows that well-planned AI security solutions can be cost-effective for organizations of any size.

CONCLUSION

The integration of Artificial Intelligence into cybersecurity marks a pivotal advancement in safeguarding digital infrastructures. AI-driven technologies—ranging from machine learning and deep learning to natural language processing—have significantly enhanced the speed, accuracy, and efficiency of threat detection, response, and risk mitigation. By automating routine tasks, analyzing massive volumes of data in real time, and adapting to evolving threats, AI empowers organizations to proactively defend against increasingly sophisticated cyberattacks. However, the use of AI in cybersecurity is not without limitations. Challenges such as model interpretability, data privacy concerns, adversarial AI threats, and the high computational cost of AI systems must be carefully addressed. Furthermore, malicious actors are now leveraging AI to launch more advanced and evasive attacks, creating a new arms race in the digital domain. To ensure AI remains a force for good in cybersecurity, it is crucial to develop explainable and transparent models, implement robust ethical frameworks, and foster global regulatory cooperation. The future of cybersecurity lies in a balanced synergy between human expertise and AI capabilities—where intelligent systems augment, not replace, human decision-making. By understanding both the strengths and vulnerabilities of AI-powered security systems, stakeholders can build resilient, adaptive, and ethically sound defense architectures. In an era where cyber threats are escalating in frequency and complexity, AI is not just an advantage—it is a necessity.

Future research should focus on developing autonomous, self-healing cybersecurity systems capable of real-time adaptation to emerging threats. Emphasis must be placed on explainable and privacy-preserving AI to enhance transparency and trust. Collaboration among governments, academia, and industry is vital to establishing global security standards. Exploring federated learning and quantum-resistant algorithms can strengthen data protection. Ultimately, integrating human expertise with intelligent automation will ensure resilient and adaptive cyber defense.

LIST OF ABBREVIATIONS

AI Artificial Intelligence

SOAR Security Orchestration Automation, and Response
IDS Intrusion Detection Systems
CNNs Convolutional Neural Networks
RNNs Recurrent Neural Networks
SOMs Self-Organizing Maps
DGAs Domain Generation Algorithms
CPS Cyber-Physical Systems
GANs Generative Adversarial Networks
DBNs Deep Belief Networks
EDR Endpoint Detection and Response
UBA User Behaviour Analytics
SVM Support Vector Machines
NLP Natural language processing
DaC Detection-as-Code
MTTR Mean Time To Respond
MTTD Mean Time To Detect

REFERENCES

[1] I.H. Sarker, A.S.M. Kayes, S. Badsha, H. Alqahtani, P. Watters, and A. Ng, "Cybersecurity data science: an overview from machine learning perspective", *J. Big Data,* vol. 7, no. 1, p. 41, 2020. [http://dx.doi.org/10.1186/s40537-020-00318-5]

[2] K. Terala, Chinnaswamy C.N., N. Arjun, J. Dev Vikas, and S. Mohammad Khaja, "Digital twins for brain tumor detection using MRI images by deep learning", *2024 4th International Conference on Advancement in Electronics & Communication Engineering (AECE),* 2024.

[3] A.T. Somnathe, V.T. Selvi, N.G. Stepha, M.T. Kingslin, F.M. Inamdar, and C.S.R. Pundru, "An intelligent traffic conflict prediction using deep learning with long-term evolution access data", *2025 3rd International Conference on Smart Systems for applications in Electrical Sciences (ICSSES),* 2025. [http://dx.doi.org/10.1109/ICSSES64899.2025.11010032]

[4] T.T. Nguyen, V.J. Reddi, and D. Arp, "Machine learning for network anomaly detection: A survey", *ACM Comput. Surv.,* vol. 55, no. 1, pp. 1-36, 2022. [http://dx.doi.org/10.1145/3487892]

[5] G. Arun, P.C.S. Reddy, N. Budati, B. Rebecca, S. Perumalla, and V.B. Gujar, "A deep learning framework for diabetes prediction: PIMA indian dataset", *2024 International Conference on Innovative Computing, Intelligent Communication and Smart Electrical Systems (ICSES),* IEEE, 2024.

[6] S. B. Latha, Y. Sucharitha, I. A. Tayubi, K. Shekar, D. Pandey, and R. V. Sudhakar, "Virtual learning analysis using complex rule-based approach in the context of cloud computing," In: *2025 3rd International Conference on Communication, Security, and Artificial Intelligence (ICCSAI)*, vol. 3, pp. 1110–1115, Greater Noida, India, 04–06 Apr. 2025. [http://dx.doi.org/10.1109/ICCSAI64074.2025.11064645]

[7] B. Elov, A. Dauletov, Y. Sucharitha, F. Khalilova, M. Latipova, and M. Abdullayeva, "An intelligent traffic management of vehicles using deep learning approach in smart cities", *in 2025 3rd*

International Conference on Integrated Circuits and Communication Systems (ICICACS), pp. 1-5, 2025.
[http://dx.doi.org/10.1109/ICICACS65178.2025.10967703]

[8] M. Almukaynizi, E. Yilmaz, and J. Zambreno, "An overview of SOAR: Security orchestration, automation and response", *IEEE Secur. Priv.,* vol. 18, no. 6, pp. 38-45, 2020.

[9] R. Kumar, M. Singh, and M.S. Hossain, "AI-powered vulnerability management: A predictive approach", *J. Cyber Security Technol,* vol. 6, no. 2, pp. 122-140, 2022.

[10] M. Indrasenareddy, N. S. Bohra, S. Mukherjee, Y. Sucharitha, M. Yesubabu, and M. L. Prasad, "Working toward a comprehensive approach for ensuring security and privacy in artificial intelligence," In: *Leveraging Artificial Intelligence in Cloud, Edge, Fog and Mobile Computing*, 2025, pp. 3–18, Auerbach Publications.
[http://dx.doi.org/10.1201/9781032703718]

[11] R. Samrin, K.A. Kumar, N. Deepthi, C. Mithra, Y. Sucharitha, and G.K. Thakur, "A hybrid deep learning based framework for prediction of rice yield through integration of biophysical parameters and optical remote sensing data in India", *J. Atmospheric and Solar-Terrestrial Physics,* vol. 279, p. 106734, 2026.
[http://dx.doi.org/10.1016/j.jastp.2026.106734]

[12] A. Nangunuri, A.T. Somnathe, B. Prasanthi, E.L. Mercy, S.V. Ramanan, and P.C.S. Reddy, "A novel meta-learning ensemble framework for cancer classification using convolution neural networks", *2024 International Conference on Electronics, Computing, Communication and Control Technology (ICECCC),* IEEE, 2024.
[http://dx.doi.org/10.1109/ICECCC61767.2024.10593843]

[13] F. Doshi-Velez, and B. Kim, "Towards a rigorous science of interpretable machine learning", *arXiv preprint arXiv: 1702.08608,* 2017.

[14] P. Ravali, P.C.S. Reddy, and P. Praveen, "An efficient neuro-framework for brain tumor classification using a CNN-based self-supervised learning approach with genetic optimizations", *Curr. Neuropharmacol.,* vol. 23, 2025.
[http://dx.doi.org/10.2174/011570159X378103250806214613]

[15] L. Floridi, J. Cowls, M. Beltrametti, R. Chatila, P. Chazerand, V. Dignum, C. Luetge, R. Madelin, U. Pagallo, F. Rossi, B. Schafer, P. Valcke, and E. Vayena, "AI4People—An ethical framework for a good AI society: Opportunities, risks, principles, and recommendations", *Minds Mach.,* vol. 28, no. 4, pp. 689-707, 2018.
[http://dx.doi.org/10.1007/s11023-018-9482-5] [PMID: 30930541]

[16] P. S. Muller, Y. Sucharitha, S. Kottapally, G. Ismoilova, L. Rakhimova, and P. C. S. Reddy, "A Novel Financial Market Prediction Framework Based on Deep Learning for Accurate Trend Forecasting", In: *Information Systems for Intelligent Systems*. ISBM 2025, A. Iglesias, J. Shin, N. Bhatt, A. Joshi, (eds) Information Systems for Intelligent Systems. ISBM 2025. Lecture Notes in Networks and Systems, vol 1748. Springer, Cham.
[http://dx.doi.org/10.1007/978-3-032-12990-1_5]

[17] A. T. Somnathe, M. Parameshwari, S. Pattem, S. N. Koka, S. Abdurakhmanova, and P. C. S. Reddy, "An Attention-Based Deep Learning Framework for Gold Price Prediction Using Time Series Data", In: *Information Systems for Intelligent Systems*. ISBM 2025, A. Iglesias, J. Shin, N. Bhatt, A Joshi (eds) Information Systems for Intelligent Systems. ISBM 2025. Lecture Notes in Networks and Systems, vol 1743. Springer, Cham.
[http://dx.doi.org/10.1007/978-3-032-13006-8_6]

[18] W. Wang, Y. Sheng, J. Wang, X. Zeng, X. Ye, Y. Huang, and M. Zhu, "HAST-IDS: Learning hierarchical spatial-temporal features using deep neural networks to improve intrusion detection", *IEEE Access,* vol. 6, pp. 1792-1806, 2018.
[http://dx.doi.org/10.1109/ACCESS.2017.2780250]

[19] N. Moustafa, and J. Slay, "UNSW-NB15: A comprehensive data set for network intrusion detection systems", *Proc. MilCIS,* pp. 1-6, 2015.

[20] A. Javaid, Q. Niyaz, W. Sun, and M. Alam, "A deep learning approach for network intrusion detection system", *Proc. 9th EAI Int. Conf. Bio-inspired Info. & Comms Tech,* 2016.
[http://dx.doi.org/10.4108/eai.3-12-2015.2262516]

[21] P.C.S. Reddy, Y. Sucharitha, and A. Vivekanand, "Customer churn prevention for E-commerce platforms using machine learning-based business intelligence", *Recent Adv. Electr. Electron. Eng.,* vol. 17, no. 5, pp. 456-465, 2024.

[22] T. Hashni, and T. Amudha, "Leveraging Machine Learning for accurate Precipitation Forecasting", *Procedia Computer Science,* vol. 259, pp. 1523-1532, 2025.
[http://dx.doi.org/10.1016/j.procs.2025.04.107]

[23] A.T. Somnathe, C.S.R. Pundru, A. Kiran, and R. Gowda, "Ensemble deep learning framework for the traffic accidents duration prediction", *2024 Global Conference on Communications and Information Technologies (GCCIT),* IEEE, 2024.

[24] G. Apruzzese, P. Laskov, E. Montes de Oca, W. Mallouli, L. Brdalo Rapa, A.V. Grammatopoulos, and F. Di Franco, "The role of machine learning in cybersecurity", *Digit. Threats,* vol. 4, no. 1, pp. 1-38, 2023.
[http://dx.doi.org/10.1145/3545574]

[25] R. Sommer, and V. Paxson, "Outside the closed world: On using machine learning for network intrusion detection", *IEEE Symp. Sec. & Privacy,* pp. 305-316, 2010.
[http://dx.doi.org/10.1109/SP.2010.25]

[26] N.N. Abbas, T. Ahmed, S.H.U. Shah, M. Omar, and H.W. Park, "Investigating the applications of artificial intelligence in cyber security", *Scientometrics,* vol. 121, no. 2, pp. 1189-1211, 2019.
[http://dx.doi.org/10.1007/s11192-019-03222-9]

[27] R. Parameswari, M. Mudarakola Lakshmi Prasad, B. Balamurugan, C. Ramesh, M. Ramesh Babu, M. Meruva Sreenivasulu, and P.C.S. Reddy, "Prediction of coronary artery calcium with CT-images using deep learning", *in 2024 International Conference on Integration of Emerging Technologies for the Digital World (ICIETDW),* 2024.
[http://dx.doi.org/10.1109/ICIETDW61607.2024.10941586]

[28] S. Suresh, V. Prabhu, V. Parthasarathy, R. Boddu, Y. Sucharitha, and G. Teshite, "A novel routing protocol for low□energy wireless sensor networks", *Journal of Sensors,* vol. 2022, no. 1, p. 8244176, 2022.
[http://dx.doi.org/10.1155/2022/8244176]

[29] A. Gadupudi, M.L. Prasad, G.Y. Vybhavi, S.N. Koka, S. Mukherjee, and P.C.S. Reddy, “An efficient provable massive data migration approach under secure cloud storage,” In: *Proc. Int. Conf. Intelligent Systems & Networks (ICISN 2024)*, Singapore: Springer Nature, Lecture Notes in Networks and Systems, vol. 1077, pp. 270–276, 2024.
[http://dx.doi.org/10.1007/978-981-97-5504-2_32]

[30] J. Zhang, and C. Li, "Adversarial examples: Opportunities and challenges", *IEEE Trans. Neural Netw. Learn. Syst.,* vol. 31, no. 7, pp. 2578-2593, 2020.
[PMID: 31722487]

[31] Z. Pan, and P. Mishra, "Explainable AI for cybersecurity: State of the art, challenges and opportunities", *Future Gener. Comput. Syst.,* vol. 139, pp. 13-39, 2023.

[32] M. Mohammadi, A. Al-Fuqaha, S. Sorour, and M. Guizani, "Deep learning for IoT big data and streaming analytics: A survey", *IEEE Commun. Surv. Tutor.,* vol. 20, no. 4, pp. 2923-2960, 2018.
[http://dx.doi.org/10.1109/COMST.2018.2844341]

[33] G. Canfora, E. Medvet, F. Mercaldo, and C.A. Visaggio, "Detection of malicious web pages using system calls sequences", *International Conference on Availability, Reliability, and Security,* Springer

International Publishing: Cham, pp. 226-238, 2014.
[http://dx.doi.org/10.1007/978-3-319-10975-6_17]

[34] AlEroud and G. Karabatis, "Network anomaly detection using rough sets and self-organizing maps", *Int. J. Inf. Secur.*, vol. 17, pp. 401-417, 2018.

[35] J. Wu, Y. Zou, X. Zhang, J. Liu, W. Sun, and G. Du, "Dependency-aware task offloading strategy via heterogeneous graph neural network and deep reinforcement learning", *IEEE Internet Things J.*, vol. 12, no. 13, pp. 22915-22933, 2025.
[http://dx.doi.org/10.1109/JIOT.2025.3549441]

[36] K. Narendra, "Leveraging artificial intelligence for real-time fraud detection in financial transactions: A fintech perspective", *World Journal of Advanced Research and Reviews,* vol. 3, no. 3, pp. 115-127, 2019.
[http://dx.doi.org/10.30574/wjarr.2019.3.3.0129]

[37] D. Narsina, and C.S.G. Jaya, "S. S. M. G. N. Venkata, A. Manikyala, S. Kothapalli, K. Devarapu, M. Rodriguez, and R. R. Talla. “AI-driven database systems in fintech: enhancing fraud detection and transaction efficiency.”", *Asian Accounting and Auditing Advancement,* vol. 10, no. 1, pp. 81-92, 2019.

[38] B. Kim, M. Wattenberg, J. Gilmer, C. Cai, J. Wexler, F. Viegas, and R. Sayres, "Interpretability beyond feature attribution: Quantitative testing with concept activation vectors (TCAV)", *in Proc. 35th Int. Conf. Mach. Learn.*, vol. 80, pp. 2668-2677, 2018.

[39] X. Wang, J. Li, X. Kuang, Y. Tan, and J. Li, "The security of machine learning in an adversarial setting: A survey", *J. Parallel Distrib. Comput.*, vol. 130, pp. 12-23, 2019.
[http://dx.doi.org/10.1016/j.jpdc.2019.03.003]

[40] Q. Liu, P. Li, W. Zhao, W. Cai, S. Yu, and V.C.M. Leung, "A survey on security threats and defensive techniques of machine learning: A data driven view", *IEEE Access,* vol. 6, pp. 12103-12117, 2018.
[http://dx.doi.org/10.1109/ACCESS.2018.2805680]

[41] S. Zhou, C. Liu, D. Ye, T. Zhu, W. Zhou, and P.S. Yu, "Adversarial attacks and defenses in deep learning: From a perspective of cybersecurity", *ACM Comput. Surv.*, vol. 55, no. 8, pp. 1-39, 2023.
[http://dx.doi.org/10.1145/3547330]

[42] E.V.N. Jyothi, M. Kranthi, S. Sailaja, U. Sesadri, and N. Sridhar, "An adaptive intrusion detection system in industrial internet of things (IIoT) using deep learning", *2024 1st International Conference on Innovative Sustainable Technologies for Energy, Mechatronics, and Smart Systems (ISTEMS),* IEEE, 2024.

[43] V. Sukhavasi, A.C. Mouli, D.V. Juneja, Y. Sucharitha, S.S. Joshi, and S. Dey, “Establishing ensemble learning models for daily rainfall forecasting,” In: *2024 International Conference on Innovative Computing, Intelligent Communication and Smart Electrical Systems (ICSES)*, Chennai, India, 12–13 Dec. 2024, pp. 1–6.
[http://dx.doi.org/10.1109/ICSES63760.2024.10910429]

[44] A.A. Cardenas, J.P. Shoukry, and L.P. Carloni, "Cyber–physical systems security. ", *ACM Trans. Cyber-Phys. Syst,* vol. 1, no. 1, pp. 1-28, 2016.

[45] M. Emec, and M.H. Özcanhan, "A hybrid deep learning approach for intrusion detection in IoT networks", *Adv. Electr. Comput. Eng.*, vol. 22, no. 1, pp. 3-12, 2022.
[http://dx.doi.org/10.4316/AECE.2022.01001]

[46] M. Ring, D. Schlör, D. Landes, and A. Hotho, "Flow-based network traffic generation using Generative Adversarial Networks", *Comput. Secur.*, vol. 82, pp. 156-172, 2019.
[http://dx.doi.org/10.1016/j.cose.2018.12.012]

[47] M.D. Basith, P. Praveen, and P.C.S. Reddy, "Adaptive deep Q-GAN framework for enhanced breast cancer detection in medical imaging", *Biomedical Signal Processing and Control,* vol. 112, p. 108638, 2026.
[http://dx.doi.org/10.1016/j.bspc.2025.108638]

[48] K. Srinivas, N. Prasanth, R. Trivedi, N. Bindra, and S.P. Raja, "A novel machine learning inspired algorithm to predict real-time network intrusions", *Int. J. Inf. Technol.,* vol. 14, no. 7, pp. 3471-3480, 2022.
[http://dx.doi.org/10.1007/s41870-022-00925-w]

[49] B. Biggio, and F. Roli, "Wild patterns: Ten years after the rise of adversarial machine learning", *Pattern Recognit.,* vol. 84, pp. 317-331, 2018.
[http://dx.doi.org/10.1016/j.patcog.2018.07.023]

[50] A. Ajao, O. Jonathan, and E. Adetiba, "The applications of federated learning algorithm in the federated cloud environment: A systematic review", In: *2024 International Conference on Science, Engineering and Business for Driving Sustainable Development Goals (SEB4SDG)* IEEE, 2024, pp. 1-15.
[http://dx.doi.org/10.1109/SEB4SDG60871.2024.10629812]

[51] A. Mahindru, and A.L. Sangal, "FSDroid:- A feature selection technique to detect malware from Android using Machine Learning Techniques", *Multimedia Tools Appl.,* vol. 80, no. 9, pp. 13271-13323, 2021.
[http://dx.doi.org/10.1007/s11042-020-10367-w] [PMID: 33462535]

[52] P. Huang, and D. Yung, "Explainable AI for digital forensics", *IEEE Access,* vol. 10, pp. 34121-34132, 2022.

[53] M.A. Altuncu, F.K. Gulagiz, H. Ozcan, O.F. Bayir, A. Gezgin, A. Niyazov, M.A. Cavuslu, and S. Sahin, "Deep learning based DNS tunneling detection and blocking system", *Adv. Electr. Comput. Eng.,* vol. 21, no. 3, pp. 39-48, 2021.
[http://dx.doi.org/10.4316/AECE.2021.03005]

[54] K. Yun, H. Yun, S. Lee, J. Oh, M. Kim, M. Lim, J. Lee, C. Kim, J. Seo, and J. Choi, "A study on machine learning-enhanced roadside unit-based detection of abnormal driving in autonomous vehicles", *Electronics (Basel),* vol. 13, no. 2, p. 288, 2024.
[http://dx.doi.org/10.3390/electronics13020288]

[55] E. Khatri, C.R. Babu, and S.K. Reddy, "Applying a hybrid deep learning framework to efficient stock price prediction", *2024 4th International Conference on Mobile Networks and Wireless Communications (ICMNWC),* IEEE, 2024.

[56] M.K. Shaik, "Brain tumor classification using unet deep neural networks from 3D MRI images", *2024 International Conference on Electronics, Computing, Communication and Control Technology (ICECCC),* IEEE, 2024.

[57] A. Gadupudi, M.L. Prasad, S.K. Nadgaundi, C.S.R. Pundru, S. Sharma, and N. Sharma, "A deep learning framework for human disease prediction using microbiome data", *2024 International Conference on Integrated Circuits and Communication Systems (ICICACS),* IEEE, 2024.
[http://dx.doi.org/10.1109/ICICACS60521.2024.10498711]

[58] V.K. Bukkarayasamudram, P.C.S. Reddy, and K. Arun Kumar, "Quantum computing revolution in healthcare: a systematic review of applications, issues and future directions", *Artif Intell Rev,* vol. 58, p. 389, 2025.
[http://dx.doi.org/10.1007/s10462-025-11381-w]

CHAPTER 4

Enhancing Cybersecurity in AI-Driven Environments: The Role of English Language Proficiency

Ranjit Kumar Elamadurthi[1], **Goddumarri Suryanarayana**[2] and **Pundru Chandra Shaker Reddy**[3,*]

[1] *Department of English, Vardhaman College of Engineering, Hyderabad, Telangana, India*

[2] *Symbiosis Institute of Technology, Hyderabad Campus, Symbiosis International University, Hyderabad, Telangana, India*

[3] *Amity School of Engineering and Technology, Department of CSE, Amity University, Noida, Uttar Pradesh, India*

Abstract: How firms detect, analyze, and respond to attacks has changed as cybersecurity systems incorporate AI. In the age of technology, human language abilities, especially English ability, are undervalued. In AI-driven cybersecurity scenarios, English proficiency affects threat interpretation, incident response, end-user interaction, and interface design. Linguistic clarity improves AI system communication, reducing miscommunication and speeding up multinational security operations. Standardized English is essential for understanding, expressing, and interpreting cybersecurity information in multilingual teams where AI relies on language inputs for correctness. Poor language abilities might mess up the procedure and miss subtle social engineering dangers. The report highlights the necessity for language ability to identify and address complex digital requirements by assessing current issues. Based on real-life case studies, NLP technology, and human-AI interaction models, the research recommends language training and English communication standards for cybersecurity procedures. The findings demonstrate the need for an interdisciplinary strategy that combines language and technological skills to improve cyber defense techniques in a changing digital world.

Keywords: Artificial Intelligence, Cyber-security, Communication, English Language Proficiency, Human-AI Interaction, Language-Aware Systems, Natural Language Processing (NLP), Security Protocols.

* **Corresponding Author Pundru Chandra Shaker Reddy:**, Amity School of Engineering and Technology, Department of CSE, Amity University, Noida, Uttar Pradesh, India; E-mail: chandu.pundru@gmail.com

Pundru Chandra Shaker Reddy, Yadala Sucharitha, & Thillaiarasu N (Eds.)

INTRODUCTION

The advent and rapid proliferation of Artificial Intelligence (AI) technologies have ushered in a transformative era across various sectors, with cybersecurity emerging as one of the most profoundly affected domains. In the wake of escalating cyber threats and the ever-expanding digital landscape, organizations and governments alike are increasingly relying on AI-based solutions to safeguard their digital infrastructure. Unlike traditional cybersecurity tools that often operate reactively, AI-driven systems adopt a more dynamic, proactive, and adaptive posture, thereby fundamentally reshaping the paradigms of threat detection, incident response, and risk mitigation.

At the core of these systems lie cutting-edge computational paradigms such as Machine Learning (ML), Deep Learning (DL), and Natural Language Processing (NLP). These technologies empower cybersecurity systems with the ability to autonomously analyze large volumes of data, identify anomalies, detect patterns indicative of malicious activities, and even forecast potential threats before they materialize. For example, machine learning algorithms can continuously learn from historical attack data and behavioral logs to fine-tune their detection capabilities, while deep learning models, through convolutional or recurrent neural networks, can discern intricate, non-linear relationships within massive datasets that may elude human analysts [1]. Meanwhile, NLP enables the real-time parsing and interpretation of unstructured data from threat reports, darknet forums, phishing emails, and incident response documentation, thereby enriching situational awareness.

These advancements have not only enhanced the scalability and efficiency of cybersecurity operations but also significantly improved the resilience of digital ecosystems against an evolving and increasingly sophisticated landscape of cyberattacks. Modern threat actors—whether cybercriminal groups, state-sponsored adversaries, or hacktivists are employing complex Tactics, Techniques, and Procedures (TTPs), including polymorphic malware, zero-day exploits, AI-generated phishing content, ransomware-as-a-service (RaaS), and Advanced Persistent Threats (APTs). In such a context, traditional rule-based systems are often insufficient. AI-infused tools, by contrast, possess the capability to autonomously evolve and adapt in response to these dynamic challenges, making them indispensable in the contemporary cyber defense arsenal [2].

Despite the remarkable capabilities of these AI-enhanced cybersecurity frameworks, it is essential to recognize that their effectiveness is not solely contingent upon the sophistication of their algorithms, the speed of their processing units, or the granularity of their data sources. Rather, a critical yet often overlooked factor lies in the human element, the cybersecurity professionals who develop, configure, maintain, and operate these complex systems. In other words, no matter how advanced an AI system may be, its operational utility, accuracy, and long-term relevance ultimately depend on the human decisions that guide its development and deployment.

This is where language, and specifically, English language proficiency, plays a crucial, though frequently underestimated, role. As cybersecurity becomes increasingly globalized, English has emerged as the *lingua franca* of the field. It serves as the principal medium for technical documentation, academic research, cybersecurity standards, cross-border communication, and the dissemination of real-time threat intelligence. From foundational texts like the MITRE ATT and CK framework and the NIST Cybersecurity Framework to vendor-specific documentation for tools such as TensorFlow, PyTorch, and Splunk, English dominates the informational and communicational infrastructure of cybersecurity [3].

Furthermore, collaboration among cybersecurity professionals rarely occurs within national silos. Cybersecurity operations now often span across geographies and time zones, with multinational teams working in tandem to respond to threats, share Indicators Of Compromise (IOCs), perform digital forensic analyses, and coordinate incident response strategies. These multinational collaborations depend heavily on clear and timely communication—much of which is conducted in English. In this context, a lack of proficiency in English can act as a barrier to effective communication, potentially leading to misinterpretations, delays in response, or incorrect configurations that can expose systems to risk [4].

The implications of this linguistic component are far-reaching. Cybersecurity practitioners who are not proficient in English may struggle to interpret critical security alerts, understand complex threat intelligence reports, or implement best practices outlined in international standards. Moreover, emerging cybersecurity professionals in non-English-speaking regions may face additional hurdles in accessing state-of-the-art AI tools and training resources, many of which are published exclusively in English. This linguistic gap can thus inadvertently widen the global cybersecurity skills gap, leaving certain organizations or regions more vulnerable to attacks.

In light of these observations, this work aims to explore the intricate and underexplored relationship between English language proficiency and cybersecurity efficacy in AI-driven environments. It argues that English language skills are not peripheral but foundational to the successful implementation and operation of AI-infused cybersecurity systems. By examining real-world case studies, academic literature, and empirical data, it seeks to provide a comprehensive framework for understanding how language shapes the capacity of professionals to engage with AI tools, interpret cybersecurity protocols, and participate in collaborative defense efforts.

In sum, as AI continues to redefine the landscape of cybersecurity, it is imperative to consider not only the technological dimensions but also the human and linguistic factors that underpin the success of these systems. Effective cybersecurity in the AI era demands not only algorithmic precision but also communicative clarity, a dual requirement that elevates English language proficiency from a soft skill to a critical operational competency [4].

In the complex, fast-paced, and highly interconnected world of cybersecurity, English has emerged as more than just a common language. Instead, it has become an essential infrastructure underpinning the operation, communication, and development of digital security practices. The cybersecurity landscape is no longer bounded by national borders or isolated technological ecosystems. Instead, it is a globally orchestrated domain where teams, tools, protocols, and threats traverse linguistic and cultural boundaries in real time. In this context, English serves not only as a technical medium but also as a socio-linguistic bridge enabling collaboration, innovation, and strategic action.

English is deeply embedded in nearly every aspect of cybersecurity operations. It is the primary language used in drafting technical documentation, user manuals, white papers, and research reports associated with both traditional and AI-driven cybersecurity tools. Whether it's reading the documentation of widely used AI frameworks like *TensorFlow, PyTorch, Scikit-learn*, or *Keras,* or interpreting outputs from sophisticated threat detection platforms, cybersecurity professionals are invariably required to navigate technical English with a high degree of fluency. This extends to understanding and also implementing security policies and standards, such as the *NIST Cybersecurity Framework, ISO/IEC 27001,* and *GDPR compliance guidelines*, all of which are primarily authored and distributed in English [5].

The necessity of English fluency becomes even more pronounced when considering the cross-border nature of cyber threats and the corresponding need for global cooperation. As organizations and nation-states grapple with common adversaries, which include ransomware gangs, state-sponsored cyber-espionage units, and distributed denial-of-service (DDoS) attackers, sharing threat intelligence has become a cornerstone of effective cyber defense. This collaboration frequently occurs through English-dominated platforms and institutions such as the *MITRE ATT&CK Framework, the Forum of Incident*

Response and Security Teams (FIRST), and *US-CERT* advisories. English proficiency in these cases becomes a prerequisite not just for understanding but also for contributing to and benefiting from collective cybersecurity intelligence.

Despite the ubiquity of English in cybersecurity-related documentation and communication, the significance of English language proficiency as a critical success factor in cybersecurity operations has been markedly underexamined. Most scholarly and technical discourse continues to prioritize algorithmic performance, data quality, and hardware capabilities, often neglecting the essential role of human linguistic competence. Yet, the effectiveness of AI-driven cybersecurity systems is not merely a function of how well machine learning algorithms detect anomalies or how quickly a threat can be mitigated autonomously. It is also significantly influenced by how well human operators can interact with, interpret, and optimize these systems; an interaction that, in most global settings, is mediated in English [6].

This work posits that English language proficiency is a foundational yet frequently underappreciated pillar of cybersecurity resilience, particularly in the context of AI-augmented systems. It argues that the ability to read, write, and communicate in English, especially within the nuanced context of technical jargon and cybersecurity lexicon, can determine the efficacy of how AI tools are adopted, managed, and improved. Proficient cybersecurity practitioners must not only comprehend system outputs and error messages but also be capable of writing clear, concise, and actionable incident reports, configuring tools using documentation, and participating in knowledge-sharing communities such as GitHub, Stack Overflow, or global threat intelligence forums.

Linguistic barriers, whether stemming from limited vocabulary, misinterpretation of syntax, or unfamiliarity with cultural idioms, can introduce critical vulnerabilities. A misread command-line instruction or misunderstood AI model parameter could result in improper configurations, thereby weakening the defensive posture of an organization. Likewise, the inability to quickly synthesize and act on a security bulletin written in high-level English during a cyber incident can delay responses, exacerbate breaches, and ultimately increase organizational risk.

Moreover, linguistic proficiency also plays a decisive role in multinational cybersecurity teams, where effective collaboration under pressure is key. In global enterprises, Security Operations Centers (SOCs) are often distributed across time zones and continents. Analysts from India, the United States, Eastern Europe, and East Asia may be required to respond to threats in a coordinated fashion [7]. In such settings, English not only acts as the operational language but also carries with it the implicit expectations of clarity, nuance, and fluency that can affect interpersonal dynamics, decision-making speed, and overall efficiency. Miscommunication caused not by technical shortcomings but by linguistic misunderstandings can not only severely hamper incident response but also undermine team cohesion and delay critical mitigation steps.

Given these considerations, this work explores the multiple intersections between English language proficiency and the broader effectiveness of cybersecurity practices in AI-driven environments. It examines how linguistic competence directly contributes to the proper configuration of AI-based security platforms, facilitates continuous learning and adaptation, and enables participation in the global discourse on cybersecurity threats and defense mechanisms. The work also highlights the growing need for cybersecurity training programs, academic curricula, and certification courses to integrate English language support and instruction as a formal component of technical education.

In doing so, the work aims to fill a vital gap in both academic literature and industry practices by providing a framework for understanding English language proficiency as a form of *cybersecurity capital:* a resource as critical as computational power, network infrastructure, or algorithmic efficiency. It offers a multidisciplinary analysis drawing from applied linguistics, cybersecurity engineering, AI ethics, and international communication studies to illuminate the mechanisms through which language skills enhance or impede cybersecurity resilience.

To this end, several key questions are addressed:

- What specific aspects of English language proficiency are most critical for cybersecurity professionals working with AI tools?
- How does limited English comprehension affect the interpretation of AI-generated insights or threat intelligence?
- In what ways can language training programs be optimized to support technical skill development in cybersecurity?
- What policy-level changes could help promote more linguistically inclusive cybersecurity infrastructures?

By unpacking these questions, the work not only underscores the pivotal role of language in securing digital systems but also sets the stage for more inclusive and effective strategies in cybersecurity education, workforce development, and global coordination.

The Role of AI in Modern Cybersecurity

AI has transformed Cybersecurity by enabling proactive and adaptive defenses against an evolving threat landscape. Technologies such as ML, DL, and NLP power tools like Splunk, CrowdStrike's Falcon, and Palo Alto Networks' Cortex XDR, which are widely used for threat detection, incident response, and risk management. These systems analyze vast datasets in real time, identifying patterns indicative of threats such as zero-day exploits, Advanced Persistent Threats (APTs), ransomware, and distributed denial-of-service (DDoS) attacks. For instance, ML-based IDS can detect anomalies by learning normal network behavior, while NLP-driven SIEM platforms process unstructured log data to generate actionable insights [8].

However, the sophistication of these tools introduces complexity in their configuration and operation. Professionals must define parameters such as anomaly detection thresholds, feature extraction pipelines, or false positive suppression rules, all articulated in technical English within Graphical User Interfaces (GUIs) or Command-Line Interfaces (CLIs). Technical documentation, such as user manuals for TensorFlow-based security tools or configuration guides for Splunk, is predominantly in English, requiring practitioners to interpret specialized terminology accurately. For example, configuring an ML-based IDS involves setting hyperparameters like learning rates, decision boundaries, or regularization coefficients, as detailed in English-language resources [9]. English proficiency ensures that these specifications are correctly implemented, optimizing the system's ability to detect threats effectively.

Beyond configuration, AI systems generate outputs in the form of alerts, logs, visualizations, or reports, which require contextual understanding to prioritize and act upon. A fluent command of English enables practitioners to discern critical insights, such as distinguishing between benign anomalies and malicious activities. For instance, a SIEM platform may flag a spike in network traffic as a potential DDoS attack, but only a nuanced understanding of the English-language alert description can clarify whether it's a false positive due to legitimate user activity or a genuine threat requiring immediate action [9]. Misinterpreting these outputs due to linguistic limitations can delay responses or lead to incorrect prioritization, compromising security [10].

Moreover, deep learning models have shown particular promise in identifying sophisticated threats, including polymorphic and metamorphic malware. Convolutional Neural Networks (CNNs), for instance, have been utilized to treat malware binaries as images, allowing security tools to visually classify and detect new threats [11]. Similarly, Recurrent Neural Networks (RNNs) and Long Short-

Term Memory (LSTM) architectures are employed to detect anomalies in time-series data such as user login behaviors, data access patterns, and financial transactions. These models offer enhanced precision and recall, reducing false positives and improving the efficiency of Security Information and Event Management (SIEM) systems.

Secondly, AI plays a crucial role in automating responses to detected threats, which is vital for reducing mean time to detection (MTTD) and mean time to response (MTTR). In traditional systems, incident response requires human analysts to manually assess alerts, prioritize incidents, and initiate countermeasures. AI systems, however, enable Security Orchestration, Automation, and Response (SOAR) platforms to autonomously correlate events, assess threat severity, and deploy appropriate responses—such as isolating compromised endpoints or revoking access credentials—without human intervention [12]. This automation not only accelerates the response cycle but also helps organizations contend with the ongoing cybersecurity talent shortage by alleviating the burden on human analysts. English proficiency is vital in AI-driven cybersecurity as it ensures accurate interpretation of AI outputs, clear communication, and proper protocol execution. Since most AI tools use English, linguistic clarity reduces errors, prevents miscommunication, and enhances collaboration in global teams.

In addition, AI is increasingly being used to enhance endpoint security and Intrusion Prevention Systems (IPS). Behavioral AI models monitor endpoints to detect abnormal usage, such as a user accessing sensitive files outside business hours or from an unusual location. These deviations are flagged or acted upon instantly. Tools like CrowdStrike Falcon and Microsoft Defender use such behavioral models in conjunction with threat intelligence feeds to provide adaptive, real-time protection [13].

AI also strengthens authentication and identity management systems. Through continuous authentication mechanisms, AI models analyze biometric, behavioral, and contextual data—such as keystroke dynamics, mouse movement, and geolocation—to verify user identities seamlessly. This approach enhances both security and user experience by minimizing reliance on static credentials, which are prone to theft and misuse [14].

Configuration and Optimization of AI Systems

Configuring AI-driven Cybersecurity tools requires precise interpretation of English-language documentation and interfaces. For example, Palo Alto Networks' Cortex XDR allows users to customize threat detection models by adjusting parameters like "confidence thresholds" or "behavioral analytics weights," terms defined in English technical manuals [15]. Misinterpreting these terms can lead to misconfigurations, such as setting overly permissive thresholds that fail to detect subtle threats or overly restrictive rules that generate excessive false positives, overwhelming security teams. A 2023 case study of a European financial institution revealed that a team with limited English proficiency misconfigured an AI-powered firewall due to misinterpreting the term "stateful inspection," resulting in a 15% increase in undetected intrusions.

English proficiency also enables professionals to leverage advanced features of AI tools. For instance, CrowdStrike's Falcon platform offers behavioral analytics to detect insider threats, but its documentation, written in English, requires familiarity with terms like "lateral movement" or "privilege escalation" [16]. Practitioners who struggle with these terms may underutilize such features, diminishing the system's ability to adapt to evolving threats. Conversely, fluent professionals can fully exploit these capabilities, enhancing detection accuracy and operational efficiency.

Human Factors in AI-Driven Cybersecurity

While AI technologies have revolutionized cybersecurity by automating threat detection, analysis, and response, human factors remain a critical and often underemphasized component in the effectiveness of these systems. AI is not a replacement for human judgment but rather an augmentation tool that relies on human input for training, interpretation, and ethical oversight. The interaction between users, security professionals, and AI-driven systems determines the overall success or vulnerability of a cybersecurity framework. Human behavior—shaped by awareness, motivation, decision-making patterns, and communication abilities—often serves as the weakest link in the security chain, especially when trust in AI systems is either excessive or unwarranted [17].

One of the most persistent human-related vulnerabilities in cybersecurity is susceptibility to social engineering attacks. Despite advancements in AI-driven intrusion detection systems (IDS), phishing attacks continue to succeed due to user error or misinterpretation of language-based cues. Studies show that even sophisticated users can be deceived by well-crafted phishing messages, particularly when language is tailored to mimic internal communication styles or exploit authority biases [18]. When users lack sufficient training or language proficiency, their ability to critically evaluate such messages diminishes, increasing organizational risk.

Another human factor that significantly affects AI-driven cybersecurity systems is cognitive load. As AI tools provide a constant stream of alerts and data visualizations, users may experience alert fatigue or information overload, which can result in critical oversights or poor decision-making. In particular, if AI-generated alerts are overly technical or linguistically complex, users with limited language or domain knowledge may misinterpret their meaning or ignore them entirely. This issue is further complicated in multilingual or cross-cultural work environments, where cybersecurity communication—primarily in English—may not be equally accessible to all stakeholders [19]. Linguistic clarity ensures an accurate understanding of security alerts and AI outputs, reducing ambiguity in threat interpretation. It enables precise communication, quick response, and minimizes errors that could lead to missed or misjudged cyber threats.

Thus, optimizing cybersecurity in AI-driven environments necessitates a socio-technical approach—one that integrates user education, language accessibility, cognitive ergonomics, and ethical oversight alongside technological innovation. Without addressing the human dimensions of cybersecurity, even the most advanced AI systems risk failure due to misaligned user behavior or communication breakdowns.

Collaboration and Knowledge Sharing

Cybersecurity is a collaborative field, with global teams working together to address threats. English serves as the primary language for communication in international forums, incident response teams, and open-source communities like GitHub, where security advisories and patches are shared [20]. For instance, during a coordinated response to a global APT campaign, teams across different countries must share findings, logs, and mitigation strategies in English to ensure alignment. Linguistic barriers can hinder this process, leading to miscommunication or delayed action.

Open-source communities further highlight the importance of English proficiency. Platforms like GitHub host discussions on vulnerabilities in AI libraries, such as TensorFlow or PyTorch, which are conducted in English. Professionals fluent in English can contribute to these discussions, report issues, or adopt community-driven patches, strengthening their organization's security posture. Conversely, those with limited proficiency may struggle to engage, missing critical updates that could prevent exploits [21].

Compliance and Threat Intelligence

AI-driven systems often operate in regulated industries, such as finance or healthcare, where compliance with standards like NIST 800-53 or ISO/IEC 27001 is mandatory. These standards, along with threat intelligence feeds from sources like MITRE's CVE database, are primarily in English (NIST, 2023; ISO/IEC 27001, 2022). Proficiency enables professionals to interpret these resources accurately, ensuring that AI systems align with regulatory requirements and incorporate the latest threat intelligence. For example, a 2024 report on a new malware variant was published in English on the CVE database, but a team with limited language skills failed to update their IDS rules in time, resulting in a data breach [22].

NLP-driven features, such as chatbots or log analysis tools, also rely on English inputs and outputs. For instance, IBM's QRadar Advisor uses NLP to provide English-language recommendations for threat mitigation [23]. Professionals with strong English skills can query these systems effectively, extracting actionable insights to counter threats like phishing or malware.

Importance of English Language Proficiency in AI-Driven Cybersecurity

Global Standardization of Cybersecurity Terminology

English plays a pivotal role as the global lingua franca in the Cybersecurity domain, serving as the primary language through which critical frameworks, threat intelligence, and industry standards are communicated. Foundational resources such as the MITRE ATT&CK® knowledge base, the NIST Cybersecurity Framework, and international standards like ISO/IEC 27001 are all predominantly authored in English. These documents are not merely technical manuals; they provide essential guidance on the classification of adversary tactics, the implementation and evaluation of security controls, and the management of risks and vulnerabilities across complex digital infrastructures.

Professionals operating in this field must engage with these materials on a daily basis, making a high level of English language proficiency crucial for effective comprehension and application. Without adequate linguistic skills, Cybersecurity personnel may misinterpret key concepts, potentially leading to flawed decision-making. For example, confusion between terminologies such as "privilege escalation" and "access control failure" can result in an incorrect assessment of the severity or nature of a security breach. This can, in turn, hinder timely and appropriate responses to ongoing cyber threats.

A concrete illustration of this issue can be seen in the frequent misinterpretation of the MITRE ATT&CK tactic labeled "Lateral Movement." If a Cybersecurity professional interprets this tactic simply as an unauthorized login attempt, they may fail to recognize the broader implication that an attacker is actively moving across systems within a network after an initial compromise. Such a misunderstanding can significantly delay the identification and containment of an attack, allowing adversaries to deepen their access and cause more damage [24]. Poor language skills can cause miscommunication with AI systems by leading to incorrect command inputs, ambiguous queries, and misunderstanding of AI-generated outputs. This can result in inaccurate threat analysis, delayed responses, or faulty security actions. Inconsistent or unclear language also reduces the AI's ability to interpret intent correctly, weakening overall cybersecurity effectiveness.

In essence, it is evident that English proficiency is not merely an academic requirement but a functional necessity in Cybersecurity. Mastery of technical English ensures that professionals can accurately interpret threat models, implement defense protocols, and collaborate effectively across international teams in real time.

Effective Use of AI-Powered Security Tools

AI tools have become integral to modern Cybersecurity systems, especially in functions such as anomaly detection, threat intelligence, malware analysis, and phishing prevention. A large portion of these tools relies heavily on Natural Language Processing (NLP) capabilities, which are predominantly trained on English-language datasets [25]. As a result, these systems typically generate and process information—such as system logs, alerts, and commands—in English. This poses a significant challenge for users with low English language proficiency. When Cybersecurity alerts, logs, or command-line outputs are presented in technical English, non-native speakers may struggle to interpret or respond to them accurately. This communication gap can compromise the efficiency and reliability of security responses. For instance, an AI-generated alert stating, "Unauthorized shell execution attempt *via* SSH tunnel," may appear unclear or misleading to someone not proficient in English. Such a misinterpretation could lead to the missed detection of a serious lateral movement attack, potentially exposing the network to further exploitation. In environments where quick and accurate interpretation of AI-generated outputs is crucial, language barriers can diminish the operational value of these technologies. Thus, English language proficiency plays a crucial role not only in configuring AI-driven Cybersecurity tools but also in ensuring effective real-time threat response and mitigation.

Cross-Border Cyber Collaboration

Cybersecurity threats transcend national borders, making international collaboration not just beneficial but essential. In a globalized digital ecosystem, cyberattacks can originate from any part of the world and rapidly spread across continents, targeting systems, data, and infrastructure indiscriminately. As a result, timely and effective collaboration between countries is crucial in identifying, mitigating, and responding to these threats. This is where English proficiency plays a pivotal role. Organizations such as Computer Emergency

Response Teams (CERTs), international threat intelligence sharing platforms, and multinational Cybersecurity task forces rely heavily on English as the common language of communication. It ensures that information related to threat indicators, vulnerabilities, and mitigation strategies can be quickly and accurately exchanged, minimizing delays caused by language barriers.

A notable example of this occurred during the 2017 WannaCry ransomware attack. Cybersecurity experts from the United Kingdom, India, the United States, and other countries coordinated efforts in real-time, sharing critical indicators of compromise (IoCs) and defensive measures—primarily in English. This rapid, coordinated response was vital in containing the damage. Had there been a lack of a common language, the resulting delays and misinterpretations could have led to significantly higher losses. Thus, English proficiency is not merely a soft skill—it is a strategic asset in global Cybersecurity defense.

Technical Documentation and Incident Reporting

In the Cybersecurity and Artificial Intelligence (AI) domains, professionals are expected to draft precise and comprehensive documents such as vulnerability reports, security advisories, and AI model documentation—most of which are authored in English. The clarity and accuracy of these documents are critical for effective communication, collaboration, and timely risk mitigation. A lack of English language proficiency can lead to vague, misleading, or incomplete descriptions that obscure the root cause of an issue and delay appropriate responses. In highly technical environments, ambiguity can compromise the effectiveness of incident response teams and hinder coordinated efforts across departments or organizations.

For example, consider a vague report that simply states, "the code got accessed." This statement lacks clarity, specificity, and actionable detail. In contrast, a more proficient and precise description, such as "unauthorized remote access occurred *via* Remote Desktop Protocol (RDP) on TCP port 3389," provides a clear understanding of the threat vector and supports more targeted mitigation efforts. The latter description enables system administrators and security teams to identify vulnerable entry points, assess the extent of the breach, and apply appropriate security patches or firewall rules. Thus, strong English communication skills are not just preferable but essential in ensuring accurate documentation and effective Cybersecurity risk management in AI-driven environments.

Advantages and Disadvantages of English Language Proficiency in Enhancing Cybersecurity in AI-Driven Environments

In today's digital age, where cyber threats are constantly evolving and AI technologies are increasingly integrated into Cybersecurity strategies, English language proficiency has become more vital than ever. As the global lingua franca, English plays a central role in shaping Cybersecurity frameworks, facilitating international collaboration, and enabling access to critical knowledge repositories, technical documentation, and threat intelligence. Most AI-driven tools, protocols, and global standards—such as the MITRE ATT&CK® framework, ISO/IEC 27001, and NIST guidelines—are documented in English, requiring precise comprehension for effective implementation. However, this dominance of English also creates notable challenges for non-native speakers, who may struggle with interpreting technical language, responding to incidents swiftly, or fully understanding complex AI-generated reports. In Cybersecurity, where accuracy and clarity are essential, language gaps can lead to miscommunication, errors, or delays in threat response. Addressing these linguistic barriers is crucial to building a globally inclusive and secure AI-driven Cybersecurity ecosystem.

Advantages

i. Improved Access to Global Cybersecurity Knowledge and Tools

English language proficiency is crucial for Cybersecurity professionals, as it grants access to the majority of global research, technical documentation, and open-source tools. According to Elsevier (2021) [26], over 80% of Cybersecurity-related content, including threat intelligence reports, security framework guidelines, and academic studies, is authored in English. This dominance makes English the de facto language of Cybersecurity, and fluency in it enables professionals to stay informed about emerging threats, innovative tools, and industry best practices.

International standards and frameworks, such as those published by the National Institute of Standards and Technology (NIST) and the MITRE ATT&CK framework, are predominantly available in English. These resources are essential for building effective Cybersecurity systems, understanding attacker methodologies, and implementing appropriate defense strategies. Without adequate English proficiency, professionals risk misinterpreting crucial details or being unable to engage with the latest global developments in the field. This language barrier can hinder their ability to collaborate, adopt up-to-date solutions, or comply with international Cybersecurity standards. Therefore, strengthening

English skills is a vital step toward enhancing Cybersecurity capabilities in an interconnected digital world.

ii. Enhanced Communication in Multinational Cybersecurity Operations

Cybersecurity operations frequently require cross-border collaboration, especially in addressing large-scale cyber threats like ransomware, phishing, and Distributed Denial of Service (DDoS) attacks. In these complex and often high-stakes environments, English functions as the primary medium of communication, facilitating seamless coordination among globally dispersed security teams. The ability to communicate effectively in English becomes crucial for ensuring that all stakeholders can interpret and respond to threats promptly and accurately.

Research highlights the significant role of English proficiency in enhancing technical communication during real-time Cybersecurity activities such as incident response, threat analysis, and coordinated countermeasures [27]. Their findings reveal that strong English skills improve the precision and efficiency of communication within Security Operations Centers (SOCs), particularly in critical areas like log reporting, ticketing systems, and the preparation of technical documentation, all of which are typically structured in English. By minimizing miscommunication and reducing errors in data interpretation, English proficiency directly contributes to faster, more accurate threat detection and resolution. Ultimately, it strengthens the operational capacity of Cybersecurity teams operating in multinational contexts.

iii. Facilitates Integration with AI and Machine Learning Models

In AI-driven Cybersecurity environments, English serves as a foundational element, particularly in the development and application of Natural Language Processing (NLP) models. These models play a crucial role in tasks such as spam filtering, phishing detection, sentiment analysis, and extracting threat intelligence from vast amounts of unstructured text. The majority of NLP training datasets and corpora are predominantly in English, making language proficiency a vital asset for Cybersecurity professionals. Proficiency in English enhances a specialist's ability to interpret and fine-tune NLP tools, ensuring more accurate detection and response to security threats. As has been noted, AI tools trained on English textual data tend to perform significantly better than those trained in multilingual or non-English contexts [28]. Therefore, Cybersecurity analysts with strong English language skills are more capable of leveraging the full potential of AI models, leading to more robust and responsive Cybersecurity measures in both local and global security landscapes. Standardized English ensures clear, consistent communication in multilingual cybersecurity teams, reducing misunderstandings and errors. It enables accurate interpretation of threats and faster, coordinated incident responses.

iv. Boosts Career Opportunities and Certification Access

Proficiency in English is vital for professionals seeking to advance in the Cybersecurity field, as many globally recognized certifications are conducted exclusively in English. Renowned certifications such as CISSP (Certified Information Systems Security Professional) by $(ISC)^2$, CEH (Certified Ethical Hacker) by EC-Council, and Security+ by CompTIA are not only career-defining credentials but also require a strong command of English to comprehend complex terminology, assessment criteria, and technical documentation. These certifications significantly enhance employability, professional credibility, and global mobility. Furthermore, active engagement in international Cybersecurity activities, such as conferences, webinars, Capture The Flag (CTF) competitions, and collaborative coding or threat analysis projects on platforms like GitHub, demands effective English communication skills. These forums are essential for knowledge exchange, staying updated with emerging threats, and networking with experts across the world. As highlighted, English fluency opens doors to cutting-edge learning and participation in the global Cybersecurity ecosystem [29].

Disadvantages

i. Exclusion of Non-Native Speakers from Cybersecurity Participation

Despite its advantages, the predominance of English in the Cybersecurity domain presents significant challenges for non-native speakers, particularly in regions with limited English proficiency. While English serves as the lingua franca for Cybersecurity documentation, frameworks, and communication, it can become a barrier that excludes capable professionals from fully engaging with critical resources. Many skilled individuals may struggle to comprehend essential materials such as threat advisories, vulnerability disclosures, and technical standards, thereby limiting their ability to effectively respond to or prevent cyber threats. This linguistic gap hinders their participation in global Cybersecurity initiatives, training programs, and collaborative platforms, reducing their contribution to international security efforts.

Inadequate English proficiency can lead to the misinterpretation of security alerts, guidelines, and policies [20]. Such misunderstandings increase the likelihood of non-compliance and create opportunities for cyber attackers to exploit vulnerabilities. This situation reinforces a global digital divide, where regions with lower English literacy face greater Cybersecurity risks. Ultimately, the reliance on English, though beneficial for standardization, inadvertently restricts inclusivity and undermines the collective global response to cyber threats. Addressing this issue is critical for achieving comprehensive Cybersecurity resilience.

ii. Underrepresentation of Localized Threat Intelligence

Most threat intelligence datasets, reports, and case studies are primarily documented in English, which creates a significant language bias in global Cybersecurity practices. As a result, cyber incidents occurring in non-Englis--speaking regions are frequently underreported or inadequately represented. This linguistic imbalance leads to a lack of diverse and region-specific data, which in turn limits the effectiveness of AI systems designed for threat detection and analysis. AI models trained predominantly on English-language datasets are often ill-equipped to identify threats that are unique to specific cultural or linguistic contexts. For instance, phishing attacks or fraud schemes that rely on local dialects, cultural references, or region-specific behavioral patterns may go undetected due to insufficient exposure during model training. The over-reliance on English in training language models, emphasizing that such practices embed linguistic and cultural biases within AI systems, is strongly criticized [30]. In Cybersecurity, this can compromise the accuracy and inclusiveness of AI-driven tools, particularly in multilingual environments. Consequently, there is an urgent need to diversify linguistic data sources to enhance the global reliability of AI-powered Cybersecurity mechanisms.

iii. Reduced Comprehension of AI Outputs and Model Interpretability

Many AI-driven Cybersecurity tools are designed and operate primarily in English. Their interfaces, including system logs, threat alerts, and interactive dashboards, present information using technical English terminology. For Cybersecurity professionals who are non-native English speakers, this language barrier can hinder their ability to fully understand critical outputs. As a result, their response time to cyber incidents may be delayed, and the accuracy of their decisions could be compromised. This challenge becomes even more pronounced when dealing with advanced AI features such as SHAP (SHapley Additive exPlanations) values or attention-based visualizations, which are often presented with English annotations and explanations. These components are crucial for interpreting the decision-making processes of AI models, especially in high-stakes environments like Cybersecurity. However, users with limited English proficiency may find such explanations opaque or confusing, thereby reducing both the interpretability and trustworthiness of the AI systems [31]. Consequently, the lack of English proficiency becomes a significant barrier to the adoption and effective use of AI-powered Cybersecurity tools, particularly in regions that could benefit most from enhanced digital protection.

iv. Increased Susceptibility to Phishing and Social Engineering

Phishing emails and malicious messages are designed to deceive users by manipulating linguistic nuances and social cues. These messages often imitate legitimate communication, using formal tone, technical jargon, or persuasive language to appear credible. Users with limited English language proficiency may struggle to identify these subtle cues, making them more vulnerable to falling for such scams. They may misinterpret key phrases, overlook grammatical inconsistencies, or fail to detect manipulative language tactics employed by cybercriminals.

A notable study revealed that non-native English speakers are particularly susceptible to phishing attacks, especially when the messages use complex grammatical structures or intentionally misleading language [32]. The study emphasized that even when users had general Cybersecurity awareness, their limited ability to comprehend intricate English expressions significantly increased their risk of deception. This demonstrates that language proficiency plays a critical role in cyber defense.

The inability to decode deceptive language or distinguish between genuine and fraudulent communication can result in users unknowingly disclosing sensitive information. Therefore, enhancing English language competence is essential not only for communication but also for reinforcing Cybersecurity awareness and resilience in digital environments.

v. Cognitive Load and Learning Fatigue

Non-native English speakers in the Cybersecurity field frequently face significant challenges due to language barriers. Much of the critical Cybersecurity documentation, training materials, and communication is predominantly authored in English, which necessitates these professionals to invest extra cognitive effort to comprehend and translate complex technical content. This additional mental workload leads to increased fatigue, which can adversely impact their ability to efficiently learn new concepts and apply them effectively in real-world scenarios. Consequently, this linguistic strain often diminishes their overall productivity and engagement in advanced Cybersecurity training programs or research activities.

A survey conducted focusing on Security Operations Center (SOC) analysts highlighted the detrimental effects of linguistic overload on performance [33]. The findings revealed that multilingual Cybersecurity teams experience slower response times and higher burnout rates, primarily because team members must process and produce English-language content under stressful conditions. This ongoing pressure not only hampers effective communication but also undermines team cohesion and operational efficiency. Addressing language proficiency challenges is, therefore, essential to improving both individual and team outcomes in the Cybersecurity domain.

While English language proficiency offers substantial advantages in Cybersecurity, such as access to resources, enhanced collaboration, and compatibility with AI systems, it also imposes significant limitations on inclusivity, accessibility, and global cyber resilience. In AI-driven environments, where precision, automation, and timely action are vital, linguistic disparities can exacerbate risks and deepen inequalities. Addressing these challenges calls for strategic interventions, including the localization of AI models, multilingual training resources, and inclusive Cybersecurity policies.

Challenges in Enhancing Cybersecurity in AI-Driven Environments

The evolution of Cybersecurity, particularly with the advent of AI, has introduced complex technical ecosystems requiring professionals to engage with advanced tools, real-time data, and global threat intelligence. Central to this engagement is effective communication—most critically in English, which remains the dominant language in Cybersecurity literature, protocols, frameworks, and AI interfaces. However, the reliance on English in Cybersecurity operations presents several **linguistic, technical, educational, and socio-political challenges**, especially in multilingual and non-English dominant contexts.

This section explores the multifaceted challenges that limit the role and development of English language proficiency in AI-driven Cybersecurity environments.

Linguistic Barriers in Understanding Technical Jargon

One major challenge in Cybersecurity is the linguistic complexity embedded in its discourse. Professionals in this field must understand and use a specialized vocabulary filled with technical terms, acronyms, and idiomatic expressions, which can be especially difficult for non-native English speakers. Terms like "buffer overflow," "zero-day exploit," and "SQL injection" often lack direct translations or equivalent concepts in other languages, increasing the difficulty of comprehension [34]. This dual challenge of interpreting advanced technical content while overcoming English language barriers creates a significant cognitive load, which can slow down decision-making and responses to cyber threats. For example, an AI-generated alert stating "Obfuscated PowerShell script detected" may be misunderstood or misinterpreted by someone not fully proficient in English, potentially causing critical delays in executing containment measures. Thus, language proficiency is vital in ensuring clear and timely communication within Cybersecurity operations, reducing risks caused by misunderstandings.

Dependence on English in AI Models and Tools

Most AI-driven Cybersecurity tools—such as Intrusion Detection Systems (IDS), phishing detection platforms, and Security Information and Event Management (SIEM) systems—are primarily trained using English-language datasets. As a result, these tools generate outputs, classify threats, and provide recommendations mainly in English. This reliance on English poses a significant challenge for Cybersecurity professionals who possess strong technical skills but have limited proficiency in English. Such users may struggle to accurately interpret AI-generated logs, alerts, and threat narratives, which can lead to incorrect responses or delayed action. Moreover, they might depend heavily on translation tools, which can introduce errors or misunderstandings, further complicating timely threat mitigation. Study highlights that the effectiveness of AI models depends heavily on the quality and diversity of their training data; a bias toward English limits their usability in non-Anglophone regions [35]. This language barrier, therefore, reduces the global accessibility and reliability of AI-driven Cybersecurity solutions, underscoring the need for more inclusive multilingual training data and interfaces.

Uneven Global Access to English-Based Cybersecurity Education

Access to Cybersecurity education and training that integrates English for Specific Purposes (ESP) is unevenly distributed worldwide. In many developing countries, especially in rural or underfunded institutions, technical programs often neglect the importance of English proficiency. This language gap creates significant barriers for aspiring Cybersecurity professionals. While they may have strong skills in areas like networking, ethical hacking, or programming, their limited English comprehension hinders their understanding of course materials, certification exams such as CISSP and CEH, and job-related communications predominantly offered in English. This disparity restricts their opportunities for career advancement and participation in the global Cybersecurity community. Research highlights that Cybersecurity personnel with limited English skills tend to have lower confidence and perform poorly in handling technical documentation and engaging in international collaboration [36]. Addressing this language divide is crucial to creating equitable access to Cybersecurity education and fostering a competent workforce worldwide.

Insufficient Policy Recognition of Language Skills

Many national Cybersecurity frameworks prioritize the development of technical competencies such as malware analysis, network forensics, and threat mitigation, yet they often overlook the critical role of language proficiency in professional growth. This gap results in the systemic neglect of language-based challenges within training and capacity-building programs. For instance, the NIST Cybersecurity Framework [37], while robust in outlining technical and procedural standards, does not explicitly address linguistic competencies or communication training. It assumes a default level of English proficiency among its users, an assumption that may not hold true globally. Consequently, educational institutions and organizations tend to deprioritize English language instruction in their Cybersecurity curricula. Research highlights the impact of this oversight, revealing that limited English proficiency among Cybersecurity professionals is closely linked to reduced confidence and diminished performance, particularly in tasks requiring technical documentation, cross-border coordination, and engagement in international Cybersecurity communities [38].

Machine Translation Limitations in Technical Contexts

Despite significant advancements in machine translation tools like Google Translate, these systems continue to face challenges when dealing with technical jargon and domain-specific terminology, particularly in fields like Cybersecurity. Literal translations often fail to capture the contextual meaning of phrases, leading to confusion or misinterpretation. For example, a sentence such as "SQL injection vulnerability in login.php" may be inaccurately translated into another language, especially if the tool mishandles proper nouns, file names, or code elements. Such distortions compromise the clarity of critical Cybersecurity information. This becomes problematic when precise communication is essential for identifying threats, implementing security measures, or documenting incidents. As a result, professionals in the Cybersecurity domain are often discouraged from relying entirely on automated translation tools. Instead, they recognize the importance of possessing strong English language proficiency or seeking domain-specific translation solutions to ensure the accurate exchange of technical knowledge. This underlines the role of language accuracy in securing digital infrastructure.

Cultural and Psychological Barriers

In many cultures, professionals working in Cybersecurity may avoid seeking clarification in English due to fear of embarrassment, loss of face, or being judged professionally. This psychological barrier significantly increases the risk of miscommunication, particularly during critical tasks such as incident response, threat mitigation, or forensic investigations. In a study [39], authors highlight that communication hesitancy among team members during security drills can directly undermine the efficiency of AI-powered incident management systems, which rely on timely and accurate human inputs. When professionals are reluctant to speak up or clarify technical terms, system responses may be delayed or flawed. Moreover, language insecurity discourages capable individuals from taking leadership roles or actively participating in international Cybersecurity forums. As a result, the global discourse on Cybersecurity often lacks the perspectives and contributions of non-native English speakers. This not only limits diversity but also narrows the scope of collaborative innovation and inclusive policy development in the field.

Challenges in AI Model Training for Non-English Threats

AI systems predominantly trained in English often face limitations when dealing with phishing emails or social engineering attacks written in other languages. This linguistic bias creates a dual vulnerability. Firstly, non-English-speaking users may find it challenging to interact effectively with English-centric AI tools, leading to miscommunication or misuse. Secondly, AI models trained mainly on English datasets are less likely to detect threats that are linguistically or culturally adapted to local contexts. As a result, cybercriminals exploiting regional languages and cultural nuances can bypass detection mechanisms more easily, leaving organizations exposed to sophisticated and localized attacks. The lack of multilingual competence in these AI systems undermines their ability to offer comprehensive protection in diverse linguistic environments. In a study [40], authors highlight that the integration of multilingual training in Cybersecurity-focused AI models remains a significantly underexplored area. Addressing this gap is critical to building globally resilient Cybersecurity frameworks capable of defending against multilingual threat vectors.

The growing reliance on AI in Cybersecurity has highlighted the importance of English language proficiency, but it has also exposed significant challenges. From linguistic and educational barriers to software limitations and cultural factors, the obstacles are multifaceted and deeply embedded in existing systems.

Strategies for the effectiveness of the English Language

Given the critical role of English proficiency, structured approaches are necessary to embed language development into Cybersecurity ecosystems.

English for Specific Purposes (ESP) in Cybersecurity Curricula

English for Specific Purposes (ESP) involves teaching English that is customized to meet the language needs of specific professional fields. In the domain of

Cybersecurity, ESP modules are designed to enhance learners' understanding of specialized vocabulary, technical documentation, log analysis, and effective communication during security incidents. These modules help professionals accurately interpret and convey complex information. For example, a Cybersecurity training institute in South Korea partnered with language experts to develop tailored ESP content. The program included instruction in malware classification terminology, ethical hacking expressions, and structured Cybersecurity report writing. This collaboration ensured that learners not only acquired technical knowledge but also developed the linguistic competence required for clear and precise communication in professional Cybersecurity environments.

Benefits:

- Enhances comprehension of tools and documentation.
- Improves team communication and crisis response.
- Increases the employability of graduates in global roles.

Controlled Natural Language (CNL) for Documentation

Controlled Natural Language (CNL) is a simplified form of English with restricted grammar and vocabulary, aimed at reducing ambiguity and complexity. It is particularly useful in AI-generated Cybersecurity reports to improve clarity and accessibility, especially for non-native English speakers. For instance, a direct alert like "System X was accessed from unknown IP Y at 02:45 UTC" is far easier to understand than a vague message such as "Anomalous remote intrusion potentially observed." By using CNL, organizations can ensure that critical threat information is communicated clearly and efficiently. Tools such as Acrolinx and the Simplified Technical English (STE) guidelines can help integrate CNL into automated documentation systems, making Cybersecurity communication more effective and universally comprehensible.

Multilingual Support in AI Tools

Although English remains the primary language in Cybersecurity, incorporating multilingual support in AI-powered tools significantly enhances accessibility for non-English speakers. AI interfaces equipped with translation capabilities can deliver security alerts in both English and the user's native language, allowing for better comprehension and quicker responses. For example, Google's Chronicle SIEM system integrates translation APIs to display log events in multiple languages while preserving an English audit trail for standardized documentation and global collaboration. This dual-language approach not only ensures users can understand critical information immediately but also encourages gradual English language acquisition in a technical context. By combining clarity with inclusivity, this strategy promotes both effective threat response and the development of essential English proficiency over time in Cybersecurity environments.

Peer Learning and Language Mentorship Programs

Peer-led initiatives play a vital role in enhancing English proficiency in real-world Cybersecurity environments. By pairing fluent English speakers with non-native professionals, these programs create opportunities for collaborative learning and skill development. Activities such as joint report writing, threat modeling, and reviewing code comments help bridge linguistic gaps while simultaneously strengthening technical communication. These real-time, task-based interactions improve vocabulary, comprehension, and professional articulation, which are critical in the fast-paced Cybersecurity domain. For instance, Security Operations Centers (SOCs) in the Philippines have successfully implemented buddy systems, where senior analysts mentor junior team members not only in technical practices but also in English language usage [41]. This dual-focus mentorship has been shown to enhance operational efficiency, reduce errors due to miscommunication, and build team confidence. Such models highlight how language learning can be seamlessly integrated into Cybersecurity workflows through structured peer engagement.

Benefits include:

- Reduced miscommunication during incident response.
- Enhanced confidence in participating in global discussions.
- On-the-job English language immersion.

Gamification and Simulations

Gamified learning and AI-driven simulations are revolutionizing Cybersecurity education by immersing learners in realistic, English-language-based scenarios. Activities like phishing simulations, Capture the Flag (CTF) competitions, and mock incident response drills provide hands-on experience while enhancing both technical skills and English proficiency. These simulations require learners to interpret system logs, analyze reports, and respond to command-line instructions—all in English—developing their ability to navigate real-world Cybersecurity challenges. For example, the U.S. CyberPatriot program uses scenario-based games to train students in defending networks, emphasizing accurate comprehension and communication. As learners make decisions under pressure, they not only sharpen their problem-solving abilities but also improve their language fluency in technical contexts. This integrated approach to learning supports deeper engagement and retention, making it especially effective for non-native English speakers aspiring to excel in global Cybersecurity environments.

Public Awareness Campaigns Using Multimodal English

To effectively reach a wider audience—including non-technical users, first responders, and the general public—Cybersecurity awareness campaigns should use simplified English, supported by visuals, infographics, and AI-generated narratives. These tools help demystify complex concepts and promote better understanding and engagement. For example, the UK's National Cybersecurity Centre (NCSC) develops animated videos and infographics in plain English to educate people about password security, phishing threats, and safe online practices. Such accessible content increases awareness and encourages safer digital behavior. In multilingual societies like India, offering these materials in English alongside regional languages not only broadens reach but also supports English language learning. This dual-language approach enhances digital literacy, particularly among users new to Cybersecurity. Overall, integrating simplified language with engaging visual content ensures that crucial security information is understood and acted upon by diverse communities across educational and linguistic backgrounds.

National Cybersecurity Policies Emphasizing Language Training

Governments need to acknowledge English proficiency as a critical component of national Cybersecurity resilience. Incorporating English language training, especially technical English, into capacity-building programs strengthens the ability of Cybersecurity professionals to understand and respond to threats effectively. Educational institutions should be encouraged and incentivized to teach technical English to prepare future professionals for the global Cybersecurity landscape. For example, India's Cyber Surakshit Bharat initiative integrates communication modules focused on Cybersecurity terminology and cyber hygiene in English, helping government officials improve their technical communication skills. Embedding language policy within Cybersecurity strategies ensures that workforce readiness can be scaled globally, enabling better collaboration across international teams and more efficient use of widely accepted Cybersecurity frameworks. Ultimately, proficiency in English enhances clarity, precision, and coordination in Cybersecurity efforts, making it an indispensable part of the national defense infrastructure.

Case Studies Highlighting Implementation

Case Study 1: Estonia's Cybersecurity Readiness

Estonia, a global leader in e-governance, emphasizes English proficiency in its national Cybersecurity policy. Training programs include ESP modules and English-language certification for government employees, enabling seamless collaboration with NATO's Cooperative Cyber Defence Centre of Excellence (CCDCOE).

Case Study 2: Cybersecurity in Multilingual Africa

Countries like Kenya and Nigeria, despite having multilingual populations, conduct most Cybersecurity education in English due to its dominance in international frameworks. Local universities incorporate Cybersecurity labs with English-driven virtual labs and simulation tools.

Impact: Graduates from these programs have better success in passing global certification exams and working with international cyber response teams.

CONCLUSION

In the rapidly evolving field of cybersecurity shaped by advancements in Artificial Intelligence (AI), English language proficiency has become a critical factor for effective defense. English serves as the lingua franca for global communication, documentation, and collaboration, underpinning essential frameworks like MITRE ATT&CK®, the NIST Cybersecurity Framework, and ISO/IEC 27001 standards, which are predominantly authored in English. Limited English skills can lead to misinterpretations of technical concepts—such as "privilege escalation" versus "access control failure"—potentially weakening an organization's security posture. Furthermore, AI-driven tools heavily rely on Natural Language Processing (NLP) to analyze unstructured data like threat reports and advisories. Cybersecurity professionals with strong English skills are better equipped to interact with AI systems, enhancing threat detection and response. Since cyber adversaries often communicate in English, proficiency is also vital for timely threat identification and disruption.

International cooperation is central to combating cyber threats, making English proficiency essential for seamless cross-border communication and coordinated responses. Programs like India's Cyber Surakshit Bharat initiative exemplify how integrating English communication modules into cybersecurity training can boost workforce readiness. Beyond individual skills, fostering an organizational culture that encourages English communication improves documentation, incident reporting, and knowledge sharing, supporting agility in AI-driven environments. In conclusion, strengthening cybersecurity resilience requires the simultaneous advancement of technical expertise and English proficiency. Policymakers and educators must embed language development into cybersecurity strategies to bridge knowledge gaps, optimize AI-human collaboration, and defend digital infrastructures worldwide against increasingly sophisticated threats.

REFERENCES

[1] I.H. Sarker, "Machine learning: Algorithms, real-world applications and research directions", *SN Comput. Sci.,* vol. 2, no. 3, p. 160, 2021.
[http://dx.doi.org/10.1007/s42979-021-00592-x] [PMID: 33778771]

[2] V.K. Bukkarayasamudram, P.C.S. Reddy, and K. Arun Kumar, "Quantum computing revolution in healthcare: a systematic review of applications, issues and future directions", *Artif Intell Rev,* vol. 58, p. 389, 2025.
[http://dx.doi.org/10.1007/s10462-025-11381-w]

[3] G. Arun, P.C.S. Reddy, N. Budati, B. Rebecca, S. Perumalla, and V.B. Gujar, "A deep learning framework for diabetes prediction: PIMA indian dataset", In: *Proc. 2024 International Conference on Innovative Computing, Intelligent Communication and Smart Electrical Systems (ICSES)* IEEE., 2024, pp. 1-6.

[4] P. S. Muller, Y. Sucharitha, S. Kottapally, G. Ismoilova, L. Rakhimova, and P. C. S. Reddy, "A Novel Financial Market Prediction Framework Based on Deep Learning for Accurate Trend Forecasting", In: *Information Systems for Intelligent Systems*. ISBM 2025, A. Iglesias, J. Shin, N. Bhatt, A. Joshi, (eds) Information Systems for Intelligent Systems. ISBM 2025. Lecture Notes in Networks and Systems, vol 1748. Springer, Cham.
[http://dx.doi.org/10.1007/978-3-032-12990-1_5]

[5] J. Park, and H. Jang, "The impact of english language proficiency on technical communication in cybersecurity operations", *Journal of Cybersecurity Education, Research and Practice,* vol. 2022, no. 1, p. 4, 2022.

[6] R. Samrin, P.C.S. Reddy, K.A. Kumar, N. Deepthi, C. Mithra, S.B. Latha, Y. Sucharitha, and G.K. Thakur, "A hybrid deep learning based framework for prediction of rice yield through integration of biophysical parameters and optical remote sensing data in India", *J. Atmos. Sol.-Terr. Phys.,* vol. 279, p. 106734, 2026.
[http://dx.doi.org/10.1016/j.jastp.2026.106734]

[7] P.C. Shaker Reddy, and Y. Sucharitha, "IoT-enabled energy-efficient multipath power control for underwater sensor networks", *Int. J. Sens. Wirel. Commun. Control,* vol. 12, no. 6, pp. 478-494, 2022.
[http://dx.doi.org/10.2174/2210327912666220615103257]

[8] A.T. Somnathe, V.T. Selvi, N.G. Stepha, M.T. Kingslin, F.M. Inamdar, and P.C.S. Reddy, "An intelligent traffic conflict prediction using deep learning with long-term evolution access data", In: *Proc. 2025 3rd International Conference on Smart Systems for applications in Electrical Sciences (ICSSES)* IEEE, 2025, pp. 1-6.
[http://dx.doi.org/10.1109/ICSSES64899.2025.11010032]

[9] M.D. Basith, P. Praveen, and P.C.S. Reddy, "Adaptive deep Q-GAN framework for enhanced breast cancer detection in medical imaging", *Biomed. Signal Process. Control,* vol. 112, p. 108638, 2026.
[http://dx.doi.org/10.1016/j.bspc.2025.108638]

[10] T. Tobiyama, Y. Yamaguchi, H. Shimada, T. Ikuse, and T. Yagi, "Malware process detection using LSTM based analysis of system call sequence", In: *Proc. IEEE 22nd Int. Conf. Comput. Commun. Netw. (ICCCN)*Waikoloa, HI, USA, 2016, pp. 1-8.
[http://dx.doi.org/10.1109/ICCCN.2016.7568492]

[11] Z.B. Akhtar, and A.T. Rawol, "Enhancing cybersecurity through AI-powered security mechanisms", *IT journal research and development,* vol. 9, no. 1, pp. 50-67, 2024. [http://dx.doi.org/10.25299/itjrd.2024.16852]

[12] I.U. Wada, G.O. Izibili, T. Babayemi, A. Abdulkareem, O.M. Macaulay, and A. Emadoye, "AI-driven cybersecurity in higher education: A systematic review and model evaluation for enhanced threat detection and incident response", *World Journal of Advanced Research and Reviews,* vol. 25, no. 3, pp. 2233-2245, 2025. [http://dx.doi.org/10.30574/wjarr.2025.25.3.0989]

[13] K. Shaukat, S. Luo, V. Varadharajan, I.A. Hameed, and M. Xu, "A survey on machine learning techniques for cybersecurity in the last decade", *IEEE Access,* vol. 8, pp. 222310-222354, 2020. [http://dx.doi.org/10.1109/ACCESS.2020.3041951]

[14] A. Shahana, R. Hasan, S.F. Farabi, J. Akter, M.A. Al Mahmud, F.T. Johora, and G. Suzer, "AI-driven cybersecurity: Balancing advancements and safeguards", *Journal of Computer Science and Technology Studies,* vol. 6, no. 2, pp. 76-85, 2024. [http://dx.doi.org/10.32996/jcsts.2024.6.2.9]

[15] U. Hasan, Z.Z. Arab, M.Z. Arab, and S.A. Sharma, "Exploring the impact of AI-powered educational technologies on English language proficiency: Ethical, practical, and pedagogical dimensions in higher education", in K. Arai, Ed., *Proc. Future Technologies Conference (FTC) 2025, vol. 3, Lecture Notes in Networks and Systems*, vol. 1677. Cham, Switzerland: Springer, 2026. [http://dx.doi.org/10.1007/978-3-032-07995-4_40]

[16] M. Palanisamy, and R. Krishnan, "Cybersecurity challenges and AI solutions", *Int. J. Eng. Adv. Technol.,* vol. 8, no. 6, pp. 3120-3124, 2019.

[17] P.C. Reddy, and A.S. Babu, "Survey on weather prediction using big data analystics", in *Proc. 2017 Second International Conference on Electrical, Computer and Communication Technologies (ICECCT)*, 2017, pp. 1–6. IEEE.

[18] R.V. Reddy, G.S. Monisha, A.M. Ali, P.Y. Devi, M.V. Madhusudhan, and Y. Sucharitha, "Empirical method for thyroid disease prediction using a deep learning techniques", *2023 IEEE 8th International Conference for Convergence in Technology (I2CT),* IEEE, pp. 1-5, 2023. [http://dx.doi.org/10.1109/I2CT57861.2023.10126291]

[19] G. Anjaneyulu, P.C.S. Reddy, P. Praveen, S. Banoth, D. Pandey, and S.N. Koka, "A hybrid optimization deep learning frame work for efficient stock market forecasting", *2025 International Conference on Advanced Computing Technologies (ICoACT),* IEEE., pp. 1-6, 2025. [http://dx.doi.org/10.1109/ICoACT63339.2025.11004655]

[20] S.B. Latha, C. Dastagiraiah, A. Kiran, S. Asif, D. Elangovan, and P.C.S. Reddy, "Expression of concern for: an adaptive machine learning model for walmart sales prediction", *2023 International Conference on Circuit Power and Computing Technologies (ICCPCT),* IEEE., pp. 1-1, 2023.

[21] D.A. Greitzer, and D.A. Frincke, "Combining traditional cybersecurity audit data with psychosocial data: Towards predictive modeling for insider threat mitigation", *Insider Threats in Cybersecurity,* vol. 49, pp. 85-113, 2010.

[22] A.M. Dreheeb, and H. El Tajouri, "Role of artificial intelligence in enhancing cyber security", *Bani Waleed University Journal of Humanities and Applied Sciences,* vol. 10, no. 3, pp. 121-129, 2025. [http://dx.doi.org/10.58916/jhas.v10i3.842]

[23] P.C. Shaker Reddy, and Y. Sucharitha, "An energy-saving data transmission approach based on migrating virtual machine technology to cloud computing", *Recent Advances in Electrical & Electronic Engineering (Formerly Recent Patents on Electrical & Electronic Engineering),* vol. 17, no. 6, pp. 573-581, 2024. [http://dx.doi.org/10.2174/2352096516666230713163440]

[24] V. Sukhavasi, and V. Dondeti, "Sarcasm detection using hybrid deep learning framework based on

word-emoji embeddings", *2024 International Conference on Recent Innovation in Smart and Sustainable Technology (ICRISST),* IEEE., pp. 1-6, 2024.
[http://dx.doi.org/10.1109/ICRISST59181.2024.10921793]

[25] G. Anjaneyulu, C.S.R. Pundru, and P. Praveen, "A hybrid deep reinforcement learning framework for stock market prediction", *2024 4th International Conference on Mobile Networks and Wireless Communications (ICMNWC),* IEEE, pp. 1-5, 2024.
[http://dx.doi.org/10.1109/ICMNWC63764.2024.10872342]

[26] A.A.S. Balla, M. AbdAlgane, A.O.A. Ahmed, and E. Osman, "AI-driven innovations in adult EFL learning: Exploring potentials and practicalities", *International Journal of Interactive Mobile Technologies,* vol. 19, no. 8, 2025.
[http://dx.doi.org/10.3991/ijim.v19i08.52295]

[27] S. Yadala, C.S.R. Pundru, and V.K. Solanki, "A novel private encryption model in IoT under cloud computing domain", *The International Conference on Intelligent Systems & Networks,* pp. 263-270, 2023.Singapore
[http://dx.doi.org/10.1007/978-981-99-4725-6_33]

[28] W. Kasri, Y. Himeur, H.A. Alkhazaleh, S. Tarapiah, S. Atalla, W. Mansoor, and H. Al-Ahmad, "From vulnerability to defense: The role of large language models in enhancing cybersecurity", *Computation,* vol. 13, no. 2, p. 30, 2025.
[http://dx.doi.org/10.3390/computation13020030]

[29] R. Jesudas, "Empowering language learning: The role of AI in enhancing language skills", in *Proc. Int. Conf. on Modelling Strategies in Mathematics (ICMSM 2024), AIP Conference Proceedings*, vol. 3306, no. 1. AIP Publishing LLC, 2025.

[30] A.S.E. AbuSahyon, A. Alzyoud, O. Alshorman, and B. Al-Absi, AbuSahyon, Alia Sa'ad Eldin, Abdelhadi Alzyoud, Omar Alshorman, and Basim Al-Absi, "AI-driven technology and chatbots as tools for enhancing English language learning in the context of second language acquisition: A review study", *International Journal of Membrane Science and Technology,* vol. 10, no. 1, pp. 1209-1223, 2023.
[http://dx.doi.org/10.15379/ijmst.v10i1.2829]

[31] Z.B. Akhtar, and A.T. Rawol, "Enhancing cybersecurity through AI-powered security mechanisms", *IT journal research and development,* vol. 9, no. 1, pp. 50-67, 2024.
[http://dx.doi.org/10.25299/itjrd.2024.16852]

[32] M.A. Mallik, and S.K. Reddi, "Stock market trend prediction using an explainable deep learning approach", In: *Proc. 2025 Int. Conf. Knowledge Engineering and Communication Systems (ICKECS)* IEEE, 2025, pp. 1-6.

[33] P. C. S. Reddy, A. Sureshbabu, and Y. Sucharitha, and G. S. Narayana "A personalized artificial neural network for rice crop yield prediction," in *Artificial Intelligence and Data Science in Recommendation System: Current Trends, Technologies and Applications*, A. Majumder, J. L. Sarkar, and A. Majumder, Eds. Singapore: Bentham Science Publishers, 2023, pp. 272–295.
[http://dx.doi.org/10.2174/9789815136746123010017]

[34] M.H. Alalawi, "Enhancing cybersecurity awareness in the United Arab Emirates: An assessment of current practices and the development of an AI-enhanced mobile application," M.S. thesis, United Arab Emirates University, 2024.

[35] E.V.N. Jyothi, "An adaptive intrusion detection system in industrial internet of things (IIoT) using deep learning", In: *Proc. 2024 1st International Conference on Innovative Sustainable Technologies for Energy, Mechatronics, and Smart Systems (ISTEMS)* IEEE, 2024.
[http://dx.doi.org/10.1109/ISTEMS60181.2024.10560245]

[36] C. V. S. Babu, and D. Vincey, "The future of english language learning: leveraging AI for enhanced learning experiences", *AI Applications for English Language Learning,* pp. 415-460.

[37] P.C.S. Reddy, S. Yadala, and S.N. Goddumarri, "Development of rainfall forecasting model using

machine learning with singular spectrum analysis", *IIUM Engineering Journal,* vol. 23, no. 1, pp. 172-186, 2022.
[http://dx.doi.org/10.31436/iiumej.v23i1.1822]

[38] N. Sari, "The role of artificial intelligence (AI) in developing English language learner's communication skills", *J. Educ.,* vol. 6, no. 01, pp. 750-757, 2023.

[39] A.M.S. Moybeka, N. Syariatin, D.P. Tatipang, D.A. Mushthoza, N.P.J.L. Dewi, and S. Tineh, "Artificial Intelligence and English classroom: the implications of AI toward EFL students' motivation", *Edumaspul: Jurnal Pendidikan,* vol. 7, no. 2, pp. 2444-2454, 2023.
[http://dx.doi.org/10.33487/edumaspul.v7i2.6669]

[40] A. T. Somnathe, M. Parameshwari, S. Pattem, S. N. Koka, S. Abdurakhmanova, and P. C. S. Reddy, "An Attention-Based Deep Learning Framework for Gold Price Prediction Using Time Series Data", In: *Information Systems for Intelligent Systems*. ISBM 2025, A. Iglesias, J. Shin, N. Bhatt, A. Joshi (eds) Information Systems for Intelligent Systems. ISBM 2025. Lecture Notes in Networks and Systems, vol 1743. Springer, Cham.
[http://dx.doi.org/10.1007/978-3-032-13006-8_6]

[41] B. Chukwu, "AI-driven risk management: Strengthening cybersecurity and market stability in the US financial sector", *World Journal of Advanced Research and Reviews,* vol. 17, pp. 1967-1976, 2021.
[http://dx.doi.org/10.30574/wjarr.2025.28.1.3647]

CHAPTER 5

Leveraging Social Networks for Cyber Threat Intelligence: Attack Trends, Cybersecurity Threat Detection Challenges, AI-Based Solutions, and Potential Opportunities in X

Sri Rekha Uppuluri[1,*] and **Sasanko Sekhar Gantayat**[1]

[1] *School of Computer Science & AI, SR University, Warangal, Telangana, India*

Abstract: The increasing prevalence of cyber-attacks is a direct result of the ubiquitous nature of social media platforms like X (previously Twitter). This threat has prompted a plethora of research on ways to analyze X data for cyber-attack detection and prediction. This study primarily addresses the implementation of Artificial Intelligence (AI) approaches for anticipating future cyber risks on X. We argue that a semantic attention is more advantageous for this step of the method, even though character-level feature extraction approaches are copious. Our findings highlight the pervasiveness of social networks as a platform for the propagation of both valuable information and numerous security risks. Social media plays a significant role in spreading these cybercrime dangers; thus, addressing them must be a top priority. Our research shows that social media may be a powerful tool for cyber threat awareness and response. Data summarization levels, algorithm complexity, anticipation scope, kinds of cybersecurity threats, feature-extraction strategies, scalability over time, and performance measures are some of the important components that are generally under-evaluated in current studies. Examining current gaps and trends in this field, this chapter mainly seeks to discover AI algorithms employed for cyber threat detection on X. The study's findings on cyber threat dynamics and assault group methodology are useful for enhancing cybersecurity. It provides practical consequences for cybersecurity practitioners, law enforcement agencies, and lawmakers dedicated to protecting the digital environment, and highlights the crucial role of social networks in modern cyber-attack landscapes.

Key Terms: Anomaly detection, AI, Attack trends, Cybersecurity, NLP, Security &privacy, Social media, Twitter, Threat detection.

[*] **Corresponding Author Sri Rekha Uppuluri:**, School of Computer Science & AI, SR University, Warangal, Telangana, India; E-mail: 2403c50122@sru.edu.in

Pundru Chandra Shaker Reddy, Yadala Sucharitha, & Thillaiarasu N (Eds.)

INTRODUCTION

The introduction of AI has brought strong defenses as well as formidable threats, radically altering the cybersecurity scene. Despite AI's greatness in areas such as incident response, user authentication, and anomaly detection, bad actors are finding ways to leverage it to launch more complex assaults [1]. As a result of the intricate relationship between AI and human enemies, the threat landscape is always changing. A major threat to organizations is the rise of AI-powered attacks that may evade conventional defenses. A combination of sophisticated threat intelligence, flexible defenses, and a solid ethical foundation is necessary for effective countermeasures. Better threat detection, automated responses, and augmented human analysts are all possible outcomes of defensive AI deployment. However, cautious risk management is required due to issues including algorithmic bias, data privacy concerns, and the possibility of attacks driven by AI. Prioritizing regulatory compliance, industry standards, and collaboration is essential for enterprises to effectively harness the promise of AI in cybersecurity [2]. Investing in cybersecurity education and training is vital to establishing a knowledgeable workforce skilled in tackling evolving threats. The best way to reduce the dangers posed by AI and create a more robust digital environment is to close the gap between the two fields [3]. In recent years, social media platforms' cybersecurity has grown into a top priority. This is happening at the same time as the cybersecurity industry is seeing phenomenal growth, increasing by a factor of 35 in the last decade. The rising threat landscape is reflected in this increase in cybersecurity spending. Unfortunately, cybercrime has been on the rise alongside the expansion of the digital economy [4]. Data breaches put social media platforms and their users at risk, and the proliferation of internet and social media apps has given attackers additional possibilities to commit such crimes. The monetary loss due to cyberattacks is anticipated to triple from 2015 levels, reaching roughly USD 10.5 trillion per year by 2025, if the present trend continues [5]. Fig (**1**) shows the global investment in cybersecurity from 2017 to 2024.

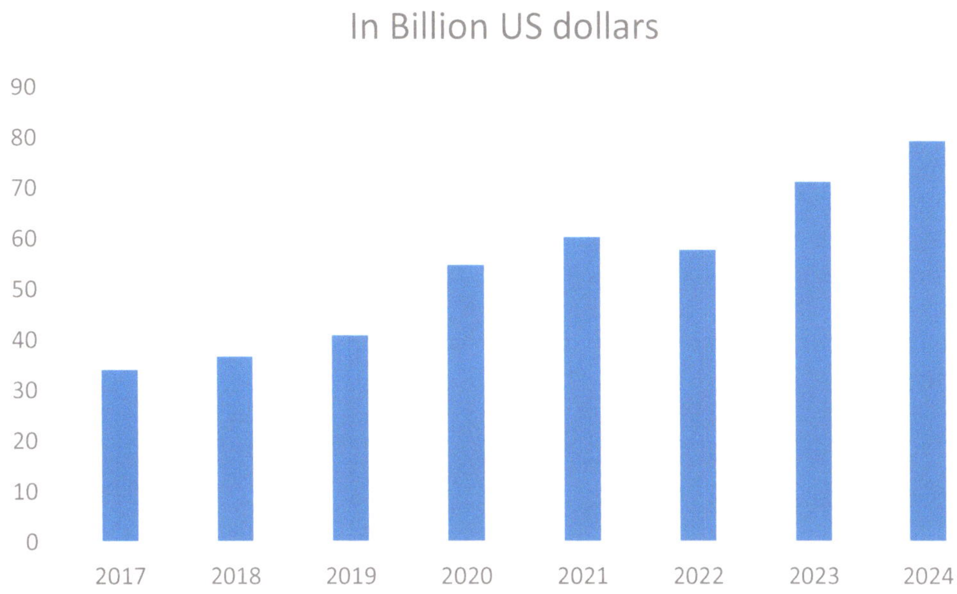

Fig. (1). Worldwide cybersecurity expenditure from 2017 to 2024.

Data analysis, pattern recognition, and automated processing are three areas where Artificial Intelligence (AI) technology excels, making it a formidable tool in the fight against cybersecurity threats [6]. Cybersecurity threat detection systems can improve their ability to spot unusual activity, uncover previously unseen dangers, and instantly adjust to changing assault patterns by utilizing technologies like deep learning and machine learning. Both the false alarm rate and the accuracy of threat detection are significantly reduced by this.

An authoritative resource for classifying and organizing newly discovered vulnerabilities according to the Common Vulnerability Exposures (CVE) standard, the National Vulnerability Database (NVD) helps businesses prioritize their efforts to fix these vulnerabilities. New research, however, suggests that the NVD might not get regular updates. Indeed, it is not uncommon for newly found vulnerabilities to be discussed on social media sites such as Twitter prior to their public disclosure on NVD, frequently without a CVE or prior to the appropriate announcement of a CVE [7]. By keeping tabs on and analyzing conversations happening within the cybersecurity community on Twitter, experts can get a head start in discovering exploitable flaws. This could help them find security holes before the NVD makes them public.

Members of the Cyber Threat Intelligence (CTI) group on Twitter can act as social sensors by listening in on group chats in real time; this can help investigators learn more about cyberattacks and vulnerabilities. The conversations are illustrated by two tweets in Fig (**2**). By delving into Twitter's mountain of CTI data, businesses can better understand attack behaviors, trends, and public opinion, all of which can help them strengthen their proactive cyber defense and incident response protocols [8]. But in the midst of all those unstructured tweets, it's easy to miss the evidence and trends. It would be impractical and take too much time to manually analyze such unstructured data. Automating this procedure is essential in the CTI application space to alleviate cybersecurity experts' information overload caused by dealing with large amounts of unstructured documents.

Fig. (2). Tweets related to potential cyber threats.

The proliferation of social-media sites like X, LinkedIn, and TikTok in the modern era is indicative of how we feel about sharing personal information online. Nevertheless, there is an increasing danger associated with this convenience: cyber-attacks [9]. When criminals launch cyber-attacks, they are attempting to acquire sensitive data, such as users' information, by means of technology. Unauthorized online activity can be facilitated by this stolen data. Potential entry points for fraudsters include information that has been lost, stolen, or skimmed. The proliferation of cyber risks is directly proportional to the growth of social media platforms, creating a formidable obstacle for users and platforms alike [10]. X is a collection of web-based tools that let individuals create profiles, either fully or partially visible to the public, and then link up with a network of other users so that they may see and exchange content from each other's profiles. Each service has its own unique way of associating X connections.

A wide variety of X with shared characteristics is appearing more frequently. The three main features of social networks are as follows: (1) the ability to make one's profile public or partially public (according to the platform's restrictions), (2) the ability to create a network of contacts with other users, and (3) the ability to navigate the network by clicking on links. X has been the target of numerous cyberattacks that have compromised user identities or eroded network trust and privacy [11]. Hackers and other attackers target X for a variety of reasons, including but not limited to: financial, ideological, personal, political, emotional, commercial, and entertainment. There have been a lot of solutions developed by security organizations and researchers in response to the growing number of cyber threats. To safeguard X users from potential dangers posed by compromised multimedia data, there are a number of options, such as watermarking [12], Steg-analysis [13], among others. The usual hazards are also mitigated by established technologies like spam detection and phishing detection. In addition to commercial solutions like small surveillance and social protection apps, there are also certain well-established security measures in X, such as authentication procedures [14] and privacy settings. The static nature of old information security solutions centered on digital signatures and heuristics makes them inadequate [15]. On the other hand, X is not well-protected against cybersecurity risks using current technologies. This issue arises for two main reasons. One interesting aspect is the wide range of word meanings and contexts used in tweets, which is not surprising given the character constraint of 140 and the adaptability of people's writing styles [16]. The second issue is that individuals use hashtags inappropriately, and the number of various and confusing advertising tweets is high. Cybersecurity vulnerabilities can be hard to spot in tweets for these reasons. As social media has grown in popularity, cybersecurity has emerged as a major issue [17]. An increasingly common means of disseminating this kind of danger has been X-based event detection, with academics making considerable use of X as a database for the sake of event analysis and extraction. Several methods have been suggested for X cybersecurity threat identification, with an emphasis on qualities, frequency, and multimodal X hashtags. But there aren't any thorough assessments of important criteria, including prediction scope, cybersecurity threat kind, and feature extraction method [18].

Identifying AI-based approaches to cyber threat detection on X is the primary emphasis of this article. We also intend to look into the current trends and gaps in this field. Cyber threat detection on X has seen a dearth of review publications in recent years. The use of ML and DL for the purpose of X cyber threat identification is the focus of this review [19].

The main thing this article has to provide is a curated library of recent research on various cyber-attacks and the technology used to detect them. Scholars are given a clear picture and a firm groundwork for additional research into the application of AI to identify and reduce cyber dangers, as it details present difficulties and knowledge gaps.

The following categories best describe the research's contributions:

- An examination of anomaly detection, classification, and analysis methodologies, as well as ML, DL, and metaheuristic approaches to cyber-attack detection.
- Sixty academic articles covering cybersecurity and the application of basic AI techniques were reviewed and critically examined during the last four years.
- Data sets, strategies for decreasing data complexity, ways of sorting data, methods for comparison, performance measurement, and cybersecurity focus were some of the factors considered to evaluate the paper.
- Assessing publicly available cybersecurity datasets and primarily categorizing the kinds observed in these statistics.
- You may easily comprehend the different methodologies and outcomes by referring to the comparative tables that organize the studies' essential aspects.
- A summary that talks about the problems with current AI technologies in cybersecurity and how to fix them in the future

Important context regarding cyber dangers to X is provided by this paper. Following a general introduction to cybersecurity risks in X, this section delves into the unique difficulties and dangers faced by this platform. Before describing the technique employed in this work, we take a look at the incentives that drive cyber threats on X. Cyber threat solutions are subsequently studied, with an emphasis on the most current findings. After that, suggestions for future methods and a review of the gaps in the current literature are given. Additionally, the survey's drawbacks are addressed. The conclusion is the last section of this work.

LITERATURE REVIEW

In this literature study, we look at how cybercrime is classified, how social networks have changed the game, and how important threat intelligence is for dealing with the increasing dangers. Additionally, it outlines the most recent findings in data analysis and artificial intelligence, offering a framework for comprehending how to construct efficient anti-cybercrime programs.

Classification of Cybercrime Phenomenon

For a comprehensive understanding of cybercrime and its effects on the world economy, its categorization is crucial. Modern endpoint attacks are complex, multi-stage heists that impact companies of any size. Crypto mining assaults have made it easier for unauthorized users to gain access to corporate networks, and ransomware attacks, which target small firms in particular, have been on the rise [20]. Huge data breaches, expensive ransomware payments, and a more complicated threat landscape have all been observed in the last year, as cybercriminals have considerably expanded their techniques.

In addition, the sophistication of data crimes committed by network hackers has grown, with the introduction of tactics like sniffing and social engineering that make it harder for cyber police to detect and track them [21]. These all-inclusive categories provide researchers with a framework for understanding the complex nature and broad impact of cybercrimes.

The Process of Cyber Threat Intelligence

According to Seker, threat intelligence is “knowing the enemy's goals, strategies, and tactics to defend vital assets” [22]. In order to deal with the variety and growing number of cyber dangers, Choo looked at ideas like routine activity theory. Cyber intelligence was defined and modeled in a study [23], which took a business-oriented approach to the topic. A customized threat intelligence infrastructure for identification and monitoring was built in a study [24], based on their examination of quick botnet behavior patterns. In order to assess existing technologies and draw attention to their shortcomings from a scientific standpoint, the authors of a study [25] suggested a taxonomy system for threat-sharing technologies. The research highlighted the necessity of threat intelligence in navigating the complicated cybersecurity landscape and its transdisciplinary character.

According to the research we looked at, threat intelligence is all about methodically gathering, evaluating, and interpreting data in order to manage and anticipate risks to information security. It is believed that this process necessitates stages including gathering, processing, analyzing, and distributing [26]. Additionally, it has been proven that automated systems are great at gathering technical data, but that evaluations involving several sources of information require human participation. There is a growing demand for comprehensive analysis to separate useful insights from noise in the ever-increasing volume of technical data. Hence, to verify social network data, we employ both automated and human-assisted approaches.

SOCIAL MEDIA-DRIVEN CYBER THREAT INTELLIGENCE

Using AI and NLP, Sufi built a system that can analyze social media posts to create a cyber threat index for an entire country. To understand the context of social-media tweets about cyber-attacks and electronic warfare, this framework uses the latest innovations in NLP and AI. The next step is to create a country-level index utilizing keyword-based index building techniques. To better prepare the nation for cybersecurity threats, this method gives decision makers data they can use [27]. Since Sufi's study is highly relevant to our present research goals and gives useful pointers for future field investigations, we will make sure to cite and incorporate its discoveries. Phishing, malware, and identity theft are commonplace due to the personal information that is often abused on popular platforms like Facebook and Twitter, which pose distinct cybersecurity threats. According to Orlowska, cyber threats can originate from and target social media platforms, so it's crucial to monitor these platforms as part of Cyber Threat Intelligence (CTI) frameworks to find and fix these vulnerabilities [28].

Social media plays a multi-faceted role in political conflict, involving both the diffusion of information and cybersecurity. The Russian-Ukrainian conflict showed how social media can be both a blessing and a curse in information operations; therefore, Kyrgos stressed the importance of public education on operational security to avoid accidental disclosures. This highlights how social media may both help with situational awareness and pose serious security dangers in areas of conflict [29]. Similarly, statistics from this study reveal that the Syrian Electronic Army (SEA) appeared frequently on Twitter due to its highly publicized and extensively publicized cyberattacks targeting Western media outlets, government websites, and major social networking platforms. The pro-Assad hacktivist group SEA used these attacks to spread propaganda and discredit opposition narratives, strengthening the position of the Syrian government during the civil war. The massive user base of social media platforms has resulted in heightened privacy and identity theft concerns, according to a study conducted in [30]. To counter these dangers, they suggest defenses based on artificial intelligence and machine learning, and they back the incorporation of these technologies into CTI systems for social media in order to make them more resistant to cyberattacks [31].

At the same time, cybersecurity is facing new hurdles due to the proliferation of misinformation on social media. Watney stressed the significance of a legal framework that includes the cybersecurity implications of disinformation and explains how targeted measures can lessen the damage to national security [32]. This study partially overcomes these concerns by selecting reputable accounts and picking relevant keywords. Unfortunately, there is yet no foolproof way to check the accuracy of all the data sets. This new research highlights how social networks are becoming more important in CTI, showing how they can both reveal important danger information and be exploited.

AI TECHNOLOGIES IN CYBERSECURITY

In recent years, numerous fields have made extensive use of AI, a technology capable of imitating human intelligence [33]. The ML, DL &NLP are at its heart; these technologies can investigate gigantic bulks of data, spot patterns, and anticipate trends and future events automatically. When it comes to real-time threat recognition and processing massive amounts of complicated data, Artificial Intelligence (AI) offers several benefits in the cybersecurity industry.

Cybersecurity threats are constantly changing in nature and level of sophistication due to the rapid advancements in information technology. Signature libraries have long been used to identify common malware like viruses and worms, but newer forms of malware like Advanced Persistent Threats (APTs), zero-day assaults, and social engineering evade detection. A significant threat to conventional cybersecurity defenses is the increasing sophistication of attackers, who are employing tactics such as encrypted traffic, evading conventional safeguards, and capitalizing on zero-day flaws. The cybersecurity profession is constantly searching for smarter and more automated solutions due to these changes [34]. Cybersecurity is progressively incorporating AI technology to enhance threat detection and response capabilities in response to the increasingly sophisticated nature of cyber-attacks. Intrusion Detection Systems (IDS), spam filters, and malware detectors were the original users of Artificial Intelligence (AI) with the purpose of automatically classifying and detecting suspicious activity using machine learning techniques [35]. These early implementations have proven that AI may enhance detection accuracy and reaction time, making up for the deficiencies of more conventional security methods.

From gathering and analyzing threat intelligence to detecting, responding to, and recovering from threats in real time, AI technology is currently present in every facet of cybersecurity. Intelligent countermeasures, real-time threat detection and prediction, and automated processing of large amounts of security data are all capabilities of AI-driven security solutions [36]. Deep learning models, for instance, can sift through mountains of network traffic data in search of unusual trends, while reinforcement learning algorithms can fine-tune security settings and make real-time adjustments to safeguards. In order to keep up with the ever-evolving security dangers posed by artificial intelligence, the cybersecurity sector is always testing out new use cases [37].

CHALLENGES AND FUTURE ADVANCES OF AI IN CYBERSECURITY THREAT DETECTION IN TWEETER

Cybersecurity is a method for protecting people's and businesses' data against unauthorized access [38]. Cyber Threat Intelligence (CTI) is a relatively new discipline that has emerged within the cybersecurity community. Academics and CTI researchers in security operations centers and security service providers have been focusing more and more on Cyber Threat Intelligence (CTI) as a cybersecurity component [39]. Gaining an advantage over cyber threat actors is the main goal of CTI. Early identification of harmful activities is expedited at the tactical and operational levels by CTI, ideally before an attacker gets a foothold in the network. At the most high-level strategic level, CTI helps decision-makers make sense of and gain insight into the pertinent threat situation. The civilian, commercial sector alternative to the long-standing Intelligence Community's (IC) defensive counter-intelligence is CTI, in essence [40].

Tweets, picture and video sharing, and e-commerce capabilities are just a few of X's many features that have made it an essential part of many people's daily lives online. People are vulnerable to a myriad of cyber dangers and security issues due to the platform's extensive use. These possible dangers will be described in the section that follows [41]. Fig (**3**) shows that X is vulnerable to multiple types of security threats. Cybercriminals target X because it is a major social media platform with a large user base and fast information sharing. The numerous cyber dangers that the platform faces are examined in this section. Numerous cyberattacks, notably, have taken root on X.

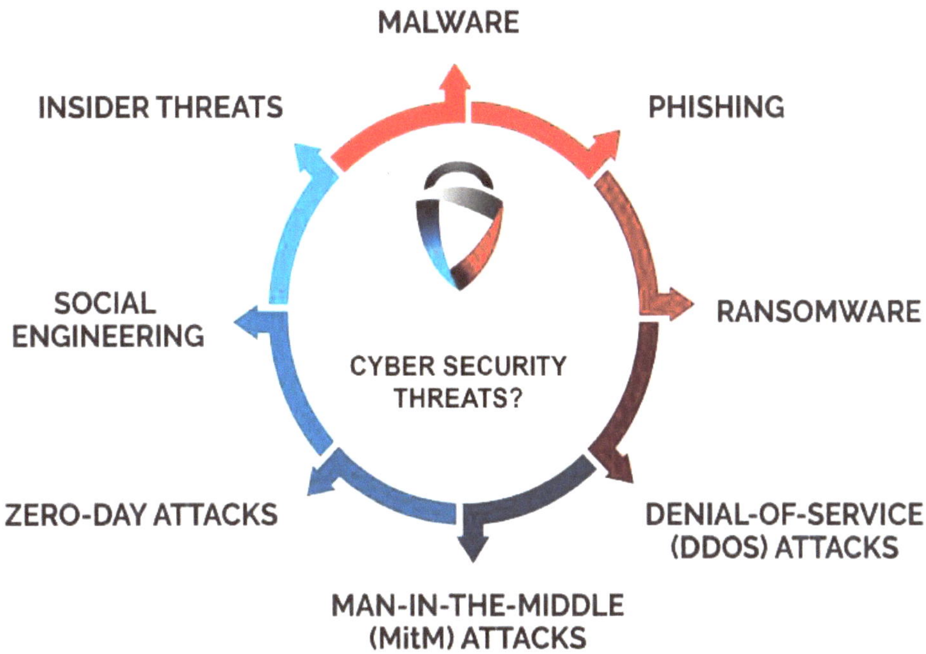

Fig. (3). Various types of cybersecurity attacks.

Concerns about personal information security and privacy arise as major obstacles to implementing AI for cybersecurity threat detection. The massive amounts of data used for threat detection—including user actions, system logs, network traffic, etc.—may include private information. We must immediately address the pressing issue of how to safeguard large data sets from unauthorized access or disclosure during the training and deployment of models [42]. There is a need for more research into how to guarantee the detection model's accuracy and efficiency while protecting data privacy, although privacy-preserving techniques like federated learning and differential privacy are making their way into the cybersecurity field. Despite their superiority in threat detection, AI models are vulnerable to malicious assaults. By creating adversarial samples or some other means, an attacker can trick the model into making incorrect decisions, which will cause the security system to fail. The detection system's efficacy is diminished, and security protections can be exploited by such hostile attacks. So, making AI models more resilient [43].

Many people view AI models, and deep learning models in particular, as mysterious "black boxes" whose decisions defy explanation. Model interpretability is of the utmost importance in cybersecurity, as security specialists frequently need to validate and interpret threat detection results. On top of that, compliance standards are tightening up as more and more sectors and fields use AI to detect security threats [44]. A crucial challenge that needs to be addressed in the future is how to make models more interpretable while simultaneously improving their performance to meet different kinds of privacy and security standards. Security staff are being progressively equipped with model visualization tools and Explainable Artificial Intelligence (XAI) to better comprehend and have faith in detection outcomes. Artificial Intelligence (AI) has great potential for use in cybersecurity threat detection [45]. Threat detection systems that integrate AI, quantum computing, and blockchain technology are just one example of how cross-field multidisciplinary collaboration is paving the way for increasingly inventive applications.

CORE STRATEGIES TO AI IN THREAT DETECTION

Thanks to its robust data investigation and trend recognition abilities, AI technology substantially enhances the efficiency and accuracy of cybersecurity threat detection. The DL processes complicated unstructured data through multi-layer neural networks, ML can learn threat features from massive amounts of labelled data, and integrated learning and multimodal approaches combine numerous data sources and algorithms to further improve detection's resilience and adaptability [46].

ML in Threat Detection

To train models to detect known threat categories in fresh data, supervised learning, a popular machine learning technique, uses labeled datasets. Supervised learning finds extensive application in cybersecurity for tasks including intrusion detection, spam filtering, and virus identification. The model can learn and identify the traits of harmful behaviors using a huge volume of labelled normal and anomalous data; this allows it to successfully differentiate between legitimate traffic and threat activities during real-time detection [47]. The interpretability and high accuracy of this method are its main strengths, but it may have limitations when it comes to new or unknown threats and is dependent on the amount and quality of labelled data. Instead of using labeled datasets, unsupervised learning looks for patterns and outliers in the data's inherent structure. Anomaly and intrusion detection are two of the most common uses of unsupervised learning in cybersecurity. This sort of learning is well-suited to identifying unknown threat types. These methods can detect possible security concerns by identifying behaviors that deviate from regular patterns of behavior. Unsupervised learning's strength is in its capacity to identify undiscovered dangers; yet, it requires optimization in conjunction with other techniques due to its high false positive rate [48].

Situations calling for ongoing learning and adaptability to changing environmental factors are well-suited to reinforcement learning, a machine learning approach to dynamic decision-making. Reinforcement learning interacts with the environment to maximize the security protection effect in network threat detection by continuously adjusting the detection approach. One application of reinforcement learning is optimizing defense strategies in response to evolving assault methods or dynamically adjusting intrusion detection systems' alert thresholds [49]. Transfer learning is a strategy that employs learned knowledge to cope with new tasks, and is predominantly apt for application in circumstances when data is limited or training costs are high. When it comes to cybersecurity, migration learning is a game-changer. It takes threat detection expertise from one domain (like financial security) and applies it to another (like healthcare security), speeding up the effectiveness of detection models. Nevertheless, in order for knowledge migration to be effective, migration learning presents a challenge: picking the right level of similarity between the source and target domains.

DL in Threat Detection

One area where deep learning really shines is in the detection of cybersecurity threats; thanks to its architecture of multi-layer neural networks, it can automatically extract and learn aspects of complicated data. When it comes to processing image and traffic data, Convolutional Neural Networks (CNNs) are widely utilized. They have the potential to detect qualities like malicious code or odd network behavior. On the flip side, RNNs and their improved version, LSTMs, excel at handling time-series data and are well-suited to use cases like tracking network activity logs and identifying ongoing dangers [50]. These neural network models improve detection accuracy and response time by deep learning of massive amounts of data, allowing them to spot dangers that are difficult to detect using standard methods.

By compressing and reassembling the input data, an auto-encoder, an unsupervised learning model, develops a latent representation of the data. One typical application of auto-encoders in cybersecurity is anomaly detection, which involves finding patterns in user behavior or network traffic that shouldn't be there. An increase in the reconstruction error, which may indicate danger, occurs when the input data deviates substantially from typical data patterns [51]. To improve the detection model's capabilities through adversarial training, Generative Adversarial Networks (GANs) use a discriminator and a generator to produce false data that looks and acts like actual data. In the realm of cybersecurity, GANs have dual purposes: first, by creating attack samples to strengthen the detection model; second, by impersonating the detection system to perform adversarial tests, which can assess and increase the system's ability to protect itself [52]. The threat detection process is shown in Fig (**4**).

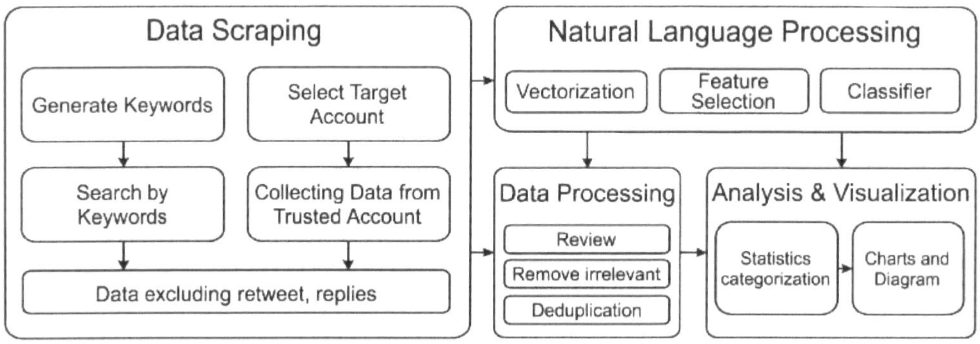

Fig. (4). Workflow diagram of the threat detection process.

By leveraging pre-trained models, migration learning is able to rapidly construct efficient threat detection models with minimal data, in contrast to deep learning models that normally demand substantial amounts of data and computer resources for training. Cybersecurity tasks like malware classification or abnormal traffic detection often employ pre-trained models that have been trained on large-scale datasets. Deep learning models can enhance detection results, swiftly adapt to new threat scenarios, and inherit knowledge from pre-trained models through migration learning. By streamlining the training process, we can save time and resources while also enhancing the model's generalizability to handle a wide range of security risks [53].

An ideal deep learning model for analyzing network architecture and detecting threats is the Graph Neural Network (GNN), which focuses on processing graph-structured input. When it comes to cybersecurity, GNNs are great for processing structured data like social networks and computer networks. They can capture the links between nodes and use that information to find possible dangers. One application of GNN is the detection of suspicious network traffic patterns, which might lead to the identification of hidden hostile nodes or attack vectors. In terms of threat detection, GNN offers new ideas and tools for network security protection by understanding the relationships in complicated network architectures better than existing methods.

Necessity of NLP

When it comes to evaluating social network unstructured text data, which can provide significant insights into cyber threat intelligence, NLP has become a crucial tool. The NLP similarity models play a crucial role in detecting instances of plagiarism, making relevant recommendations, and finding user questions that are similar. There is still a lack of knowledge on how to successfully set up cyber-attack intelligence programs inside organizations, even with these advancements. The NLP is an important subfield of AI that employs ML models to understand human speech [54]. Among the many uses for these models are the following: proposing relevant resources for journalistic research, detecting plagiarism by comparing digital documents, recognizing comparable user inquiries in online forums, and detecting similarities between user profiles and social media posts. We elucidated the process of using machine learning models to evaluate text and derive valuable insights in our study. The goal is to train algorithms to pick up on subtleties in human speech so that they can grasp complete phrases and read between the lines to determine meaning, whether that be emotions or intentions [55]. Areas including advertising, voice translation, customer service, and suspect profiling stand to benefit greatly from this capability.

Usages of NLP Technologies

The study's recommended NLP approaches are the backbone of the system's architecture. Analyzing data, creating phase-specific representations, vectorizing it, selecting features, and evaluating classifiers are all steps that make use of natural language processing.

Privacy Concerns

Using social media data from X for cyber threat detection raises major privacy issues. AI-based analysis may expose personal information or infer user identities without consent. Large-scale data mining increases the risk of misuse, breaches, and ethical violations. Ensuring anonymization, secure storage, and compliance with privacy laws like GDPR is essential. Balancing effective threat detection with individual privacy protection remains a key challenge in AI-driven cybersecurity research.

ENTHUSIASMS OF THE CYBER THREATS ON TWITTER

Hackers, acting out of a variety of motives, have grown into a serious problem for X users. These can embrace revenge, financial gain, entertainment, or contribution to hacktivist movements that protest certain concerns. For nefarious intentions, some hackers even participate in cyberwarfare or espionage. These attacks can have major consequences for people and businesses regardless of why they happen. As a result, X users must be aware of these drivers and actively protect their online identity [56]. In Fig. (**5**), we can see the many kinds of motivations.

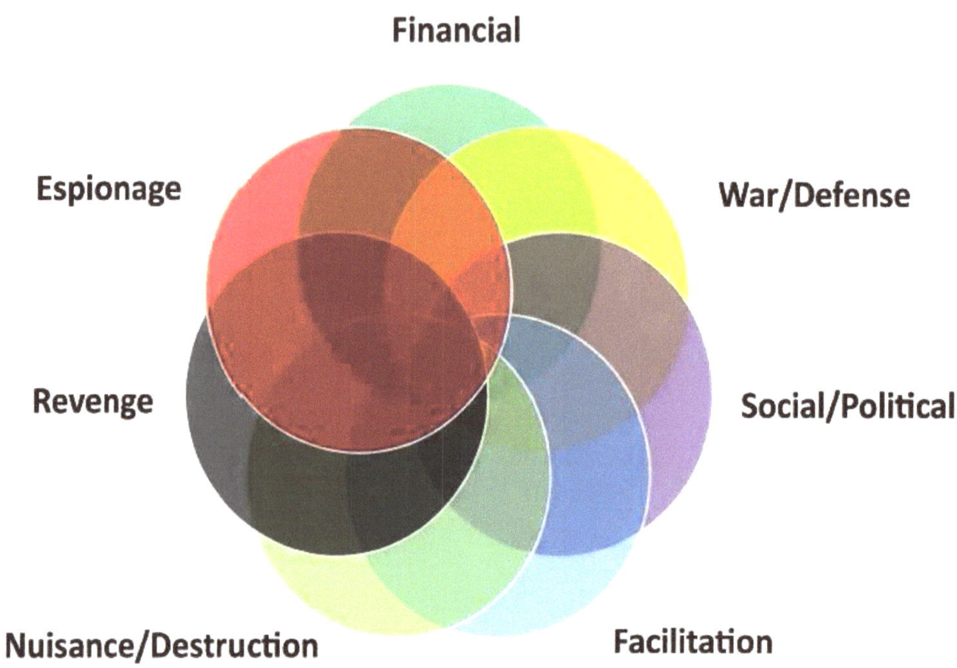

Fig. (5). Motivations of the cyber attackers.

X SECURITY: ML/DL SOLUTIONS

Finding important vulnerability features and reviewing previous research that has used DL and X. data to detect cyber-attacks are the main goals of this section. We will begin with a quick introduction to susceptibility recognition and exploitation, and then we will analyze this prior research in depth.

Discovery of Vulnerabilities and Exploits on X

Vulnerabilities and exploits are problematic security flaws. Software systems are rife with flaws, and exploits are born out of these vulnerabilities. Additional research is needed to determine the source of these security problems and create effective ways to mitigate them [57]. This will help us understand these weaknesses better. This section analyzes the marginal variation between different notions of weaknesses in order to prioritize system security. It is critical to establish efficient systems for uncovering security issues promptly because the majority of them are time-sensitive. Saving time and effort, this allows us to prioritize the deployment of resources towards fixing the vulnerability [58]. One aspect that researchers use to forecast the chance of an exploit for known vulnerabilities is the common vulnerability and exposure identifier (CVE-ID).

Ethical concerns include potential violations of user privacy, data misuse, and surveillance without consent. Monitoring social media may expose personal information or misinterpret legitimate user activity as threats. Balancing security needs with individual rights, ensuring data transparency, and complying with privacy laws are essential to maintain ethical integrity in cybersecurity monitoring.

Discovery of Security Content

X is a well-known platform for social media where millions of people all over the globe contribute content. Nevertheless, the dissemination of misinformation or propaganda by malevolent individuals raises security concerns. Several approaches, including ML algorithms, human expert assessment, and natural language processing, have been suggested by researchers to identify security-related information on X. The goal of these suggestions is to make it easier to identify harmful content and guarantee that the information shared on X is secure and trustworthy. Here we will take a look at some of the literature that has suggested ways to identify security-related content on X. There was research done by them [59]. I presented a new method for locating occurrences by studying document distribution and the existence of bursty keywords. The authors stressed that event detection systems should use both spatial and temporal factors.

Attack trends on social networking platforms evolve as cybercriminals adapt to user behavior, platform algorithms, and emerging technologies. They exploit trending topics, viral content, and social engineering tactics to spread malware, phishing links, or misinformation. Attackers increasingly use AI-generated content and bots to automate and personalize attacks, making them harder to detect. As security measures improve, attackers shift to new vulnerabilities, leveraging psychological manipulation and data leaks to maintain effectiveness.

LIMITATIONS AND FUTURE WORK

Limitations

Several restrictions limited the study's ability to draw firm conclusions. The change from X to Twitter was a major problem since it made the API cost money to access tweets. An important limitation of the study was the fact that this adjustment drastically reduced the amount of data that could be collected and examined. Despite our desire for a more extensive dataset, we are faced with the challenge of circumventing the access constraints that this modification imposes. Data may also be lacking in diversity and neutrality due to the study's reliance on a single social media platform. Findings may not be representative of the full scope due to the limited data set.

Methodological issues included the potential for incorrect feature extraction or misclassification of pertinent tweets during preprocessing. Additionally, Arabic tweets were not included in this analysis; it solely dealt with English tweets. An issue that persists is the generalizability of the results to settings or areas outside of the Arab world. In conclusion, the study had to meticulously handle ethical concerns, such as privacy concerns about gathering and analyzing user data from social networks and the dangers of retaining and processing sensitive information.

Threat intelligence from social networks enables early detection of emerging cyber threats and attacker activities. It provides real-time insights that help organizations anticipate risks, strengthen defenses, and respond proactively to potential attacks.

Future Work

Future study attempts to address these constraints by increasing the scope of data collecting beyond X (previously Twitter) to include additional social networks such as Facebook, LinkedIn, Telegram, and deep/dark web forums. More accurate and thorough results will be produced by this method since it increases data diversity and objectivity. If we want a more complete dataset, we need to go over the limitations of premium APIs. To address the study's limitations and provide a more comprehensive understanding of the themes examined, data from other platforms should be integrated. Future studies will also focus on improving methods, with the goal of creating more advanced natural language processing approaches to enhance data cleaning and feature extraction. Specifically, research will include establishing ways to safely scrape content from deep Web forums and training deep learning algorithms. Databases on the web are used for the purpose of comparing these records with data found on the surface of the web. Improving classification algorithms will also include manually annotating a larger dataset sample and making it publicly available. Researchers will be able to foresee alterations and new patterns if they are successful in predicting future trends. Taking a look ahead will improve the analysis and help us understand these trends better, as they could change in the future. The methodology must be tested outside of the Arab world to determine its adaptability and generalizability, and industry-specific analysis must be carried out to find targeted risks. A continual effort is required to develop procedures that safeguard user privacy and adhere to international data protection laws and ethical principles, while also prioritizing ethical and legal considerations. By taking an all-encompassing strategy, we can lessen the likelihood of unethical outcomes and increase the reliability, validity, and generalizability of future research.

CONCLUSION

The proliferation of security breaches in recent years has made attack detection and monitoring an absolute necessity for any company. Different research has employed countless methodologies to notice cybersecurity vulnerabilities in X, including ML, NLP, and social network analysis. The reliability of their results is compromised because of the discrepancies in their data gathering methods, classification strategies, and assessment criteria. More research is desirable to create reliable and effective recognition algorithms, and proper assessment criteria are important to measure their success. This study set out to examine and contrast different efforts at real-time X streaming data extraction of information about present and future security attacks. Scope of detection, analysis of semantic features, algorithm complexity, degree of information condensation, scalability, and efficacy were some of the aspects of cybersecurity techniques that were considered in the study as they pertain to real-world scenarios. In order to make the most of the security information that is released on X, this study suggested certain enhancements.

This chapter argues that a semantic effort is more advantageous for this step of the process, even though character-level feature extraction approaches are abundant. There has to be more research since no study has succeeded in improving all of these areas of feedback. We propose areas for future research and work in this area using deep learning. In the end, it comes down to offering a synopsis of cybersecurity issues, DL remedies, and X platform opportunities. We suggest additional study and solutions for X cyber-threat identification utilizing DL approaches based on our survey.

REFERENCES

[1] D. Kavitha, and S. Thejas, "AI enabled threat detection: Leveraging artificial intelligence for advanced security and cyber threat mitigation", *IEEE Access,* vol. 12, no. 7, pp. 173127-173136, 2024.

[2] O. Alsodi, X. Zhou, R. Gururajan, A. Shrestha, and E. Btoush, "From tweets to threats: A survey of cybersecurity threat detection challenges, ai-based solutions and potential opportunities in X", *Appl. Sci. (Basel),* vol. 15, no. 7, p. 3898, 2025. [http://dx.doi.org/10.3390/app15073898]

[3] P. Chillakuru, M. Madiajagan, K.V. Prashanth, S. Ambala, P.C. Shaker Reddy, and J. Pavan, "Enhancing wind power monitoring through motion deblurring with modified GoogleNet algorithm", *Soft Comput.,* vol. 28, no. 23-24, pp. 13965-13975, 2024. [http://dx.doi.org/10.1007/s00500-023-08358-8]

[4] P. S. Muller, Y. Sucharitha, S. Kottapally, G. Ismoilova, L. Rakhimova, and P. C. S. Reddy, "A Novel Financial Market Prediction Framework Based on Deep Learning for Accurate Trend Forecasting", In: *Information Systems for Intelligent Systems.* ISBM 2025, A. Iglesias, J. Shin, N. Bhatt, A. Joshi, (eds) Information Systems for Intelligent Systems. ISBM 2025. Lecture Notes in Networks and Systems, vol 1748. Springer, Cham. [http://dx.doi.org/10.1007/978-3-032-12990-1_5]

[5] S. Kulkarni, G.K. Thakur, K. Bhargavi, C.R. Babu, G.B. Madhavi, and C.S.R. Pundru, "A hybrid deep learning framework for gastrointestinal tract classification based on endoscopic images", In: *Proc. 2024 2nd World Conf. Communication & Computing (WCONF)* Raipur, India, Jul. 12–14, 2024, pp. 1-6. [http://dx.doi.org/10.1109/WCONF61366.2024.10692196]

[6] R. Samrin, P.C.S. Reddy, K.A. Kumar, N. Deepthi, C. Mithra, S.B. Latha, Y. Sucharitha, and G.K. Thakur, "A hybrid deep learning based framework for prediction of rice yield through integration of biophysical parameters and optical remote sensing data in India", In: *J. Atmos. Solar-Terrestrial Phys.* vol. 279. , 2026, p. 106734. [http://dx.doi.org/10.1016/j.jastp.2026.106734]

[7] A Kanaan, A L-H Ahmad, A Alorfi, and M Aloun, "Cybersecurity resilience for business: a comprehensive model for proactive defense and swift recovery", In: *Proc. 2024 2nd International Conference on Cyber Resilience (ICCR)* IEEE, 2024, pp. 1-7.

[8] S. Sowjanya, I.S. Reddy, C. Muralikrishna, T.S.L. Prasad, P.C.S. Reddy, and V. Sharma, "Bioacoustics signal authentication for e-medical records using blockchain", In: *2024 International Conference on Knowledge Engineering and Communication Systems (ICKECS)* vol. 1. IEEE, 2024, pp. 1-6.

[9] I.H. Sarker, "Introduction to AI-driven cybersecurity and threat intelligence", In: *AI-driven cybersecurity and threat intelligence: Cyber automation, intelligent decision-making and explainability.* Springer Nature Switzerland: Cham, 2024, pp. 3-19. [http://dx.doi.org/10.1007/978-3-031-54497-2_1]

[10] O.U. Khan, S.M. Abdullah, A.O. Olajide, A.I. Sani, M.W.F. Shah, A.A. Ogunola, and M.D. Lee, "The future of cybersecurity: Leveraging artificial intelligence to combat evolving threats and enhance digital defense strategies", *J. Comput. Anal. Appl.,* vol. 33, no. 8, 2024.

[11] H. Hussain, M. Kainat, and T. Ali, "Leveraging AI and machine learning to detect and prevent cyber security threats", *Dialogue Social Science Review,* vol. 3, no. 1, pp. 881-895, 2025.

[12] G. Arun, P.C.S. Reddy, N. Budati, B. Rebecca, S. Perumalla, and V.B. Gujar, "A deep learning framework for diabetes prediction: PIMA indian dataset", *2024 International Conference on Innovative Computing, Intelligent Communication and Smart Electrical Systems (ICSES),* IEEE, 2024.

[13] M.D. Basith, P. Praveen, and P.C.S. Reddy, "Adaptive deep Q-GAN framework for enhanced breast cancer detection in medical imaging", *Biomedical Signal Processing and Control,* vol. 112, p. 108638, 2026. [http://dx.doi.org/10.1016/j.bspc.2025.108638]

[14] A. Spyros, I. Koritsas, A. Papoutsis, P. Panagiotou, D. Chatzakou, D. Kavallieros, T. Tsikrika, S. Vrochidis, and I. Kompatsiaris, "AI-based holistic framework for cyber threat intelligence management", *IEEE Access,* vol. 13, pp. 20820-20846, 2025. [http://dx.doi.org/10.1109/ACCESS.2025.3533084]

[15] A Tanikonda, B K Pandey, S R Peddinti, and S Rao, "Advanced AI-driven cybersecurity solutions for proactive threat detection and response in complex ecosystems", *Journal of Science & Technology,* vol. 3, no. 1, 2022. [Online]. Available: https://ssrn.com/abstract=5102358 [http://dx.doi.org/10.2139/ssrn.5102358]

[16] M. Aminu, A. Akinsanya, D.A. Dako, and O. Oyedokun, "Enhancing cyber threat detection through real-time threat intelligence and adaptive defense mechanisms", *International Journal of Computer Applications Technology and Research,* vol. 13, no. 8, pp. 11-27, 2024.

[17] D. Patil, "Artificial intelligence in cybersecurity: Enhancing threat detection and prevention mechanisms through machine learning and data analytics", *SSRN,* p. 5057410, 2024.

[18] G R Kumar, S B Latha, P C S Reddy, and Y Sucharitha, "Multi-agent IoT-based system for intelligent vehicle traffic management using wireless sensor networks", *Recent Advances in Electrical &*

Electronic Engineering, vol. 17, no. 5, pp. 515-522, 2024.

[19] A. Singh, and S.K. Dubey, "Analytical approach towards cybersecurity through AI-enabled threat intelligence", *2024 11th International Conference on Reliability, Infocom Technologies and Optimization (ICRITO),* IEEE, pp. 1-6, 2024. [http://dx.doi.org/10.1109/ICRITO61523.2024.10522422]

[20] S. Lee, A.H.M. Aisha, and K. Kim, "Leveraging Social Networks for Cyber Threat Intelligence: Analyzing Attack Trends and TTPs in the Arab World", *IEEE Access,* 2024.

[21] G.K. Thakur, L.P. Mudarakola, M. Sreenivasulu, V. Krishna B, I.R. Raja, I.A. Tayubi, and Y. Sucharitha, "An enhanced prediction framework for blood-brain barrier permeability: DeePred-BBB", *Recent Patents on Engineering,* vol. 19, no. 9, p. E18722121342031, 2025. [http://dx.doi.org/10.2174/0118722121342031250218042131]

[22] N. Sun, M. Ding, J. Jiang, W. Xu, X. Mo, Y. Tai, and J. Zhang, "Cyber threat intelligence mining for proactive cybersecurity defense: A survey and new perspectives", *IEEE Commun. Surv. Tutor.,* vol. 25, no. 3, pp. 1748-1774, 2023. [http://dx.doi.org/10.1109/COMST.2023.3273282]

[23] C. Madhavram, E.P. Galla, J.R. Sunkara, S.K. Rajaram, and G.K. Patra, "AI-driven threat detection: Leveraging big data for advanced cybersecurity compliance", *SSRN,* p. 5029406, 2022.

[24] P. Alaeifar, S. Pal, Z. Jadidi, M. Hussain, and E. Foo, "Current approaches and future directions for Cyber Threat Intelligence sharing: A survey", *Journal of Information Security and Applications,* vol. 83, p. 103786, 2024. [http://dx.doi.org/10.1016/j.jisa.2024.103786]

[25] G.P. Kumar, B. Sridevi, P.S. Dhanaselvam, K. Kavitha, P. Karthikeyan, and B. Karthikeyan, "Art of network monitoring and security enhancement using AI-driven tools", In: *Utilizing AI in Network and Mobile Security for Threat Detection and Prevention.* IGI Global Scientific Publishing, 2025, pp. 43-58. [http://dx.doi.org/10.4018/979-8-3693-9919-4.ch003]

[26] O.J. Adeyeye, I. Akanbi, I. Emeteveke, and O. Emehin, "Leveraging secured AI-driven data analytics for cybersecurity: Safeguarding information and enhancing threat detection", *International Journal of Research Publication and Reviews,* vol. 5, no. 10, pp. 3208-3223, 2024. [http://dx.doi.org/10.55248/gengpi.5.1024.2911]

[27] V.K. Bukkarayasamudram, P.C.S. Reddy, and K. Arun Kumar, "Quantum computing revolution in healthcare: a systematic review of applications, issues and future directions", *Artif Intell Rev,* vol. 58, p. 389, 2025. [http://dx.doi.org/10.1007/s10462-025-11381-w]

[28] A. Zacharis, V. Katos, and C. Patsakis, "Integrating AI-driven threat intelligence and forecasting in the cyber security exercise content generation lifecycle", *Int. J. Inf. Secur.,* vol. 23, no. 4, pp. 2691-2710, 2024. [http://dx.doi.org/10.1007/s10207-024-00860-w]

[29] Aftab Arif, A. Arif, and A.R.A. Khan, "AI's revolutionary role in cyber defense and social engineering", *International Journal of Multidisciplinary Sciences and Arts,* vol. 3, no. 4, pp. 57-66, 2024. [http://dx.doi.org/10.47709/ijmdsa.v3i4.4752]

[30] A. Kumar, and K. Guleria, "Leveraging machine learning algorithms for threat detection using AI-enhanced cybersecurity datasets", *2024 4th International Conference on Technological Advancements in Computational Sciences (ICTACS),* IEEE, pp. 483-488, 2024. [http://dx.doi.org/10.1109/ICTACS62700.2024.10840478]

[31] A.H. Salem, S.M. Azzam, O.E. Emam, and A.A. Abohany, "Advancing cybersecurity: a comprehensive review of AI-driven detection techniques", *J. Big Data,* vol. 11, no. 1, p. 105, 2024. [http://dx.doi.org/10.1186/s40537-024-00957-y]

[32] B Elov, A Dauletov, Y Sucharitha, F Khalilova, M Latipova, and M Abdullayeva, "An intelligent traffic management of vehicles using deep learning approach in smart cities", In: *2025 3rd International Conference on Integrated Circuits and Communication Systems (ICICACS)*. IEEE, 2025, pp. 1-5.
[http://dx.doi.org/10.1109/ICICACS65178.2025.10967703]

[33] M. A. Wani, "AI and NLP-empowered framework for strengthening social cyber security", In: *Recent Advancements in Multimedia Data Processing and Security: Issues, Challenges, and Techniques* IGI Global, 2023, pp. 32-45.

[34] S. R. Sindiramutty, K. R. V. Prabagaran, N. Z. Jhanjhi, and R. K. Murugesan, "Threat intelligence and information sharing", In: *Utilizing Generative AI for Cyber Defense Strategies*, 2023, p. 191.

[35] U.I. Okoli, O.C. Obi, A.O. Adewusi, and T.O. Abrahams, "Machine learning in cybersecurity: A review of threat detection and defense mechanisms", *World Journal of Advanced Research and Reviews,* vol. 21, no. 1, pp. 2286-2295, 2024.
[http://dx.doi.org/10.30574/wjarr.2024.21.1.0315]

[36] O.A. Ajala, C.C. Okoye, O.C. Ofodile, C.A. Arinze, and O.D. Daraojimba, "Review of AI and machine learning applications to predict and Thwart cyber-attacks in real-time", *Magna Scientia Advanced Research and Reviews,* vol. 10, no. 1, pp. 312-320, 2024.
[http://dx.doi.org/10.30574/msarr.2024.10.1.0037]

[37] T. Zaid, and S. Garai, "Emerging trends in cybersecurity: a holistic view on current threats, assessing solutions, and pioneering new frontiers", *Blockchain Healthc. Today,* vol. 7, pp. 10-30953, 2024.
[PMID: 38715765]

[38] A. Gadupudi, M.L. Prasad, G.Y. Vybhavi, S.N. Koka, S. Mukherjee, and P.C.S. Reddy, "An efficient provable massive data migration approach under secure cloud storage", *The International Conference on Intelligent Systems & Networks,* pp. 270-276, 2024.Singapore
[http://dx.doi.org/10.1007/978-981-97-5504-2_32]

[39] S S Goswami, S Mondal, R Halder, J Nayak, and A Sil, "Exploring the impact of artificial intelligence integration on cybersecurity: A comprehensive analysis", *Journal of Industrial Intelligence,* vol. 2, no. 2, pp. 73-93, 2024.
[http://dx.doi.org/10.56578/jii020202]

[40] P C S Reddy, and Y Sucharitha, "A design and challenges in energy optimizing CR-wireless sensor networks", *Recent Advances in Computer Science and Communications,* vol. 16, no. 5, pp. 82-92, 2023.
[http://dx.doi.org/10.2174/2666255816666221104115024]

[41] Y. Sucharitha, and P.C. Shaker Reddy, "An autonomous adaptive enhancement method based on learning to optimize heterogeneous network selection", *Int. J. Sensors Wirel. Commun. Control,* vol. 12, no. 7, pp. 495-509, 2022.
[http://dx.doi.org/10.2174/2210327912666221012154428]

[42] P.C. Shaker Reddy, and Y. Sucharitha, "IoT-enabled energy-efficient multipath power control for underwater sensor networks", *Int. J. Sensors Wirel. Commun. Control,* vol. 12, no. 6, pp. 478-494, 2022.
[http://dx.doi.org/10.2174/2210327912666220615103257]

[43] K. Achuthan, S. Ramanathan, S. Srinivas, and R. Raman, "Advancing cybersecurity and privacy with artificial intelligence: current trends and future research directions", *Front. Big Data,* vol. 7, p. 1497535, 2024.
[http://dx.doi.org/10.3389/fdata.2024.1497535] [PMID: 39703783]

[44] Y Sucharitha, Y Vijayalata, and V K Prasad, "Predicting election results from Twitter using machine learning algorithms", *Recent Advances in Computer Science and Communications,* vol. 14, no. 1, pp. 246-256, 2021.
[http://dx.doi.org/10.2174/2666255813999200729164142]

[45] G. Waizel, "Bridging the AI divide: The evolving arms race between AI-driven cyber attacks and AI-powered cybersecurity defenses", In: *Proc. Int. Conf. Machine Intelligence & Security for Smart Cities (TRUST)* vol. 1. , 2024, pp. 141-156.

[46] F. O'Connell, "Data-driven cybersecurity: AI-based predictive models for threat intelligence and risk mitigation", *International Journal of AI, BigData, Computational and Management Studies,* vol. 3, no. 1, pp. 21-31, 2022. [http://dx.doi.org/10.63282/3050-9416.IJAIBDCMS-V3I1P103]

[47] S. Suresh, V. Prabhu, V. Parthasarathy, R. Boddu, Y. Sucharitha, and G. Teshite, "A novel routing protocol for low-energy wireless sensor networks", *J. Sens.,* vol. 2022, no. 1, pp. 1-8, 2022. [http://dx.doi.org/10.1155/2022/8244176]

[48] S. Yadala, C.S.R. Pundru, and V.K. Solanki, "A novel private encryption model in IoT under cloud computing domain," in *Intelligent Systems and Networks: ICISN 2023*, T. D. L. Nguyen, E. Verdú, A. N. Le, and M. Ganzha, Eds., Lecture Notes in Networks and Systems, vol. 752, Singapore: Springer, 2023, pp. 341–354. [http://dx.doi.org/10.1007/978-981-99-4725-6_33]

[49] Y. Sucharitha, Y. Vijayalata, and V.K. Prasad, "Analysis of early detection of emerging patterns from social media networks: A data mining techniques perspective," in *Soft Computing and Signal Processing*, J. Wang, G. Reddy, V. Prasad, and V. Reddy, Eds., Advances in Intelligent Systems and Computing, vol. 900, Singapore: Springer, 2019, pp. 13–27. [http://dx.doi.org/10.1007/978-981-13-3600-3_2]

[50] A.T. Somnathe, V.T. Selvi, N.G. Stepha, M.T. Kingslin, F.M. Inamdar, and P.C.S. Reddy, "An intelligent traffic conflict prediction using deep learning with long-term evolution access data", In: *Proc. 2025 3rd International Conference on Smart Systems for applications in Electrical Sciences (ICSSES)* IEEE, 2025, pp. 1-6. [http://dx.doi.org/10.1109/ICSSES64899.2025.11010032]

[51] R. Thilagavathy, P.N. Renjith, R.V.S. Lalitha, M.Y.B. Murthy, Y. Sucharitha, and S.L. Narayanan, "[Retracted] A novel framework paradigm for EMR management cloud system authentication using blockchain security network", *Soft Comput.,* pp. 1-9, 2023. [http://dx.doi.org/10.1007/s00500-023-07958-8]

[52] B. Mohammed, "The impact of Artificial Intelligence on cyberspace security and market dynamics", *Brazilian Journal of Technology,* vol. 7, no. 4, pp. e74677-e74677, 2024. [http://dx.doi.org/10.38152/bjtv7n4-019]

[53] S. Zeadally, E. Adi, Z. Baig, and I.A. Khan, "Harnessing artificial intelligence capabilities to improve cybersecurity", *IEEE Access,* vol. 8, pp. 23817-23837, 2020. [http://dx.doi.org/10.1109/ACCESS.2020.2968045]

[54] R. Tarade, and S. Das, "Cybersecurity in the age of AI—Enhancing defences for today's threats," in *Critical Phishing Defense Strategies and Digital Asset Protection*, Brij B. Gupta, Ed., Hershey, PA, USA: IGI Global, 2025, p. 309.

[55] A. Al Siam, M. Alazab, A. Awajan, and N. Faruqui, "A comprehensive review of AI's current impact and future prospects in cybersecurity", *IEEE Access,* vol. 13, pp. 14029-14050, 2025. [http://dx.doi.org/10.1109/ACCESS.2025.3528114]

[56] M. Reddy, and K. Desai, "Leveraging AI for cloud security: An analysis of emerging threat detection and prevention techniques", *East.-Eur. J. Eng. Technol.,* vol. 3, no. 1, pp. 28-35, 2024.

[57] Y. Sucharitha, Y. Vijayalata, and V. Kamakshi Prasad, "Analysis of early detection of emerging patterns from social media networks: A data mining techniques perspective," in *Soft Computing and Signal Processing*, J. Wang, G. Reddy, V. Prasad, and V. Reddy, Eds., Advances in Intelligent Systems and Computing, vol. 900, Singapore: Springer, 2019, pp. 13–27. [http://dx.doi.org/10.1007/978-981-13-3600-3_2]

[58] R.Y. Rani, M.L. Prasad, I.S. Reddy, I.A. Tayubi, G. Sultan, and P.C.S. Reddy, "Early prediction and diagnosis cardiovascular disease using deep learning models", In: *2024 International Conference on Emerging Technologies in Computer Science for Interdisciplinary Applications (ICETCS)* IEEE., 2024, pp. 1-6.
[http://dx.doi.org/10.1109/ICETCS61022.2024.10543851]

[59] G. Anjaneyulu, C.S.R. Pundru, and P. Praveen, "A hybrid deep reinforcement learning framework for stock market prediction", In: *2024 4th International Conference on Mobile Networks and Wireless Communications (ICMNWC)* IEEE, 2024.
[http://dx.doi.org/10.1109/ICMNWC63764.2024.10872342]

CHAPTER 6

Securing The Digital Frontier: A Comprehensive Guide to Modern Security Operations Centers (SOC)

Diivyaam Shah[1,*], **Kiran Dodiya**[1] and **Kapil Kumar**[1]

[1] *Department of Biochemistry and Forensic Science, Gujarat University, Ahmedabad, Gujarat, India*

Abstract: An organization's cybersecurity infrastructure relies on a Security Operations Centre (SOC) in an age of fast cyber threat evolution. This chapter examines how SOCs protect against malware, ransomware, and advanced persistent threats as the first line of defense. A SOC monitors, analyzes, and responds to cybersecurity incidents, assesses alerts, and prioritizes threats by severity. A SOC's success depends on analysts and operations teams working together with integrated tools, processes, technologies, and policies to protect infrastructure. A modern Security Operations Centre (SOC) uses advanced threat intelligence, security automation, and orchestration technologies to detect and respond to threats. Security Operations Centers (SOCs) use various technologies and cybersecurity frameworks, including NIST, FedRAMP, FISMA, and MITRE ATT and CK, to improve security. These guidelines govern the SOC's plans and methods to prevent data breaches and assaults. SOC teams encounter obstacles from detection to investigation, containment, eradication, and recovery during cybersecurity incidents. It details the incident lifecycle, including SOC analysts' reaction processes and tools and techniques for speedy, effective, and complete action. This chapter examines the SOC operational lifecycle, highlights challenges in detection, investigation, and recovery, and introduces an AI-driven model to enhance efficiency, accuracy, and adaptability in threat response. It further emphasizes human–machine collaboration, skill development, and the integration of emerging technologies to build predictive and autonomous AI-augmented security environments.

Keywords: AI and ML, Analysts, Frameworks, Incident Response, SIEM, SOAR, SOC Lifecycle, SOC Team, SOC, Triage Specialist.

[*] **Corresponding Author Diivyaam Shah,**: Department of Biochemistry and Forensic Science, Gujarat University, Ahmedabad, Gujarat, India; E-mail: shahdivyam2912@gmail.com

Pundru Chandra Shaker Reddy, Yadala Sucharitha, & Thillaiarasu N (Eds.)

INTRODUCTION

What is SOC?

The Security Operation Centre, also known as a Computer Emergency Response Team or Computer Security Incident Response Team, is dedicated to monitoring and analysing activity on networks, servers, endpoints, databases, applications, websites, and other systems that connect to your network, either locally or from a remote location. It is the first line of Defence that assesses different types of alerts and determines whether they're real or false positives. If implemented correctly, it can provide an overarching solution for detecting and mitigating an attack [1].

The role of SOC in Modern Cybersecurity

SOC does not just focus on developing a security strategy, designing a security architecture, or implementing protective measures. It is responsible for operational components of enterprise information security, improving the business's security posture through its products and services by introducing security as a shared responsibility [2]. A team that makes the most important strategic decisions at the time of an attack, when the attacker is attempting to breach a company's security to harm or steal their data, thereby ruining their reputation in the market and potentially leading to monetary loss.

Evolution of SOC in the Digital Age

From the 1970s to the early 2000s, traditional SOC, also known as a Network Operations Centre (NOC), primarily focused on incident detection and response, which included managing network devices and monitoring performance. In the early 2000s, after the introduction of Information Security Management Standards (ISMS) compliance, which was added to the objectives of the SOC. With the introduction of SIEM (Security Information and Event Management) platforms, which allowed analysts to collect logs centrally, automated alert generation based on predefined rules helped improve threat detection. As more sophisticated threats emerged and attackers became more advanced, SOC needed to change their strategies to incorporate advanced analysis, threat intelligence, and detection, along with active threat hunting, to detect and prevent advanced persistent threats in the late 2000s [3]. Presently, with the adoption of AI and ML, which has helped in faster detection and alert with minimal false positives. SOAR Security Orchestration, Automation, and Response tools help make an easy and simplified incident response workflow (Fig. **1**).

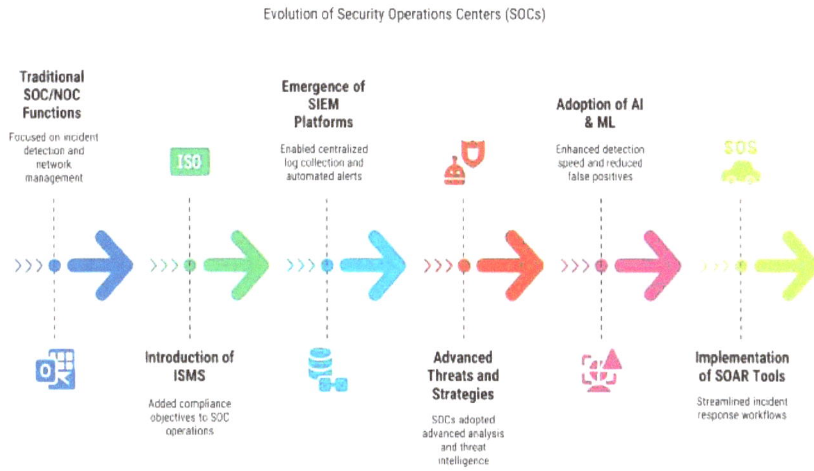

Fig. (1). Evolution of SOC in the digital era.

Literature Review

In the current world of evolving cyber threats, a Security Operations Centre (SOC) must also evolve rapidly to face such threats effectively. Traditionally, Security Operations Centers (SOCs) detected and responded to known threats only; however, in the modern approach, with the help of AI and other security tools, SOCs can actively identify and mitigate risks—the shift from reactive to proactive has helped improve SOC response times [4].

Regarding key components of SOCs, AI and ML have become core technologies in modern-era SOCs, enabling the investigation of incidents, triage of alerts, and recommendation of mitigations with high accuracy. ML algorithms are trained to detect APTs and reduce false positives, thereby achieving a higher percentage of accurate detections in the IT environment. Active defence strategies depend heavily on threat intelligence, which involves gathering, analysing, and disseminating information about potential threats. The integration of Extended Detection and Response (XDR), Zero Trust Architecture (ZTA), and Threat Intelligence Centres (TICs) collectively enhances the effectiveness of operations by enabling better prediction and mitigation of threats [5]. Automation helps streamline the incident response process and reduces human workload by speeding up the process of generating incident reports, providing background intelligence, and suggesting remediation steps. Orchestration tools integrate various security products, allowing for seamless communication and a coordinated response. Even after advancements, human expertise is highly required in SOCs as AI and humans work together to make ethical decisions, which helps solve problems such as AI bias [6].

Security strategies help the SOC work efficiently. Threat hunting involves actively searching for threats within an organisation's IT environment, rather than relying on generating alerts that could be false positives, thereby wasting time. This strategy involves threat intelligence, behavioural analysis, and threat detection tools to identify threats before they occur, staying ahead of the curve. Organisations that do not have an adequate amount of resources to build and maintain a dedicated SOC opt for Security Operation Centre as a Service (SOCaas), providing access to advanced monitoring, threat detection, and incident response capabilities, allowing organisations to improve their cybersecurity posture without any need for high investments in infrastructure and personnel [7].

A SOC is nothing without tools and technology: SIEM tools that provide real-time monitoring and analysis of security events, collecting and analyzing data from multiple sources to identify potential threats. XDR is an enhanced and refined version of Endpoint Detection and Response, combining data from various sources, including endpoints, networks, and cloud environments, to provide comprehensive visibility and more accurate threat detection and response, and using Natural Language Processing for analyzing data, generating incident reports, and recommending remediation processes, thereby increasing the efficiency and effectiveness of SOCs [8].

Considering Challenges: The effectiveness of AI and ML depends on the quality of data used for training. Poor data quality and biased datasets can lead to false predictions and faulty decision-making. The use of AI raises ethical concerns regarding transparency, accountability, and potential bias. AI systems, when operated under human direction, should adhere to ethical standards to ensure responsible deployment.

THE ANATOMY OF A SUCCESSFUL SOC

Core components: People- Collaborative efforts between Analysts and the Operations Team

Security Operations is a collaborative effort between the analytical team and the operations team that integrates tools, processes, and technology. A SOC team consist of Tier 1- Triage specialist: one who collects incoming raw data as well as review alarms and alerts to determine if they are false positive or not, they are the ones who determine the level of the alert generated and if it needs to be escalated further to tier-2 or can be controlled by them, Tier 2-Incident Responder: they are the ones who takes high priority calls and conducts an in-depth assessment for the incidents escalated by tier-1 analysts. Tier 3- Threat Hunter: One with the most experience and responsibility in the whole team, they handle major incidents escalated by tier-2 by performing or supervising the process of vulnerability assessment and penetration testing to identify attack vectors, possible threats, and security gaps, also every small or big incident occurring and data provided by both tier-1 and tier-2 are reviewed by this tier. SOC Manager: One who manages and supervises all tiers and provides guidance when needed. They are also responsible for hiring and training new team members, reporting to the CISO (Chief Information Security Officer), and top-level management [9].

Process

A typical SOC must follow its organisation's well-defined process to function correctly and effectively in its daily shifts. A process essentially includes identification and detection: analyze and classify alerts according to their severity. If a suspected malicious alert is identified, it will be considered an incident, and an investigation will be conducted. Investigation: Search for the root cause and its impact, which helps analysts understand the incident and determine the best response method. Respond and Mitigation: Analysts need to respond and mitigate the incident by performing the required actions according to the policies and mitigation plan created by the SOC team collectively. Post-incident recovery and improvements: The phase where the team works on restoring systems and data to how they were before, where they perform system restoration, data recovery, account remediation, network analysis and clean-up, vulnerability patching, incident reporting, and policy updating [10].

Technology and Policies

Technologies used by SOC are Security Information and Event Management (SIEM), Endpoint Detection and Response (EDR), Network Intrusion Detection Systems (NIDS), Network Intrusion Prevention Systems (NIPS), Security Orchestration, Automation and Response (SOAR), Security Analytics Platforms, Vulnerability Assessment Tools, Identity and Access Management (IAM), Firewalls, Honeypots, etc. A SOC team creates and follows numerous policies that help maintain security and prevent data loss. Some of these policies include Access Control Policies, Role-Based Access Control (RBAC), Alert Management Policies, Threat Detection Policies, Incident Response Policies, and Compliance Policies [11].

KEY TECHNOLOGIES IN SOCS

A Security Operations Centre relies heavily on various technologies, each with its own functions and benefits. Here technology consist of all the components present in the organisations for data storage and its security such as: **Network Devices:-** switches, routers, servers, hosts, proxies, **Virtualization Technologies:-** hypervisors, cloud environments, **Operational Technologies:-** sensors, actuators,

Physical Security Techs:- Security Cameras, **Other Software's:-** databases, mail servers, identity and access management etc. Although these technologies are used in the organisation other technologies helps in securing and defending from outside threats such as – (1) **Threat Intelligence platforms (TIPs):** it collects data from all available sources and keeps updating itself that helps identifying malicious threats, domains, file-hashes and other possible attack vectors and assigns them risk scores based on which the SOC team focuses on the most critical ones, TIPs can be integrated with SIEM, EDR and Firewall to help analysts detect and respond on time (ex. Recorded future, ThreatConnect). (2) **Security Information and Event Management (SIEM):** A system that collects and analyse security event logs from firewall, servers, network devices, applications and endpoints using predefined rules with the help of AI analysis solutions that correlates the events and detects suspicious activities with reduced false positive alerts, also helps SOC analysts to rebuild the timeline and figure out the root cause of the incident (ex. Splunk, Microsoft Sentinel). (3) **Security Orchestration, Automation and Response (SOAR):** It is used to enhance the efficiency of SOC by automating the incidence response and workflow with the help of predefined rules to respond common threats automatically, it also gathers additions information from other integrated tools like TIPs and SIEM to enhance threat analysis and automates basic repetitive tasks to free up humans so that they can focus on more complex problems and investigations (ex. Palo Alto Cortex XSOAR, Splunk SOAR). (4) **Endpoint Detection and Response (EDR):** It is mainly responsible for monitoring, detecting and responding to the threats over endpoint devices, it tracks all the processes, changes in the files, network connections and user behaviour patterns on its dedicated endpoint by using machine learning to identify abnormal activities due to which it isolates compromised endpoints and ends any malicious processes, it can also integrate with other SOC tools to function more efficiently (ex. CrowdStrike Falcon, Sentinel One). (5) **Network Monitoring and Intrusion Detection Systems (IDS/IPS):** It detects and prevents any malicious activity over the organisation's network, by analysing the network traffic at packet level, comparing network activity against familiar attack signatures, and using behaviour analysis to identify suspicious patterns and threats to which is automatically blocked and mitigated by IPS (ex. SNORT (IDS), Palo Alto Networks NGFW (with IDS/IPS capability)) (Fig. **2**).

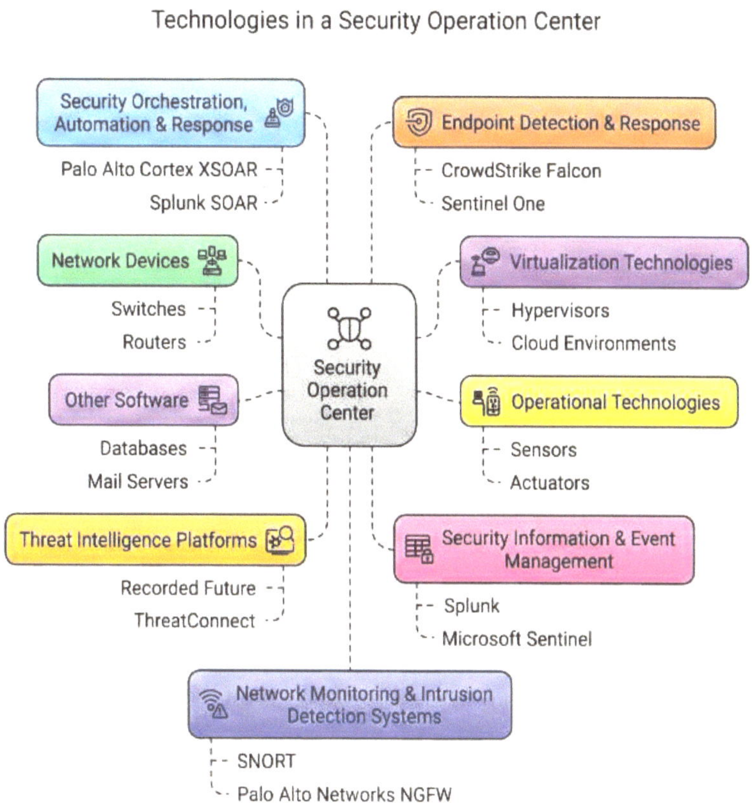

Fig. (2). Technologies in SOC.

UNDERSTANDING CYBER SECURITY FRAMEWORKS FOR SOCS

NIST Cybersecurity Framework

The National Institute of Standards and Technology's cybersecurity framework provides a set of guidelines designed to help assess and improve an organisation's security posture and better manage and reduce its cybersecurity risk [12]. The core reason of NIST is to provide a set of guidelines that can be implemented regardless of the organisation's size, from minor to medium-sized businesses and multi-national companies. Developed in the US, this framework has five main functions, such as:-

(Identify): understand cybersecurity risks and critical assets by conducting risk assessment and classifying information systems and establishing governance structure of policies, **(Protect):** By deploying endpoint protection, data security measures, access control measures and training employees to ensure secure operations, **(Detect):** Use tools like SIEM to track and monitor threats continuously, also conduct VA and PT, **(Respond):** With a proper incident response plan one can contain and mitigate the impact of incident without heavy loss of data or finance, **(Recover):** Affected systems and services should be restored after any incident as soon as possible to reduce downtime [13]. NIST provides an SOC team to continue monitoring an organisation's security posture systematically.

Federal Risk and Authorisation Management Program (FedRAMP)

The US government program provides a standardised security assessment, authorisation, and monitoring process for cloud products and services. FedRAMP is primarily administered by the US government, with other organisations, including NIST, DHS, DOD, and OMB, working together as the Joint Authorisation Board to advise, develop, and maintain security standards. It instructs and oversees cloud service providers to perform regular scans and audits for potential security threats. Cloud Service Providers need to conduct regular audits and security scans, while SOC teams analyse cloud logs for possible security threats. FedRAMP has four security baselines: 1) High, with a set of 421 advanced protection controls for mission-critical federal data. 2) Moderate: with a set of 325 controls for sensitive but unclassified data. 3) Low: with a set of 125 basic controls for publicly available data. 4) LI-SAAS (Low Impact): with a set of 36 security controls [14].

Federal Information Security Modernisation Act (FISMA)

A US Federal law enforced by the Office of Management and Budget (OMB) and Department of Homeland Security (DHS) that directs government agencies and contractors to establish, implement, and maintain a strong cybersecurity measure to secure Federal data. To address new and evolving threats, the original FISMA (Federal Information Security Management Act of 2002) was updated with the Modernisation Act of 2014. The primary goals for the new FISMA were to implement a risk-based approach, improve coordination, enforce accountability and compliance, and continue monitoring security threats [15]. To do so Risk Management Framework was introduced developed by NIST in SP 800-37 which included six steps of security management: **1) Categorization:** ensuring that sensitive information and High Value Assets (HVA) are given highest level of security which is why systems are divided into 3 levels of risk: a)Low, b) Moderate, c) High depending on the level of impact if the information or information system is compromised, **2) Security Control Selection:** access controls, encryption, auditing and incident response, **3) Implementation:**

deployment of selected tools ensuring it is implemented according to the policy framework, **4) Assessment:** making sure that implemented tools are up and running properly a security assessment and audit should be conducted that helps in identifying gaps and vulnerabilities, **5) Authorization:** every agencies deploying their tools or policies must have Authority-to-Operate(ATO), **6) Continues Monitoring:** implementing live-monitoring and timely audits using automated tools [16].

MITRE ATT&CK (Adversarial Tactics, Techniques, and Common Knowledge)

A globally accessible knowledge base of adversary tactics and techniques based on real-world incidents that allows a SOC team to understand and plot cyberattacks based on the attacker's techniques. **1) Tactics:** Here, attackers have high-level objectives to gain initial access, privilege escalation, and data exportation. The attacker can achieve initial access through phishing and the exploitation of public-facing applications by running malicious scripts or code. **2) Techniques:** the specific methods used by the attacker to achieve their goal through dumping credentials to steal login details of personnel in the organisation by using commands in PowerShell or scripting Python scripts to execute attacks. The framework depicts the attack behaviours of known threat groups, allowing a SOC team to plan and prepare their defence mechanisms for each attack technique. This helps them take proactive decisions and improve incident response [17].

SOC INCIDENT LIFECYCLE

Detection: Identification of Threats in Early Stages

Detecting potential threats that could cause significant harm to an organisation as early as possible is the first step in the SOC incident lifecycle. Analysing and classifying the alert according to severity, which, if found malicious, will be considered as an incident. This stage involves working with security tools and techniques to monitor network traffic, logs, and other sources with the help of Security Information and Event Management (SIEM), Intrusion Detection Systems (IDS), Intrusion Prevention Systems (IPS), Endpoint Detection and Response (EDR), User Behaviour Analysis (UBA), and other threat intelligence feeds. Suspicious login attempts from unknown IP addresses, unauthorised file access and modifications, increased network traffic, and malware alerts generated by endpoint security solutions are some of the indicators that, if worked on promptly, potential threats can be responded to quickly, minimising the damage before it escalates or can be avoided entirely [18]. The SOC framework in cybersecurity is shown in Fig. (**3**).

Fig. (3). Cybersecurity Frameworks for SOC.

Investigation: Analysing the Scope and Impact

Identifying the root cause of the incident enables analysts to understand it and determine the most effective response methods, such as quarantine, avoidance, or restoration of systems. This stage includes processes like 1) Prioritizing the alert based on severity, 2) Examining system and network logs, 3) identifying and quarantining affected system from the network to stop further harm, 4) If malicious malware found escalating it towards Tier 2 analysts so that they can reverse engineer it to understand its ability and effects, 5) Correlate different alerts if any larger attack is detected [19]. Determining how the incident happened? What systems or data have been affected? Is any data stolen, modified, or deleted? Was any backdoor created? Is everything resolved at the end before moving to the containment and response procedure?

Containment: Minimizing Damage

Once an incident is confirmed, to prevent excessive damage, it should be contained as soon as possible. Strategies to contain any incident vary depending on the type of attack and what procedure (Incident response plan) a SOC team follows. A containment procedure can be short-term or long-term. Short-term containment is applied where immediate actions must be taken, such as identifying and disconnecting the affected system from the network to stop the attack from spreading further. Long-term containment is applied with in-depth planning, such as patching vulnerabilities, updating security, and implementing additional monitoring. A containment process involves different steps to be completed, such as: isolating infected systems or servers from the network to stop further spread, adding malicious IP - attackers' IP and other suspicious domains to the firewall blocklist/blacklist, disposing of affected user accounts that the attacker might have access to, concealing found malwares using endpoint security tools for further investigations [20].

Eradication: Removing the Threat

Contained threats must be destroyed or removed from the systems to eliminate the presence of the attacker from the organization's network environment. This process includes removal of malware and malicious files from affected systems using endpoint protection and antivirus tools, remove backdoors or scheduled task that attacked may have setup to regain access which SOC must identify and remove, update security information about the attack vector to prevent attack due to similar cause, ask employees to reset their passwords and enforce Multi-Factor Authentication (MFA), update security policies to prevent such attacks from happening again in future. This process is done to ensure systems are clean before moving to the recovery process [21].

Recovery: Restoring Normal Operations

The final step of the process is to restore affected systems, and the organization returns to normal operations. Restoring deleted or modified data from available backup after checking if any modification or deletion was not done in the backup data, if you are confident about the cleanup, proceed forward to restart the work back to normal as it was before, work on loopholes discovered, and enhance your security from lessons learned. Recovering and restoring the data is an important part of the process to ensure business continuity (Fig. **4**).

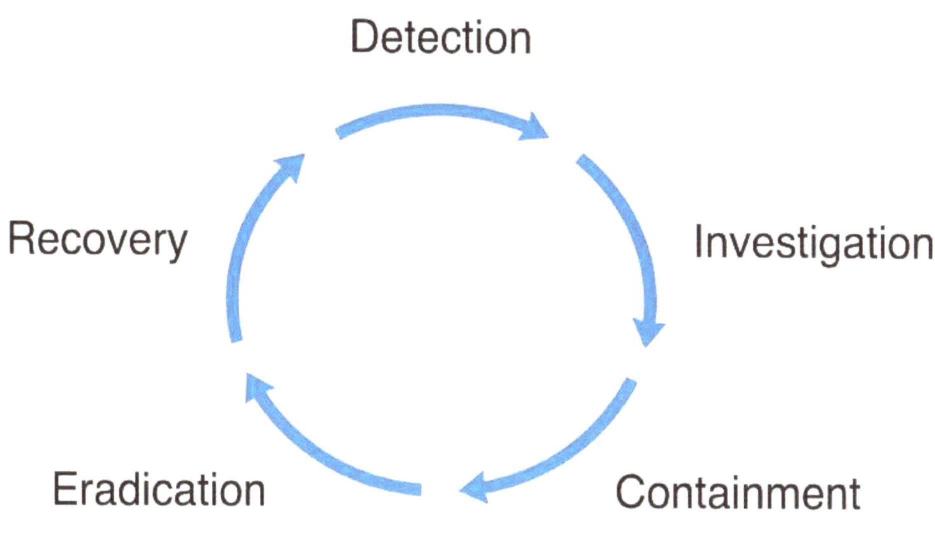

Fig. (4). SOC incident lifecycle.

SOC INCIDENT MITIGATION STRATEGIES AND AUTOMATION

Mitigation Strategies for Different Cybersecurity Attacks

Depending on the type of incident or attack occurring within the organisation, a SOC team must strategise a mitigation plan and respond to it according to their playbook. Some common threats that a SOC team faces often and their mitigation plan are as follows: **1) Ransomware Attack:** An attack that encrypts the data and demands ransom against its decryption key – The affected system must be separated and isolated from the network to prevent further spread, malicious domain and IP associated with the ransom attack must be blocked, using Endpoint Detection and Response (EDR) and other security tools try to remove the ransomware, if the Remote Desktop Protocol was exploited turn it off immediately, use and implement a blocklist and allowlist to prevent unauthorised software and application execution, restore the data from clean and secure offline backups to prevent reinfection. **2) Phishing attack:** tricking users into revealing credentials or installing malware by sending fraudulent emails – SPF, DMARK, DKIM and other email security solutions should be used to filter malicious emails, compromised user credentials should be reset immediately to prevent attacker from reaccessing the network or data, Multi-factor Authorization (MFA) should be implemented to prevent unauthorised access, phishing domains and fraudulent URLs should be blocked, employees security awareness training should be conducted. **3) Insider Threat:** Employees or contractors intentionally or unintentionally misusing access to steal data or sabotage the systems – Least Privilege Access should be enforced restricting users to only necessary data, User Behaviour Analytics (UBA) should be implemented to detect abnormal access patterns, Data Loss Prevention tools can help in monitoring file transfers and data exfiltration, audit logs should be used to track suspicious activity, background checks should be held for employees with access to sensitive data. **4) DOS/DDOS Denial of Service Attacks:** Flooding of the network or application with traffic to disrupt data. Web Application Firewall should be deployed to filter malicious traffic, malicious IP addresses found on filtering the traffic should be blocked, rate-limiting and traffic filtering should be implemented for critical services, and DDOS mitigation services like Cloudflare and AWS Shield should be used. **5) Data breach and Unauthorized access:** Weak security controls lead to access, theft, and leaking of confidential data - forensic analysis should be conducted to discover what data was compromised, sensitive data should be encrypted to prevent unauthorized access, reset passwords, and implement MFA, regulatory bodies and affected users should be informed if legally required. **6) Zero-day exploits:** An unknown vulnerability is exploited by the attacker before its patch is available. Zero-day attack indicators should be monitored using threat intelligence feeds. Security solutions, such as web-application firewalls, should be used to apply virtual patching. Suspicious behaviour should be detected and monitored using Intrusion Prevention Systems (IPS).

Automation in SOC Response

Automating repetitive and time-consuming tasks to enhance the speed, precision, and efficiency of security operations using AI, Machine Learning, and Orchestration, allowing analysts to focus on more critical, complex, and strategic tasks. Automation allows for streamlining the process, eliminating manual errors, and utilising resources more efficiently. Operational costs can be reduced by automating tasks, optimising workflows, and scaling, which improves the return on investment (ROI). Integrating real-time threat intelligence allows proactive identification and response to emerging threats. Upon detection of a threat, predefined actions such as isolating compromised devices and blocking malicious traffic can be initiated automatically without human intervention. As cyber threats evolve, using automated tools such as: 1) SOAR: Security Orchestration, Automation and Response – automating incident response workflow by integrating multiple security tools helps in sending suspicious files to a sandbox environment, restraining it from doing any harm, isolating infected devices, extracting malicious URLs, and blocking them in firewalls. 2) Machine learning and AI help correlate security events faster than humans by scanning patterns of attacks and identifying unusual behaviours in network traffic and user activities [22].

CHALLENGES FACED BY A MODERN SOC TEAM

Handling the Increasing Volume and Complexity of Alerts

CHALLENGES

Thousands of alerts are generated daily from various security tools, leading to alert fatigue, which can result in a significant number of false positives, wasting the time and resources of analysts and leaving real threats unnoticed. Fileless malware, multi-staged attacks, and encrypted communication are used by threat actors to evade detection, making it difficult for analysts to correlate data and detect highly advanced attacks due to insufficient context [23].

SOLUTION

AI-driven threat detection and behaviour analysis help reduce noise and prioritise real threats, automate alert triage, and enhance alerts with contextual data. This is achieved by leveraging SOAR solutions, SIEM rules, baselines, and anomaly detection algorithms, which should be regularly updated and refined to improve accuracy.

Maintaining 24/7 Coverage with Limited Resources

CHALLENGES

A significant skill gap is causing difficulties in hiring, retaining, and training qualified Security Operations Centre (SOC) analysts. Long shifts, high-stress environments, and the constant discovery of new threats cause fatigue in employees, leading to their departures. A significant amount of resources, including employee personnel, technology, and infrastructure, is required to run a SOC 24/7, which incurs substantial operational costs. Relying on a traditional manual process slows down response time.

SOLUTION

Rotating shifts between employees, regular wellness and health monitoring, and training regularly reduce employees' burnout. Implementing hybrid SOC models by associating with a Managed Security Service Provider (MSSP) that helps in-house employees work more efficiently. 24/7 monitoring without a whole in-house staff can be implemented using MDR (Managed Detection and Response). Reducing analyst workload by automating repetitive tasks using AI and ML.

Integrating Threat Intelligence into SOC Workflows

CHALLENGES

Filtering relevant information of threat intelligence is difficult, as it is received from multiple sources. Threat intelligence that is raw and newly added to the database, which cannot be immediately acted on, requires additional improvement and upgrades in knowledge. Flawless integration of TI feeds is essential, which can be challenging as some SIEM and SOC solutions struggle with it. Some SOCs lack automation to update threat intelligence, which hinders their effectiveness and efficiency.

SOLUTION

A Threat intelligence platform helps analyse and make threat intelligence practical. Indicators of Compromise can be mapped in real-time using AI to create alerts and logs. Collaborating and connecting with industry threat sharing groups to keep updated on recent events.

Adapting to New Threats and Attack Vectors

CHALLENGES

The continued development of new attack vectors, such as zero-day exploits, AI-driven attacks, and living-off-the-land techniques, presents a daily challenge for analysts to adapt. Attackers find new ways to gain entry into organisations as they migrate to cloud computing, remote work, and an increase in the use of IoT devices. Behavioural analysis is essential, as there may be malicious or angry employees who attempt to harm, compromise accounts, or cause accidental data leaks, which should be considered by any Security Operations Centre (SOC) team. Monitoring cloud environments, SaaS applications, and supply chain security can be challenging, and many Security Operations Centre (SOC) teams struggle to implement it effectively.

SOLUTION

Red teams and threat hunters must proactively search for threats rather than relying on reactive monitoring and detecting anomalies beyond traditional signature-based methods by implementing User and Entity Behaviour Analysis (UEBA). Monitoring misconfigurations and vulnerabilities in a cloud environment can be done using Cloud Security Posture Management (CSPM). Insider attacks can be minimised by implementing Zero-Trust Principles.

BUILDING AN EFFECTIVE SOC TEAM

Skillsets and Roles within a SOC

Cybersecurity professionals with specialised skills together build an effective SOC team that defends an organisation from cyber threats. Key roles in a SOC team include: a) SOC Manager – The person in charge of supervising all operations, including staffing, budget, and strategies, ensuring compliance with industry policies and regulations, and informing senior management of security risks and incidents. b) SOC Analysts (L1, L2, L3) -L1 - Tier 1 (triage specialists): Monitors security alerts and performs initial investigation using SIEM tools and escalates the event details to the next tier if required. L2 - Tier 2 (Incident Responders): Conducts forensic analysis to find out the impact of the threat by investigating security incidents in-depth. L3 - Tier 3 (Threat Hunters): Updates the detection mechanism to prevent future attacks by identifying Advanced Persistent Threats and unknown malware. c) Threat Intelligence Analysts: Based on threat intelligence, provide security recommendations by gathering information on emerging threats and attacker Tactics, Techniques, and Procedures (TTP). d) Forensics Analysts: Retrieve deleted or hidden evidence from compromised systems and perform a digital forensic investigation to determine the source of the attack. e) Security engineer: ensures the proper incorporation of security controls across the IT infrastructure, including SIEM solutions, firewalls, and security tools, which are also developed and maintained by them. f) Compliance and Risk analysts: They conduct security audits and risk assessments to ensure that security policies comply with regulatory requirements [24].

Recruitment and Training of Analysts

Careful recruitment and continuous training are essential for building a strong SOC team that can keep pace with evolving cyber threats. Hiring the best candidates with the required skill sets, which organisations should look for the following: 1) A person with a background in cybersecurity, computer science, or information technology. 2) Knows how to work with SIEM, Firewall, IDS/IPS, etc. 3) Knows network protocols, malware analysis, and scripting languages. Once hired, analysts must be given continuous training to upskill their knowledge by 1) working with hands-on labs and simulations, and having real-world scenarios practised in a sandbox environment. 2) train to identify and analyse emerging threats. 3) Training in different groups, such as red *vs.* blue teaming. As threats evolve rapidly, analysts must stay updated on which organisations should: 1) Encourage employees to take industry certifications and advance training courses. 2) Provide access to cyber conferences to gain knowledge from industry experts. 3) Start a brainstorming session within the team to share their knowledge [25].

Developing a Security Culture Across the Organisation

Responding to incidents is not the only purpose of a SOC team; they must also try to make the entire organisation aware of those incidents and how to avoid them. To do so, a SOC must follow the following steps: 1) Security awareness training should be held within the organisation, where employees must be trained to identify phishing emails, social engineering attacks, and insider threats. 2) Strong password policies, Multi-Factor Authentication (MFA), and Access Control

Secure coding practices should be implemented to avoid vulnerabilities in the software development process. 3) Creating an environment where employees feel comfortable reporting any security concerns, where clear guidelines should be provided on how to report suspicious incidents. 4) Prioritising cybersecurity by allocating sufficient budget and resources should be done by management to establish a cybersecurity governance framework that aligns with business goals. 5) Adopting a zero-trust architecture in the organisation can help enhance security controls [26].

ENHANCING THE SOC CAPABILITIES WITH ADVANCED TOOLS

The Role of Artificial Intelligence and Machine Learning

Transforming the Security Operations Center by enabling faster threat detection, analysis, and response using Artificial Intelligence and Machine Learning can help the team in the following ways: a) Analyzing a vast amount of data in real time, identifying anomalies and suspicious activities more efficiently with the help of AI and ML instead of following traditional rule-based systems. b) AI-powered systems can differentiate between benign and malicious activities by using and learning from historical data provided to them. c) Analysing historical attack patterns, ML models predict potential future threats, which helps SOCs to avoid risks. d) Identifying insider threats and Advanced Persistent Threats (APT) can be done easily as AI-powered tools help detect deviations in normal user behaviour [27].

Automation and Orchestration for Improved Efficiency

Streamlining SOC operations, reducing response time, and improving efficiency by implementing automation and orchestration can have numerous benefits, such as: a) Enabling automated containment and remediation of threats using Security Orchestration, Automation, and Response (SOAR) platforms reduces the burden on the SOC team. b) Correlating alerts from multiple sources, ensuring extensive analysis of security events can be done by integrating SIEM systems. c) Playbook helps automate common investigation steps, allowing analysts to focus on more complex threats. d) Minimising human error and ensuring compliance with security policies helps maintain consistency in responding to threats [28].

Integrating Threat Hunting Capabilities

Threat Hunting involves searching for indicators of compromise and tactics, techniques, and procedures used by attackers. a) SOC teams identify emerging threats and tailor their defences accordingly by integrating threat intelligence platforms (TIPs). b) Advanced threat hunting supports AI-driven behaviour analysis to identify stealthy attacks, rather than relying solely on signature-based detection. c) MITRE ATT and CK improve the ability to detect, analyse, and respond to threats. d) Collaborating and sharing intelligence with industry peers to stay ahead of the time and attackers.

CASE STUDIES IN SOC OPERATIONS

Responding to a Ransomware Attack

In February 2023, the City of Oakland, California, was attacked by the Play Ransomware Group, launching a double-extortion ransomware attack that encrypted municipal systems and exfiltrated sensitive data, threatening to publish the data unless the ransom was paid. This attack involved two major key points: 1) The attackers locked the critical file systems using encryption to disrupt city operations, and 2) They stole sensitive city data before encrypting the files and demanded extortion money. The attack had a severe impact on Oakland's municipal operations as several systems went offline, impacting services such as emergency response, IT and administrative services, and Payment processing systems. As emergency services were disrupted, law enforcement agencies experienced delays in responding to calls, and other crimes increased in the city. Personal and financial data of government employees were stolen and later found on the dark web. Oakland's SOC and IT team on detecting the ransomware attack executed a multi-phase response strategy to contain and mitigate the attack for which step taken were: 1) Incident containment and system isolation: To include the damage and isolate the systems they disconnected the infected systems to avoid things getting sideways, put an halt to the working of critical municipal services for time being to contain the spread, also deployed endpoint detection and response (EDR) tools to identify other infected endpoints if any available. 2) Threat analysis and investigation: To analyse and investigate the initial entry point, type of ransomware variant used, and the extent of data stolen, a forensic investigation was conducted in coordination with law enforcement agencies and cybersecurity firms for a deeper investigation. 3) Data recovery and system restoration: Backup systems were verified and assessed for integrity checks, ensuring they weren't compromised, and strengthened network defences before bringing municipal systems back online. 4) Public communication and Legal compliance: Affected employees and residents were notified through public statements to keep citizens informed about the incident, ensuring that other legal and compliance measures were in place. 5) Long-term cybersecurity improvements: Implementation of access control with Multi-Factor Authentication (MFA), usage of email security filters to prevent phishing attacks in the future, development of backup and disaster recovery strategies for future reference, and employee awareness training. This incident highlighted several cybersecurity loopholes and challenges faced by the Oakland Government in eradicating the incident, such as a Weak cybersecurity posture that underscored a lack of readiness against modern ransomware or other cyberattacks, a need for defensive strategies that emphasize the importance of network segmentation, Multi-Factor Authentication (MFA), and real-time monitoring. A data breach raised concerns about identity theft and fraud against employees and residents of the city. The attack indicated a rising trend of cybercriminals targeting public sector institutions. This incident highlights the importance of why municipal governments must invest in advanced threat detection, including AI-driven Security Operations Centre (SOC) monitoring, regular audits, and effective patch management. Implementing zero-trust architecture, which limits access to confidential and critical data, is also crucial. Additionally, developing and adopting a robust incident response plan is critical in achieving faster response times and minimising damage [29].

Detecting and Mitigating Advanced Persistent Threat

The SolarWinds supply chain attack, also known as Sunburst, is a sophisticated cyber espionage campaign credited to the Russian foreign intelligence service (SVR) and specifically to the APT 29, also known as the Cosy Bear group, which was discovered in December 2020 and has been ongoing since March 2020. A widely used IT monitoring and management software, SolarWinds Orion, was compromised by hackers who injected a backdoor into legitimate software updates. The back door provided persistent access to numerous organisations, including U.S. government agencies, MNC companies, and cybersecurity firms, as the attack is considered one of the most significant supply chain attacks in history. Let's examine how the attack occurred: 1) Initial compromise: A so-called legitimate update was used to insert malicious code into the SolarWinds Orion software, which was digitally signed and delivered through official SolarWinds update channels, making it difficult to detect. 2) Malware Deployment: The malicious update was installed by around 18,000 customers, from which high-value targets were selected and exploited further. Once installed, the backdoor created a private communication channel with the attacker's Command and Control (C2) server, after which the malware remained dormant for up to 2 weeks to evade detection. 3) Lateral Movement and Data Exfiltration: Stolen credentials and privilege escalation were used to gain persistent access to Microsoft 365 email accounts, enabling the exfiltration of sensitive data from U.S. government agencies and major corporations. 4) Covering Tracks: The hackers mimicked legitimate network traffic, removed logs, and encrypted communications to remain undetected. On discovering the attack multiple associate teams and cyber security firms initiated incident response and mitigation measures such as: a) Identification and Detection: A company named FireEye first detected the attack when they noticed an unauthorised access in their tools while multiple Indicators of Compromise (IoCs) including malware hashes and IP addresses were detected, security teams started analysing network traffic logs and endpoint behaviour to identify compromised systems. **2) Containment Measures:** All malicious updates were disabled and removed from critical infrastructure. Compromised systems were isolated, and suspicious credentials were revoked. Implementation of network segmentation was done to prevent further damage. **3) Eradication and Remediation:** Sunburst and other malware were removed from infected systems, Microsoft revoked stolen certificates, and compromised accounts were reset. Threat hunting operations were carried out to detect any backdoors. **4) Policy and Infrastructure Hardening:** Executive orders were issued to improve supply chain security. Organisations adopted Zero-Trust Architecture (ZTA) and Multi-Factor Authentication (MFA), along with behavioural analysis, to enhance security. This attack highlighted the importance of a zero-trust security model, continuous monitoring, and the utilisation of threat intelligence, as well as the strengthening of security measures [30].

THE FUTURE OF SOCS: TRENDS AND INNOVATION

The Security Operations Centre (SOC) plays a crucial role in modern cybersecurity by continuously evolving to counter emerging threats. Evolving with time, trends, and innovation will help SOCs function better in the future.

The Shift Towards Cloud-Native Security Operations

With the increase in organisations migrating to cloud environments, traditional SOC models are adapting to a cloud-based approach. Cloud-optimised SOCs utilise cloud infrastructure, enabling scalability and flexibility. Key features include: 1) Distributed Security Monitoring: Monitoring threats across multiple environments, including hybrid and multi-cloud infrastructures, helps SOCs gain a broader and more dynamic view of threats, enabling real-time threat detection and response. 2) Centralised log management: Cloud-based security tools collect logs from various sources, enhancing threat visibility, which enables analysts to work with data from multiple cloud applications, endpoints, and network traffic, providing a consolidated security posture. 3) Seamless Integration with Cloud Providers: Built-in security features provided by cloud service providers help SOC teams simplify security operations and automate threat response workflows. 4) Serverless Security Operations: Reducing infrastructure costs, SOCs can enhance detection and response mechanisms without deploying and maintaining dedicated servers, resulting in improved resource utilisation and scalability. 5) Enhanced Incident Response in Cloud Environment: Automated incident response tools, such as Security Orchestration, Automation, and Response (SOAR) platforms, help in responding to threats faster, reducing the time attackers spend crawling within a cloud environment [31].

The role of Automation and AI in SOC Evolution

Increase in volume and complexity of cyber threats have called for adoption of Artificial Intelligence (AI) and Automation within SOC which helps enhance SOC's efficiency through: 1) Threat Intelligence and Prediction: AI algorithm can analyse a large number of datasets and identify attack patterns to predict potential threats while Machine Learning (ML) models processes and correlates threat intelligence from multiple sources which helps SOC teams to anticipate cyber threats before they rise rapidly. 2) Behaviour Analytics: ML models detect inconsistencies in user and network behaviour, which helps identify insider threats and Advanced Persistent Threats (APTs). Meanwhile, AI analyses standard behaviour patterns and flags any differences that might indicate malicious activity. 3) AI-Enhanced Threat Hunting: AI can help detect sophisticated attacks, such as fileless malware, by recognising slight variations in system behaviour. 4) Reduction of False Positives: AI filters out false alarms, allowing analysts to focus on real threats and prioritising alerts based on risk levels and attack patterns. 5) Natural Language Processing (NLP) for threat analysis: to increase the ability to make informed decisions quickly, AI-powered NLP can help analyse reports, threat intelligence feeds, and security logs to derive usable data. 6) Adaptive Security Measures: AI adapts security mechanisms that continuously learn and evolve based on emerging threats, allowing SOCs to implement dynamic security controls that adjust in real-time to mitigate new attack techniques [32].

Preparing for Future Cyber Threats: What's next for SOCs?

As cyber threats evolve, the SOC must adopt forward-thinking strategies to stay ahead of the curve. Future SOC innovations include: 1) Zero-trust security model: The traditional perimeter-based security model is becoming outdated. The zero-trust approach is the future, where every user, device, and application must continually verify its legitimacy before gaining access to resources, which decreases the risk of insider threats and unknown access within the network. 2) Extended Detection and Response (XDR): XDR platforms collect and compare data from various sources, including endpoint, network, and cloud environments, providing a broader view of the threat landscape. 3) Quantum-resistant Security: Quantum computing poses a serious challenge to existing encryption standards, for which the SOCs must develop and explore quantum-resistant cryptographic algorithms and upgrade their security protocols accordingly. Government and organisations will have to invest in quantum-safe encryption techniques to safeguard sensitive data. 4) Cybersecurity Mesh Architecture: The cybersecurity mesh approach means that security controls are decentralised yet interconnected across multiple environments. This architecture ensures that security is compatible across all environments, including cloud, on-premises, and hybrid infrastructures, providing greater adaptability against cyber threats. 5) Human-AI collaboration: As AI and automation play a key role in enhancing SOC capabilities, human expertise remains incomparable. With AI-driven insights and human decision-making, SOC analysts can focus on high-priority threats, strategic response planning, and critical investigations. **5) Treat Intelligence sharing and collaboration:** SOCs must increasingly participate in global threat intelligence sharing initiatives, connecting with industry peers, government agencies, and cybersecurity organisations to actively identify and mitigate emerging threats. **6) Automated Deception Technologies:** Deploying automated deception techniques such as honeypots and decoy networks to lure attackers and analyse their tactics and techniques, which will provide valuable intelligence while mitigating the impact of real incidents. **7) Regulatory and Compliance Adaptation:** SOCs will need to stay ahead of compliance requirements with the help of automated compliance monitoring and reporting tools, which will enable organisations to adhere to frameworks such as GDPR, CCPA, and NIST. **8) Big Data Analytics:** provides SOC with a thorough insight into the entire IT environment, helping to detect suspicious activity and potential threats across different systems and domains. This enables real-time data processing, providing SOC with immediate insights.

CONCLUSIONS

The Security Operations Centre is a crucial component of an organisation's cybersecurity strategy, providing real-time monitoring, detection, and response to cyber threats, ensuring the organisation's security posture remains strong. A recap regarding the roles, components and challenges for SOCs are as follows: 1) The Role of SOC: 24/7 threat monitoring of IT infrastructure to detect suspicious activities and identifying Indicators of Compromise (IoCs), Security breaches must be identified and mitigated before they intensified, gathering and analysing the threat intelligence data to future attacks, ensuring compliance to regulatory standards such as GDPR, HIPPA, PCI-DSS and NIST frameworks, conducting forensics investigation to analyse attack patterns, discover threat actors and obtain evidence for legal or investigation purpose. Combining these functions into a single dedicated team helps in rapid response to security incidents and mitigates damage from cyber threats. 2) Key components of SOC: Security Information and Event Management systems (SIEM) - collects and analyse logs from different sources to detect irregularities, Intrusion Detection and Prevention Systems (IDPS) - Monitors and blocks possible attacks in real time, Threat Intelligence Platforms (TIPs) - Collects and Process external threats to enhance active defences, Endpoint Detection and Response (EDR) - Identifies threat on device level, Network Security Tools: firewall, IDS/IPS and packet inspection tools, SOAR – automates threat response to reduce manual workload and response time,

Skilled Security Analysts and threat hunters – human expertise remains necessary for interpreting alerts, identifying attacks and active threat hunting, Incident Response Plan (IRP) - well strategised procedures for handling security incidents efficiently. 3) Challenges faced by a SOC: Alert Fatigue – Large numbers of alerts lead to burnout and missed threats, Skill Shortage – Lack of experienced professionals makes it challenging to hire and operate an effective SOC, Evolving Threat Landscape – Continuously evolving threat landscape and new attack techniques makes ti essential for SOC to adapt quickly, Budget Limitations - organisations allocate a limited amount of resources for SOC infrastructure, staffing and tools, False positive and False Negative – a large amount of false alerts leads to inefficiency while undetected threats increases significant risks.

The chapter concludes by recommending continuous upskilling of cybersecurity professionals, the adoption of intelligent automation for faster incident handling, and the implementation of adaptive AI models to strengthen proactive threat defense and organizational resilience.

LIST OF ABBREVIATIONS

SOC Security Operations Centre

AI Artificial Intelligence

ML Machine Learning

SOAR Security Orchestration Automation, and Response

SIEM Security Information and Event Management

XDR Extended Detection and Response

ZTA Zero Trust Architecture

UEBA User and Entity Behavior Analytics

NLP Natural Language Processing

IoT Internet of Things

C2 Command and Control

MFA Multi-Factor Authentication

TIP Threat Intelligence Platform

API Application Programming Interface

GDPR General Data Protection Regulation

CCPA California Consumer Privacy Act

REFERENCES

[1] M.D. Basith, P. Praveen, and P.C.S. Reddy, "Adaptive deep Q-GAN framework for enhanced breast cancer detection in medical imaging", *Biomed. Signal Process. Control.*, vol. 112, p. 108638, 2026. [http://dx.doi.org/10.1016/j.bspc.2025.108638]

[2] I.P.E.D. Nugraha, "A review on the role of modern SOC in cybersecurity operations", *Int. J. Curr. Sci. Res. Rev.,* vol. 4, no. 5, pp. 441-448, 2021. [http://dx.doi.org/10.47191/ijcsrr/V4-i5-13]

[3] L.N. Kaliyaperumal, "The evolution of security operations and strategies for building an effective SOC", *ISACA Journal,* vol. 5, pp. 1-9, 2021.

[4] C. Bassey, E.T. Chinda, and S. Idowu, "Building a scalable security operations center: A focus on open-source tools", *Journal of Engineering Research and Reports,* vol. 26, no. 7, pp. 196-209, 2024. [http://dx.doi.org/10.9734/jerr/2024/v26i71203]

[5] A. Boussaksou, and M. Sethi, "Securing the digital frontier: ML-based hierarchical classification of malicious network activities", In: *Proc. 2025 IEEE Int. Conf. Comput. Electron. Elect. Eng. Appl. (IC2E3)* Srinagar Garhwal, India, 2025, pp. 1-6. [http://dx.doi.org/10.1109/IC2E364273.2025.11005893]

[6] V.K. Bukkarayasamudram, P.C.S. Reddy, and K. Arun Kumar, "Quantum computing revolution in healthcare: a systematic review of applications, issues and future directions", *Artif Intell Rev,* vol. 58, p. 389, 2025. [http://dx.doi.org/10.1007/s10462-025-11381-w]

[7] B. Al-Sada, A. Sadighian, and G. Oligeri, "MITRE ATT&CK: State of the art and way forward", *ACM Comput. Surv.,* vol. 57, no. 1, pp. 1-37, 2025. [http://dx.doi.org/10.1145/3687300]

[8] V. Saravanan, S.K. James, V.S. Pandi, J. Shakila, and S. Banumathi, "Securing the digital frontier: An analysis of cybersecurity strategies and obstacles,", In: *Proc. 2025 Int. Conf. Comput. Commun. Inf. Technol. (ICCCIT)* Indore, India, 2025, pp. 741-746. [http://dx.doi.org/10.1109/ICCCIT62592.2025.10928088]

[9] A.T. Somnathe, V.T. Selvi, N.G. Stepha, M.T. Kingslin, F.M. Inamdar, and P.C.S. Reddy, "An intelligent traffic conflict prediction using deep learning with long-term evolution access data", In: *Proc. 2025 3rd Int. Conf. Smart Syst. Appl. Elect. Sci. (ICSSES)*, 2025, pp. 1-6. [http://dx.doi.org/10.1109/ICSSES64899.2025.11010032]

[10] N. Mohamed, "Artificial intelligence and machine learning in cybersecurity: a deep dive into state-o--the-art techniques and future paradigms", *Knowl. Inf. Syst.,* vol. 67, pp. 6969-7055, 2025. [http://dx.doi.org/10.1007/s10115-025-02429-y]

[11] B. Elov, A. Dauletov, Y. Sucharitha, F. Khalilova, M. Latipova, and M. Abdullayeva, "An intelligent traffic management of vehicles using deep learning approach in smart cities", *Proc. 2025 3rd Int. Conf. Integr. Circuits Commun. Syst. (ICICACS),* 2025. [http://dx.doi.org/10.1109/ICICACS65178.2025.10967703]

[12] S.S. Shinde, G.M. Kale, S.L. Nalbalwar, and S.B. Deosarkar, "Navigating the cyber battlefield: Understanding threats and safeguarding digital frontiers", In: *Proc. 2024 Int. Conf. Elect. Electron. Comput. Technol. (ICEECT)* vol. 1. Greater Noida, India, 2024, pp. 1-6. [http://dx.doi.org/10.1109/ICEECT61758.2024.10739310]

[13] J. Kinyua, and L. Awuah, "AI/ML in security orchestration, automation and response: Future research directions", *Intelligent Automation & Soft Computing,* vol. 28, no. 2, pp. 527-545, 2021. [http://dx.doi.org/10.32604/iasc.2021.016240]

[14] P. Purohit, A. Chouhan, and K. Sutaria, "Defending the digital frontier: Combating cyber warfare and DoS attacks with CNN and DPI", *AIP Conference Proceedings,* vol. 3288, no. 1, p. 040002, 2025. [http://dx.doi.org/10.1063/5.0291145]

[15] G. Arun, P.C.S. Reddy, N. Budati, B. Rebecca, S. Perumalla, and V.B. Gujar, "A deep learning framework for diabetes prediction: PIMA indian dataset", *2024 International Conference on Innovative Computing, Intelligent Communication and Smart Electrical Systems (ICSES),* IEEE., pp. 1-6, 2024.

[16] Katkuri, and Srinivas, "Securing the digital frontier: Legal analysis of cybersecurity, data privacy and cyber forensics in India", *Indian J. Public Admin,* vol. 71, no. 1, pp. 75-91, 2025.
[http://dx.doi.org/10.1177/00195561241284886]

[17] V.K. Bukkarayasamudram, P.C.S. Reddy, and K. Arun Kumar, "Quantum computing revolution in healthcare: a systematic review of applications, issues and future directions", *Artif Intell Rev,* vol. 58, p. 389, 2025.
[http://dx.doi.org/10.1007/s10462-025-11381-w]

[18] A. Shah, R. Ganesan, S. Jajodia, H. Cam, and S. Hutchinson, "A novel team formation framework based on performance in a cybersecurity operations center", *IEEE Trans. Serv. Comput.,* vol. 16, no. 4, pp. 2359-2371, 2023.
[http://dx.doi.org/10.1109/TSC.2023.3253307]

[19] S. Yadala, C.S.R. Pundru, and V.K. Solanki, "A novel private encryption model in IoT under cloud computing domain", In: *Proc. Int. Conf. Intell. Syst. Netw. (ICISN)*, 2023, pp. 263-270.Singapore
[http://dx.doi.org/10.1007/978-981-99-4725-6_33]

[20] M. Raimondi, G. Longo, A. Merlo, A. Armando, and E. Russo, "Training the maritime security operations centre teams", In: *2022 IEEE Int. Conf. Cyber Secur. Resilience (CSR)*, 2022, pp. 388-393.*IEEE*, , 2022.
[http://dx.doi.org/10.1109/CSR54599.2022.9850324]

[21] K. Razzaq, and M. Shah, "Advancing cybersecurity through machine learning: A scientometric analysis of global research trends and influential contributions", *J. Cybersecur. Priv.,* vol. 5, no. 2, 2025.
[http://dx.doi.org/10.3390/jcp5020012]

[22] R. Thilagavathy, P.N. Renjith, R.V.S. Lalitha, M.Y.B. Murthy, Y. Sucharitha, and S.L. Narayanan, "A novel framework paradigm for EMR management cloud system authentication using blockchain security network", *Soft Comput.,* pp. 1-9, 2023.
[http://dx.doi.org/10.1007/s00500-023-07958-8]

[23] A. Yusuf, "Examining the role of organizational culture in shaping security practices: A case study of tertiary institutions", *J. Adv. Res. Multidiscip. Stud. (JARMS),* vol. 4, no. 4, pp. 191-202, 2024.
[http://dx.doi.org/10.52589/JARMS-NVZ29VAY]

[24] A. Abisoye, J.I. Akerele, P.E. Odio, A. Collins, G.O. Babatunde, and S.D. Mustapha, "Using AI and machine learning to predict and mitigate cybersecurity risks in critical infrastructure", *Int. J. Eng. Res. Dev.,* vol. 21, no. 2, pp. 205-224, 2025.

[25] S. Suresh, V. Prabhu, V. Parthasarathy, R. Boddu, Y. Sucharitha, and G. Teshite, "A novel routing protocol for low-energy wireless sensor networks", *J. Sens.,* vol. 2022, no. 1, pp. 1-8, 2022.
[http://dx.doi.org/10.1155/2022/8244176]

[26] R Samrin, P C S Reddy, K Arun Kumar, N Deepthi, C Mithra, S Bhargavi Latha, Y Yadala, and G K Thakur, "A hybrid deep learning based framework for prediction of rice yield through integration of biophysical parameters and optical remote sensing data in India", *J. Atmos. Solar-Terr. Phys.,* vol. 279, p. 106734, 2026.
[http://dx.doi.org/10.1016/j.jastp.2026.106734]

[27] K. Kaushik, S. Tayal, A. Bhardwaj, and M. Kumar, *Advanced Smart Computing Technologies in Cybersecurity and Forensics* 1st ed. CRC Press, 2021.
[http://dx.doi.org/10.1201/9781003140023]

[28] M.A. Mahmoud Ahmed, and N.A. Md Yunus, "Securing the IoT frontier: Exploring the limitation and future directions in cybersecurity", *Int. J. Internet Broadcast. Commun.,* vol. 16, no. 2, pp. 1-9, 2024.
[http://dx.doi.org/10.7236/IJIBC.2024.16.2.1]

[29] M. Khayat, E. Barka, M. Adel Serhani, F. Sallabi, K. Shuaib, and H.M. Khater, "Empowering security operation center with artificial intelligence and machine learning—a systematic literature review",

IEEE Access, vol. 13, pp. 19162-19197, 2025.
[http://dx.doi.org/10.1109/ACCESS.2025.3532951]

[30] G. Nagar, "The evolution of security operations centers (SOCs): Shifting from reactive to proactive cybersecurity strategies", *Int. J. Sci. Res. Manag. (IJSRM),* vol. 6, no. 9, pp. 100-115, 2018.
[http://dx.doi.org/10.18535/ijsrm/v6i9.ec03]

[31] Y. Sucharitha, P.C.S. Reddy, and G. Suryanarayana, "Network intrusion detection of drones using recurrent neural networks", *Drone Technol.: Future Trends Pract. Appl.,* pp. 375-392, 2023.
[http://dx.doi.org/10.1002/9781394168002.ch15]

[32] S Malik, P K Malik, and A Naim, "Opportunities and challenges in new generation cyber security applications using artificial intelligence, machine learning and blockchain", In: *Next-Generation Cybersecurity: Blockchain Technologies,* K Kaushik, I Sharma, Eds., Springer: Singapore, 2024.
[http://dx.doi.org/10.1007/978-981-97-1249-6_2]

CHAPTER 7

ML-based Endpoint Security: Advancing from Reactive Defense to Proactive Protection

S Nancy Lima Christy[1], **C Santhosh Kumar**[2], **P Esaiarasi**[3], **N Gurusamy**[4], **N Shanmugapriya**[5] and **K Madhan**[6,*]

[1] *Department of Computer Science and Engineering, SRM Institute of Science and Technology, Chennai, Tamil Nadu, India*

[2] *Department of Electronics and Communication Engineering, Mailam Engineering College, Mailam, Tamil Nadu, India*

[3] *Department of AI and DS, Sri Shanmugha College of Engineering and Technology, Sangakiri Salem, Tamil Nadu, India*

[4] *Department of Computer Science and Engineering, Dhanalakshmi Srinivasan University, Tamil Nadu, India*

[5] *Department of Information Technology, St. Joseph's College of Engineering, Chennai, Tamil Nadu, India*

Abstract: The rapidly changing cybersecurity environment makes enterprise system endpoints the main targets that cybercriminals use to gain access illegally. Web-based work and mobile devices, as well as IoT technologies, have substantially increased the potential attack space for endpoints. Modern cyber threats, along with ransomware-induced service attacks and fileless malware, and adversary artificial intelligence threats, diminish the effectiveness of traditional detection signatures at the endpoint. This chapter examines Artificial Intelligence that reinforces the defense at the endpoint to evolve towards predictive defense from conventional reactive controls. With machine learning partnered with natural language processing, along with behavioural analytics, AI enables real-time detection of threats, along with automation of incident response, while introducing security controls that adjust based on moving attack targets. It explains how AI-powered Endpoint Detection and Response technologies aid organizations in conducting anomaly detection coupled with active prevention of lateral movement activity, and realize threat response times that are prompt. The analysis displays how endpoint AI tools ought to be strategically added to enterprise threat intelligence systems to provide complete defense situational awareness and joint protection across all sections of the organization. The article discusses the ethical dimensions as well as regulatory positions while illustrating how generative AIs can evolve into systems that heal themselves while running autonomously to defend

* **Corresponding Author K. Madhan:** Department of Information Technology, St. Joseph's College of Engineering, Chennai, Tamil Nadu, India; E-mail: madhanckn@gmail.com

Pundru Chandra Shaker Reddy, Yadala Sucharitha, & Thillaiarasu N (Eds.)

endpoints. The chapter provides essential guidance to organizations that want to develop AI-based automated endpoint security capabilities within the context of contemporary cyber defense.

Keywords: Artificial Intelligence, Cybersecurity, Cyber Threats, Endpoint Detection, Endpoint security, Generative AIs, IoT technologies, Reactive Defense.

INTRODUCTION

The role of endpoint security in IT, as endpoint devices' security, became a key element of enterprise cybersecurity, as the traditional network barrier continues to disappear. From an endpoint protection aspect, things were relatively easy at first with a reliance on antivirus software to pick up and clean threats. But since endpoints were becoming more complicated and attackers were as well, endpoint security moved from chiefly being a process to keep the organization's desktop computers safe against malware and spyware [1]. This redirection embodies not only the evolving nature of cyber defense technologies but, more fundamentally, the shift from concentrating primarily upon known threats all the way to perceiving and responding to the unknown and evolving ones. This shift in defense strategies from basic baseline approaches to intelligent, adaptive, proactive models based on Artificial Intelligence (AI) demonstrates the mounting demand for intelligent, adaptive, and proactive models to safeguard enterprise endpoints [2].

This chapter aims to explore the transformative role of AI in redefining endpoint security. With the growing complexity of cyberattacks and the limitations of traditional reactive defense mechanisms, ML-based approaches offer intelligent, adaptive, and predictive capabilities that are essential for modern endpoint protection. The theme or focus of the chapter is on how the AI technologies– including Machine Learning (ML), Deep Learning (DL), and Reinforcement Learning (RL) enable proactive threat detection, automated response, and continuous security improvement.

Through the organization of the discussion into focused sections, this chapter provides both theoretical and practical insights. The primary objective of the chapter is as follows:

- To establish a comprehensive understanding of how AI augments endpoint security frameworks.
- To help cybersecurity professionals and researchers better defend against contemporary and future threats.

The chapter is organized as follows: Section 1 introduces the evolution of endpoint security, covering traditional endpoint protection mechanisms, the rise of API, and the shift from reactive to predictive security. Section 2 discusses the fundamentals of AI in cybersecurity, offering insights on the role of ML in threat classification, DL for malware detection, and RL in adaptive security models. Section 3 highlights ML-based endpoint detection and response-related concepts like behavioural analysis for endpoint anomaly detection, automated threat containment and remediation, and EDR integration in threat intelligence platforms. Section 4 concentrates on real-time threat detection using AI with in-depth analysis on stream processing for live data monitoring, predictive analysis for zero-day threats, and AI for phishing and social engineering detection. Section 5 is intended for the scope of AI in endpoint threat hunting, covering other concepts like data enrichment and correlation, identifying lateral movements in networks, and the use of graph analytics for threat tracing. Finally, Section 6 concludes the chapter by outlining the concepts discussed throughout, expressing the scope and fundamentals of AI in endpoint security.

The evolving cybersecurity landscape has made enterprise endpoints key targets for attackers, with web-based systems, mobile devices, and IoT expanding the threat surface. Traditional signature-based defenses are ineffective against modern threats like ransomware, fileless malware, and adversarial AI. Artificial Intelligence (AI) enhances endpoint protection through machine learning, natural language processing, and behavioral analytics, enabling real-time threat detection, automated response, and adaptive defenses. Real-world examples include **CrowdStrike Falcon**, which uses ML-based behavioral analytics to detect abnormal activities and prevent breaches, and **Microsoft Defender for Endpoint**, which applies deep learning and global threat intelligence to isolate compromised devices swiftly. The chapter concludes that AI-powered endpoint security, supported by ethical and regulatory compliance, predictive modeling, and skilled workforce development, is vital for building resilient, adaptive, and proactive cyber defenses.

EVOLUTION OF ENDPOINT SECURITY

Traditional Endpoint Protection Mechanisms

The early phase of digital security relied heavily on signature-based antivirus programs for endpoint protection. These tools worked by cross-referencing files and processes on a device against a database of known threat signatures. If a match was found, the system would quarantine or delete the suspected file. This worked well enough in an era where strains of malware were fewer and, in many cases, could be grouped together by their telltale attributes. More protective measures were added around this primitive AV, local firewalls, and heuristic analysis were introduced. Heuristic approaches tried to find signs of malicious behaviour based on existing rules and user behaviours, but they simply lacked the flexibility to catch new attacks [3].

The fundamental limitation of such legacy mechanisms was that they relied upon historical information. Signature-based systems inherently responded to threats only after they had already been identified. Polymorphic methods, which change the malware each time it is run, tended to stay under the radar. Unfortunately, these legacy systems worked predominantly in separate silos, with minimal integration, correlation, or context of information between the network devices or the global threat landscape. As threats evolved to be more sophisticated and spread at greater velocities, however, what we came to realize was that implementing static, standalone defense would be inadequate to protect enterprise environments from constantly changing attacks [4].

Rise of Advanced Persistent Threats (APTs)

APTs were a game-changer in cyber warfare. APTs are distinct from conventional malware due primarily to the difference in nature, intent, and capacity for both immediate and long-term effect, as compared with traditional malware, which focuses on both quick effect and wide distribution. These types of threats are usually seen from very organized threat actors, such as nation-state sponsored groups or cybercriminal syndicates, who look to penetrate particular organizations and remain undetected for long periods [5]. APT campaigns often start with extensive reconnaissance work and then move to the staging of an initial compromise *via* phishing, social engineering, or zero-day exploits, and culminate in data exfiltration or the disruption of critical systems [6].

The most dangerous aspect of APTs is the capability to remain unnoticed while executing the lateral movements in the network. They are often fileless, using trusted tools within the operating system, or existing only in system memory, thus evading typical antivirus and firewall methods. Also, these attacks are intended to be dynamic, changing their behaviour based on the defensive measures employed by the security teams [7]. The emergence of APTs revealed the fatal weaknesses of conventional endpoint protection and the need for something more intelligent, more responsive, able to identify low levels of signs of compromise, correlate events over time and across systems, and respond quickly to contain a threat and eliminate it. These threats required a drastic shift in the way endpoint security was treated.

Shift from Reactive to Predictive Security

In a specific event, organizations began to realize the ineffectiveness of reactive security, and the greater cybersecurity community began a move forward toward predictive and proactive models of defense. It also meant being able to transition past signature-based detection mechanisms that had defined security programs up until that time—this was largely a byproduct of advances in both artificial intelligence and machine learning. Instead, predictive endpoint security focuses on detecting anomalous behaviour patterns that indicate a potential threat to the system, even if there is no known signature associated with the threat. Instead of being trained exclusively on historical data, AI models examine real-time information from diverse sources such as user activity, system logs [8].

This proactive approach changes how endpoint security works. Instead of just waiting for known threats, these predictive systems learn from their surroundings and tweak their detection settings on the fly. They can spot zero-day exploits, see new types of malware, and react to fresh attack methods almost in real-time. Plus, ML-based endpoint protection often links up with larger security setups, like threat intelligence platforms and SIEM systems, giving a complete view and coordinated responses across the company. By automating threat containment and fixing issues, predictive security cuts down on how much human input is needed, speeds up incident response times, and strengthens overall Defenses. This shift is a big step forward in tackling more nimble and ongoing cyber threats [9].

The radar chart shown in Fig. (**1**) compares traditional endpoint protection mechanisms with AI-based predictive security approaches. The chart covers five key areas of endpoint protection: how quickly threats are detected; the coverage of threats; adaptability; false positive rate (embedded for clarity); and real-time response. Conventional approaches showcase average detection speed and false-positive control—yet their adaptability and real-time responses are also rated low. This reflects their dependence on rigid rule sets and slow response to new threats. Ultimately, the shift highlights how AI-enabled security models are better equipped to respond, adapt, and provide more complete threat coverage.

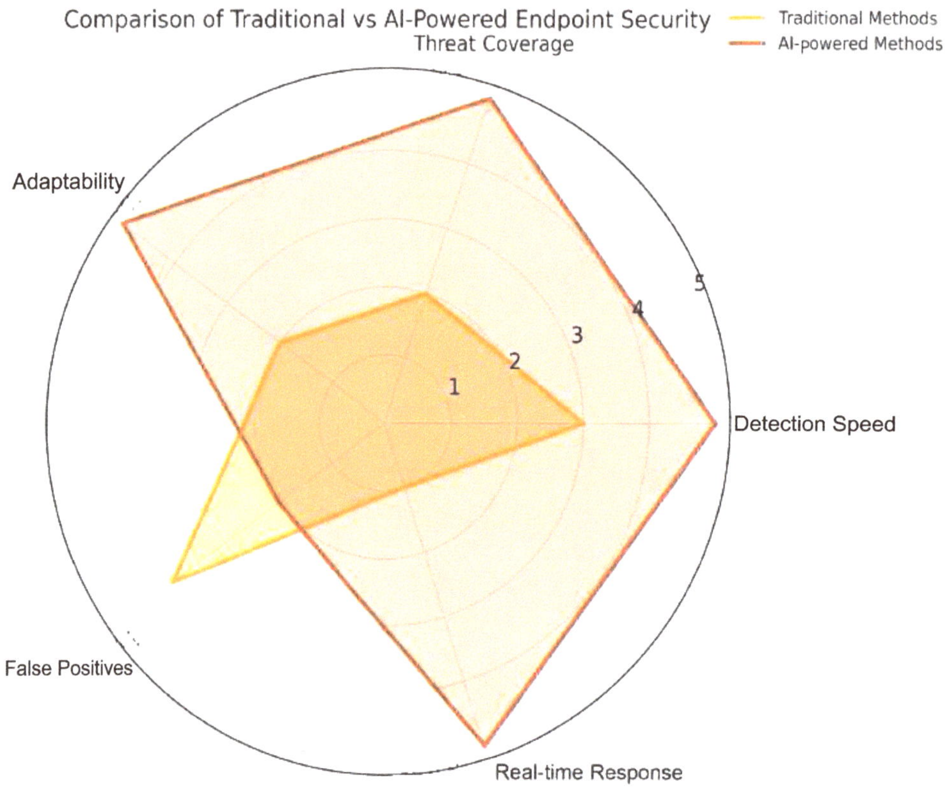

Fig. (1). Comparison of traditional *vs*. AI-powered endpoint security.

Fig. (**2**) shows the same performance indicators, but in a more detailed side-b--side format. Each bar indicates the strength of traditional versus AI approaches. AI systems are rated a perfect 5 out of 5 for detection speed, coverage of all threats, and real-time response capabilities among other areas, indicating an increasing capacity to identify and counter threats in real time and proactively. Traditional systems also fall short in these aspects, especially real-time response, given their reactive nature and reliance on already known threat signatures. This bar chart supports the argument for moving enterprises toward AI-scaled endpoint security technologies that can keep up with evolving threats accurately and nimbly. Table **1** shows comparative approaches in various aspects of protection.

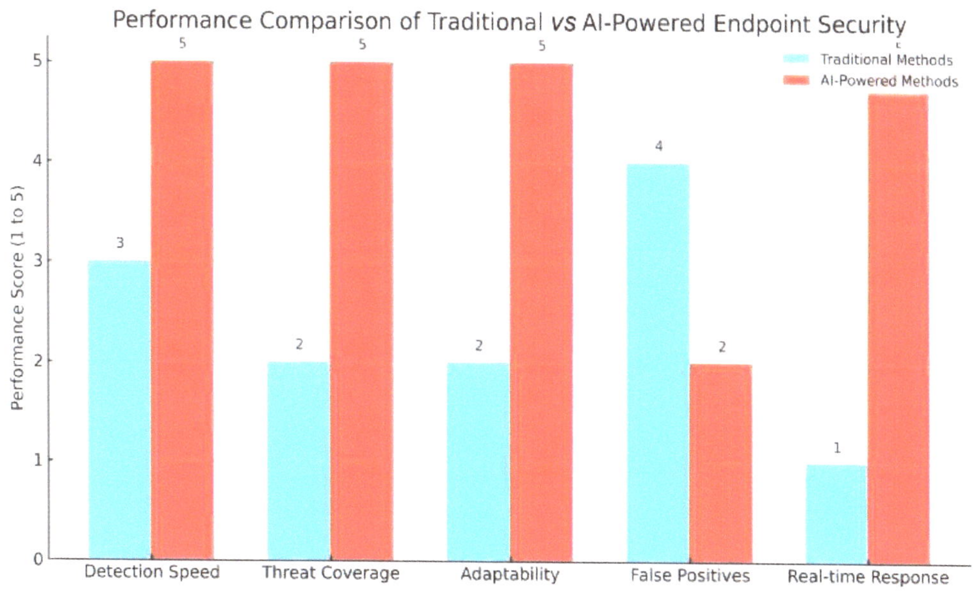

Fig. (2). Performance comparison of traditional *vs.* AI-powered endpoint security.

Table 1. Comparative analysis of traditional *vs.* AI-powered endpoint protection approaches.

Aspect	Traditional Endpoint Protection	AI-Powered Endpoint Protection
Threat Detection Speed	Moderate detection speed, as it relies on signature matching.	High speed due to behavioral patterns and anomaly analysis.
Threat Coverage	Limited overage is effective only for known malware and static threats.	Broad coverage, including known, unknown (zero-day), polymorphic, and fileless threats.
Adaptability	Low adaptability due to static rule sets and manual updates.	High adaptability with machine learning and reinforcement learning models
False Positive Rate	Low FPR tuned for known threats, but may miss unknowns.	FPR improves with model fine-tuning.
Response Mechanism	Responds only after a threat is identified, making it Reactive.	Proactive mode of operation, anticipating and mitigating threats based on prediction models.
Integration Capabilities	Minimal capabilities, as it operates in silos and lacks context-sharing.	High with integration of SIEMs, threat intelligence platforms, and centralized security frameworks.
Detection of APTs	Unable to identify lateral movements or fileless intrusions.	Strong detection of APTs due to behavioral analysis and long-term pattern recognition.

(Table 1) cont.....

Aspect	Traditional Endpoint Protection	AI-Powered Endpoint Protection
Maintenance and Update Frequency	High maintenance is required as constant signature updates are needed manually or semi-automatically.	Lower maintenance as models continuously learn and update automatically.
Human Involvement	High reliance on manual analysis and intervention.	Due to automated detection, remediation, and self-learning, human dependency is low.
Overall Effectiveness	Limited effectiveness and struggles with modern attack vectors.	Comprehensive effectiveness is better suited for evolving and dynamic threat environments.

AI FUNDAMENTALS IN CYBERSECURITY

Artificial Intelligence is a game-changer in the domain of cybersecurity and brings forth powers that could not be achieved by traditional means. With these two major facets of data—data-driven intelligence and adaptive learning—AI provides a solid foundation for detecting, analysing, and mitigating a wide range of cyber threats. Static rule-based defense has not been enough as adversaries are coming up with more and more sophisticated attack methods. AI fills that void with responses that can be dynamic and context-aware, adapting as the threat does. This section explains how the core areas of AI, i.e., Machine Learning, Deep Learning, and Reinforcement Learning, are revolutionizing present-day cybersecurity practices, notably with the use of endpoint defense, threat detection, and auto-decisions [10].

Role of Machine Learning in Threat Classification

You see, Machine Learning, as you know it, works in a key role to digest volumes of data and detect classes of threat through pattern matching. Machine Learning creates a main functionality that allows systems to explore learning based on historical data and identify suspicious activities and anomalous behaviours in real-time scenarios. Cybersecurity ML models are trained on varied inputs such as network traffic logs, user behaviour profiles, and file attributes [11]. Successful training teaches these models to be able to distinguish between normal function of the system and intrusions (even zero-day attacks) without relying on previously known attack vectors or unknown small deviations from expected behaviour. ML excels at processing difficult data sets and does not need any specific programming instructions based on various threats. Supervised learning classifiers use sets with mixed known good, known bad samples to train the likelihood of the input supplied to be harmful. These methods, like unsupervised learning, mostly concentrate on use case scenarios like anomaly detection, where this kind of approach responds to unknown sources of threats based on data points. ML is thus crucial to the automation of the threats' classification with an exceptionally low false positive rate, where the functionality of the security teams is made significantly more productive [12].

The fact that ML models can extract new information at all times enables organizations to update systems and protect against evolving methods of attacks without relying on archaic signature information. This process of continuous learning enables organizations to protect known threats as well as educate themselves to face sophisticated intrusion activities. Machine Learning, due to its dynamic nature, can be an intrinsic technology to create strong cybersecurity solutions that can effectively counter potential attacks.

Deep Learning for Malware Detection

Cybersecurity systems have achieved significant advances through Deep Learning technology because it functions similarly to human brain structures while serving as a subset of Machine Learning methods. Deep models surpass conventional methods since they handle data representation learning with no human manual input and find implicit data patterns that are beyond human detection capabilities [13].

Deep learning models that include Convolutional Neural Networks (CNNs) and Recurrent Neural Networks (RNNs) examine binary files along with code sequences and system logs to be used for malware detection purposes.CNN software executes outstanding binary-to-image conversion for malware analysis, which leads to the detection of visible behavioural indicators important for security investigation. RNNs process sequences of data, such as API call trails or network session logs, because the event order serves to differentiate between standard activity and security threats.

Deep learning achieves superior success by recognizing diverse malware types, both known and unknown. This technology functions excellently to identify polymorphic and metamorphic malware because these threats regularly transform their manifestation to avoid signature-detection solutions. Deep learning systems can identify anomalies with the help of autoencoders and generative models to generate simulated attack paths to constitute an enhanced defense feature. Deep learning models will be more accurate and faster at detecting malware due to the increase in computing power alongside more readily available huge training sets of data. Their ability to directly learn from raw data makes the tools seamlessly deployable, along with enhanced detection accuracy that sets them up as necessary cybersecurity infrastructure components [14].

Reinforcement Learning in Adaptive Security Models

Reinforcement Learning offers a brand-new way of handling cybersecurity by concentrating on decision-making through trial-and-error interaction with a nonlinear and dynamic environment. Unlike supervised or unsupervised learning, it is not based on labelled data or on previously used labelled datasets. In contrast, the agent trains to pick out the quality motion by maximizing cumulative rewards over time. In the world of cybersecurity, it involves the development of highly intelligent solutions that can learn and evolve through the experiences of defensive manoeuvres that occurred before [15]. One of the most promising uses of reinforcement learning is the creation of adaptive models of security that change dynamically to respond to live threats effectively with fluidity and autonomy. Take, for example, an RL deployable inside of an endpoint security system where it can learn to decide whether or not to quarantine a process, escalate an alert, or isolate a device from the network. These choices are made with ongoing assistance in feedback from the system, a threat was wiped out, or legitimate operations were disrupted. As the days go by, the agent adjusts its policy to balance security effectiveness with operational efficiency [16].

Reinforcement learning is also very relevant in scenarios like automated penetration testing, cybersecurity deception, and dynamic resource allocation. In such cases, the RL agent can model and explore attacker behaviour in safe virtual neighbourhoods before it places said scenarios into the production systems. This ability to experiential learning lets defenders predict an offense sequence and proactively reinforce weak sides [17]. Additionally, Reinforcement learning helps in the generation of self-healing systems capable of autonomously recovering from an attack by reconfiguring the components, rolling back the malicious changes, or restoring the compromised data. As the complexity and scope of cyber threats evolve, RL can unlock the potential to independently and adaptively take defensive actions. Its integration into endpoint protection, as well as broader threat intelligence capabilities, is an all the more significant step toward the creation of cyber-resilient systems that operate efficiently under times of uncertainty and enmity [18].

To illustrate the feats of Modern Security Systems, the workflow in Fig. (**3**) demonstrates the processing pipeline of AI techniques (i.e., ML, DL, and RL) applied, and the final result is multi-layered network protection. You are trained on data until September 2023. The process starts by collecting data from various sources like network logs, endpoint sensors, and user activity traces. That is succeeded by data preprocessing—normalization, noise reduction, and transformation to prepare the dataset for algorithmic ingestion. From there, the workflow splits into three paths, specific to the AI technique used. The bottom line is that, even in the ML branch, the features need to be extracted and fine-tuned before going to any supervised or unsupervised learning model. Once trained, these models facilitate efficient classification of threats and produce responses based on previously learned patterns of attack [19]. Manual feature selection is not necessary in the DL branch; raw data is fed to the deep neural networks. Through several hidden layers of interconnected nodes, these networks draw in complex characteristics and make inferences on potential threats (*e.g.*, malware, anomalies, *etc.*).

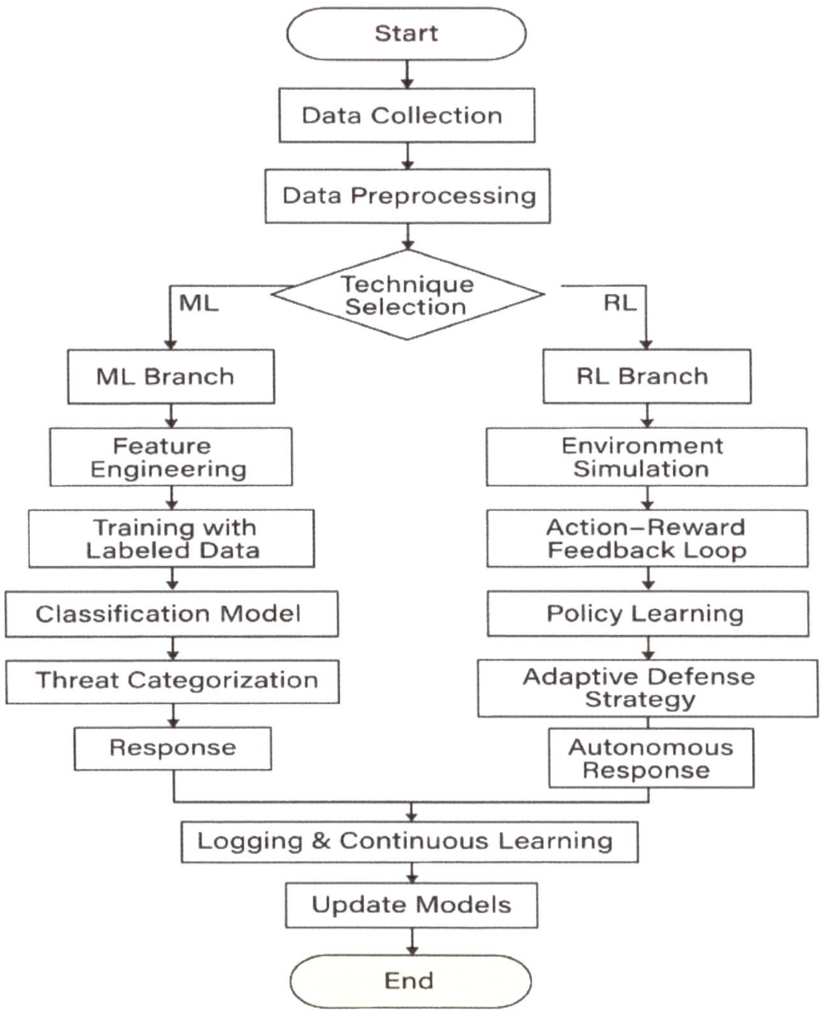

Fig. (3). Workflow of AI techniques in cybersecurity.

The net result is a high-accuracy malware or other anomaly detection system that recognises known threats and threats never seen before. The RL part takes a completely different approach by using an environment simulation method. It is here that the model is trained on a cyber kill chain, from which it learns through reinforcement feedback loops derived from in-system interactions over the cyber kill chain. Then, gradually, it gets the best possible policy for adaptive defense, which enables it to autonomously decide when and how to act during an active threat scenario. This would have a pipeline of data collection with human decision-makers helping to make those systems better over time with logs, feedback, and updates based on observations. Lather, rinse, repeat — this cyclical approach builds the resilience and responsiveness of the cybersecurity ecosystem, allowing it to advance alongside the threat landscape [20].

Fig. (**4**) summarizes the comparison of ML, DL, and RL based on their performance when used in cybersecurity applications. These are the dependencies on data, accuracy of threat detection, adaptability, response time, and autonomy of decisions. ML had relatively good performance in response time and data sufficiency, as it works well on labelled data and is less computationally complex. Nevertheless, it is not as good as Reinforcement Learning at making its own decisions. Deep Learning was superior with respect to detection performance and adaptability because it can learn very complex structures from raw data, like malware binaries or logs of network traffic. Reinforcement Learning, although slower in response time, has the highest score in adaptability and decision autonomy, being able to learn and update knowledge on the fly in case the threat circumstances change.

ML-BASED ENDPOINT DETECTION AND RESPONSE (EDR)

With the changing face of the cyber threat landscape, conventional endpoint defense systems never managed to stay abreast of next-gen approaches to attacks. This has prompted the introduction of AI-powered Endpoint Detection and Response (EDR) systems that ensure an intelligent, proactive, and adaptive defense strategy. ML-based EDR solutions can sift through vast amounts of endpoint data in real-time, recognize malicious trends, and initiate relevant, automated responses. AI-based EDR systems continue to learn from emerging threats, which allows them to evolve in reaction, unlike the legacy ones dependent on static signatures or previously established rules. This empowers them to not only detect ongoing attacks but also anticipate future intrusions before they inflict significant damage [21].

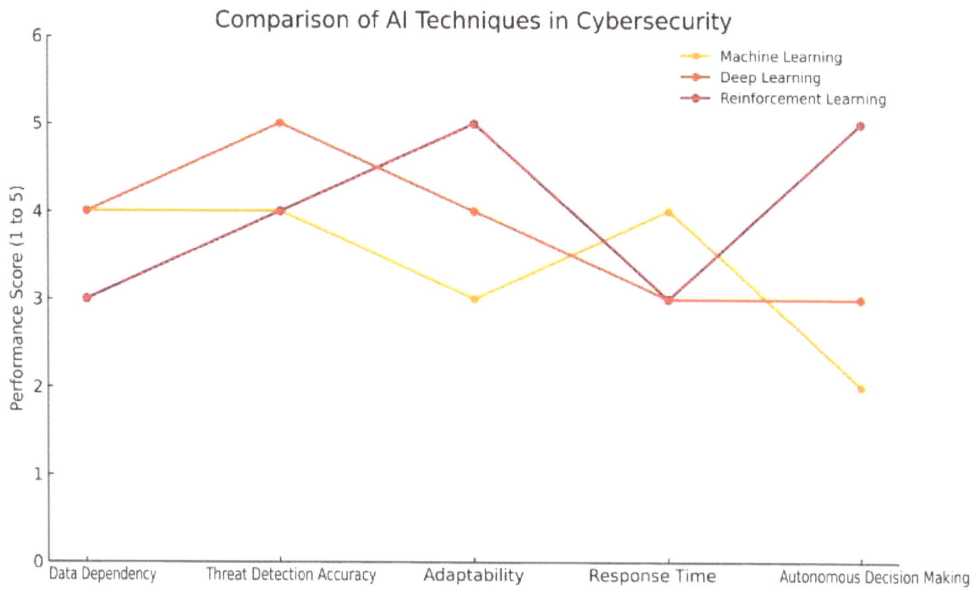

Fig. (4). Comparison of AI techniques in cybersecurity.

Behavioural Analysis for Endpoint Anomaly Detection

A big part of AI-powered EDR is behavioural analysis. Instead of just hunting down known bad signatures, it looks for weird activity on endpoints. So, it monitors user behaviour, the apps they use, how they access files, and what's going on across different endpoints. AI algorithms, especially those using machine learning, figure out what "normal" looks like for each device or user.

When something seems off—like unauthorized file access, odd processes running, or strange login times—the system flags it as a potential threat.

Machine learning algorithms identify malicious behavior on endpoints by analyzing patterns in system activities, network traffic, and user behavior. They learn from historical data to recognize anomalies—such as unusual file access, process execution, or data transfers—that deviate from normal behavior, flagging them as potential threats for further investigation.

Behavioural analysis can spot new, sneaky threats like fileless malware or insider problems that traditional methods might overlook. And since AI models get regular data updates, they become better at distinguishing harmless quirks from real threats. This means fewer false alarms and more useful alerts from the EDR system. In short, ML-based behavioural analysis moves endpoint security away from just reacting to a more proactive way of monitoring and preventing issues.

Automated Threat Containment and Remediation

Beyond detection, AI-powered EDR solutions permit prompt, as well as automatic, response to known dangers. The moment an anomaly, or even a confirmed attack, is detected, the EDR instrument can respond automatically in under minutes. Actions may include disconnection of the affected device from the network, stopping malignant programs, or restricting user permissions. These steps are critically important to contain the malware and prevent ongoing destruction during an investigation. Besides containment, the remediation function of AI-powered EDR systems can reverse changes done by the malware, restoring files from backup copies or deploying security updates live. This is where the 'AI' part is critical, as it needs to decide on the best response given the type and severity of threat, historic incident data, and knowledge of the particular system. This provides rapid responses as well as relieving humans who would be investigating and responding to do so.

ADRs eliminate the impact and disruption to operations by automating the containment and remediation process, increasing the organization's resiliency. This capability is useful in any type of mass attack, like ransomware, where being able to quickly respond can be the difference between a small impact and an entire system takeover [22]. Anomaly detection plays a crucial role in AI-based endpoint security by identifying deviations from normal system or user behavior that may indicate a cyber threat. It enables early detection of previously unseen or zero-day attacks that traditional signature-based systems might miss, enhancing proactive threat prevention and response.

EDR Integration with Threat Intelligence Platforms

The potential for ML-based EDR solutions is vastly enhanced when they are part of Threat Intelligence Platforms (TIPs). These platforms consolidate threat information from several outside sources—including open-source intelligence, commercial feeds, and governmental advisories—and add context about known malware families, attack campaigns, threat actor descriptions, and Indicators Of Compromise (IOCs). Integration of EDR systems with TIPs improves the quality of detection and prioritization by allowing real data from threat actors to accompany the anomalies detected to enrich them further. This integration enables EDR platforms to discover threats at lightning speed and also offer an understanding of the bigger picture. This enriched intelligence becomes the basis for the AI algorithms to adjust their models in real time, making fine-tuned predictions for a more effective and targeted approach to defensive mechanisms. In addition, such integrations enable collaborative defense, which is to share anonymized threat data that enables organizations to contribute to a group cybersecurity posture. Thus, AI-powered EDRs are no longer mere internal defense, but actually part of a worldwide cybercrime fight. As a result, this inter-communication allows endpoint protection systems to become more dynamic, proactive, and in line with the evolving threat landscape [23].

Fig. (**5**) is a line graph illustrating the comparison of the three primary components of AI-powered Endpoint Detection and Response technologies, specifically Behavioural Analysis, Automated Remediation, and Integration with Threat Intelligence Platforms. This comparison is made relative to five performance measures of Detection Accuracy, Response Time, False Positive Reduction, Threat Contextualization, and Autonomous Remediation, each scored between 1 and 5. While Behavioural Analysis scores high in Detection Accuracy and False Positive Reduction, clearly indicating that it is good at detecting subtle anomalies and minimizing alert fatigue, it scores low, comparatively, in Autonomous Remediation, since this process is primarily intended for detection, not action. Automated Remediation scores highly in Response Time and Autonomous Remediation, which attests to the fact that it is fast to respond and act independently upon detection of threats. On the contrary, Integration with TIPs scores highly in Threat Contextualization, indicating that it enhances situational awareness through the correlation of local detection with worldwide threat knowledge. This graph illustrates the individual contributions of each EDR component to the protection of endpoints, as well as the importance of having all three combined to take an all-around approach to security.

In Fig. (**6**), we replicate Find, Shape, and Verify component details from the previous line chart Fig. (**5**), but now we present this information in a bar chart for greater clarity in comparing details for each of the three ML-based EDR components. Each set of bars plots a performance metric, so we can see where each component leads or lags. Behavioural Analysis Outperforms in Detection Accuracy and False Positive Reduction, reinforcing its effectiveness in recognizing anomalous behaviour patterns and reducing excessive alerts. Automated Remediation leads in Response Time and Autonomous Remediation, demonstrating its power in executing rapid and intelligent actions following detection." On the other hand, EDR Integration with TIPs received a perfect score in Threat Contextualization, showcasing its ability to amplify local detections with global intelligence feeds. Data facilitating an EDR strategy and its techniques show how to combine and integrate EDR techniques for optimal endpoint security. Illustrating how the three components are compared helps understand how they stand and help and support each other.

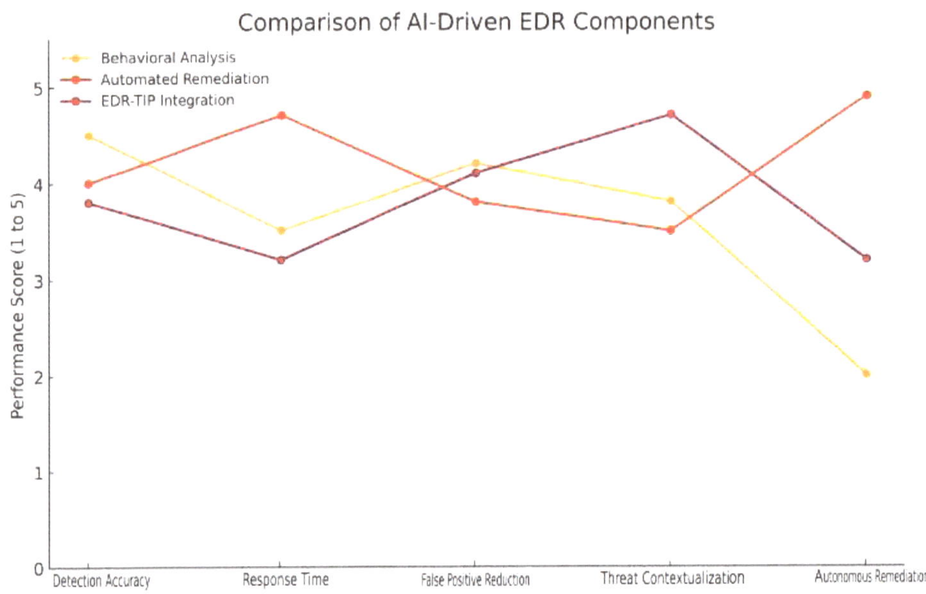

Fig. (5). Comparison of ML-based EDR components.

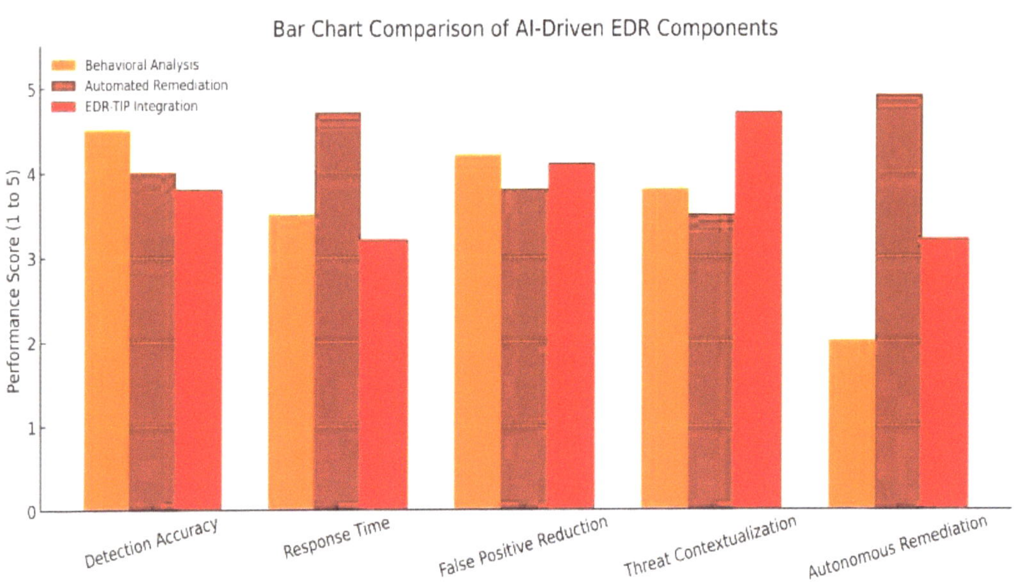

Fig. (6). Bar chart comparison of ML-based EDR components.

REAL-TIME THREAT DETECTION USING AI

With the threat landscape evolving to become wider and faster, organizations have realized that to stay ahead of malicious activities, they need to make the move towards real-time threat detection, one in which they can identify and mitigate threats nearly instantaneously. In this space, AI has become a critical enabler, providing capabilities that rule-based systems fall short of. AI systems are designed to work in real time; they can analyze live data streams, detect slight deviations from patterns, and respond to an attack in as little as a few seconds. Whereas traditional tools tend to respond only after some harm is done, AI [24].

Stream Processing for Live Data Monitoring

Contemporary cyber defense systems rely heavily upon the process of analyzing and processing data in real time. Stream processing is the method that makes this possible through the processing of the streams of data as they are created, unlike waiting until these are aggregated into batches. AI extends the process of stream processing through the application of machine learning and deep learning techniques directly on the real-time data streams, so that the system is able to identify anomalies or suspicious activity as it occurs.

This is highly effective in situations like monitoring of traffic, where AI models can immediately identify sudden spikes in data, unusual access queries, or anomalous communication patterns. AI, along with tools such as Apache Kafka or Apache Flink, enables scalable, distributed processing platforms to handle large amounts of high-velocity data. These systems can change detection models dynamically based on live feedback, learning from each incident and getting better with time. Organizations can thus intercept threats at the early stage, minimizing the time between detection and response to seconds [25].

Predictive Analytics for Zero-Day Threats

One of the main challenges in the realm of cybersecurity is finding zero-day threats, vulnerabilities, or exploits that are unknown to security vendors and for which there is neither a patch nor a signature in place. Traditional systems fail in those scenarios because they are based on known threat profiles. But AI-designed predictive analytics is an auxiliary, in that it utilizes immense records to uncover marks of unclear or rising chances on the premise of conduct and setting versus specific trademarks [26].

Using historical information, system telemetry, and anomaly detection methods, AI is able to forecast potential weaknesses or untypical activity patterns that replicate known attack behaviour, possibly an unknown threat. Supervised learning methods can be used to train models to identify the patterns, i.e., your older zero-day exploits (not yet seen exploits), and unsupervised learning detects out-of-band activity that could mean a new threat. Predictive analytics employs probabilistic models to forecast the likelihood of another piracy attack, allowing the information security team to prepare and strengthen its defense too. This approach enables companies to take a proactive security stance, massively reducing the time it takes to identify and address anything that is new and unknown to bother the organization [27].

AI for Phishing and Social Engineering Detection

Attacks that exploit human vulnerabilities use phishing along with social engineering as their most successful methods over technical intrusions. The main threat from these techniques exists because they use human deception to make people perform dangerous actions like clicking on harmful links or giving away sensitive information. AI establishes an effective defense method that allows systems to detect suspicious content together with irregular communication signals and deceptive patterns employed in phishing schemes.

Natural Language Processing (NLP) operates as an AI subset to analyse the text within emails and websites, as well as messages by identifying abnormal language use and grammatical errors, together with urgent warnings and known phrasing elements associated with fraud. Machine learning models are trained with thousands of phishing samples before acquiring new samples perpetually so that they can counter sophisticated attacks that can beat conventional filtering systems. AI real-time processing supports operational sender legitimacy assessments that involve domain validation checks along with metadata inspection. AI technologies integrated with the email gateways, along with the defense at endpoints, and the filters at the browser, build effective vulnerability mitigations along with human-targeted cyber threats. AI acts as an assistive tool in user training programs by marking potentially dangerous content while providing instant feedback, which develops a staff group that better understands security threats.

The split between the three primary areas of AI-based real-time threat detection is depicted in Fig. (7) *via* a pie graph. The graph is divided into three slices representing the three primary methods: Stream Processing for Live Data Monitoring occupies 35% of the area, whereas Predictive Analytics for Zero-Day Threats occupies 40%, and AI for Phishing and Social Engineering Detection occupies 25%. The figures depict the way these solutions are relevant directly, as well as in practice, to present-day cybersecurity setups. The predictive analysis of zero-day threats constitutes the greatest segment (40%) in this sector because it stands as one of the most essential preventative measures for identifying unknown cyberattacks. Whole companies depend on artificial intelligence-driven models that enable organizations to identify exploits before public disclosure or implementation of security updates. The percentage of Stream Processing usage in Live Data Monitoring stands at 35%. The real-time tracking of high-speed network and endpoint data streams depends essentially on this monitoring technique. Security systems obtain basic and rapid threat detection capabilities through AI algorithms employed in stream processing platforms.

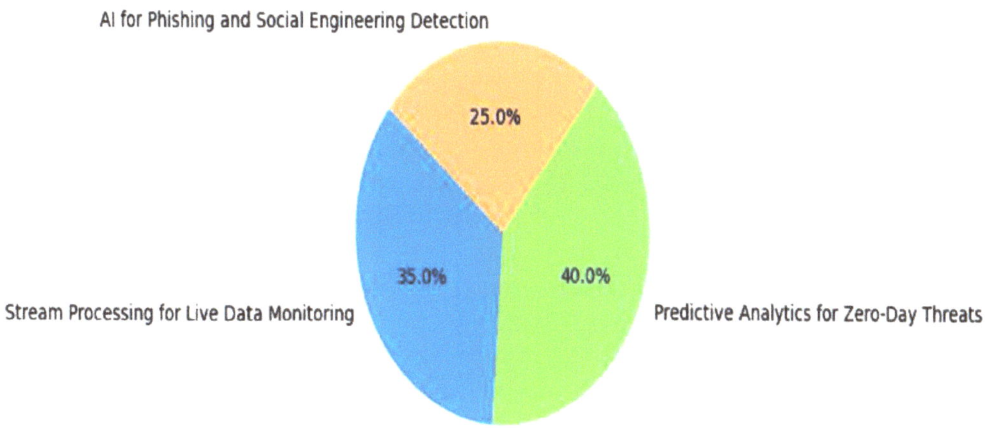

Fig. (7). Focus areas in real-time threat detection using AI.

AI for Phishing and Social Engineering Detection represents 25% of the market share because human-targeted attack protection has become increasingly important. The limited scope of this domain produces significant effects since numerous social engineering assaults use methods that overcome technological defenses. Enterprises require an AI-based cybersecurity strategy that integrates predictive intelligence capabilities with real-time monitoring capabilities and human-oriented threat detection systems to safeguard their environment appropriately.

AI IN ENDPOINT THREAT HUNTING

Endpoint threat hunting is quite crucial in the current world of cybersecurity. It's not so much about stopping the attacks–it's more about actively seeking out the blind spots that the automatic vulnerabilities could skirt around. And with the addition of AI, the threat hunters now possess a number of additional tools. AI enables the security teams to shift from just monitoring for stuff to go wrong to drilling into the data. They must be able to analyze boatloads of endpoint/ data, find out-of-the-ordinary behaviour, and correlate disparate threat indicators. Smart and continuous way of hunting really raises the situational awareness, accelerates detection of misbehaviours, and shortens dwell time within an organization's network. This segment explores how AI aids endpoint hunting, particularly focusing on the likes of data enhancement, network motion analysis, and even more remarkable methods like Graph Analytics [28].

Data Enrichment and Correlation

One of the major challenges for endpoint threat hunters is the analysis of the massive volumes of data that are aggregated from multiple endpoints and may include user activity event logs, application execution, and even processes running. AI addresses this problem by enriching and correlating the data, transforming raw telemetry into meaningful, actionable intelligence. An example of data enrichment is contextualizing raw data points, like having geolocation, reputation scores, or asset criticality associated with an IP address or user account. AI puts this on steroids by automating the analysis of these datasets and using threat intelligence to assign levels of risk to them. On top of that, the enriched data can be linked by machine learning models to many endpoints and correlations that a human analyst would not necessarily need. Failed login attempts by a single user from different machines could be innocent, but in combination, they could indicate a distributed brute-force attack. An APT action may also be a combination of low-severity anomalies identified by AI. Giving context to this understanding, hunters are then able to recognize sneaky attacks that rely on "piecemeal and hidden behaviour" [29].

Identifying Lateral Movement in Networks

Attackers who are successful at breaching an initial endpoint tend to shift laterally between systems to acquire additional privileges with the ultimate objective of accessing valuable resources. Current security tools find it challenging to identify these behaviours because these activities duplicate typical administrative procedures. Artificial Intelligence provides real-time analysis of lateral movement activities through behavioural patterns, authentication logs, file access trails, and network connections. AI systems trained with standard behavioural patterns can recognize when abnormal movements occur, which might indicate unethical lateral operations. When a device or user begins to access systems that it has never touched before during unexpected operational times while exercising increased permission levels, an AI-based warning could be generated. These models show the capability to detect known lateral movement tools such as

PsExec and RDP tunnelling and credential dumping utilities, even if they were obfuscated or concealed. AI-based endpoint solutions prevent lateral movement by continuously monitoring device behavior and network interactions to detect abnormal access patterns. They use machine learning to identify unauthorized privilege escalations or suspicious connections and automatically isolate compromised endpoints, stopping threats from spreading across the network.

AI platforms can track attacker dwell time, which helps them anticipate what is going to be the next move based on correlated earlier intrusion patterns. Sudden threat hunters are able to identify and contain compromised endpoints in neighbouring nodes before the attacker has any time to make further damage. The earliest discovery of lateral movement becomes possible with AI, which directly interferes with one of the most important stages of cyber-attack progression.

Use of Graph Analytics for Threat Tracing

Security analysts need a tool that can model the relationships between users, systems, processes, and events in order to detect emergent threats in highly complex enterprise environments. Graph analytics, one branch of AI that visualizes relationships between all data points and follows threats through networks, is especially good at this. In threat hunting, this methodology helps to visualize the entire kill chain from the initial entry point to lateral spread and ultimate payload execution. Graph-based AI models consider data as nodes (*e.g.*, user nodes, IP address nodes, application nodes) and edges (*e.g.*, a user check-in event, file transfers, or communication sessions). With this framework, the system can make fast decisions about central nodes, unusual connections, and the origins of suspicious behaviour. For instance, if an endpoint gets compromised through a phishing email, then graph analytics will identify the compromised user account, the attachment used, the processes it spawned out of the attachment, and all the endpoints contacted post this, essentially creating a visual representation of the path the attacker took. Through a unique combination of relational intelligence, temporal sequencing, and behaviour scoring, however, AI allows for the quick reconstruction of attack timelines and reveals hidden pivot points. Such analysis aids in real-time threat response, forensic investigations, and reinforcing future defensive measures [30].

Based on earlier calculations on cost and time savings, the bar chart in Fig (**8**) shows the total operational efficiency improvement (in %) on 3 core threat hunting tasks when AI is used. 70% more efficiency in data enrichment and correlation: Looking for signs of malware or IP of a malware (which has already been purchased) to automate log analysis and to match it with threat intelligence. AI capabilities of behavioural monitoring and anomaly detection provide an 85%

enhancement towards Lateral Movement Detection. The highest impact is noted in Graph-Based Threat Tracing, with a 90% gain, as AI efficiently maps complex relationships and uncovers attack chains faster than manual methods. This visualization reflects how AI reduces manual effort and enhances decision-making speed across threat hunting workflows [31, 32].

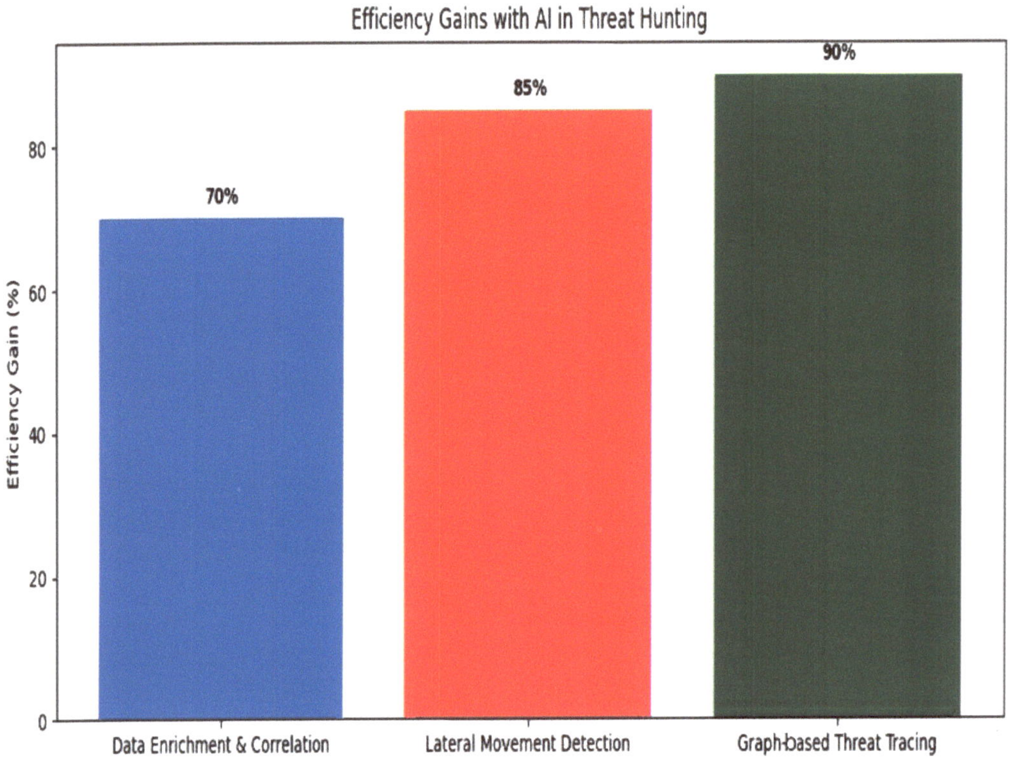

Fig. (8). Efficiency gains with AI in threat hunting.

The line graph in Fig. (**9**) compares detection speed across the same three AI-enabled tasks. Detection speed–indicated as a performance score out of 100, describes how fast threats can be detected. This function scores highest at 95 with the help of AI-augmented Graph-Based Threat Tracing that provides real-time visualization and tracing paths of an attack. Lateral Movement Detection scores second at 80, as AI models quickly identify unusual network traversal patterns. Data Enrichment and Correlation is 60, a modest but significant improvement. In summary, this graph emphasizes how AI speeds up the visibility of a threat, especially if it is a complex threat chain [33].

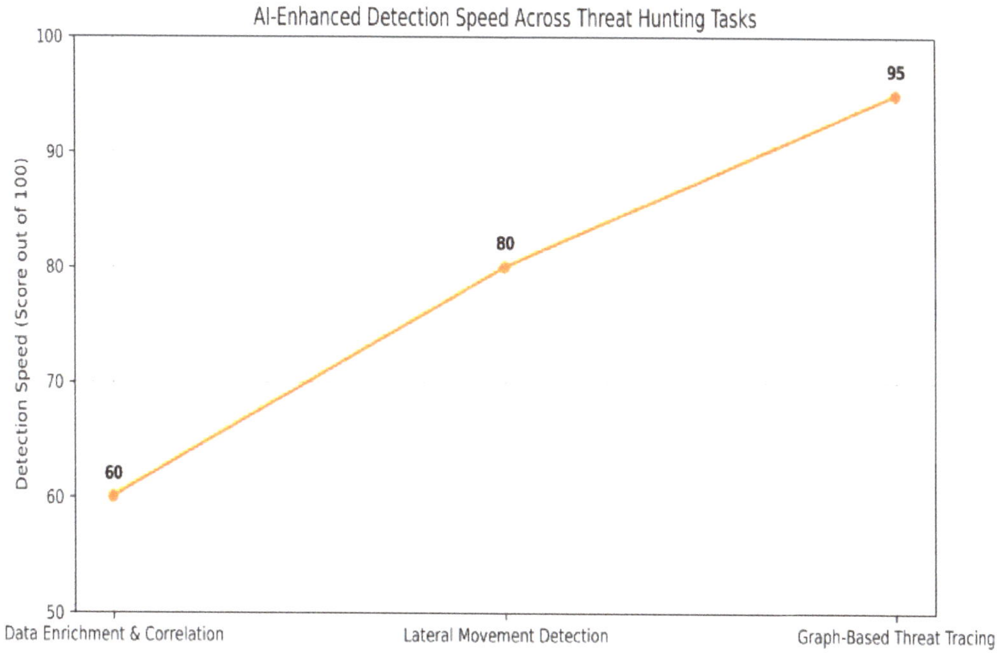

Fig. (9). Detection speed across threat hunting tasks.

Open Research Challenges and Future Directions

Despite the significant advancements that AI has brought to endpoint security, several open research challenges remain. These challenges must be addressed to fully harness the potential of AI technologies for creating a robust, scalable, and trustworthy endpoint defense mechanism [34].

Data Quality and Availability

AI models require large volumes of high-quality, labelled data for the training process; however, accessing diverse and real-world endpoint threat data is difficult due to privacy concerns, data sensitivity, and organizational silos. Developing privacy-preserving techniques could be a key direction to overcome this in the near future [35].

Adversarial Attacks against AI Models

Attackers are now targeting the AI systems through adversarial input crafted to fool models. More resilient AI models and adversarial-aware training techniques are needed to defend against such manipulation.

False Positives and Model Explainability

Although AI-based systems detect a broader spectrum of threats, they often struggle with high false positive rates, especially in earlier stages. Additionally, the "Black-box" nature of many models makes it difficult for security analysts to understand where the model went wrong in making decisions. Research into explainable AI and human-in-the-loop systems is essential for improving trust and transparency [36].

Resource Constraints on Endpoints

Many AI models require significant computing power, which is often not available on lightweight or legacy endpoints. Optimized AI models for edge computing and resource-constrained environments remain a vital research area. Looking ahead, hybrid approaches combining symbolic reasoning, graph analysis, and deep learning may offer more robust security frameworks. In parallel, the use of ethical AI, regulatory frameworks, and collaborative intelligence will shape the future of endpoint security [37].

CONCLUSION

In the current chapter, amid increasing threats on the Internet, endpoint security methods employed by many enterprises today have proven inadequate to meet compliance and security standards. In this chapter, we've underlined how the adoption of Artificial Intelligence into endpoint protection solutions presents a paradigm shift in the world of cybersecurity. AI helps organizations move from reactive to predictive and adaptive defense strategies, enabling real-time detection, analysis, and response to threats—minimizing damage and speeding up incident response time. We explored AI methods such as machine learning, behavioural analytics, and natural language processing. These systems can identify subtle anomalies, assist with difficult-to-detect attack patterns, and evolve to evolving threats. A portfolio of Endpoint Detection and Response (EDR) solutions shows just how pivotal AI has become in helping minimize the dwell time of attackers before they move laterally within networks. Lastly, an AI-enhanced endpoint solution leveraged within an overarching cybersecurity platform provides greater context and enables a coordinated defense and compliance with regulatory requirements. The huge upsides—agility, scalability, and resilience—outweigh the downsides, including ethical considerations, data privacy, and transparency of AI governance, among many others. The secret sauce of the cybersecurity future is that far from being an adjunct to endpoint security, AI is the underlying structure of this future class of such defense. In an increasingly hostile digital world, organizations that transition to an AI-powered, endpoint-first cyber model will realize they can more effectively protect digital assets and adapt to changing threat vectors.

REFERENCES

[1] S. Rangaraju, "Secure by intelligence: Enhancing products with AI-driven security measures", *EPH-Int. J. Sci. Eng.,* vol. 9, no. 3, pp. 36-41, 2023.

[2] M.A. Mahmoud Ahmed, and N.A. Md Yunus, "Securing the IoT frontier: Exploring the limitation and future directions in cybersecurity", *Int. J. Internet Broadcast. Commun.,* vol. 16, no. 2, pp. 1-9, 2024. [http://dx.doi.org/10.7236/IJIBC.2024.16.2.1]

[3] S.B. Latha, Y. Sucharitha, I.A. Tayubi, K. Shekar, D. Pandey, and R.V. Sudhakar, "Virtual learning analysis using complex rule-based approach in the context of cloud computing", In: *Proc. 2025 3rd Int. Conf. Commun., Secur., Artificial Intell. (ICCSAI).*, 2025, pp. 1110-1115. [http://dx.doi.org/10.1109/ICCSAI64074.2025.11064645]

[4] A. T. Somnathe, M. Parameshwari, S. Pattem, S. N. Koka, S. Abdurakhmanova, and P. C. S. Reddy, "An Attention-Based Deep Learning Framework for Gold Price Prediction Using Time Series Data", In: *Information Systems for Intelligent Systems.* ISBM 2025, A. Iglesias, J. Shin, N. Bhatt, A Joshi (eds) Information Systems for Intelligent Systems. ISBM 2025. Lecture Notes in Networks and Systems, vol 1743. Springer, Cham. [http://dx.doi.org/10.1007/978-3-032-13006-8_6]

[5] S.M. Doğan, A. Koçak, and M. Alkan, "Detection and mitigation of cyber-attacks in software defined networks using machine learning/deep learning: a systematic literature review, research challenges and future directions", *Int. J. Inf. Secur,* vol. 24, p. 209, 2025. [http://dx.doi.org/10.1007/s10207-025-01114-z]

[6] Aladiyan, "Digital safeguards: Unravelling the complex interplay between emerging threats and proactive cyber defense strategies", *J. Internet Serv. Inf. Secur.,* vol. 15, no. 1, pp. 348-360, 2025.

[7] Y. Sucharitha, P.C.S. Reddy, and G. Suryanarayana, “Network intrusion detection of drones using recurrent neural networks,” in Drone Technology: *Future Trends and Practical Applications*, S. N. Mohanty, J. V. R. Ravindra, G. Surya Narayana, and C. R. Pattnaik, Eds., Hoboken, NJ, USA: Wiley-Scrivener, 2023, pp. 375–392. [http://dx.doi.org/10.1002/9781394168002.ch15]

[8] H. Khan, "Balancing proactive and reactive strategies in cyber threat intelligence with ML-based predictive analytics", *East. Eur. J. Multidiscip. Res,* vol. 1, no. 1, pp. 46-59, 2024.

[9] Y.I. Alzoubi, A. Mishra, and A.E. Topcu, "Research trends in deep learning and machine learning for cloud computing security", *Artif Intell Rev,* vol. 57, p. 132, 2024. [http://dx.doi.org/10.1007/s10462-024-10776-5]

[10] N. Palanivel, K. Madhan, P.T. Sivashankar, C. Santhosh Kumar, and R. Sarath Kumar, "Enhanced QR CODE scanning and blockchain technology for drug packaging system", In: *Proc. 2024 Int. Conf. Syst., Comput., Autom. Netw. (ICSCAN)*, 2024, pp. 1-5.Puducherry, India [http://dx.doi.org/10.1109/ICSCAN62807.2024.10894169]

[11] A. Hozouri, A. Mirzaei, and M. Effatparvar, "A comprehensive survey on intrusion detection systems with advances in machine learning, deep learning and emerging cybersecurity challenges", *Discov Artif Intell,* vol. 5, p. 314, 2025. [http://dx.doi.org/10.1007/s44163-025-00578-1]

[12] G. Arun, P.C. Shaker Reddy, N. Budati, B. Rebecca, S. Perumalla, and V.B. Gujar, "A Deep learning framework for diabetes prediction: PIMA Indian dataset", In: *Proc. 2024 Int. Conf. Innov. Comput., Intell. Commun. Smart Electr. Syst. (ICSES)* Chennai, India, 2024, pp. 1-6. [http://dx.doi.org/10.1109/ICSES63760.2024.10910386]

[13] P.C.S. Reddy, G.L.P.K. Suryanarayana, and S. Yadala, "Data analytics in farming: rice price

prediction in Andhra Pradesh", *2022 5th International Conference on Multimedia, Signal Processing and Communication Technologies (IMPACT),* IEEE, pp. 1-5, 2022.

[14] K. Tallam, "Transforming cyber defense: Harnessing agentic and frontier AI for proactive, ethical threat intelligence", *arXiv preprint arXiv:2503.00164,* 2025.

[15] S.R. Pulyala, "From detection to prediction: AI-powered SIEM for proactive threat hunting and risk mitigation", *Turkish Journal of Computer and Mathematics Education (TURCOMAT),* vol. 15, no. 1, pp. 34-43, 2024. [http://dx.doi.org/10.61841/turcomat.v15i1.14393]

[16] N. Mohamed, "Artificial intelligence and machine learning in cybersecurity: a deep dive into state-o--the-art techniques and future paradigms", *Knowl Inf Syst,* vol. 67, pp. 6969-7055, 2025. [http://dx.doi.org/10.1007/s10115-025-02429-y]

[17] N. Patel, and K. Ethan, "ML-based threat detection: Enhancing cloud security with cutting-edge technologies", *Int. J. Trend Sci. Res. Dev,* vol. 4, no. 1, pp. 1362-1374, 2019.

[18] S. Thilagavathy, P. N. Renjith, R. V. S. Lalitha, M. Y. B. Murthy, Y. Sucharitha, and S. L. Narayanan, "A novel framework paradigm for EMR management cloud system authentication using blockchain security network", *Soft Computing,* pp. 1-9, 2023.

[19] A.T. Somnathe, V.T. Selvi, N.G. Stepha, M.T. Kingslin, F.M. Inamdar, and P.C.S. Reddy, "An intelligent traffic conflict prediction using deep learning with long-term evolution access data", In: *Proc. 2025 3rd Int. Conf. Smart Syst. for Appl. in Electr. Sci. (ICSSES)*, 2025, pp. 1-6. [http://dx.doi.org/10.1109/ICSSES64899.2025.11010032]

[20] R. Samrin, P.C.S. Reddy, K.A. Kumar, N. Deepthi, C. Mithra, S.B. Latha, Y. Sucharitha, and G.K. Thakur, "A hybrid deep learning based framework for prediction of rice yield through integration of biophysical parameters and optical remote sensing data in India", *J. Atmos. Solar-Terrestrial Phys.,* vol. 279, p. 106734, 2026. [http://dx.doi.org/10.1016/j.jastp.2026.106734]

[21] Rossi and G. Bianchi, "AI-Enhanced Cybersecurity Proactive Measures against Ransomware and Emerging Threats", *Innovative: Int. Multidiscip. J. Appl. Technol,* vol. 2, no. 11, pp. 77-92, 2024.

[22] M.D. Basith, P. Praveen, and P.C.S. Reddy, "Adaptive deep Q-GAN framework for enhanced breast cancer detection in medical imaging", *Biomedical Signal Processing and Control,* vol. 112, p. 108638, 2026. [http://dx.doi.org/10.1016/j.bspc.2025.108638]

[23] P. Ravali, P.C.S. Reddy, and P. Praveen, "An efficient neuro-framework for brain tumor classification using a CNN-based self-supervised learning approach with genetic optimizations", *Current Neuropharmacology,* vol. 24, no. 4, 2025. [http://dx.doi.org/10.2174/011570159X378103250806214613]

[24] K. Madhan, and N. Shanmugapriya, "Real time object detection in low light environment using adaptive image information enhancement algorithm", *International Research Journal of Multidisciplinary Scope,* vol. 5, no. 1, pp. 62-73, 2024. [http://dx.doi.org/10.47857/irjms.2024.v05i01.0145]

[25] G. Boyraz, *Endpoint detection and response essentials: Explore the landscape of hacking, defense, and deployment in EDR*, Softcover ed., Packt Publishing, 2024.

[26] S. Yalamati, "Fortifying cybersecurity: Harnessing AI for advanced threat detection and predictive analytics," in *Cutting-Edge Solutions for Advancing Sustainable Development: Exploring Technological Horizons for Sustainability—Part 1.* Bentham Science Publishers, 2025, pp. 190–207.

[27] M. Santhiya, M. Sindhuja, R. Jegatha, and J. Manikandan, "An effective automated framework for oral cancer detection by enhanced convolutional neural networks", In: *Proc. 2023 12th Int. Conf. Adv. Comput. (ICoAC)* IEEE, 2023, pp. 1-7. [http://dx.doi.org/10.1109/ICoAC59537.2023.10249983]

[28] B. Elov, A. Dauletov, Y. Sucharitha, F. Khalilova, M. Latipova, and M. Abdullayeva, "An intelligent traffic management of vehicles using deep learning approach in smart cities", In: *Proc. 2025 3rd Int. Conf. Integrated Circuits and Communication Systems (ICICACS)*Raichur, India, 2025, pp. 1-5. [http://dx.doi.org/10.1109/ICICACS65178.2025.10967703]

[29] M. J, and J. K, "Enhancing lung nodule classification: A novel CViEBi-CBGWO approach with integrated image preprocessing", *Journal of Digital Imaging,* vol. 37, no. 5, pp. 2108-2125, 2024. [http://dx.doi.org/10.1007/s10278-024-01074-1] [PMID: 38526706]

[30] D. Patil, "Artificial intelligence in cybersecurity: Enhancing threat detection and prevention mechanisms through machine learning and data analytics", *SSRN Electronic Journal,* 2024. Available from: https://ssrn.com/abstract=5057410

[31] A. Tanikonda, B.K. Pandey, S.R. Peddinti, and S.R. Katragadda, "Advanced ML-based cybersecurity solutions for proactive threat detection and response in complex ecosystems", *J. Sci. Technol.,* vol. 3, p. 1, 2022.

[32] A. Aladiyan, "Digital safeguards: Unravelling the complex interplay between emerging threats and proactive cyber defence strategies", *Journal of Internet Services and Information Security,* vol. 15, no. 1, pp. 348-360, 2025. [http://dx.doi.org/10.58346/JISIS.2025.I1.022]

[33] O. Marimuthu, P. Ravi, and S. Janarthanan, "Application of AI and ML in threat detection", In: *rotecting and Mitigating Against Cyber Threats: Deploying Artificial Intelligence and Machine Learning*Hoboken, NJ, USA: Wiley, 2025, p. 29. [http://dx.doi.org/10.1002/9781394305216.ch2]

[34] E. Indra, C. Geetha, N. Palanivel, K. Madhan, and J. Magesh Kumar, "Cloud-based secure interoperability of electronic health records sharing by using clinical document architecture", In: *Proc. 2024 Int. Conf. Systems, Computation, Automation and Networking (ICSCAN),* Puducherry, India, 2024, pp. 1-5. [http://dx.doi.org/10.1109/ICSCAN62807.2024.10894197]

[35] V. Sukhavasi, A.C. Mouli, D.V. Juneja, Y. Sucharitha, S.S. Joshi, and S. Dey, "Establishing ensemble learning models for daily rainfall forecasting", In: *Proc. 2024 International Conference on Innovative Computing, Intelligent Communication and Smart Electrical Systems (ICSES)* IEEE., 2024, pp. 1-6. [http://dx.doi.org/10.1109/ICSES63760.2024.10910429]

[36] V.K. Bukkarayasamudram, P.C.S. Reddy, K. Arun Kumar, R.M. Jagadish, S. Sharma, M. Lakshmi Prasad, Y. Sucharitha, I.A. Tayubi, and G.K. Thakur, "Quantum computing revolution in healthcare: A systematic review of applications, issues and future directions", *Artificial Intelligence Review,* vol. 58, p. 389, 2025. [http://dx.doi.org/10.1007/s10462-025-11381-w]

[37] S. M. Shaffi, S. Vengathattil, J. N. Sidhick, and R. Vijayan, "AI-Driven security in cloud computing: enhancing threat detection, automated response, and cyber resilience", *arXiv preprint arXiv:2505.03945,* 2025.

CHAPTER 8

Sentiment Analysis with AI: Approaches, Datasets, Applications, Limitations, Challenges, and Future Directions

Nikita Gaur[1,*] and **Sridhar Chintala**[1]

[1] *School of Computer Science & AI, SR University, Warangal 506371, Telangana, India*

Abstract: One important area of NLP is Sentiment Analysis (SA), which involves classifying texts as either positive, negative, or neutral. Organizations must understand the sentiments underlying these ideas in order to make informed decisions, especially with the rise of online platforms where people can freely share their views and opinions. Improved customer happiness, stronger brand reputation, and more money can be achieved when businesses understand the feelings behind consumers' perceptions and attitudes towards their products and services. Political analysts can also use sentiment analysis to learn how the public feels about various parties, candidates, and policies. The financial sector can also make use of sentiment research to forecast stock prices and spot investment opportunities by analyzing news stories and social media posts. Including preprocessing approaches, feature extraction techniques, classification strategies, commonly utilized datasets, and investigational results, this chapter offers an overview of the newest breakthroughs in sentiment analysis. In addition, this chapter explores the difficulties of SA datasets, as well as their limitations and potential for further study. This chapter also offers insightful information about the current status of sentiment analysis, which is important for researchers and practitioners alike, because of the field's significance. Researchers and interested parties can use this document as a resource for up-to-date information on sentiment analysis and how the subject is evolving.

Keywords: AI, Deep learning, Machine learning, NLP, Opinion mining, Sentimental analysis, Social media, Text processing.

INTRODUCTION

The exponential evolution of the Internet over the past decade has occasioned an overwhelming volume of online comments; understanding the feelings of netizens

* **Corresponding Author: Nikita Gaur:** Research Scholar, School of Computer Science & AI, SR University, Warangal, Telangana, India; E-mail: 2403c50120@sru.edu.in

Pundru Chandra Shaker Reddy, Yadala Sucharitha, & Thillaiarasu N (Eds.)

through these comments is crucial to societal progress and stability. Emerging as a reply to this trend is SA expertise. Opinion mining, or SA, is a significant subfield in NLP that aims to automatically extract and assess viewpoints and sentiment from text. The advancement of AI cannot be achieved without SA [1]. We can find positive, neutral, and negative sentiments, which can be further subdivided into numerous subtypes. From a linguistic standpoint, studies involving sentiment analysis can make use of a wide range of natural languages, including English, Chinese, and many more. The only way for machines to respond intelligently is for them to study and comprehend human facial expressions, which will ultimately benefit humans. The growth of online social networks, e-commerce, banking, healthcare, and government all rely on SA [2]. Comments on websites are skyrocketing since most people's lives are now online. Public belief oversight and decision-making in many businesses can be aided by automatically scrutinizing tens of thousands of notes and recording the psychological thinking of contributors proficiently, rapidly, and cheaply.

An area of study within natural language processing known as sentiment analysis is concerned with the automatic detection and classification of feelings and opinions conveyed in written language. The proliferation of social-media platforms has greatly enhanced the accessibility of public thoughts and sentiments. As a result, sentiment analysis has become an indispensable tool for understanding public sentiment in many fields, including commerce, politics, and others. Preprocessing, feature extraction, and classification are three key processes in the SA process. Stop words, special characters, and digits are among the irrelevant information that are cleaned out of the raw text data through the preprocessing [3]. Tools like GloVe, word2vec, fastText, and Term Frequency-Inverse Document-Frequency (TF-IDF) are utilized to convert the text input into features during this step as well. The ML strategies, as well as DL models like RNN and LSTM, are used to categorize the processed text into feelings in the feature extraction stage.

Deep learning models like **LSTM** and **Transformers** enhance sentiment analysis by capturing contextual and semantic relationships in text. **LSTMs** retain long-term dependencies to interpret meaning across word sequences, while **Transformers** use attention mechanisms to analyze all word relationships simultaneously. This contextual understanding enables more accurate detection of sentiment, even in complex or ambiguous expressions.

To find out how the general population feels about a topic, Sentiment Analysis (SA) uses tools from the fields of NLP, Computational Linguistics (CL), and text analytics to extract opinions and other subjective information from source materials and then labels them as positive/negative or neutral. The intersection of computers and human natural languages is the focus of NLP, a subfield of AI and linguistics [4]. By gleaning valuable insights from natively produced texts, NLP bridges the gap between machines and humans. Using several online data sources, SA aims to collect and analyze knowledge from personal data, reviews, and feedback. Sentence level, document level, and feature level are the three levels of SA. The goal here is to assign a favorable, negative, or neutral attitude to each opinion derived from a sentence, document, or aspect. Consequently, one can classify the methods according to their reliance on lexicons, machine learning, hybrid approaches, or, more recently, deep learning [5]. One method relies on algorithms trained on machine learning to identify and extract sentiment from data, while another uses a lexicon of sentiment terms, such as enhancement and negation, to count the number of positive and negative words in the data and determine the polarity of each phrase.

On the other hand, this approach relies on gleaning information from a statement that contains strongly held opinions. In the first stage of the deep learning-based approach, terms are learned by embedding them in the text corpus. The second stage uses these word embeddings to generate semantic composition interpretations of sentences using various deep learning approaches. Applying ML strategies greatly improves SA [6]. In this approach, a computer program is trained to carry out specific tasks, and it is said that the program has learned from its experience if and only if its measurable performance on these tasks improves over time. So, the data is the basis for the machine's decisions and forecasts. When training a model with labeled data is possible, a supervised learning strategy is utilized; otherwise, unsupervised learning is employed when the dependability of labeled data is questionable [7].

There are new opportunities to grasp people, groups, and society as a whole, thanks to the data collected from social media, which is currently the most dynamic signal base of human activity. Now more often referred to as "big social data," the vast amounts of data produced by social media use exhibit computational properties such as large quantity, noise, and dynamic nature [8]. Due to its unique properties, it necessitates the application of appropriate computational methods for analysis. Using SA on social network data, we can see if there's any societal drift in people's opinions, perceptions, and expectations. Organizations are increasingly utilizing SA with ML approaches on social network data to get insight into user sentiment and opinion shared on these platforms, as well as to predict future organizational trends and identify areas for strategy change for improved efficiency and effectiveness [9]. From keeping tabs on how people feel about a certain business to seeing how people feel about certain political or social issues to seeing trends and patterns in user opinions—which can help with decision-making—it has many potential uses.

Sentiment analysis supports threat detection by identifying emotional patterns that signal potential risks or hostile intent. Negative or aggressive sentiments in communications, social media posts, or online forums can indicate insider threats, radicalization, or planned attacks. By monitoring sentiment trends, security systems can detect early warning signs and respond proactively to emerging threats.

Examining relevant literature published between 2018 and 2022, this study aims to gather empirical and practical evidence and shed light on the use of ML for SA in social networks. By doing so, we can assess the phenomenon's scientific merit, validity, and social impact in other contexts, and thus establish a state-of-the-art level of analysis [10]. The theoretical underpinnings of the methodologies, models, and algorithms outlined in the reviewed literature are not supported by this study, and neither are the concepts themselves defined. Fig. (**1**) shows the three key sections of this chapter: methodology, applications, and challenges.

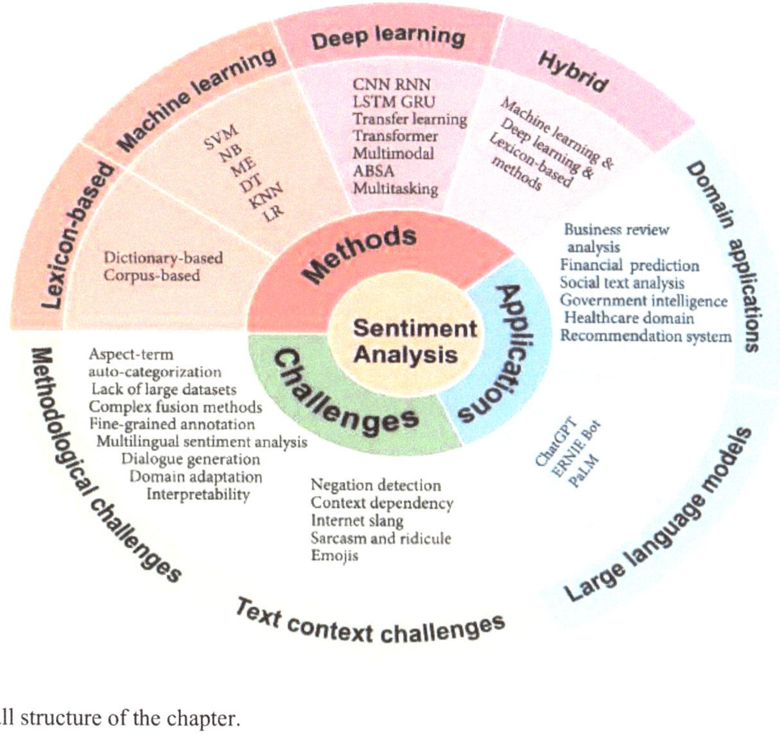

Fig. (1). Overall structure of the chapter.

A thorough overview of the most current developments in sentiment analysis is provided in this chapter. This study differs from others in that it classifies the examined works according to three distinct approaches: traditional machine learning, deep learning, and ensemble learning. Datasets, feature extraction methods, classification strategies, and preprocessing techniques are all covered in detail in this study, along with experimental results for each [11]. Also covered in this study are the common sentiment analysis datasets and the problems with them, the shortcomings of previous efforts, and where the area could go from here in terms of research.

This paper primarily contributes to the following areas:

- A thorough review of recent research on sentiment analysis, including conventional, deep, and ensemble learning approaches; an examination of these studies' preprocessing processes, feature extraction models, classification methods, datasets, and applications;
- A detailed examination of the most popular sentiment analysis datasets and the difficulties associated with them; finally, a review of the present literature's limitations and recommendations for future research in this area.

The rest of the piece is organized like this: The review of literature and the reasons for doing it are presented in Section II. The third section covers the various datasets that are utilized in sentiment analysis. Section IV offers the sentimental analysis's practical applications. Part V delves into the difficulties encountered and potential avenues for further research. Section VI presents the research discussions. In Section VII, the study comes to a close.

LITERATURE REVIEW

The present state of sentiment analysis algorithms is summarized in this section. It is the goal of SA to extract and classify the underlying feelings conveyed in written works. Preprocessing the raw text data, extracting features, and classifying them are all necessary procedures to complete this assignment. In order to normalize the text data and remove any extraneous or noisy parts, data preparation is a crucial step in sentiment analysis [12]. During this stage, methods including stemming, lemmatization, and eliminating stop words and special characters are employed. After the text data has been cleaned, it is turned into features or embeddings and put into the classifier to predict sentiment. It is important to consider the sentiment analysis task's unique needs and use case while selecting a classifier. In this part, we take a look back at the previous research on sentiment analysis, comparing and contrasting the various approaches taken for preprocessing, feature extraction, and classification [13]. As a first step in utilizing ML strategies for SA, preparing the text input to remove unnecessary information and standardize it is essential. To make the text usable by machine learning classifiers, feature extraction methods like TF-IDF and N-grams are used to convert it to numerical features. Decision trees, logistic regression, SVMs, NBs, and RFs are among the most popular classifiers used for SA.

Following the feature extraction process, the authors of a study [14] used multinomial naive Bayes to analyze sentiment in Tweets. They tested their method on the sentiment140 dataset, which includes 1.6M tweets that were tagged as neutral, positive, or negative. After dividing the dataset into a 9:1 training-testing ratio, the authors found that the multinomial NB model reached an accuracy of 87%. Also using naive Bayes, the authors of [15] examined Twitter reviews written by customers. The naive Bayes model attained a 77% accuracy rate after undergoing preprocessing processes such as tokenization and stemming. These works show that ML strategies, especially the NB classifier, are useful in sentiment analysis. For the purpose of SA, researchers in [16] tested the efficacy of two well-known ML strategies—NB and SVM—on Amazon customer evaluations. Before being represented by the a priori algorithm, the text data underwent preprocessing to eliminate stop words. With a precision of 91% *vs* 84%, NB was determined to be the superior model. On the IMDb dataset, the maximum entropy technique reached an accuracy of 88%, while on the sentiment dataset, it reached 90%. The findings demonstrated that the decision tree achieved 84% accuracy, AdaBoost 67% accuracy, and the support vector machine 82% accuracy [17].

Compared the efficacy of various ML models for sentiment analysis in an additional study [18]. C5.0, k-NN, SVM, LDA, classification and regression trees, and random forest were among the models used. After collecting a dataset of 1,150 product review Tweets, the authors performed preprocessing operations such as stemming, case folding, and amputation of stop words and punctuation. The text was subsequently fed into various models in the form of a term-document matrix. Among the decision tree algorithms tested, classification and regression trees demonstrated the best performance with an accuracy of 88.99%. A number of ML strategies for SA were thoroughly evaluated in a related work [19]. Several models were utilized, such as decision tree, k-NNs, LR, AdaBoost, Gaussian-NB, and random forest. A total of 14,640 tweets mentioning Indian Airlines were compiled and categorized as favorable, negative, or neutral by the writers. Methods like lemmatization and stopword removal were used to preprocess the text. The results demonstrated that boosting models outperform other models when it comes to sentiment classification accuracy, with the AdaBoost model reaching the best exactness of 92%. For sentiment analysis, the authors of a study [20] contrasted the efficacy of two ML strategies: multinomial-NB and SVC with linear kernels. About 10,000 tweets, including both positive &negative sentiment as well as neutral ones, were gathered from Twitter to make up the dataset. Methods, including stemming, URL, and stop-word removal, were used to preprocess the text. According to the findings, SVC was more accurate (82.48%) than multinomial-NBs (76.56%).

The authors of the study that looked into homosexuality in Indonesia suggested using an SVM approach to analyze the sentiment of Tweets about it [21]. The dataset was prepared using TF-IDF features, which involved removing stop words, lemmatization, and stemming. The SVM approach demonstrated an outstanding 99.5% accuracy on the dataset, according to the results. The SVM, NBs, and KNN were the three ML strategies that were compared in a study [22] for sentiment analysis. The dataset was split 80/20 between train and test, and it consisted of all the tweets on the 2019 Indonesian presidential candidates. Parsing text, tokenizing data, and mining text were all part of the preparation stages. In terms of accuracy, the findings demonstrated that naive Bayes achieved 75.58%, KNN 73.34%, and SVM 63.99%. The author of the study [23] used a Twitter dataset pertaining to Indian Railways to examine the efficacy of four ML models: C4.5, NB, SVM, and RF. There were three categories of sentiment in the dataset: positive, negative, and neutral. Among the methods tested, SVM produced the best outcomes at 91.5% accuracy, followed by C4.5 at 89.5%, RFt at 90.5%, and NB at 89%.

The SA using DL has been the subject of multiple surveys and review articles. An evaluation was conducted in 2023. An excellent overview of DL strategies and their use in SA was provided [24]. However, the limitations of current methods of SA based on DL and analytical analysis were not addressed. A recent review article from 2022 discussed sentiment analysis methods and their uses, but it glossed over the deep learning strategy. In 2022, there was another study that discussed several deep learning methods, their shortcomings, and potential problems in the future; however, this one did not include any data analysis [25]. In 2020, Dang published a review paper that summarizes DL-based SA, including the outcomes of many deep learning models' experiments, but fails to adequately address the research gaps that exist in the field. The year 2020 saw the publication of a review article on opinion mining using deep learning by [26]. Although the study provides a solid evaluation of the results of the performance, it is lacking in other analyses, research gaps, and specifics regarding the findings. A review study using Twitter data and soft computing was released in [27]. While the paper's analysis is well-done and covers a variety of tools, domains, and characteristics, the information regarding research gaps and strengths is lacking. The well-known datasets, important dataset attributes, taxonomy of SA models, levels of analysis, and deep learning models were detailed in a 2019 review article [28].

SENTIMENT ANALYSIS DATASETS

To train and evaluate SA models, sentiment analysis datasets are essential. There are a number of openly available and extensively utilized SA datasets that have been useful resources, even though some SA works employ datasets that were collected by the authors themselves [29]. Internet Movie Database (IMDb), Sentiment140, SemEval-2017 Task 4, and Twitter US Airline Sentiment are among these datasets.

Internet Movie Database (IMDb)

An extensive and evenly distributed set of 50,000 movie reviews may be found in the Internet Movie Database (IMDb) dataset. Half of the 25,000 reviews in this dataset are favorable, and the other half are negative. The dataset has been divided in half. Given the intricate structure of the reviews in this dataset, sentiment analysis models face a formidable hurdle [30]. It can be difficult for algorithms to reliably ascertain the general sentiment of a review because the movie reviews in the IMDb dataset contain both narrative and subjective comments. There are two columns in the dataset labeled "review" and "sentiment," and sentiment analysis models have an additional challenge due to the intricate language used in reviews [31].

Twitter US Airline Sentiment

It was compiled by CrowdFlower in 2017 and provides an extensive archive of consumer evaluations for six prominent American airlines. Academics in the subject are always on the lookout for new datasets like this one because it gives a great tool for testing sentiment analysis models in practical settings [32]. There are 23,363 observations in the positive sentiment class, 9,178 in the negative sentiment class, and 30,99 in the neutral sentiment class in this dataset. Since most samples fall into the negative sentiment category, this dataset presents a significant problem in terms of class imbalance, which in turn can impact the precision of sentiment analysis models. The dataset's Tweets are brief and informal, adding to the problems caused by class imbalance, which further complicates matters for sentiment analysis models [33]. Due to their informal tone and brief length, tweets sometimes omit key contextual and emotionally charged words. Because of these difficulties, sentiment analysis models may incorrectly categorize Tweets, making it harder to extract meaningful emotions from these messages.

Sentiment140

Stanford University's Sentiment140 dataset [34] compiles extensive customer sentiment data mined from Twitter. There are 1.6M samples total, with an equal number of positive and negative sentiments. Tweets in the Sentiment140 dataset are often brief and casual, which might be difficult for SA models to handle. Because tweets are usually shorter and more informal than other types of communication, the tone of the message could be unclear. Sentiment analysis models may fail to correctly determine a Tweet's sentiment since they fail to capture key phrases or context that convey the sentiment [35].

SemEval-2017 Task 4

When it comes to testing SA models on text data from social media, the International Workshop on Semantic Evaluation (SemEval) is the place to go. Since 2013, sentiment analysis on Twitter has been one of the main jobs hosted by SemEval. As mentioned in [36], the most recent version of this shared task is the SemEval-2017 Task 4 dataset. Its dataset contains data in both English and Arabic, setting it apart from earlier SemEval datasets that just contained English data. Focusing on the English section of the dataset was the primary aim of the paper's writers.

APPLICATIONS OF SENTIMENT ANALYSIS

Business Domain

The field of business analysis greatly benefits from SA. As an example, sentiment analysis can help businesses enhance their products and services by collecting customer feedback and enhancing market tactics. Also, buyers may use the study to compare items and get a better idea of what to buy. So, it's not just for product companies. In order to identify potential factors that affect the accuracy of sentiment categorization, the authors of another study [37] examined Chinese online reviews across different areas. Additionally, for a decade, they have compiled meal reviews posted by Amazon.com customers. The research categorized evaluations into eight emotions—surprise, trust, anticipation, anger, fear, sadness, disgust, and joy—using the NRC emotion lexicon. The financial market and stock price forecasts were also informed by sentiment analysis. It is possible to forecast stock price patterns by analyzing all market news. Weibo, blogs, Twitter, the news, and many other platforms provide numerous opportunities to gather datasets. The use of news in predicting the direction of stock price trends was documented in a review [38]. As a general rule, trends rose in response to positive news and declined in response to negative news. Additionally, they looked at how news-related emotions affected the volume, volatility, and returns of both traditional currencies and digital ones, such as bitcoin. In light of the meteoric rise of social media platforms, it may be possible to foretell how these platforms will evolve in the future by using SA technology to sift through user comments and extract sentiment patterns expressed by keywords. During Russia's attack against Ukraine, the authors of [39] looked into Twitter sentiment analysis. Prior to categorizing the tweet evaluations, the article located databases regarding pertinent hashtags. Amidst the backdrop of increasing gasoline prices, they used machine learning techniques to examine consumer sentiment on electric vehicles.

Government Intelligence

Comments on current events, politics, and everyday life have proliferated with the rise of social media platforms online. The government can track possible public reactions by using SA to find ideas on socially hot issues or policy [40]. It would be wise for the government to come up with appropriate policies or conduct similar actions. The study looked at tweets from US city governments to see how public opinion influences their engagement with the government on social media [41]. It is often necessary to perform sentiment analysis in real-time in order to track public opinion. Using the Sentiment Political Compass (SPC), the authors of a study [42] determined the closeness of newspapers and political parties in order to study the impact of media bias on voter sentiment.

Healthcare Domain

In recent years, SA has found extensive use in the medical and therapeutic fields. Using this tool, medical personnel can better understand and treat patients by collecting and analyzing data on diseases, adverse drug responses, epidemics, and patients' emotions. With the use of sentiment analysis and maritime health data, this study presents text mining applications. The ability to visually represent patient symptoms is incredibly useful for healthcare providers and organizations [43]. Keeping track of medical records, evaluating patient input, and improving patient knowledge of issues are powerful tools. In order to model data and reviews from colon patients, the authors of another study [44] used three deep learning techniques: LSTM, GRU, and CNN. The purpose of this study is to analyze the Colon cancer datasets in order to forecast the occurrence of future diseases.

Scientometric Analysis

Within scientific citations, it seeks to understand the feelings of the writers. The application of sentiment analysis in many settings might be greatly enhanced by this area. Yet, when it comes to citations in scientific literature, South Africa has conducted very few studies. A review of sentiment analysis in scientific citations was provided by the authors of a study [45]. Several approaches were suggested, and the primary obstacles were outlined. Furthermore, the writers incorporated pertinent domains that have lately garnered significant interest, like the classification of citation functions and citation suggestion.

LIMITATIONS AND FUTURE RESEARCH PROSPECTS

Despite the fact that sentiment analysis has come a long way, there are still obstacles that prevent it from being completely accurate and useful. Problems with managing sarcastic and badly organized texts are among these constraints [46]. Other issues include reliance on annotated data, word embeddings' limits, the possibility of bias in the training data, and the absence of fine-grained sentiment analysis.

- Social media postings, slang, and snarky remarks are examples of informal and poorly structured texts that might be difficult for sentiment analysis tools to accurately analyze because they rely on well-formed and grammatically correct material. The reasons behind this are that the feelings conveyed in these works often go beyond what can be understood by superficial examination and necessitate a deeper grasp of the context.
- Coarse-Grained Sentiment Analysis: While neutral, positive, and negative categories are frequently employed in sentiment analysis, it's possible that they don't encompass the entire spectrum of human emotions and their intensities. Sentiment analysis that is more granular, such as fine-grained sentiment analysis, can reveal more subtleties in the meaning of a text by classifying emotions into more precise categories, such as joyful, sad, furious, or startled.
- Ignorance of Cultural Differences: Models for SA trained on data from one culture or language might not be able to convey the feelings conveyed in texts written in a different language or culture. This is due to the fact that culturally specific expressions, idioms, and language usage might yield inaccurate results when applied to sentiment analysis models trained on different cultures.
- Annotated data, in which people manually mark the sentiment of a document, is frequently used by sentiment analysis algorithms. On the other hand, it can be laborious and resource-intensive to gather and annotate a big dataset, which might restrict the study to a certain language or domain.
- Word embeddings have limitations when it comes to capturing the intricate links between words and their meanings in a text. Word embeddings are a prominent technique utilized in SA that relies on deep learning. Inaccurate analysis may come from a model that fails to capture the intended meaning of a text.
- One potential issue is bias in the training data utilized to train SA models. If the data is skewed, the accuracy and generalizability of the models trained on that data could be compromised. To illustrate the point, a model can develop bias if it is trained on a dataset that primarily contains texts from a certain gender or ethnicity. This bias can then cause the model to incorrectly predict messages from other groups.

Research in the future can concentrate on making sentiment analysis more precise and comprehensive in order to tackle these issues [47]. Among these goals can be the improvement of SA's applicability to social-media platforms, the development of more nuanced models for capturing texts' emotional intensity, the expansion of cross-lingual SA's scope, the handling of ambiguous and sarcastic texts, and the quantification of sentiment distribution across different topics.

- **Analysis of Sentiment at a Fine-grained Level:** Generally speaking, there are three broad categories that are present in most SA models: positive, negative, and neutral. Nevertheless, it must be expanded to encompass fine-grained SA, which encompasses varying emotional intensities like extremely positive, neutral, negative, and extremely negative. By experimenting with different deep learning architectures and methods, researchers may do sentiment analysis at a finer level. Hierarchical attention networks are one method that can do this; they can pick up on the tone of a text at various levels of detail.
- The quantification of sentiment is a significant use case for sentiment analysis. In order to help with strategic decision-making, it entails computing the topic-based polarity distributions. In order to better capture the emotion distribution across various themes, researchers can construct more complex models. You may accomplish this in a few different ways. One is to utilize topic modeling strategies to find the main subjects in a large text corpus. Then, you can use sentiment analysis to figure out how people feel about each issue.
- **Dealing with Sarcasmic and Ambiguous Texts:** Sentiment analysis algorithms have difficulties when it comes to reliably identifying sentiment in texts that are ambiguous or sarcastic. Train models to handle ambiguous and caustic texts by exploring the application of reinforcement learning approaches. This necessitates the creation of models with the ability to absorb feedback and modify their predictions appropriately.
- **Sentiment Analysis Across Languages:** At present, most SA strategies are taught using English text. The demand, however, for SA models that are multilingual, is increasing. An expanded audience could benefit from SA with the use of cross-lingual sentiment analysis, which would improve our understanding of sentiment expressed in many languages. In order to create sentiment analysis models that are multilingual, researchers can investigate transfer learning methods. One method involves training models on massive multilingual corpora before refining them for language-specific sentiment analysis.
- **Social Media Sentiment Analysis:** The sheer volume of data generated daily by social media networks makes manual processing a daunting task. If researchers want to make sentiment analysis models more accurate, they can train them on text from social media and then incorporate domain-specific embeddings.

Additionally, by utilizing user interactions and contextual information, they can train models to handle brief or loud social-media text.

- Multilingual and domain-specific datasets challenge sentiment analysis due to language diversity, cultural nuances, and specialized jargon. Models trained on one language or domain often fail to generalize, and limited labeled data in less-resourced contexts further reduces accuracy.

The area of SA can broaden its practical uses and offer useful insights into text sentiment if it overcomes these restrictions and develops more sophisticated models.

DISCUSSION

When it came to SA tasks, the researchers favored the general sentiment lexicons over the domain-specific ones. One probable explanation is the relative ease with which general sentiment lexicons can be constructed. Furthermore, the vast majority of sentiment lexicons utilized in primary research are applicable worldwide [48]. An issue with sentiment lexicons is that they need to be updated regularly to keep up with society's progress. Furthermore, lexicon-based approaches necessitate exact word-for-word matching between text and dictionary terms, which means they must deal with slang, negative expressions, spelling mistakes, and synonyms. To go beyond the restrictions of earlier lexicon-based approaches, most researchers opted for traditional deep learning and machine learning approaches for SA problems [49]. Because of its great accuracy on numerous public datasets, SVM is the ML approach most commonly employed for SA tasks. The capacity of SVM to deal with high-dimensional text features could be the explanation. But SVM's training time grows exponentially with the size of the training datasets, which is a major downside.

Additional semantic tokens and contextual information are needed for SA tasks due to their unique nature compared to other natural language processing tasks. Consequently, it is important to pay attention to crucial tokens that impact the overall attitude of the sentence context, and choosing these tokens is difficult [50]. It is possible to learn contextual information and infer textual meaning by modifying the BERT model's output layer. When the computational demands are too great, it becomes impossible to do research. The experiment was run by deleting various components of the original design to get around these problems. In a similar vein, the BERT model was used to perform SA flawlessly in numerous languages, including Russian, Arabic, German, French, and Chinese [51].

Feature extraction is essential in sentiment analysis as it converts raw text into numerical representations usable by machine learning models. **TF-IDF** highlights important sentiment-bearing words by measuring their relevance within a text, while **word embeddings** like **Word2Vec**, **GloVe**, and **BERT** capture semantic meaning and context between words. These techniques enable models to understand emotional tone, word relationships, and nuanced expressions, thereby improving the accuracy of sentiment classification.

Recent years have seen substantial performance increases attained by ABSA, a fine-grained SA study. Having said that, a number of problems persist. Conventional approaches expose the domain adaptation issue of performance reduction when the ABSA model's use domain differs from the training datasets' field. Still, it's crucial to train the right model with a large sample corpus for each task domain so it can capture the right contextual factors. Using SemEval's public benchmark datasets in the laptop and restaurant domains, about half of the ABSA research was conducted [52]. Nevertheless, ABSA models that incorporate domain-specific labels perform the best. Simply said, various domains could provide distinct interpretations to the same sentimental phrases. Hence, ABSA models that are trained on datasets specific to one domain typically fail miserably when applied to datasets from another domain. Furthermore, standard technology fails to correctly link multiple-aspect words retrieved from various comment sentences, leading to the extraction of inaccurate aspect terms [53]. Aspect extraction performance might be negatively impacted by invalid aspect extraction. To find out what the aspect and opinion terms mean, it's helpful to gather correlation information within the sentence and look at the context. The extraction of aspect terms may also benefit from models based on supervised hierarchical attention and the BERT representation. Before running ABSA, it is conceivable to include processes for sentence co-reference resolution as preprocessing [54].

Sentiment analysis is increasingly used for threat prediction and user-risk profiling. In organizations, it helps detect insider threats by identifying negative emotions such as anger or frustration in employee communications. On social media, it flags hostile or extremist language that may indicate cyberbullying or radical behavior. In cybersecurity, analyzing dark web discussions through sentiment trends can reveal early signs of planned attacks. Financial institutions use sentiment cues in customer interactions to detect fraud or risky behavior. By integrating emotional tone analysis with predictive models, sentiment analysis enables proactive identification of threats and high-risk users across digital platforms.

CONCLUSION

An exhaustive survey of research on text sentiment analysis is presented in this chapter. An overview of the three tiers of sentiment analysis—document, sentence, and aspect—was provided first. As a second point, this chapter outlined the many SA strategies and weighed the pros and cons of each. After that, we went over some of SA's uses, including its potential in the commercial world, government intelligence, the healthcare industry, and recommendation systems. Also included are some of the most cutting-edge SA big language models, such as PaLM, ERNIE Bot, and ChatGPT. After that, we went into detail about the problem's sentiment analysis, which shows that there are a lot of open questions about the field. Given its versatility, sentiment analysis has emerged as a key subfield within NLP. Traditional machine learning approaches were used in the first sentiment analysis studies to normalize the text, eliminate stop words, and represent the text using frequency-based features like TF-IDF or bag of words. Next, machine learning methods like SVM, naive Bayes, and others were used to classify the cleaned text. Researchers' attention has moved from natural language processing to deep learning techniques, though, due to developments in NLP.

There have to be more dependable language models since current sentiment analysis approaches can't handle badly organized or sarcastic messages, no matter how far the field has come. Furthermore, the majority of the present literature on SA tends to lump sentiments into broad categories like positive, negative, and neutral. However, it would be beneficial for future studies to concentrate on fine-grained SA, which could incorporate classes with different levels of emotional intensity, such as extremely positive and extremely negative. Strategic decision-making may also benefit from sentiment quantification, which involves calculating the polarity distribution of an issue. In conclusion, sentiment analysis enhances cybersecurity by detecting emotional cues linked to insider threats, radicalization, and malicious intent. When integrated with threat intelligence and behavioral analytics, it enables early threat identification and strengthens proactive cyber defense mechanisms.

DECLARATION

The English language of the article was improved with ChatGPT.

REFERENCES

[1] A. Gandhi, K. Adhvaryu, S. Poria, E. Cambria, and A. Hussain, "Multimodal sentiment analysis: A systematic review of history, datasets, multimodal fusion methods, applications, challenges and future directions", *Inf. Fusion,* vol. 91, pp. 424-444, 2023. [http://dx.doi.org/10.1016/j.inffus.2022.09.025]

[2] M. Wankhade, A.C.S. Rao, and C. Kulkarni, "A survey on sentiment analysis methods, applications, and challenges", *Artif. Intell. Rev.,* vol. 55, no. 7, pp. 5731-5780, 2022. [http://dx.doi.org/10.1007/s10462-022-10144-1]

[3] M.S. Islam, M.N. Kabir, N.A. Ghani, K.Z. Zamli, N.S.A. Zulkifli, M.M. Rahman, and M.A. Moni, "Challenges and future in deep learning for sentiment analysis: a comprehensive review and a

proposed novel hybrid approach", *Artif. Intell. Rev.,* vol. 57, no. 3, p. 62, 2024. [http://dx.doi.org/10.1007/s10462-023-10651-9]

[4] A. Alslaity, and R. Orji, "Machine learning techniques for emotion detection and sentiment analysis: current state, challenges, and future directions", *Behav. Inf. Technol.,* vol. 43, no. 1, pp. 139-164, 2024. [http://dx.doi.org/10.1080/0144929X.2022.2156387]

[5] K.L. Tan, C.P. Lee, and K.M. Lim, "A survey of sentiment analysis: Approaches, datasets, and future research", *Appl. Sci. (Basel),* vol. 13, no. 7, p. 4550, 2023. [http://dx.doi.org/10.3390/app13074550]

[6] T. Anilsagar, and S. S. A. Syed, "The evolution of sentiment analysis and conversational AI: Techniques, applications, and future research directions", *J. Syst. Eng. Electron.,* vol. 35, no. 1, .

[7] J. R. Jim, M. A. R. Talukder, P. Malakar, M. M. Kabir, K. Nur, and M. F. Mridha, "Recent advancements and challenges of NLP-based sentiment analysis: A state-of-the-art review", *Natural Language Processing Journal,* vol. 6, p. 100059. [http://dx.doi.org/10.1016/j.nlp.2024.100059]

[8] N. Rani, and R. Walia, "A comprehensive review of sentiment analysis: Techniques, datasets, limitations, and future scope", In: *2024 Sixth International Conference on Computational Intelligence and Communication Technologies (CCICT)* IEEE., 2024, pp. 403-409.

[9] M. Birjali, M. Kasri, and A. Beni-Hssane, "A comprehensive survey on sentiment analysis: Approaches, challenges and trends", *Knowl. Base. Syst.,* vol. 226, p. 107134, 2021. [http://dx.doi.org/10.1016/j.knosys.2021.107134]

[10] N.A. Sharma, A.S. Ali, and M.A. Kabir, "A review of sentiment analysis: tasks, applications, and deep learning techniques", *Int. J. Data Sci. Anal.,* pp. 1-38, 2024.

[11] K. Patel, D. Mehta, C. Mistry, R. Gupta, S. Tanwar, N. Kumar, and M. Alazab, "Facial sentiment analysis using AI techniques: state-of-the-art, taxonomies, and challenges", *IEEE Access,* vol. 8, pp. 90495-90519, 2020. [http://dx.doi.org/10.1109/ACCESS.2020.2993803]

[12] A. T. Somnathe, V. T. Selvi, N. G. Stepha, M. T. Kingslin, F. M. Inamdar, and P. C. S. Reddy, "An intelligent traffic conflict prediction using deep learning with long-term evolution access data", In: *2025 3rd International Conference on Smart Systems for Applications in Electrical Sciences (ICSSES)* IEEE, 2025, pp. 1-6. [http://dx.doi.org/10.1109/ICSSES64899.2025.11010032]

[13] Y. Mao, Q. Liu, and Y. Zhang, "Sentiment analysis methods, applications, and challenges: A systematic literature review", *J. King Saud Univ. - Comput. Inf. Sci.,* p. 102048, 2024. [http://dx.doi.org/10.1016/j.jksuci.2024.102048]

[14] A.A. Aladeemy, A. Alzahrani, M.H. Algarni, S.N. Alsubari, T.H.H. Aldhyani, S.N. Deshmukh, O.I. Khalaf, W.K. Wong, and S. Aqburi, "Advancements and challenges in Arabic sentiment analysis: A decade of methodologies, applications, and resource development", *Heliyon,* vol. 10, no. 21, p. e39786, 2024. [http://dx.doi.org/10.1016/j.heliyon.2024.e39786] [PMID: 39553679]

[15] Q.A. Xu, V. Chang, and C. Jayne, "A systematic review of social media-based sentiment analysis: Emerging trends and challenges", *Decision Analytics Journal,* vol. 3, p. 100073, 2022. [http://dx.doi.org/10.1016/j.dajour.2022.100073]

[16] G. Arun, P.C.S. Reddy, N. Budati, B. Rebecca, S. Perumalla, and V.B. Gujar, "A deep learning framework for diabetes prediction: PIMA Indian dataset", In: *2024 International Conference on Innovative Computing, Intelligent Communication and Smart Electrical Systems (ICSES)* IEEE., 2024, pp. 1-6.

[17] S. Kusal, S. Patil, J. Choudrie, K. Kotecha, D. Vora, and I. Pappas, "A systematic review of applications of natural language processing and future challenges with special emphasis in text-based

emotion detection", *Artif. Intell. Rev.,* vol. 56, no. 12, pp. 15129-15215, 2023.
[http://dx.doi.org/10.1007/s10462-023-10509-0]

[18] H.M.U. Ali, Q. Farooq, A. Imran, and K. El Hindi, "A systematic literature review on sentiment analysis techniques, challenges, and future trends", *Knowl. Inf. Syst.,* vol. 67, no. 5, pp. 3967-4034, 2025.
[http://dx.doi.org/10.1007/s10115-025-02365-x]

[19] A. Yadav, and D.K. Vishwakarma, "Sentiment analysis using deep learning architectures: a review", *Artif. Intell. Rev.,* vol. 53, no. 6, pp. 4335-4385, 2020.
[http://dx.doi.org/10.1007/s10462-019-09794-5]

[20] S. Kusal, S. Patil, J. Choudrie, K. Kotecha, D. Vora, and I. Pappas, "A review on text-based emotion detection--techniques, applications, datasets, and future directions", In: *arXiv preprint arXiv:2205.03235,* 2022.

[21] R.A. García-Hernández, H. Luna-García, J.M. Celaya-Padilla, A. García-Hernández, L.C. Reveles-Gómez, L.A. Flores-Chaires, J.R. Delgado-Contreras, D. Rondon, and K.O. Villalba-Condori, "A systematic literature review of modalities, trends, and limitations in emotion recognition, affective computing, and sentiment analysis", *Appl. Sci. (Basel),* vol. 14, no. 16, p. 7165, 2024.
[http://dx.doi.org/10.3390/app14167165]

[22] V.K. Bukkarayasamudram, P.C.S. Reddy, and K. Arun Kumar, "Quantum computing revolution in healthcare: a systematic review of applications, issues and future directions", *Artif Intell Rev,* vol. 58, p. 389, 2025.
[http://dx.doi.org/10.1007/s10462-025-11381-w]

[23] J.Y.L. Chan, K.T. Bea, S.M.H. Leow, S.W. Phoong, and W.K. Cheng, "State of the art: a review of sentiment analysis based on sequential transfer learning", *Artif. Intell. Rev.,* vol. 56, no. 1, pp. 749-780, 2023.
[http://dx.doi.org/10.1007/s10462-022-10183-8]

[24] I. A. Tayubi, D. N. Pawar, A. Kiran, P. C. S. Reddy, N. Sharma, and D. Chitra, "Facial emotion recognition using a local binary pattern based deep learning", In: *2024 2nd International Conference on Computer, Communication and Control (IC4)*, 2024, pp. 1-7.
[http://dx.doi.org/10.1109/IC457434.2024.10486509]

[25] N. Rane, S. Choudhary, and J. Rane, "Machine learning and deep learning: A comprehensive review on methods, techniques, applications, challenges, and future directions", In: *Techniques, Applications, Challenges, and Future Directions*, 2024.
[http://dx.doi.org/10.2139/ssrn.4850451]

[26] A. Ghorbanali, and M.K. Sohrabi, "A comprehensive survey on deep learning-based approaches for multimodal sentiment analysis", *Artif. Intell. Rev.,* vol. 56, no. S1, suppl. Suppl. 1, pp. 1479-1512, 2023.
[http://dx.doi.org/10.1007/s10462-023-10555-8]

[27] T.A. Al-Qablan, M.H. Mohd Noor, M.A. Al-Betar, and A.T. Khader, "A survey on sentiment analysis and its applications", *Neural Comput. Appl.,* vol. 35, no. 29, pp. 21567-21601, 2023.
[http://dx.doi.org/10.1007/s00521-023-08941-y]

[28] S.B. Latha, Y. Sucharitha, I.A. Tayubi, K. Shekar, D. Pandey, and R.V. Sudhakar, "Virtual learning analysis using complex rule-based approach in the context of cloud computing", In: *Proc. 2025 3rd Int. Conf. Commun., Security, and Artificial Intelligence (ICCSAI)* vol. 3. Greater Noida, India, 2025, pp. 1110-1115.
[http://dx.doi.org/10.1109/ICCSAI64074.2025.11064645]

[29] S. Sushma, S.K. Nayak, and M.V. Krishna, "A comprehensive review of sentiment analysis: trends, challenges, and future directions", In: *Proc. 2024 5th Int. Conf. Data Intelligence and Cognitive Informatics (ICDICI)* IEEE, 2024, pp. 1175-1181.
[http://dx.doi.org/10.1109/ICDICI62993.2024.10810919]

[30] G.K. Thakur, L.P. Mudarakola, M. Sreenivasulu, V. Krishna B, I.R. Raja, I.A. Tayubi, and Y. Sucharitha, "An enhanced prediction framework for blood-brain barrier permeability: DeePred-BBB", *Recent Patents on Engineering,* vol. 19, no. 9, p. E18722121342031, 2025. [http://dx.doi.org/10.2174/0118722121342031250218042131]

[31] A. Diwali, K. Saeedi, K. Dashtipour, M. Gogate, E. Cambria, and A. Hussain, "Sentiment analysis meets explainable artificial intelligence: a survey on explainable sentiment analysis", *IEEE Trans. Affect. Comput.,* 2023. [http://dx.doi.org/10.1109/TAFFC.2023.XXXXXXX]

[32] M. Indrasenareddy, N.S. Bohra, S. Mukherjee, Y. Sucharitha, M. Yesubabu, and M.L. Prasad, "Working toward a comprehensive approach for ensuring security and privacy in artificial intelligence", In: *Leveraging Artificial Intelligence in Cloud, Edge, Fog and Mobile Computing* Auerbach Publications, 2025, pp. 3-18. [http://dx.doi.org/10.1201/9781032703718]

[33] S. Elzeheiry, W.A. Gab-Allah, N. Mekky, and M. Elmogy, "Sentiment analysis for e-commerce product reviews: Current trends and future directions", *Preprint,* 2023. [http://dx.doi.org/10.20944/preprints202305.1649.v1]

[34] B. Elov, A. Dauletov, Y. Sucharitha, F. Khalilova, M. Latipova, and M. Abdullayeva, "An intelligent traffic management of vehicles using deep learning approach in smart cities", In: *Proc. 2025 3rd Int. Conf. Integrated Circuits and Commun. Syst. (ICICACS)*Raichur, India, 2025, pp. 1-5. [http://dx.doi.org/10.1109/ICICACS65178.2025.10967703]

[35] W. Aljedaani, E. Saad, F. Rustam, I. de la Torre Díez, and I. Ashraf, "Role of artificial intelligence for analysis of covid-19 vaccination-related tweets: Opportunities, challenges, and future trends", *Mathematics,* vol. 10, no. 17, p. 3199, 2022. [http://dx.doi.org/10.3390/math10173199]

[36] G.R. Kumar, S.B. Latha, P.C. Shaker Reddy, and Y. Sucharitha, "Multi-agent IoT-based system for intelligent vehicle traffic management using wireless sensor networks", *Recent Adv. Electr. Electron. Eng.,* vol. 17, no. 5, pp. 515-522, 2024. [http://dx.doi.org/10.2174/2352096516666230719114956]

[37] K. Sudha, S. Muthumarilakshmi, G. Kavitha, S. Hashini, and V.N. Kumar, "Sentiment analysis on text data: Methods, applications, challenges and future Directions", In: *Proc. 2023 Int. Conf. Evolutionary Algorithms and Soft Comput. Techniques (EASCT)*, 2023, pp. 1-7. [http://dx.doi.org/10.1109/EASCT59475.2023.10392868]

[38] V. Sukhavasi, A.C. Mouli, D.V. Juneja, Y. Sucharitha, S.S. Joshi, and S. Dey, "Establishing ensemble learning models for daily rainfall forecasting", In: *Proc. 2024 Int. Conf. Innov. Comput., Intell. Commun. Smart Electr. Syst. (ICSES)* Chennai, India, 2024, pp. 1-6. [http://dx.doi.org/10.1109/ICSES63760.2024.10910429]

[39] H. Huang, A. Asemi, and M.B. Mustafa, "Sentiment analysis application in e-commerce: Current models and future directions," in *Proc. 12th Int. Conf. Electronic Government and the Information Systems Perspective (EGOVIS 2023)*, Penang, Malaysia, 2023, pp. 67–72, Lecture Notes in Computer Science, vol. 14149, Springer, Cham. [http://dx.doi.org/10.1007/978-3-031-39841-4_5]

[40] M.D. Basith, P. Praveen, and P.C.S. Reddy, "Adaptive deep Q-GAN framework for enhanced breast cancer detection in medical imaging", *Biomedical Signal Processing and Control,* vol. 112, p. 108638, 2026. [http://dx.doi.org/10.1016/j.bspc.2025.108638]

[41] D. Shukla, G. Chandra, B. Pandey, and S.K. Dwivedi, "A comprehensive survey on sentiment analysis: Challenges and future insights", *J. Intell. Fuzzy Syst.,* vol. 43, no. 6, pp. 7733-7763, 2022. [http://dx.doi.org/10.3233/JIFS-213372]

[42] A. Ligthart, C. Catal, and B. Tekinerdogan, "Systematic reviews in sentiment analysis: a tertiary

study", *Artif. Intell. Rev.,* vol. 54, no. 7, pp. 4997-5053, 2021. [http://dx.doi.org/10.1007/s10462-021-09973-3]

[43] P.C. Shaker Reddy, and Y. Sucharitha, "An energy-saving data transmission approach based on migrating virtual machine technology to cloud computing", *Recent Adv. Electr. Electron. Eng.,* vol. 17, no. 6, pp. 573-581, 2024. [http://dx.doi.org/10.2174/2352096516666230713163440]

[44] M.S. Sharif, M. Theeng, M.S. Koya, and W. Elmedany, "Advancements in sentiment analysis: Insights, innovations and future directions", In: *Proc. 2024 11th Int. Conf. Future Internet of Things and Cloud (FiCloud)* IEEE, 2024, pp. 195-200. [http://dx.doi.org/10.1109/FiCloud62933.2024.00037]

[45] R. Samrin, P.C.S. Reddy, K.A. Kumar, N. Deepthi, C. Mithra, S.B. Latha, Y. Sucharitha, and G.K. Thakur, "A hybrid deep learning based framework for prediction of rice yield through integration of biophysical parameters and optical remote sensing data in India", *J. Atmos. Solar-Terrestrial Phys.,* vol. 279, p. 106734, 2026. [http://dx.doi.org/10.1016/j.jastp.2026.106734]

[46] S. Sowjanya, I.S. Reddy, C. Muralikrishna, T.S.L. Prasad, P.C.S. Reddy, and V. Sharma, "Bioacoustics signal authentication for E-medical records using blockchain", In: *Proc. 2024 Int. Conf. Knowledge Eng. Commun. Syst. (ICKECS)* vol. 1. IEEE., 2024, pp. 1-6. [http://dx.doi.org/10.1109/ICKECS61492.2024.10617376]

[47] A. Qazi, R.G. Raj, G. Hardaker, and C. Standing, "A systematic literature review on opinion types and sentiment analysis techniques", *Internet Res.,* vol. 27, no. 3, pp. 608-630, 2017. [http://dx.doi.org/10.1108/IntR-04-2016-0086]

[48] T. Hashni, and T. Amudha, "Leveraging machine learning for accurate precipitation forecasting", *Procedia Computer Science,* vol. 259, pp. 1523-1532, 2025. [http://dx.doi.org/10.1016/j.procs.2025.04.107]

[49] Z. Wang, D. Huang, J. Cui, X. Zhang, S.B. Ho, and E. Cambria, "A review of Chinese sentiment analysis: subjects, methods, and trends", *Artif. Intell. Rev.,* vol. 58, no. 3, p. 75, 2025. [http://dx.doi.org/10.1007/s10462-024-10988-9]

[50] P.P. Ray, "ChatGPT: A comprehensive review on background, applications, key challenges, bias, ethics, limitations and future scope", *Internet of Things and Cyber-Physical Systems,* vol. 3, pp. 121-154, 2023. [http://dx.doi.org/10.1016/j.iotcps.2023.04.003]

[51] P. Chillakuru, M. Madiajagan, K.V. Prashanth, S. Ambala, P.C. Shaker Reddy, and J. Pavan, "Enhancing wind power monitoring through motion deblurring with modified GoogleNet algorithm", *Soft Comput.,* vol. 28, no. 23-24, pp. 13965-13975, 2024. [http://dx.doi.org/10.1007/s00500-023-08358-8]

[52] A. Önden, M. Alnour, V. Simic, and D. Pamucar, "The evolution of sentiment analysis across various scientific disciplines: A comprehensive review based on the bibliometric technique", *Decision Making Advances,* vol. 2, no. 1, pp. 222-237, 2024. [http://dx.doi.org/10.31181/dma21202441]

[53] P. Ravali, P.C.S. Reddy, and P. Praveen, "An efficient neuro-framework for brain tumor classification using a CNN-based self-supervised learning approach with genetic optimizations", *Curr. Neuropharmacol,* vol. 23, 2025. [http://dx.doi.org/10.2174/011570159X378103250806214613]

[54] S. Surekha, R.V.S. Lalitha, M. Srikanya, S.J. Sri, R. Kinjagi, and D. Keerthana, "Deep reinforcement learning approach for autonomous vehicles to cross junctions," in *Algorithms and Computational Theory for Engineering Applications: ICACTEA 2024*, S. Rama Sree and S. Kumar, Eds., Cham, Switzerland: Springer, 2025. [http://dx.doi.org/10.1007/978-3-031-72747-4_16]

CHAPTER 9

Leveraging Artificial Intelligence and Blockchain: Feasibility of Integration, Research Issues, Applications, Challenges, and Future Directions

Rayapati Venkata Sudhakar[1], **Karibasappa Chatrapathi**[2], **Sridhar N Koka**[3], **Vijay Bhanudas Gujar**[4], **Yadala Sucharitha**[5,*] and **Mudarakola Lakshmi Prasad**[6]

[1] *Department of Computer Science and Engineering, Geethanjali College of Engineering and Technology, Hyderabad, Telangana, India*

[2] *School of Computing & Information Technology, REVA University, Bangalore, Karnataka, India*

[3] *Faculty of Business Administration, Panyapiwat Institute of Management, Pak Kret, Nonthaburi, Thailand*

[4] *Computer Science and Engineering Department, Arvind Gavali College of Engineering, Satara, Maharashtra, India*

[5] *Sharda School of Computing Science and Engineering, Department of CSE, Sharda University, Greater Noida, Uttar Pradesh, India*

[6] *Computer Science and Engineering, Institute of Aeronautical Engineering, Dundigal, Telangana, India*

Abstract: Blockchain is a decentralised ledger technology that has several applications in the financial sector, IoT, big data, cloud computing, and edge computing because of its distributed point-to-point architecture, which provides a secure and provable method for validating transactions. However, AI is progressively fostering the intelligent development of numerous sectors. Converging blockchain and AI technology has obvious benefits, since they are two of the most promising technologies in use today. Both blockchain and AI can work together to make AI smarter; AI can make blockchain more trustworthy and autonomous, and AI can make blockchain smarter. The integration of blockchain technology with AI is examined in this article from a more holistic and multi-faceted perspective. Before delving into an analysis of the potential for a blockchain-AI hybrid, we provide some context for both systems by outlining AI's history and the idea, traits, and core technology of blockchain. Our next step is to provide a synopsis of the relevant domestic and international research on blockchain and AI convergence. Following that, we will go over a few connected use cases regarding the merging of the two technologies. Additionally, the assessment covers the current state of these systems, the difficulties they continue to encounter as a

[*] **Corresponding Author Yadala Sucharitha**: Sharda School of Computing Science and Engineering, Department of CSE, Sharda University, Greater Noida, Uttar Pradesh, India; suchi.yadala@gmail.com

Pundru Chandra Shaker Reddy, Yadala Sucharitha, & Thillaiarasu N (Eds.)

result of the AI and blockchain algorithms that power them, as well as the potential areas for future research. An overview of the study area from many angles is provided by the analysis's results.

Keywords: Applications, Artificial intelligence, Blockchain, Machine Learning, Security.

INTRODUCTION

The indispensable role that blockchain and AI play in scientific innovation and industrial transformation has led to them attracting increased attention as cutting-edge technologies currently [1]. In 1956, the Dartmouth Society came up with the idea of AI technology. An integral part of computer science, AI technology seeks to model, augment, and improve upon human intellect through the study and application of technical sciences. The exponential growth of data and the remarkable advances in Machine Learning (ML), particularly Deep Learning (DL), have ushered in a new era of explosive growth in artificial intelligence in recent years. Industries like education, retail, transportation, security, and finance stand to gain greatly from artificial intelligence's prowess in analysis, prediction, judgment, and decision-making [2]. The concept of blockchain technology did not emerge until 2008, when Satoshi Nakamoto introduced Bitcoin. A distributed ledger is the basic idea behind the blockchain [3]. Without the need for an intermediary, it is able to use a decentralized consensus process in a multi-entity setting. In addition to facilitating the creation and verification of transactions in a decentralized, untrusted system, blockchain technology allows for the cost-effective development of trust [4]. For this reason alone, blockchain technology has attracted a growing number of academics.

In Fig. (**1**), we can see an overview of the AI terminology. Any system that makes decisions by consulting a database is said to have artificial intelligence (AI). It is possible to teach computers to make decisions using massive amounts of data through a branch of artificial intelligence known as machine learning (ML). An area of machine learning known as a neural network draws inspiration from the way the human brain works [5]. Inside, you'll find the building blocks of an input, multiple hidden, and output layers. The foundation of deep learning is a network of interconnected brain units called a "neural network," which employs these layers to refine feature extraction over time.

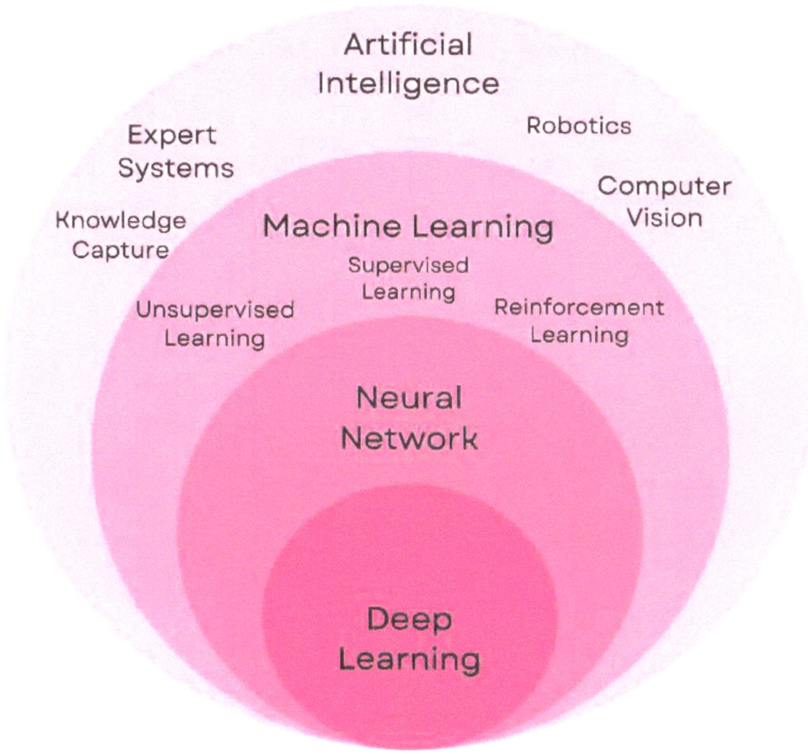

Fig. (1). Structure of the AI.

Recent developments in blockchain-related systems have opened up new possibilities for decentralized environments, even if AI has been flourishing across many industries, particularly healthcare, for the past few years. The significance of up-to-the-minute data became clear as the COVID-19 pandemic progressed [6]. Faster and faster mobile healthcare is replacing the antiquated patient-hospital-based system. This is particularly true in light of new innovations like the Internet of Medical Things (IoMT), which allow for the remote tracking and monitoring of a wide range of health conditions through smart devices [7]. Although this simplifies a lot of work and makes things more reliable, it generates and transmits a lot of sensitive medical data, which must be protected. In Fig. (**2**), we can see how AI and blockchain work together. In this setup, data is gathered by sensors and smart devices, then delivered to smart applications that analyze and predict using blockchain platforms and machine learning models [8].

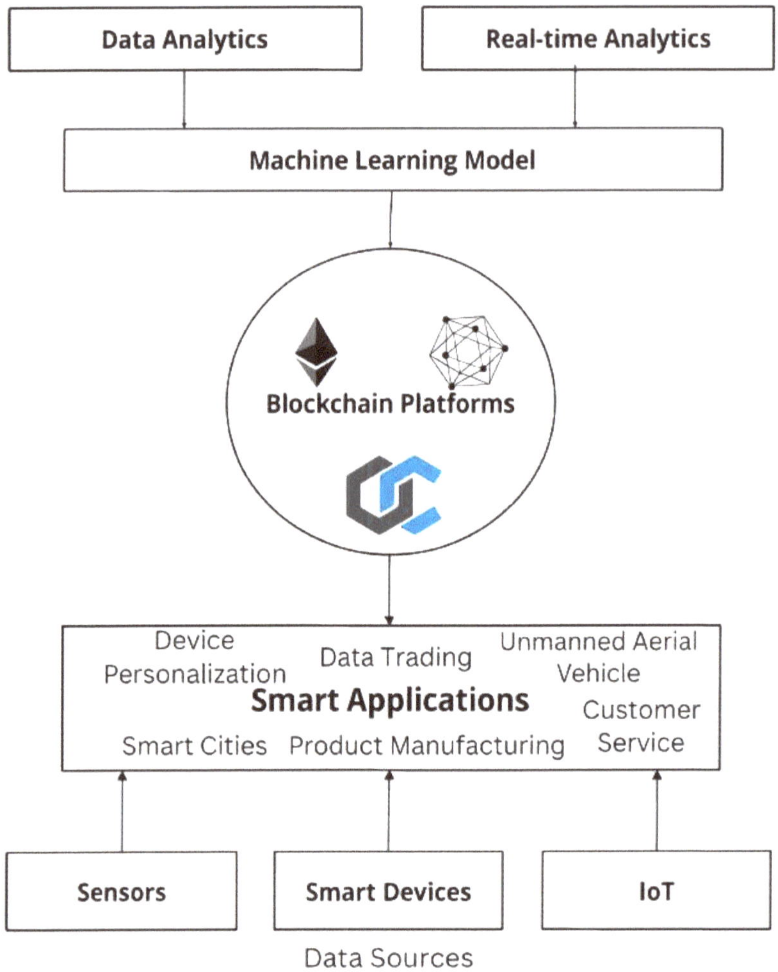

Fig. (2). AI with blockchain.

Blockchain technology has found new uses beyond the bitcoin ecosystem, where it has been shown to be an invaluable tool in achieving unprecedented security levels in a number of different contexts [9]. Similarly, blockchain technology is finding its way into many parts of the healthcare industry in this digital era. Protecting the personal information of patients—essential players in the healthcare system—is made possible by its features like smart contracts, consensus processes, decentralized exchanges, and micro-transactions. Clinical and trial outcomes, billing details, medical reports, and other similar data are examples of this type of information [10].

While both blockchain and artificial intelligence offer many potential benefits, they also have some potential downsides. While AI has challenges with interpretability and efficacy, blockchain has concerns with energy usage, scalability, privacy, security, and efficiency. Although they are distinct lines of inquiry, they might have common ground and mutually beneficial synergies. Data analysis, security, and trust are commonalities between the two systems, and they can complement one another [11]. For example, AI relies on three main components: data, algorithms, and computing power. The blockchain, with its decentralized, immutable, and anonymizing properties, can break the data island and make the data, algorithms, and computing power flow. Blockchain technology also ensures the veracity of audits and the capacity to track AI systems, in addition to the authenticity of the original data. Not only that, but blockchain can record AI decisions, which aids in AI behavior analysis and understanding, and eventually encourages AI decision-making by making it more visible, explainable, and trustworthy. With the help of AI, the blockchain may be built in a way that maximizes efficiency, security, and energy savings [12].

There has been some writing on the state of the art in AI and blockchain research up to this point. Still missing, though, is a summary or generalization of their integration work, as well as any reflection of the correlation between the two. According to the available literature, academics are interested in exploring the potential uses of blockchain technology in conjunction with artificial intelligence across a range of industries and businesses [13]. In contrast, this study takes a more holistic and multi-faceted framework to evaluate the potential of blockchain and AI working together, and it does so by collecting and demonstrating the combination points of the two across a range of research domains. This chapter primarily contributes to the following areas:

- The connection and potential for integration of blockchain technology with artificial intelligence are examined.
- We compile a thorough overview from several categories in light of the most recent local and international studies on the combination of blockchain technology with artificial intelligence.
- To explore how to combine blockchain technology with AI, we chose a number of real-world use cases and application scenarios from different industries.
- We describe the difficulties of combining Blockchain Technology (BT) with AI and mention upcoming research that will hopefully solve these obstacles.

How the rest of the chapter is organized is as follows. Section 2 delivers an outline of the fundamentals of AI and blockchain technology, respectively. In Section 3, we examine the practicality of integrating blockchain technology with

AI. Integration of AI &BT research challenges is discussed in Section 4. In Section 5, we categorized application scenarios across numerous domains. The current problems and obstacles are detailed in Section 6, and the future research development is presented in Section 7. The chapter is concluded in Section 8.

BACKGROUND STUDY

Blockchain

Since its introduction by Satoshi Nakamoto in 2008 [14], blockchain technology has evolved to include many valid transactions in each block. By preserving the cryptographic hash of the most recent block, each block in the blockchain is connected to the one before it. With a timestamp, every transaction added to the chain is permanent. Each block of transactions is connected to the record of the transaction that came before it, making the chain traceable. No change may be made to the chain once a new transaction has been inserted. A blockchain database is administered by a decentralized network of peers, rather than a central server. Each node in the network has access to a duplicate of the blockchain [15]. Hence, everyone in the network needs to double-check the chain before making any changes, such as adding a new transaction. To avoid having a transaction added to the chain that is deemed a fraud assault, it must first obtain consensus from the majority of participants. The original intention of the blockchain was to do away with the need for a reliable third party or central server. Not only in the cryptocurrency industry, but also in healthcare and the IoT, the concept of decentralization has found numerous uses [16]. The four essential features of blockchain, as outlined in a study [17], are audibility, decentralization, permanence, and anonymity. Decentralization is achieved by the consensus process applied to the blockchain, which ensures data consistency in a distributed network. Neither the operation cost nor the performance limitations brought on by the trusted authority are present in a decentralized system. Because no one can alter or remove transactions from the blockchain, and because it is easy to spot fraudulent transactions, its durability is evident. Furthermore, true identities are not required of those who participate in the blockchain [18]. To remain anonymous, they can utilize an address that is generated within the blockchain network. The linked structure of the blockchain makes it possible to audibly trace each transaction in the chain. The other two characteristics of the blockchain that were brought up by [19] are assault resistance and fault tolerance. There are three distinct varieties of blockchain networks: public, private, and conglomerate blockchains. Since the public BT is entirely decentralized, anybody can join it and take part in the consensus process. Everyone involved in a transaction can see it without revealing their identity. Public blockchains include cryptocurrencies like Bitcoin and Ethereum [20]. Because of the centralization of the private blockchain, only an authorized organization may add nodes to the network. Fast network output and secrecy are two benefits of private blockchain [21]. Among the several private permissioned blockchain platforms, Hyperledger Fabric stands out. Scalable and featuring multiple nodes, the consortium blockchain is an innovative solution. The consortium blockchain network is overseen by multiple organizations or parties in order to maintain privacy and security. The problem with a consortium is that if one member does something wrong, it could affect the whole network.

Artificial Intelligence

From 1956 to 1970, 1980 to 1990, and 2000 to the present, artificial intelligence technology has seen three peaks of progress. The technology began in 1956. The first development peaked with the 1959 proposal for machine learning. The second development peaked in the 1980s and 1990s, when the US and Japan were deeply involved in AI research. The third epoch of hasty development in AI has begun, thanks to the breakthrough of DL &RL strategies, and the exponential escalation of network data [22].

Computer algorithms that can learn and complete tasks automatically are known as Machine Learning (ML). ML is a subset of AI. In ML, a mathematical process is constructed using the attributes of historical data; when exposed to new data, the design is trained and updated. The ML model can autonomously learn patterns, modify behaviors, and make judgments without any human intervention. It is hard for a human to process and interpret all types of data, and the digital world harvests a tremendous amount of data. With the help of machine learning, massive amounts of data may be automatically processed and useful data attributes extracted. Machine learning's key benefit is that it can self-improve in response to algorithmic surprises and keeps learning from fresh training data [23]. Classification, anomaly detection, and prediction are just a few of the many common uses for machine learning techniques. Some of the most common everyday uses of ML include facial expression recognition, marketing recommendation systems, sentiment analysis, and the detection of credit card fraud [24].

Supervised, unsupervised, and RL are the three prime categories into which ML approaches fall. Labeled training data is essential for supervised learning algorithms to construct their mathematical design. After receiving input data and the anticipated outputs, the model finds the label that corresponds to the input data and extracts the relationship between the two. Afterwards, the algorithm will be able to accurately calculate the work for the unseen input data. One typical application of supervised learning is the prediction or categorization of a target outcome [25]. To train the model, unsupervised learning algorithms use unlabeled data, in contrast to supervised learning. The aim of unsupervised learning is to discover the underlying structure and insights in a dataset and then group similar pieces of data together. Unsupervised learning makes use of cluster analysis as one of its primary methods [26]. Data that are comparable to one another are grouped together in a cluster after clustering, and this cluster is distinct from the others. Since this data point does not belong to any cluster, it can be efficiently identified in this manner. The machine may be able to understand its own behavior based on input received from the ground, and the algorithm for reinforcement learning learns by interacting with the outside world [27]. Various tasks can be accomplished with different machine learning algorithms. Data analysis can benefit from supervised and unsupervised learning methods, whereas decision-making problems are best solved with reinforcement learning [28]. A prominent way to do continuous work is through deep knowledge, which has recently gained popularity. In artificial neural networks, deep learning finds its foundation. In order for the neural network to extract more complex information from its inputs, it is built with numerous layers. Three of the most popular deep learning designs include recurrent neural networks, convolutional neural networks, and deep multilayer perceptrons. Image recognition and natural language processing are two examples of fields that have made use of deep understanding due to its capacity to offer a high-level abstraction for data modeling [29].

INTEGRATION OF AI WITH BLOCKCHAIN

Among the several benefits of blockchain technology (BT) are its decentralized nature, durability, and openness. Machine learning algorithms may find new possibilities on the blockchain, which might help them provide trustworthy conclusions while protecting users' data and information. The financial sector heavily promoted blockchain [30] *via* the use of Bitcoin. Pharmaceutical production, supply chain operations, healthcare, and a plethora of other crucial industries have all adopted it in recent years. Blockchain is frequently employed to secure financial transactions and data by keeping a distributed digital ledger that records all information in an extremely secure way, whereas ML is famous for automating problem-solving through the application of statistical computer algorithms or models.

By automatically predicting what kinds of data need to be processed and saved in a chain to make instances as accessible as possible, blockchain considerably improves data safety. Data may be made encryptedly available at any time using blockchain technology, and it offers great support for standards that secure large amounts of data at various nodes. Blockchains can be vulnerable to security breaches due to their decentralized nature [31]. The main concern is that an attack might compromise the consensus process, giving a small number of mining farms control over the blocks added to the network. There is a particular danger associated with public blockchains. Because every node is identified individually and an appropriate consensus mechanism is established, private versions are protected from this attack.

Fig. (3), shows that innovative and dependable solutions in the security sphere could emerge from merging blockchain with ML. Using BT, a complete and verifiable record of a supply chain's activities can be created. Finally, machine learning can be used to analyze these contracts' behaviors in order to detect possible security vulnerabilities, which can aid in preventing the loss of funds or other assets. Using blockchain technology, one can establish "smart contracts" that, when met, will execute automatically according to specified criteria.

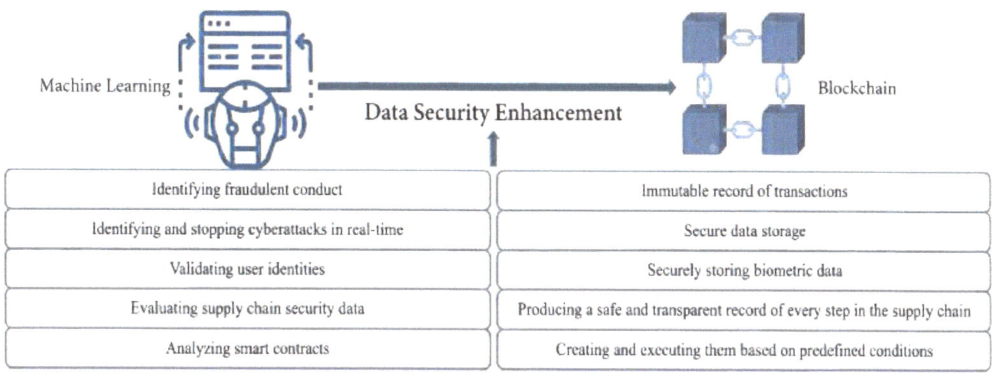

Fig. (3). AI to enhance the security in blockchain.

BT EMPOWERS AI

Transparent and Reliable Data Sources

Verifying the authenticity and trustworthiness of data sources is crucial for improving the safety of data sharing across different businesses. After validating certificates, smart blockchain technology makes sure all data on the chain is transparent by syncing the whole ledger of all nodes and by adding features like time stamps and signatures to transactions to make them easy to track. Several people have worked together to build a trustworthy conduit for exchanging information [32].

Strong Fairness Guarantee

By promoting proper system operation and guaranteeing fairness, the classic blockchain system awards tokens to miners who diligently labor for the regular operation of the system. An economic penalty will be meted out to the dishonest person, while the truthful one will receive compensation commensurate with their actions. By automatically executing predefined smart contract codes, smart blockchain technology guarantees that system members can receive proportional rewards if they honestly adhere to the agreement. Concurrently, the awards are distributed to the appropriate participants using the condition-triggered automatic transfer method, which ensures a high level of fairness for the intelligent scene involving several parties [33].

Efficient Autonomy

Blockchain is characterized by its decentralized nature as a distributed ledger system. Blockchain technology will not be under the jurisdiction of any one entity because of its decentralized nature, which eliminates the necessity for a central server or authority to supervise the whole system. By utilizing smart contracts' automatic execution features, management rules can be predefined, thereby reducing human error and the risk of attacks [34].

Privacy Protection

The risk of direct or indirect user privacy leaks is growing in tandem with the amount of data content shared on the chain [35]. Users' privacy is protected by traditional blockchain systems using pseudonyms and shuffling, but data mining and analysis still allow malevolent attackers to steal users' private information. To safeguard user information, the new smart blockchain system makes use of a number of cryptographic algorithms that have proven to be quite effective in this area.

Distributed Computing Power

In most cases, all it takes to power AI is a single computer or server. As data volumes and computational complexity continue to grow at an exponential rate, traditional computing platforms are struggling to keep up with the demands of artificial intelligence while simultaneously driving up hardware and maintenance expenses for businesses [36]. Given its distributed structure, blockchain enables the decentralization of processing resources; this, in turn, facilitates the operation of AI models across a worldwide network of decentralized nodes. An innovative wireless edge intelligence framework is suggested by another study [37] for the purpose of achieving stable and resilient edge intelligence.

AI EMPOWERS BT

Countless aspects are involved in the design and operation of BT, with security, throughput, decentralization, and other parameters all being carefully considered and traded off. With the help of AI, these decisions can be made easier, and the BT can be optimized for better governance and higher performance. On top of that, AI has the potential to make blockchain applications smarter and less prone to human mistakes [38].

Security

Everyone knows that blockchain is nearly impossible to hack unless the enemy has most of the mining privileges. Regrettably, the blockchain platform's decentralized applications' programming and operations lack sufficient security. As an example, in the DAO event [39], hackers lost $50 million because they exploited smart contract vulnerabilities and repeatedly withdrew cash. All the way through a blockchain transaction's lifetime, AI can offer security and technical support, opening up new avenues for advancement in the intelligentization of the system's security protections. Some work has been done to ensure that smart contracts are secure. In an effort to find the sweet spot between security and usability, we have automated the generation of smart contracts using AI technology. Additionally, smart contract vulnerabilities are examined using data mining and other technologies, and harmful vulnerabilities are checked using big data analysis to prevent hackers from causing economic damage. As AI becomes more integrated into the blockchain, smart contracts will become smarter and more efficient [40].

Efficiency

Numerous fully-fledged blockchain systems have found use in manufacturing, and more and more businesses are pouring resources into exploring blockchain's potential. Nevertheless, blockchain systems often encounter significant issues with basic query functions and poor query speed as a result of data storage mode limitations. Because levelDB, a data storage system optimized for write-intensive applications, is used as the foundational data storage system in the majority of blockchain systems [41]. Writing performance has improved, while reading performance has suffered. Dealing with frequent queries is becoming more required due to the proliferation of data and the expansion of blockchain applications. As a result of the underlying storage system's poor reading performance and overly fast writing performance, query performance is severely constrained. By incorporating AI algorithms, blockchain data storage methods can also be improved. In order to create a decentralized and safe network for VECON data management, the authors of [42] suggest a new TTA-CB protocol that is based on artificial intelligence. They then use a PSO algorithm to find the best data source to work with. The advent of AI has opened up new avenues for the advancement of blockchain technology. It has greatly enhanced the efficiency of blockchain applications and the speed of data queries through constant practice and learning.

RESEARCH CHALLENGES OF BLOCKCHAIN AND AI INTEGRATION

We outline and categorize the uses of blockchain and AI integration in this section.

Sharing Applications

There has been a meteoric rise in data volume since the advent of the information age, and that data is most valuable when it is in use. But the current data trust system has its flaws, which limit the safe transfer of data and slow down the industry's progress. Because of its intrinsic properties—including immutability, decentralization, and traceability—blockchain technology can give new technological ways for exchanging data. On the other hand, blockchain is typically reserved for usage as a trustworthy distributed database in more generic data-sharing applications. The blockchain's usefulness is severely diminished due to the lack of data analysis capabilities. To make up for blockchain's shortcomings and boost its use, artificial intelligence technologies can be employed.

The authors of a study [43] built a smart and secure network structure for the next generation of wireless systems by utilizing BT & AI to guarantee flexible and safe resource sharing. To overcome the issues of complexity, time variation, and unpredictability in wireless systems, AI was employed, while blockchain technology was utilized to create a distributed and secure environment for sharing resources. Specifically, the authors implemented a safe content-caching environment using the consortium blockchain and optimized cache resource use through the application of deep reinforcement learning in the architecture of the caching mechanism.

Security Applications

The prevalence of malevolent activity in the system will determine the exactness of smart contracts and enticement mechanisms as the blockchain system continues to evolve. The security of the BT is seriously compromised by these malevolent actions. On the flip side, analyzing and detecting malicious conduct will become more challenging due to the massive amounts of data generated by the blockchain. The current blockchain system can be improved by the merging of AI with blockchain [44].

Smart contracts provide a significant risk of money loss due to the possibility of incorrect code and vulnerabilities. The majority of the existing approaches to detecting vulnerabilities in smart contracts rely on ineffective methods of symbolic execution and dynamic execution. In order to identify vulnerabilities in smart contracts [45], developed SoliAudit. This approach improved the capacity to find vulnerabilities in smart contracts by combining static and dynamic testing technologies, with the help of machine learning and dynamic fuzzers. Using a different angle, a study [46] suggested a machine learning-fused vulnerability detection method that detects smart contracts using a graph neural network.

Transaction Applications

Data security is where blockchain really shines, but AI really shines when it comes to analysis, prediction, and judgment. Related fields of study, such as transaction analysis and price prediction, can benefit from combining the two. Machine learning was utilized by McNally et al. to forecast Bitcoin price trends. They achieved this by optimizing RNN and LSTM using Bayesian techniques [47]. When McNally et al. compared actual data with predictions made by the widely used ARIMA model, they discovered that nonlinear deep learning techniques had a more favorable impact. Given that Bitcoin users employed anonymous Bitcoin addresses for their transactions, analyzing correlations between these addresses proved to be a formidable challenge. In this instance, the ability to trace addresses within the Bitcoin system was made available with the proposal of a new Bitcoin address connotation mechanism in [48]. To transform the computational complexity of the discourse clustering issue into a binary classification problem, once Bitcoin addresses were extracted, it allowed the authors to lower the complexity. After that, it built a two-layer model and checked to see if the two Bitcoin addresses were associated with the same user. Lastly, addresses associated with the same user were grouped together by the system. The implementation of user identification in the Bitcoin system is made possible by a deep learning algorithm provided by a study [49] for address-user mapping. To obtain the feature vector for each address. At last, the address verification, identification, and clustering processes reveal who the address's owner is.

Deposit Applications

Due to its inherent properties, blockchain can ensure that stored digital information is authentic, intact, and credible. Smart contracts can adapt and evolve naturally with the use of AI, which can also aid in processing and data analysis. Nowadays, immunization is a must-have tool for keeping infectious diseases at bay. Public health and the safety of our nation's vaccines are interdependent. Nevertheless, vaccine record fraud and vaccine expiration are still prevalent problems in the vaccine supply chain. Consequently, a reliable mechanism for regulating vaccines is an absolute necessity. Using blockchain and ML, the authors of a study [50] created a vaccine blockchain system for this purpose. In the information management system, machine learning offers an extra way for data analysis, while blockchain technology seeks to alter the present method and build a new trust mechanism. In order to facilitate user queries regarding vaccine circulation and personal vaccination records, as well as government and institutional oversight of vaccine operations, the vaccine blockchain system was built using an Ethereum-based smart contract. Using the vaccine blockchain technology, any liability issues with the vaccination can be resolved.

Resource Management Applications

Integrating blockchain and AI into resource management systems is fraught with permutations because both technologies rely on network resources. Loung et al. suggested a deep learning-based optimal auction mechanism to distribute computing resources at the network's periphery in light of the fact that blockchain mining uses a lot of power and computational resources [51]. One way that edge computing service providers can help with mobile blockchain environments is by allowing users to offload mining work from their own devices. A multilayer neural network was built by the authors using the investigative resolution of the optimum auction as its foundation. In order to optimize the loss function, the parameters of the neural network were tuned using the estimated absenteeism as training data. Complete optimization of the blockchain system, maximum improvement of MEC security and privacy, and solution of the job offloading problem were the goals of [52]. A deep reinforcement learning technique was suggested for the stable training of neural networks.

Scalability Optimization Applications

As the volume of transactions on the blockchain continues to rise, its scalability has emerged as a critical issue that is limiting its advancement. In order to crack the scalability issue, it is crucial to choose a consensus procedure. The chosen solution for solving the blockchain network's scalability challenge is based on Byzantine fault tolerance. As an alternative to proof of work, authors of another study [53] suggested a novel paradigm for consensus group formation. Byzantine fault tolerance techniques were made possible in public blockchain networks by this consensus group. The model used a decision-theory online learning algorithm to determine each node's reputation value; then, it chose nodes with higher reputation values to serve on the consensus committee, protecting them from potential harm.

Future research should focus on scalable architectures, privacy-preserving frameworks, and energy-efficient consensus mechanisms. Enhancing interoperability, adopting post-quantum cryptography, and establishing regulatory standards will enable more secure and effective AI-blockchain integration.

Technology that slices data is another approach to growing the blockchain. In order to perform transactions in parallel, it might partition the network. For the majority of their blockchain implementations, proof-of-work consensus protocols are used to generate new blocks. A machine learning-based technique for sharing networks was suggested by a study [54]. This approach accurately and rapidly creates fragments by first mapping nodes' IP addresses to geographic coordinates and then dividing these coordinates into pieces using the k-means clustering algorithm. During intrashard communication, the propagation delay was reduced since the nodes in the spike were geographically closer. When it comes to scalability, Geo-Sharding is light-years ahead of the PoW-based slicing technique.

APPLICATION SCENARIOS

Here we present some real-world examples and scenarios from different industries.

Smart Grid

Everybody pitches in to keep the lights on *via* a smart grid, which is a component of the energy Internet [55]. However, conventional centralized grid systems do not naturally integrate with distributed energy trading, which is the present dominant trend in smart grid development. As a result, smart grids can make the transition from centralization to distribution with the support of smart blockchains' decentralized nature [56]. Smart blockchain's decentralization allows for the secure sharing of data among numerous participants and the elimination of information barriers. Smart blockchain technology also has the potential to increase market involvement while decreasing smart grid operating and maintenance expenses.

Internet of Vehicles

The role of the Internet-of-Vehicles (IoV) in smart mobility is growing as communication technologies advance. While vehicular communication through the IoV has the potential to alleviate traffic &road safety issues, there is a risk of a trust disaster and other safety risks associated with the information sharing process [57]. The growth of IoV technology can be accompanied by smart blockchain's ability to offer trust guarantees, dependable data security, and effective incentive systems. With BT, new nodes—including vehicles, humans, and SPs—are added to the network. Its immutability, transparency, and anonymity make it ideal for fostering data sharing, enhancing data security, and ensuring mutual confidence among various components.

Health Care

The expansion of the socialeconomy has coincided with a golden age in health care innovation. Nevertheless, specific issues must be addressed. Data exchange between healthcare facilities allows for more precise diagnoses and more efficient treatments, but clients have very high standards for the safety of their personal information and health records. The issues mentioned above can be resolved with blockchain technology. The immutability of the blockchain makes it an ideal tool for anti-counterfeiting and data tracking, thanks to its trust mechanism. With the blockchain, safe data sharing is possible. In order to do more thorough data analysis, AI can be utilized to uncover the data's hidden value [58].

Many sectors and application domains have seen substantial impacts from combining Blockchain with machine learning. Because healthcare typically involves massive amounts of data, machine learning techniques are very useful in this field. Human processing of medical data is going to be laborious. Ensuring the security of patients' health records and information is of the utmost importance [59]. By integrating blockchain with machine learning, healthcare organizations may automate the process of analyzing merged medical data from many sources while also addressing privacy and security concerns. Both public and private blockchains find usage in healthcare applications. Additionally, we discovered that the majority of research articles concerning healthcare-related issue prediction and disease diagnostics make use of supervised learning. These algorithms include LSTM, ANN, SVM, and DDQL. Additionally, most intelligent transportation research that integrates ML and BT fails to make use of unsupervised learning, as we have noted. To address privacy and security concerns, the e-commerce industry is exploring alternative solutions that combine Blockchain technology with machine intelligence. When it comes to supply chain management, combined BT-ML optimizes production. Public BT is utilized by the majority of blockchain types utilized in e-commerce research. We have also seen that most BT-ML-related work has limitations, such as the lack of sufficient validation in the coupled models. In the age of the IoT, businesses and organizations can accomplish long-term privacy protection by implementing blockchain technology [60].

PROBLEMS AND CHALLENGES

Here, we highlight the difficulties and issues of combining blockchain technology with AI.

Scalability

For smart blockchain applications to run well, the scalability problem must be solved. A blockchain's decentralized application (DApp) platform is essential for its operation. It will not be possible to deploy the system on a broad scale if its performance and scalability are inadequate. The three main areas of blockchain's scalability concerns include consistency issues, network latency, and performance constraints. These issues stem from the underlying assumption of data protection and decentralization [61]. The security of the blockchain depends on the majority of nodes agreeing on the details of the transactions. The blockchain will split in two if scalability is pursued in a way that doesn't take into account the distributed network's consistency requirements. As a decentralised, peer-to-peer network, blockchain scalability is severely constrained by the latency between individual nodes. Thirdly, the fundamental cause that limits the use of BT applications is the effect of transaction performance limitations on the blockchain's scalability. It is difficult to improve transaction throughput on blockchains because transactions cannot be executed in parallel to guarantee security and ultimate consistency [62].

Security and Privacy

Important concerns with blockchain applications include landing, security, and privacy protection. The data transferred between the blockchain's nodes is public and viewable by everybody, yet some users may be reluctant to provide some sensitive information because it forms the backbone of the Internet of Value. Thus, the ability to execute blockchain applications on a broad scale hinges on how user privacy can be safeguarded. Data concealment and identity confusion are two popular ways that blockchains safeguard user privacy. By utilizing privacy protection signature technologies like group signatures and ring signatures, identity obfuscation technology makes it impossible to correspond to the actual user by partially anonymizing their identity on the blockchain. To guarantee identity security, a supervisor can examine user information using the supervisor's private key when needed [63].

Data Alliance between On-Chain and Off-Chain Storage

There are two main approaches to data storage, and both have their advantages and disadvantages: traditional information systems and blockchain systems. While off-chain storage and processing systems are essential to blockchain's performance, traditional information systems rely on blockchain technology to guarantee data reliability and secure sharing. The most important thing is to make sure the data on the chain and the data off the chain are relevant and consistent, and this can only be achieved by effectively combining blockchain technology with traditional information systems. In addition, data is essential to the advancement of artificial intelligence. Many issues, including data monopolization, misuse, poor data quality, and so on, persist in artificial intelligence technologies. These issues now have new avenues for growth thanks to the involvement of blockchain technology. Successful integration of blockchain and off-chain data is crucial for real-world economic applications of AI and blockchain technology [64].

FUTURE TRENDS

Here, we anticipate future research efforts that may focus on combining blockchain technology with artificial intelligence.

Hybrid Architecture Integrating On-Chain and Off-Chain Storage

Due to many distributed scenarios, smart blockchain transaction and data storage types may eventually merge on-chain and off-chain(OC &OC) storage into a hybrid architecture. Off-chain storage offers more privacy, lower costs, and greater efficiency, but off-chain data has a hard time taking advantage of blockchain trust. Future research should focus on integrating OC and OC data closely to map chain trust to off-chain data.

Stability between Performance Upgrading and Security Guarantees

Even though BT offers numerous benefits in different areas, its actual implementation is still limited by its own performance barrier. Performance concerns, such as transaction throughput, confirmation time, and block capacity, constitute the bulk of the blockchain's technological hurdles. While directed acyclic graphs, off-chain transactions, block enlargement, and transaction sharing have all been suggested as potential answers to the blockchain's performance issues, they all run the risk of undermining the blockchain's legitimacy and security.

While the blockchain system's transaction efficiency is negatively affected, the level of privacy protection is enhanced in circumstances where better privacy protection needs are met by implementing cryptographic schemes with higher security. Finding a direct balance between improving performance and protecting privacy is a major problem for future blockchain technology developments.

Distributed Trust Construction

There is increased device collaboration and intercommunication in the blockchain-enabled application scenarios. Cooperation can only take place when both parties trust one another and have faith in the veracity of the information and identities shared. Because of its consensus process and immutability modification, blockchain technology is able to improve confidence in an open network and automatically ensures the validity and dependability of data. When a node is assigned a certain identity and function, it is necessary to verify the node's identification, which houses the device. For the blockchain scenario to work, distributed trust must be built. Verifying the identities of additional nodes decentralised from a single authority is an important area for future research.

Improve User Awareness and Legal Regulations

Chaos and bubbles are inevitable outcomes of the rapid development of blockchain technology and the relatively slow deployment of applicable industry laws. Due to deleveraging, strict oversight, and the volatile nature of the capital market, everyone is keeping an eye on the blockchain, and some illicit activities that masquerade as blockchain have been outlawed time and time again. The boundary between a coin and a chain is therefore extremely porous, and there is no universally accepted definition of blockchain technology. Therefore, it is critical to increase public awareness about blockchain technology.

AI-blockchain integration raises ethical concerns around privacy, accountability, and bias. Immutable ledgers can conflict with data protection rights, while biased AI decisions may become permanently recorded. Additionally, decentralized governance complicates responsibility, and the combined technologies increase energy consumption and environmental impact.

CONCLUSION

Blockchain and AI are two of the most innovative technologies now available. They provide complementary integration options, and each has the potential to radically alter the future of information technology. In this chapter, we provide a thorough introduction to the concepts of blockchain and artificial intelligence, analyze the feasibility of integrating the two, and summarize the research on this topic nationally and internationally. These four domains have the trait of incorporating big data and a high number of partners into the system. This article delves into several application areas, highlights the advantages of combining blockchain technology with machine learning, and tackles any restrictions that may exist. Combine machine learning's prowess with blockchain's trustworthy data storage capabilities, and you get a solution that can access data secretly and securely, allowing for more reliable categorization or prediction judgments. We conclude by highlighting potential future work and application scenarios.

LIST OF ABBREVIATIONS

IoMT Internet of Medical Things

BT Blockchain-Technology

IoV Internet-of-Vehicles

PSO Particle Swarm Optimization

NLP Natural language processing

DL Deep Learning

AI Artificial Intelligence

ML Machine Learning

REFERENCES

[1] A. Alabdulatif, M. Al Asqah, T. Moulahi, and S. Zidi, "Leveraging artificial intelligence in blockchain-based E-health for safer decision-making framework", *Appl. Sci. (Basel),* vol. 13, no. 2, p. 1035, 2023.
[http://dx.doi.org/10.3390/app13021035]

[2] N. Chandrasekaran, Radhakhrishna Somanah, Dhirajsing Rughoo, Raj Kumar Dreepaul, Tyagaraja S. Modelly Cunden, and Mangeshkumar Demkah., "Digital transformation from leveraging blockchain technology, artificial intelligence, machine learning and deep learning", In: *Proc. Fifth Int. Conf. on Information Systems Design and Intelligent Applications* vol. 2. , 2019, pp. 271-283.INDIA

[3] H. Jebamikyous, M. Li, Y. Suhas, and R. Kashef, "Leveraging machine learning and blockchain in e-commerce and beyond: benefits, models, and application", *Discover Artif. Intell.,* vol. 3, no. 1, p. 3, 2023.
[http://dx.doi.org/10.1007/s44163-022-00046-0]

[4] S. Kumar, W.M. Lim, U. Sivarajah, and J. Kaur, "Artificial intelligence and blockchain integration in business: trends from a bibliometric-content analysis", *Inf. Syst. Front.,* vol. 25, no. 2, pp. 871-896, 2023.
[PMID: 35431617]

[5] G. Arun, P.C.S. Reddy, N. Budati, B. Rebecca, S. Perumalla, and V.B. Gujar, "A Deep Learning Framework for Diabetes Prediction: PIMA Indian Dataset", *2024 International Conference on Innovative Computing, Intelligent Communication and Smart Electrical Systems (ICSES),* IEEE., 2024.

[6] M. Mascarenhas, T. Ribeiro, J. Afonso, F. Mendes, P. Cardoso, M. Martins, J. Ferreira, and G. Macedo, "Smart endoscopy is greener endoscopy: Leveraging artificial intelligence and blockchain technologies to drive sustainability in digestive health care", *Diagnostics (Basel),* vol. 13, no. 24, p. 3625, 2023.
[http://dx.doi.org/10.3390/diagnostics13243625] [PMID: 38132209]

[7] S. Yadala, C.S.R. Pundru, and V.K. Solanki, "A novel private encryption model in IoT under cloud computing domain", In: *Lecture Notes in Networks and Systems: Proc. Int. Conf. on Intelligent Systems & Networks,*, 2023, pp. 263-270.Singapore, Springer Nature Singapore
[http://dx.doi.org/10.1007/978-981-99-4725-6_33]

[8] N. Tsolakis, R. Schumacher, M. Dora, and M. Kumar, "Artificial intelligence and blockchain implementation in supply chains: a pathway to sustainability and data monetisation?", *Ann. Oper. Res.,* vol. 327, no. 1, pp. 1-54, 2022.
[PMID: 35755830]

[9] A.T. Somnathe, V.T. Selvi, N.G. Stepha, M.T. Kingslin, F.M. Inamdar, and P.C.S. Reddy, "An intelligent traffic conflict prediction using deep learning with long-term evolution access data", In: *2025 3rd International Conference on Smart Systems for applications in Electrical Sciences (ICSSES),* 2025, pp. 1-6.
[http://dx.doi.org/10.1109/ICSSES64899.2025.11010032]

[10] V. Sukhavasi, A.C. Mouli, D.V. Juneja, Y. Sucharitha, S.S. Joshi, and S. Dey, "Establishing ensemble learning models for daily rainfall forecasting," in *Proc. 2024 Int. Conf. on Innovative Computing, Intelligent Communication and Smart Electrical Systems (ICSES)*, Chennai, India, 2024, pp. 1–6, IEEE.
[http://dx.doi.org/10.1109/ICSES63760.2024.10910429]

[11] V. Hemamalini, A.K. Mishra, A.K. Tyagi, and V. Kakulapati, "Artificial intelligence–blockchain-enabled–internet of things-based cloud applications for next-generation society," in *Automated Secure Computing for Next-Generation Systems*, A. Sharma and P. Singh, Eds., Singapore: Springer, 2024, pp. 65–82.
[http://dx.doi.org/10.1002/9781394213948.ch4]

[12] S.B. Latha, Y. Sucharitha, I.A. Tayubi, K. Shekar, D. Pandey, and R.V. Sudhakar, "Virtual learning analysis using complex rule-based approach in the context of cloud computing", In: *Proc. 2025 3rd Int. Conf. on Communication, Security, and Artificial Intelligence (ICCSAI)* vol. 3. Greater Noida, India, 2025, pp. 1110-1115.
[http://dx.doi.org/10.1109/ICCSAI64074.2025.11064645]

[13] S Swati, and M Kumar, "Innovations in blockchain using artificial intelligence", In: *Blockchain and its Applications in Industry 4.0* Springer Nature: Singapore, 2023, pp. 179-210.

[14] G.K. Thakur, L.P. Mudarakola, M. Sreenivasulu, V. Krishna B, I.R. Raja, I.A. Tayubi, and Y. Sucharitha, "An enhanced prediction framework for blood-brain barrier permeability: DeePred-BBB", *Recent Patents on Engineering,* vol. 19, no. 9, p. E18722121342031, 2025.
[http://dx.doi.org/10.2174/0118722121342031250218042131]

[15] A. Ayub Khan, A. Ali Laghari, M. Rashid, H. Li, A. Rehman Javed, and T. Reddy Gadekallu, "Artificial intelligence and blockchain technology for secure smart grid and power distribution Automation: A State-of-the-Art Review", *Sustain. Energy Technol. Assess.,* vol. 57, p. 103282, 2023.
[http://dx.doi.org/10.1016/j.seta.2023.103282]

[16] S Kulkarni, P William, V Prakash, J N Dwivedi, Ed., *Leveraging Artificial Intelligence in Cloud, Edge, Fog and Mobile Computing* 1st ed. Auerbach Publications, 2025.
[http://dx.doi.org/10.1201/9781032703718]

[17] V.S. Anoop, and S. Asharaf, "Integrating artificial intelligence and blockchain for enabling a trusted ecosystem for healthcare sector", In: *Intelligent Healthcare: Infrastructure, Algorithms and Management.*Springer Nature Singapore, 2022, pp. 281-295.
[http://dx.doi.org/10.1007/978-981-16-8150-9_13]

[18] C. Qu, L. Jin, Y. Zhang, C. Fan, J. Chu, and S. Liu, "Exploration on the fusion of artificial intelligence and blockchain", In: *Proc. 2022 3rd Int. Conf. on Big Data Economy and Information Management (BDEIM 2022)*, 2023, pp. 156-163.
[http://dx.doi.org/10.2991/978-94-6463-124-1_19]

[19] B. Elov, A. Dauletov, Y. Sucharitha, F. Khalilova, M. Latipova, and M. Abdullayeva, "An intelligent traffic management of vehicles using deep learning approach in smart cities",
[http://dx.doi.org/10.1109/ICICACS65178.2025.10967703]

[20] V. Charles, A. Emrouznejad, and T. Gherman, "A critical analysis of the integration of blockchain and artificial intelligence for supply chain", *Ann. Oper. Res.,* vol. 327, no. 1, pp. 7-47, 2023.
[http://dx.doi.org/10.1007/s10479-023-05169-w] [PMID: 36718465]

[21] S Surekha, R. V. S. Lalitha, M Srikanya, S. J. Sri, R Kinjagi, and D Keerthana, "Deep reinforcement learning approach for autonomous vehicles to cross junctions", In: *Algorithms and Computational Theory for Engineering Applications,* S Rama Sree, S Kumar, Eds., Springer: Cham, Switzerland, 2025, pp. 105-112.Adv. Sci., Technol. & Innov. book series
[http://dx.doi.org/10.1007/978-3-031-72747-4_16]

[22] V.V. Vegesna, "AI-enabled blockchain solutions for sustainable development, harnessing technological synergy towards a greener future", *Int. J. Sustain. Dev. Through AI, ML IoT,* vol. 2, no.

2, pp. 1-10, 2023.

[23] N. Rane, S. Choudhary, and J. Rane, "Leading-edge artificial intelligence (AI), machine learning (ML), blockchain, and internet of things (IoT) technologies for enhanced wastewater treatment systems", *SSRN Electron. J.*, .
[http://dx.doi.org/10.2139/ssrn.4641557]

[24] A. Alabdulatif, "A novel ensemble of deep learning approach for cybersecurity intrusion detection with explainable artificial intelligence", *Applied Sciences,* vol. 15, no. 14, p. 7984, 2025.
[http://dx.doi.org/10.3390/app15147984]

[25] R Leung, "Leveraging AI and blockchain for streamlining healthcare payments", In: *Proc. 2023 5th Blockchain and Internet of Things Conference (BIOTC'23)*, Osaka, Japan. Assoc. Comput. Mach.: New York, NY, USA, 2023.
[http://dx.doi.org/10.1145/3625078.3625086]

[26] A. Sedykh, M. Podapaka, A. Sagingalieva, K. Pinto, M. Pflitsch, and A. Melnikov, "Hybrid quantum physics-informed neural networks for simulating computational fluid dynamics in complex shapes", *Machine Learning: Science and Technology 5.2,* p. 025045, 2024.
[http://dx.doi.org/10.1088/2632-2153/ad43b2]

[27] D Darwish, "Blockchain and Artificial Intelligence for Business Transformation Toward Sustainability", In: *Blockchain and its Applications in Industry 4.0* Springer Nature: Singapore, 2023, pp. 211-255.
[http://dx.doi.org/10.1007/978-981-19-8730-4_8]

[28] V. Dutta, M. Choraś, M. Pawlicki, and R. Kozik, "A deep learning ensemble for network anomaly and cyber-attack detection", *Sensors,* vol. 20, no. 16, p. 4583, 2020.
[http://dx.doi.org/10.3390/s20164583]

[29] B. Mamatha, D. Rashmi, K.S. Tiwari, P.A. Sikrant, A.A. Jovith, and P.C.S. Reddy, "Lung cancer prediction from CT images and using deep learning techniques", In: *Proc. 2023 Second International Conference on Trends in Electrical, Electronics, and Computer Engineering (TEECCON)* IEEE., 2023, pp. 263-267.
[http://dx.doi.org/10.1109/TEECCON59234.2023.10335801]

[30] R. Saxena, E. Gayathri, and L. Surya Kumari, "Semantic analysis of blockchain intelligence with proposed agenda for future issues", *International Journal of System Assurance Engineering and Management,* vol. 14, no. S1, suppl. 1, pp. 34-54, 2023.
[http://dx.doi.org/10.1007/s13198-023-01862-y]

[31] M.A. Umer, E.G. Belay, and L.B. Gouveia, "Leveraging artificial intelligence and provenance blockchain framework to mitigate risks in cloud manufacturing in industry 4.0", *Electronics (Basel),* vol. 13, no. 3, p. 660, 2024.
[http://dx.doi.org/10.3390/electronics13030660]

[32] P. Bothra, R. Karmakar, S. Bhattacharya, and S. De, "How can applications of blockchain and artificial intelligence improve performance of Internet of Things? – A survey", *Comput. Netw.,* vol. 224, p. 109634, 2023.
[http://dx.doi.org/10.1016/j.comnet.2023.109634]

[33] N. Rane, S. Choudhary, and J. Rane, "Blockchain and Artificial Intelligence (AI) integration for revolutionizing security and transparency in finance", *SSRN,* 2023p. 4644253.
[http://dx.doi.org/10.2139/ssrn.4644253]

[34] S. Markkandeyan, A.D. Ananth, M. Rajakumaran, R.G. Gokila, R. Venkatesan, and B. Lakshmi, "Novel hybrid deep learning based cyber security threat detection model with optimization algorithm", *Cyber Security and Applications,* vol. 3, p. 100075, 2025.
[http://dx.doi.org/10.1016/j.csa.2024.100075]

[35] R. Kandepu, "Leveraging filenet technology for enhanced efficiency and security in banking and insurance applications and its future with Artificial Intelligence (AI) and machine learning", *Int. J.*

Adv. Res. Comput. Commun. Eng., vol. 12, no. 8, pp. 20-26, 2023. [http://dx.doi.org/10.17148/IJARCCE.2023.12803]

[36] U. Ahmed, M. Nazir, and A. Sarwar, "Signature-based intrusion detection using machine learning and deep learning approaches empowered with fuzzy clustering", *Sci Rep,* vol. 15, p. 1726, 2025. [http://dx.doi.org/10.1038/s41598-025-85866-7]

[37] C. Krittanawong, M. Aydar, H.U. Hassan Virk, A. Kumar, S. Kaplin, L. Guimaraes, Z. Wang, and J.L. Halperin, "Artificial intelligence-powered blockchains for cardiovascular medicine", *Can. J. Cardiol.,* vol. 38, no. 2, pp. 185-195, 2022. [PMID: 34856332]

[38] N. Alkhafaji, T. Viana, and A. Al-Sherbaz, "Integrated genetic algorithm and deep learning approach for effective cyber-attack detection and classification in Industrial Internet of Things (IIoT) environments", *Arab J Sci Eng,* vol. 50, pp. 12071-12095, 2025. [http://dx.doi.org/10.1007/s13369-024-09663-6]

[39] Y. Abu Huson, L. Sierra-García, and M.A. Garcia-Benau, "A bibliometric review of information technology, artificial intelligence, and blockchain on auditing", *Total Qual. Manage. Bus. Excell.,* pp. 1-23, 2023.

[40] M.D. Basith, P. Praveen, and P.C.S. Reddy, "Adaptive deep Q-GAN framework for enhanced breast cancer detection in medical imaging", *Biomedical Signal Processing and Control,* vol. 112, p. 108638, 2026. [http://dx.doi.org/10.1016/j.bspc.2025.108638]

[41] N. Singh, and D. Adhikari, "Leveraging AI and blockchain to automate inventory auditing: Enhancing accuracy and compliance", *Int. J. Res. Appl. Sci. Eng. Technol.,* vol. 11, no. 12, pp. 1239-1247, 2023. [http://dx.doi.org/10.22214/ijraset.2023.57565]

[42] H. Maheshwari, U. Chandra, D. Yadav, A. Gupta, and R. Kaur, "Machine learning and blockchain: A promising future", *In 2023 4th International Conference on Intelligent Engineering and Management (ICIEM),* pp. 1-6, 2023. [http://dx.doi.org/10.1109/ICIEM59379.2023.10166343]

[43] M.J.I. Idian, M.K. Hassan, and A.S. Terzungwe, "Artificial intelligence, blockchain, machine learning, and customer relationship management", *Bincang Sains dan Teknologi,* vol. 2, no. 1, pp. 16-20, 2023. [http://dx.doi.org/10.56741/bst.v2i01.276]

[44] AKÇETİN, "Türkiye can leverage the power of innovation, artificial intelligence, and fintech to enhance productivity", *AJIT-e: Academic Journal of Information Technology,,* vol. 14, no. 55, pp. 335-364, 2023.

[45] C Chaka, "Fourth industrial revolution—a review of applications, prospects, and challenges for artificial intelligence, robotics and blockchain in higher education", *Research and Practice in Technology Enhanced Learning,* vol. 18, p. 002.

[46] S. Karim, S. saxena, D.A. Singh, P. Deshmukh, A.B. Lokare, O.G. Gour, A.M. Sattar, and M.K. Ranjan, "Revolutionising marketing: Leveraging blockchain and AI for impactful management", *E-Commerce for Future & Trends,* vol. 10, no. 3, pp. 26-33, 2023. [http://dx.doi.org/10.37591/ecft.v10i3.675]

[47] N. Hicham, H. Nassera, and S. Karim, "Strategic framework for leveraging artificial intelligence in future marketing decision-making", *Journal of Intelligent Management Decision,* vol. 2, no. 3, pp. 139-150, 2023. [http://dx.doi.org/10.56578/jimd020304]

[48] N.K. Jadav, T. Rathod, R. Gupta, S. Tanwar, N. Kumar, and A. Alkhayyat, "Blockchain and artificial intelligence-empowered smart agriculture framework for maximizing human life expectancy", *Comput. Electr. Eng.,* vol. 105, p. 108486, 2023. [http://dx.doi.org/10.1016/j.compeleceng.2022.108486]

[49] M.M. Moawad, M.M. Madbouly, and S.K. Guirguis, "Leveraging blockchain and machine learning to improve IoT security for smart cities", *Proc. Int. Conf. on Artificial Intelligence and Computer Vision,* pp. 216-228, 2023.Cham, Switzerland: Springer [http://dx.doi.org/10.1007/978-3-031-27762-7_21]

[50] Y. Zuo, J. Guo, N. Gao, Y. Zhu, S. Jin, and X. Li, "A survey of blockchain and artificial intelligence for 6G wireless communications", *IEEE Commun. Surv. Tutor.,* vol. 25, no. 4, pp. 2494-2528, 2023. [http://dx.doi.org/10.1109/COMST.2023.3315374]

[51] A. Mahmood, A. Al Marzooqi, M. El Khatib, and H. AlAmeemi, "How Artificial Intelligence can leverage Project Management Information system (PMIS) and data driven decision making in project management", *International Journal of Business Analytics and Security (IJBAS),* vol. 3, no. 1, pp. 180-191, 2023. [http://dx.doi.org/10.54489/ijbas.v3i1.215]

[52] R. Samrin, P.C.S. Reddy, K.A. Kumar, N. Deepthi, C. Mithra, S.B. Latha, Y. Sucharitha, and G.K. Thakur, "A hybrid deep learning based framework for prediction of rice yield through integration of biophysical parameters and optical remote sensing data in India", *Journal of Atmospheric and Solar-Terrestrial Physics,* vol. 279, p. 106734, 2026. [http://dx.doi.org/10.1016/j.jastp.2026.106734]

[53] I Ahmed, A Chehri, and G Jeon, "Artificial intelligence and blockchain enabled smart healthcare system for monitoring and detection of COVID-19 in biomedical images", *IEEE/ACM Trans. Comput. Biol. Bioinform.,* vol. 21, pp. 814-822, 2024. [http://dx.doi.org/10.1109/TCBB.2023.3294333]

[54] M.K. Brar, P.K. Jindal, M. Kumar, and P. Sharma, "Research methodology", In: *2023 International Conference on Research Methodologies in Knowledge Management, Artificial Intelligence and Telecommunication Engineering (RMKMATE)*, 2023.

[55] J.L. Woolley, "Getting along with frenemies: enhancing multi-competitor coopetition governance through artificial intelligence and blockchain", *Ind. Innov.,* vol. 30, no. 9, pp. 1156-1189, 2023. [http://dx.doi.org/10.1080/13662716.2023.2168519]

[56] V.K. Bukkarayasamudram, P.C.S. Reddy, and K. Arun Kumar, "Quantum computing revolution in healthcare: a systematic review of applications, issues and future directions", *Artif Intell Rev,* vol. 58, p. 389, 2025. [http://dx.doi.org/10.1007/s10462-025-11381-w]

[57] M. Shen, A. Gu, J. Kang, X. Tang, X. Lin, L. Zhu, and D. Niyato, "Blockchains for artificial intelligence of things: A comprehensive survey", *IEEE Internet Things J.,* vol. 10, no. 16, pp. 14483-14506, 2023. [http://dx.doi.org/10.1109/JIOT.2023.3268705]

[58] A. Majumder and J. L. Sarkar, eds., *Artificial Intelligence and Data Science in Recommendation System: Current Trends, Technologies and Applications*. Bentham Science Publishers, 2023.

[59] W. AlKhader, R. Jayaraman, K. Salah, A. Sleptchenko, J. Antony, and M. Omar, "Leveraging blockchain and NFTs for quality 4.0 implementation in digital manufacturing", *J. Manuf. Tech. Manag.,* vol. 34, no. 7, pp. 1208-1234, 2023. [http://dx.doi.org/10.1108/JMTM-05-2023-0172]

[60] R.W. Ahmad, W. Al Khader, R. Jayaraman, K. Salah, J. Antony, and V. Swarnakar, "Integrating Lean Six Sigma with blockchain technology for quality management – a scoping review of current trends and future prospects", *TQM J.,* vol. 35, no. 7, pp. 1609-1631, 2023. [http://dx.doi.org/10.1108/TQM-06-2022-0181]

[61] P.C. Reddy, S. Nachiyappan, V. Ramakrishna, R. Senthil, and M.D. Sajid Anwer, "Hybrid model using scrum methodology for software development systems", *J. Nucl. Ene. Sci. Power Generat. Techno.,* vol. 10, no. 9, p. 2, 2021.

[62] L. Zhang, "Machine learning for blockchain: Literature review and open research questions", In: *NeurIPS 2023 AI for Science Workshop*, 2023. [http://dx.doi.org/10.31219/osf.io/g2q5t]

[63] J.P. Bharadiya, "Artificial intelligence and the future of web 3.0: Opportunities and challenges ahead", *American Journal of Computer Science and Technology,* vol. 6, no. 2, pp. 91-96, 2023.

[64] P. Ravali, P.C.S. Reddy, and P. Praveen, "An efficient neuro-framework for brain tumor classification using a CNN-based self-supervised learning approach with genetic optimizations", *Curr. Neuropharmacol.* vol. 24, no. 4, 2026. [http://dx.doi.org/10.2174/011570159X378103250806214613]

CHAPTER 10

AI-Driven Cybersecurity Framework for SRI Funds: Ensuring Ethical Compliance and Risk Mitigation

Ambati Suvarna[1,*] and **Kafila**[1]

[1] *School of Business, SR University, Warangal, Telangana, India*

Abstract: Funds under the purview of socially responsible investment strive to promote ethical practices in investment and financing methods, making cybersecurity an important prerequisite for building investor confidence and ensuring compliance with laws and regulations. This paper presents an AI-based cybersecurity framework designed to advance the security, compliance, and risk management of SRI funds. It also considers risk management methods, including AI predictive analytics, mitigation of insider threats through AI, and transparency through blockchain affiliation. One main impediment for SRI funds is ensuring proper ethical compliance, warranting automation of regulatory frameworks using AI and comparative analysis of various global cybersecurity regulations on SRI investments. By way of case studies, the paper explores the transformational role of AI in cybersecurity. BlackRock's real-world case of internal AI deployment for fraud detection serves as an example of reducing financial threats and improving investor confidence using cyber-secured systems powered by AI. Along the same lines, HSBC's implementation of automation under AI ensures compliance with ESG at a pace that demonstrates the efficiency of AI in sticking to the regulations. AI improves monitoring for cybersecurity, automates compliance with ESG regulations, and links to blockchain for making secure transactions. Threats to all of these developments abound, such as AI-powered cybercrime, shifts across borders in regulation, and vagaries in ethical AI. The end of the paper provides recommendations for adopting AI strategies for a more resilient, compliant, and safe SRI investment ecosystem for fund managers.

Keywords: AI-driven cybersecurity, AI-Based Fraud Detection, Blockchain Transparency, Cyber Risk Management, ESG Regulatory Compliance, Ethical AI in Finance, SRI Fund Security, Sustainable Investment Technology.

* **Corresponding Author Ambati Suvarna:**, School of Business, SR University, Warangal, Telangana, India; E-mail: ambatisuv786@gmail.com

Pundru Chandra Shaker Reddy, Yadala Sucharitha, & Thillaiarasu N (Eds.)

INTRODUCTION

With the accelerated digitization of financial services, including SRI, data security increasingly emerged as an issue of ethical compliance and risk mitigation. Ethical SRI funds, which consider the environmental, social, and governance framework in making their investment decisions, should have a mechanism to ascertain ethical alignment amidst a cyber-attacking environment. In line with this, AI-based cybersecurity systems have increasingly assisted. Such systems intervene with real-time threat determinations, anomaly detections, and enable compliance automation [1, 2].

The environment of this paper is a compelling combination of the need for strengthening cybersecurity systems in an SRI environment where financial integrity and social responsibility coexist. The approach to designing, analyzing, and evaluating a cybersecurity framework that an AI would use to make the environment more resilient toward threats, ensure adherence to international ESG regulations, and abide by ethical AI must [3, 4]. AI brings with it groundbreaking tools for predictive analysis and fraud detection, also bringing with it new types of risks, such as adversarial attacks and algorithmic bias, that require being treated by a multidisciplinary approach [5].

This paper emphasizes a comprehensive theme: integrating ethical, regulatory, and technological safeguards into AI-powered security systems tailored for SRI funds. In doing so, it supports the broader vision of using responsible innovation to protect investor trust and regulatory adherence in sustainable finance [6].

OVERVIEW OF SRI FUNDS

Recently, there has been a great deal of attention on Socially Responsible Investment (SRI) funds, and their growth and impact have been thoroughly studied in various markets. SRI has evolved from a niche and primarily religious exclusionary practice into a mainstream risk analysis strategy for institutional and retail investors, according to [7]. However, although some researchers claim that SRI funds appear to be more promising in some areas, their actual impact on corporate behavior has also been subject to skepticism. A recent study indicated that SRI funds target firms promoting better environmental and social conduct, but do not change the behavior of firms or actively engage in shareholder proposals to effect change [8]. On the other hand, many remaining challenges are recognized by the lack of a global common taxonomy on sustainable activities, legislative clarity, and quality data for cross-industry and cross-regional comparison [7].

IMPORTANCE OF CYBERSECURITY IN FINANCIAL MARKETS

Cybersecurity is a focal discussion in the increasingly emerging financial institutions, as their common concern nowadays is frequent and sophisticated cyberattacks [9]. The rapidly developing financial technologies (FinTech) have brought tremendous changes to the financial landscape: advanced convenience and speed in service delivery, but unfortunately, exposing the sector to even more complicated issues in cybersecurity threats. Cybersecurity threats include traditional attacks from phishing to malware and sophisticated attacks like supply chain attacks, AI-driven cyber threats, and ransomware [10]. Interestingly, while cybersecurity measures are essential, there is also a concept that complements the existing paradigm of cybersecurity, called cyber-resilience. Cyber-resilience will thus enable very complex organizations to prepare for adverse events such as cyber-risk-induced external shocks, which they are supposed to withstand, recover from, and adapt to. In a nutshell, importance cannot be overestimated when it comes to financial markets and cybersecurity. It is also about the protection of private customer information, the integrity of transactions, and trust maintained in the digital financial environment [11]. A holistic approach to cybersecurity will enhance this for the financial institutions in terms of user awareness, technical measures, preparedness for incidents, and regulatory compliance to maneuver through confident resilience in a digital landscape [12]. As evolving technology transforms the relationships within the financial industry, a proactive and adaptive cybersecurity strategy in advance will guarantee the viability of the financial ecosystem against growing and more complex cyber threats [10].

ROLE OF AI IN ENHANCING SECURITY AND COMPLIANCE

AI serves as a fundamental lever to enhance security and compliance systems across multiple sectors with the additional benefits of risk management, threat detection, and regulatory compliance. In the case of hospital-integrated risk management, AI contributes to patient safety by facilitating early detection of critical conditions and enhancing clinical risk management [13]. In the sphere of cybersecurity, AI systems are doing far better than their human counterparts in dealing with increasing volumes of data, being able to detect anomalies and identify patterns that would have most likely gone unnoticed by conventional security systems, and thus improve the prediction and trend analyses to plug possible loopholes [2]. Ironically, despite the introduction of AI as a powerful tool in security and compliance, newer challenges have arisen. The introduction of AI brings with it adversarial threats, concerns regarding data privacy, and a clear view of the transparency of AI in its decision-making processes in the area of cybersecurity [2]. In healthcare, the use of AI likewise raises issues bordering on data privacy and security, as well as the need for sound cybersecurity measures

[14]. Thus, the utility of AI is poised to witness far-reaching transformations across security and compliance processes spanning different industries, from healthcare to finance. AI enhances identification of risk, automates hassle-free compliance, and fine-tunes threat detection. However, the road is laden with challenges that need to be addressed for successful realization: data quality, bias, and ethics. Organizations use AI for security and to enhance operational efficiency while ensuring regulatory compliance by developing competencies and related best practices [13, 14].

AI-DRIVEN CYBERSECURITY IN SRI FUNDS

Cybersecurity provided by AI is becoming an even more significant factor to be considered in SRI funds, which emphasizes the importance of digital security within the framework of ethical and sustainable applications of business practices. Thus, it accords with its goal of investing in companies that consider social responsibility and sustainability as a priority for their business activities. This characteristic makes for an interesting dialogue: for all that AI can bring to the enhancement of the cybersecurity industry, the very same cybersecurity suffers new vulnerabilities and threat perspectives on account of digital technological evolution, including AI. Comparison of AI models with traditional approaches is shown in Table 1. Such engagement with contradictory motives serves to strengthen calls for an adequate strategic response that will not only enable greater digital security and user privacy but also ensure ethical and regulatory matters are addressed. In this manner, the immediate paradox justifies the complexity of having AI-driven cybersecurity included in SRI funds, as the investors will weigh these technologies' possible rewards against the risks inflicted upon them. In summary, SRI funds for AI initiatives and cybersecurity must recognize the ethical implications and vulnerabilities these technologies may create. Enterprises desiring entry into the SRI portfolio must focus on the development of strong, trusted, and secure AI systems [15]. The workflow diagram of AI-driven cybersecurity in SRI funds is shown in Fig. (**1**).

Table1. Comparison of AI *vs.* Traditional cybersecurity approaches in SRI funds.

Feature	Traditional Cybersecurity	AI-Driven Cybersecurity
Data Processing	Rule-based filtering	Intelligent pattern recognition and analysis
Response Time	Delayed due to manual checks	Instantly, through autonomous systems
Adaptability to New Threats	Requires manual updates	Self-learning from evolving threats

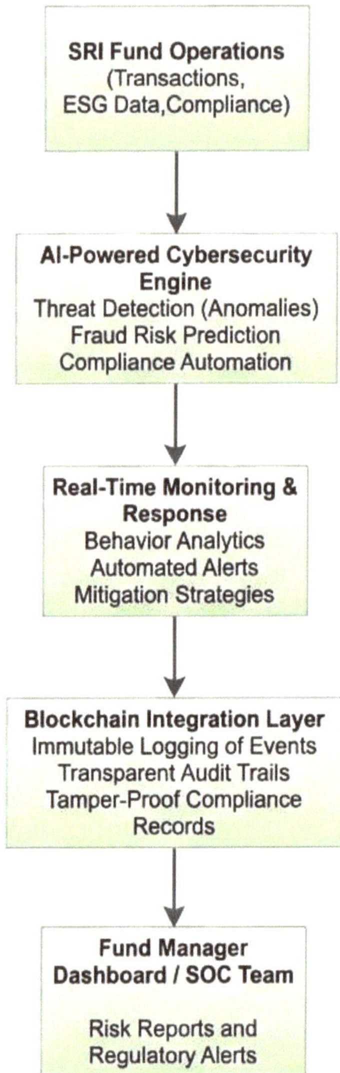

Fig. (1). Flowchart showing the integration of AI-driven cybersecurity in SRI funds.

AI applications in risk detection and fraud prevention

AI is fast being touted as the key transformational technology for risk detection and fraud prevention within different sectors, particularly financial services and e-commerce. Some features include machine learning algorithms, predictive analytics, and anomaly detection techniques that are being employed to bolster defenses against these increasingly sophisticated fraudulent activities [16]. In the financial sector, AI-enabled systems ingest vast quantities of data in real-time, identify suspicious patterns, and quickly take action to block fraudulent transactions [17]. AI can deliver high-frequency trading and predictive risk assessment with real high-speed compliance processes while making operations possible and improving market responsiveness [18]. For example, AI in banking enables operational efficiency, enhances customer experience, and allows more accurate risk assessment and fraud detection [19]. Interestingly, we also find applications of AI in detecting fraud, which is not purely confined to traditional financial services. For example, machine learning algorithms have shown great promise in addressing consumer-based fraud in e-commerce transaction detection. The AI sequential and CatBoost classifiers showed excellent performance in all metrics, with delivery status, payment type, and late delivery risks being the best features for the anomaly detection of unusual orders [20]. In multiple industries, AI is creating a new paradigm for risk detection and fraud prevention. Such expansive capabilities make it an invaluable weapon in fighting against fraud, the ability to ingest and analyze huge data sets in real time, tease out very complicated patterns, and constantly adapt itself to changing threats. However, this adoption brings challenges concerning data privacy, ethical considerations, and compliance with the decentralized regulatory framework [19, 21]. Future applications of AI in risk and fraud management systems will depend on responses to the above concerns.

AI can enhance ethical compliance and risk mitigation in Socially Responsible Investing (SRI) by enabling continuous monitoring, predictive analysis, and automated decision support. Advanced AI models can analyze vast ESG data to detect non-compliance, unethical practices, or reputational risks in real time. Natural language processing can assess company reports, news, and social media for transparency and integrity. Moreover, explainable AI (XAI) can improve accountability by providing clear reasoning behind investment decisions, ensuring alignment with ethical standards. Over time, adaptive AI systems will integrate regulatory updates automatically, offering proactive risk alerts and fostering a more transparent, compliant, and trustworthy SRI ecosystem.

Real-time monitoring for fund security

Real-time monitoring systems have been found useful in enhancing security and efficiency in several areas, such as financial asset management. Such systems could monitor critical parameters all around to minimize exposure to risks and guarantee compliance [22]. In the case of fund safety, an application of real-time monitoring systems could be the continuous observation of fund flows, asset allocations, and risk metrics. Real-time asset tracking systems have proven their worth, at least in the medical arena [23], while in finance, they open new opportunities and challenges for their use. Given the complexities of financial markets and the need for increasingly sophisticated analytical capabilities to qualify movements, interpretation of markets in real time may demand more advanced circuitry than what can be offered to track physical assets. All in all, real-time monitoring for fund security may be used with IoT and digital twin technologies to construct virtual replicas of financial systems, which can timely detect anomalies, offering alerts [24]. However, the effectiveness of such systems would depend on careful consideration of factors like data quality, analytical capabilities, and integration with existing financial management processes. More study is needed on the potential impact of real-time monitoring regarding applications for fund security.

Machine Learning Models for Threat Intelligence

Machine learning models are undeniably gaining more traction in Cyber Threat Intelligence (CTI) and detection. In this definition, these models use enhanced accuracy and efficiency to identify and classify several kinds of cyber threats, even in complex settings like the Internet of Things and large-scale Security Operations Centers (SOCs) [25, 26]. The use of ML in CTI has, by all means, proven to be an encouraging step. For instance, individuals studied 12 years of DNS query logs and presented a model for DGA traffic detection with an accuracy of 96.3% [26]. Meanwhile [25], proposed a Mayfly Optimization-Regularized Extreme Learning Machine (MFO-RELM) model for cybersecurity threat detection in IoT environments with more excellent results. Furthermore, machine learning-based analytics for security machine data is a trending area in cybersecurity to unveil advanced targeted cyber threats and reduce operational overheads. The interesting aspect is that ML models provide great advantages but also pose grounds for several challenges. These models can be prone to adversarial attacks, thus having the pressing demand for robust defense [27]. Moreover, the risk of false-positive detections is a barrier to choosing the best-suited ML algorithms for server log analytics, especially in vast setups. In conclusion, ML models seem to be emerging as important tools in cyber threat intelligence with better detection rates or efficiency. Their deployment, however, needs to be approached cautiously to assess the potential vulnerabilities and the need for continuous refinements. Further improvements would be possible through the integration of ML with other emerging technologies like explainable AI (XAI) and open-source intelligence (OSINT), enhancing the models' efficiency and trustworthiness in application to the field of cybersecurity [27, 26].

Emerging AI technologies like **deep learning**, **reinforcement learning**, and **generative AI** enhance financial cybersecurity by improving threat detection, enabling adaptive defense, and simulating attacks for risk assessment.

Explainable AI (XAI) further ensures transparency and regulatory compliance in automated security decisions.

Existing research is focused solely on AI models, or ESG outcomes are shown in Table (**2**). What this chapter tries to fill is the gap in integrated studies on AI, cybersecurity, ESG compliance, and SRI fund performance.

Table 2. Comparative analysis of existing works.

Reference	Focus Area	Strengths	Weaknesses
[6]	AI-driven cybersecurity modeling	Provides a foundational overview and research directions	Lacks application to ESG or SRI fund environments
[1]	Cybersecurity challenges with AI	Theoretical depth, practical frameworks	Limited focus on financial services
[2]	AI and compliance systems	Real-time compliance benefits discussed	No integration with blockchain or ESG
[3]	ESG performance during crises	Strong data-based ESG fund evaluation	Cybersecurity and AI applications are not addressed
[5]	AI trustworthiness and risk	Highlights regulatory and ethical risks	Lacks sector-specific examples like SRI funds
[15]	AI risk and resilience	Broad risk management techniques	Does not include experimental validation

RISK MANAGEMENT STRATEGIES

Strategies for Risk Management in AI-centric Cybersecurity for SRI Funds: The benefits of AI-enabled cybersecurity systems are immeasurable in identifying, assessing, and mitigating risks for socially responsible investment (SRI) funds. These benefits also include improved enhancements in security measures and compliance with regulations and processes for ethical decision-making [13]. Through predictive analytics, anomaly detection, and decision-making using big data, coupled with a secure and immutable ledger employable *via* blockchain, organizations can create a strong solution to existing problems in risk management [28]. Interestingly, AI has proven to play a dual role in both supplementing and compromising security mechanisms. That is to say, while AI would strengthen cybersecurity provisions, it would also be a source of new vulnerabilities and threats. It emphasizes both opportunities and dangers, by which dangers accentuate the need for framing strategy solutions, keeping ethical and regulatory dimensions in mind [15]. Such contradictory reactions only reiterate that comprehensive approaches to risk management are indefinite in AI-based cybersecurity frameworks for SRI funds. Thus, creating an AI-driven cybersecurity framework for SRI funds requires multi-dimensional approaches. It can include using AI for automatically detecting and mitigating threats, ensuring data integrity through blockchain, and dealing with ethical considerations and compliance with regulations [2, 29]. Such a framework can optimize risk management strategies within SRI funds with elevated security postures while entrenching SRI principles.

AI can balance automation with human oversight by using **Human-In-The-Loop (HITL)** systems, where AI handles routine monitoring and anomaly detection while humans review critical or ambiguous cases. Automated tools ensure speed and consistency, while human judgment addresses ethical nuances, context, and accountability. This collaboration ensures that compliance remains both efficient and aligned with ethical and regulatory standards.

AI-BASED PREDICTIVE ANALYTICS FOR FUND SECURITY

Very promising indeed, AI-based predictive analytics is drawing revolutionary changes in the various sectors concerning fund security. The whole concept of risk assessment, threat detection, and proactive decision-making is made possible by effective tools in AI. For instance, within the ambit of the financial industry, the use of AI technologies illustrates a better-precision practice speeded up such that risk and assessment procedures are facilitated towards achieving improved business continuity and operational efficiency [30]. Therefore, such systems are very effective in processing enormous amounts of data, learning anomalies, and recognizing patterns that most traditional security systems may not allow, hence invaluable for more sophisticated threats like zero-day vulnerabilities or advanced persistent threats. While benefiting a lot from fund security, it has also thrown up new challenges. Adversarial AI and AI-driven attacks need more elaboration and regulation for the systems to be made sufficiently robust against those threats [2]. Furthermore, AI-deployed cybersecurity leads to many issues like data privacy and transparency of AI decision-making processes, which emphasizes the need for responsible deployment and regulatory frameworks [2, 31]. Thus, in conclusion, by predictive analytics, fund security would be built around early threat detection, complemented by personal risk assessment and automated compliance monitoring. With machine learning algorithms and real-time data analysis, predicted assets of financial companies gain consistent protection and regulatory compliance enhancement [2, 30]. However, like any other emerging technology, AI technologies will come with a slew of ethical and security disadvantages, which should be addressed for maximum benefit from AI.

MITIGATING INSIDER THREATS AND UNAUTHORIZED ACCESS

Insider threats remain a great concern for organizations, which subjects the data security and operational integrity to considerable risk. Research has been conducted recently on the development of advanced detection and mitigation strategies in response to this evolving threat landscape [32]. Machine learning and artificial intelligence techniques appear to be promising avenues for the detection of insider threats. A hybrid frame that merges statistics with machine learning-based classification has attained an accuracy of 98.48% in detecting insider threats, outperforming many existing techniques [32]. Additionally, models like the AD-DNN, which combine adaptive synthetic sampling (ADASYN) with deep neural networks, have been introduced to enhance detection performance, particularly in handling highly imbalanced datasets. In the area of anomaly detection algorithms for user behavior modeling, unique techniques have also been useful in identifying malicious activities with limited insider threat instances.

BLOCKCHAIN INTEGRATION FOR ENHANCED TRANSPARENCY

Blockchain technology emerged as an incredible tool for ensuring utmost transparency in multiple sectors of the economy, such as supply chains, government processes, and financial systems. By using decentralised ledgers and smart contracts, blockchain is capable of giving some semblance of real-time data access tracking, data integrity, and automated compliance [33]. In food supply chains, blockchain lays down traceability and more effective recalls while taking away the chances for counterfeits and illegal trades [34]. This increased visibility and transparency generate confidence among consumers and stakeholders throughout the supply chain process [35]. Curiously, first designed to aid full transparency and uncontrolled access to data, blockchain was heavily resisted by market actors apprehensive about confidentiality [36]. This dichotomy implies that the cross-fertilisation of transparency with some opacity in the processes will be the next best for the protection of sensitive data and the confidentiality of business processes.

In government operations, anything relating to blockchain would ensure accountability, but non-technical issues of digital ID, privacy, interoperability, and regulatory support have to be resolved if any aspirations of establishing a truly transparent and accountable e-government system are to be fulfilled. The potential for linked enhancements' transparency is certainly high and shows an imposing insight into many industries. What increases the glamour of these inputs is the irrevocable record, real-time access to data, and an automatic compliance mechanism that injects enhanced trust, efficiency, and accountability. However, for something meaningful to happen, the privacy concerns, concerns over regulation, and actual needs of various stakeholders must be tackled before the path for implementation is set. The versatility of the technology will be examined to gradually infiltrate the very diverse sectors and favour the establishment of fairly transparent systems that can be held accountable [37]. The AI-based Threat Intelligence Model for SRI Funds is shown in Fig. (**2**).

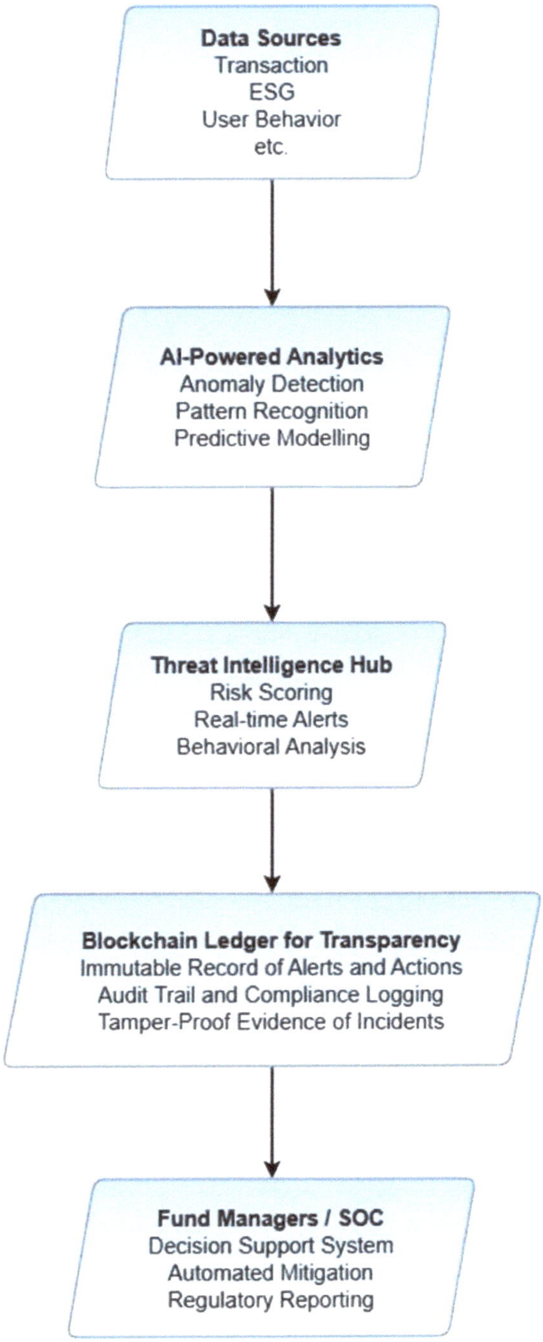

Fig. (2). AI-based threat intelligence model for SRI funds.

ETHICAL COMPLIANCE AND REGULATORY FRAMEWORK

The ethical compliance and regulatory frameworks are key ingredients in developing and implementing an AI-powered cybersecurity system for the purposes of building Socially Responsible Investment (SRI) funds. These frameworks typically govern the responsible use of AI technologies while giving direction on ethical principles and legal compliance, along with practical risk mitigation strategies [1, 2]. This is to say that AI cybersecurity systems in implementation must intend to consider the various legal frameworks on the nexus of SRI funds, such as the GDPR, HIPAA, and PCI-DSS, which in effect govern data protection and privacy issues [2]. AI integration into cybersecurity calls for an overarching risk management framework, which needs to encompass algorithmic bias, data privacy, and the embodied risks of AI attacks [1]. This would require establishing a secure threat intelligence system capable of furnishing adaptive defense measures, dispensing with ethical lenses targeting potential threats posed by AI-based cyber threats against firms' ethical compliance by means of transparency, fairness, and accountability in AI decision-making processes. The researchers, for example, will resort to XAI methods to enhance a clear understanding of the AI predictions or outputs. It is equally necessary to create a multi-stakeholder perspective, involving the policymakers, developers, and practitioners in addressing ethical issues affecting responsible AI use in cybersecurity [38]. Thus, as long as the funds themselves are ethical, the SRI would use AI-powered cybersecurity solutions in more precise ways for their risk-mitigation strategies while maintaining trust and compliance in their operations.

Ensuring Ethical AI use in SRI Funds

Ethical use of AI in SRI funds should follow the ethical principles of respect for individual agency, accountability, technical robustness, privacy, transparency, diversity, non-discrimination, and fairness [39]. These principles naturally cascade from the broader applicability of ethical norms for AI interventions like healthcare and education [40,-41]. An ethical AI-based decision-making framework would allow investment decisions by SRI funds to be ethical in their character while at the same time considering financial return. The performance of sustainable funds has been reported to be mixed, with some studies indicating the underperformance of SRI funds when compared to mutual funds with regular investing strategies. On the other hand, the recent environment has shown that some Article 9 funds under the SFDR might, against continued low levels of performance, have been capable of outperforming conventional funds during periods of crisis [3]. This shows the importance of due diligence in implementing AI-driven SRI approaches aimed at ensuring an ethical focus with a view to generating financial returns. In conclusion, the real needs of AI ethics for SRI funds should be approached from multiple angles. Fund managers ought to work out an ethical framework that deals specifically with the ethical issues of AI in finance while generally adhering to principles of responsible investment [42]. All possible avenues for doing so must be pursued, including developing guidelines for those sectors and promoting transparency regarding AI-powered decision-making, along with continuous assessment of the implications of AI for ethical and financial performance. In this way, SRI funds could exploit AI technologies to improve their investment methods while upholding their commitment to ethics and social responsibility.

Global Regulations on Cybersecurity in Financial Markets

Most cyber assaults are becoming more serious and frequent. The importance of cybersecurity rules in the financial markets has consequently risen. Globally accepted rules on cybersecurity compliance for financial institutions, being shaped by the interdependence of the financial sector itself and the demand for harmonized regulatory schemes, are gradually merging together. Regulatory frameworks have been developed in key jurisdictions "the United States, the European Union, and Asia-Pacific countries "that address data protection, incident response, and risk management mandates. In spite of this trend toward convergence, significant differences remain in regulatory schemes with a partial focus on data protection and breach notification [9]. Following the findings in [43], cooperation in the design of cybersecurity regulations between the two principal Western blocs, the US and the EU, is found to be thin. This indeed may create further possibilities for gaps or inconsistencies in the global cybersecurity regulations. Resource limitations, anomalous changing cyber threats, and a complex web of regulatory demands have been pointed out as possible challenges impeding financial service providers' journey towards cybersecurity compliance [9]. Hence, organizations are encouraged to make a real effort regarding cybersecurity, enforcing procedures for encryption, multi-factor authentication, and periodic security audits. The establishment of cybersecurity frameworks, technical defense measures, and end-user awareness training is key to safeguarding critical financial information from the imminent threat pervasive in the environment [12].

Role of AI in Automating Regulatory Compliance

AI is becoming more and more relevant in the automation of regulatory compliance for different industries, especially by providing an innovative answer to difficult problems. In the oil and gas sector, AI technologies like ML from the perspective of natural language processing and predictive analytics are facilitating data management and analysis by automating data collection, processing, and reporting, which in turn helps to increase accuracy and efficacy. The compliance monitoring systems being built using AI can trace regulatory compliance in real time, helping to lessen cases of non-compliance and penalties attached to such. With automated auditing and inspection, compliance checks will be made much easier for thorough evaluation and consistency throughout [44]. This is particularly helpful for compliance with frameworks such as GDPR, HIPAA, and PCI-DSS [2]. AI solutions provide governments with opportunities in tax compliance for alternative simplifications of all tax administration processes, in the detection of non-compliance, and in combating tax evasion. Application of machine learning algorithms can analyze huge amounts of financial information at a much greater speed and accuracy to identify such trends, which indicate VAT fraud or evasion. Likewise, AI systems empowered by natural language processing can seek potential regulatory breaches or systemic risks by surveying vast amounts of regulatory documents and financial data in the regulatory framework [45]. The other burden of AI with regulatory compliance relates to the issue of data quality and integration, cybersecurity implementations, and regulatory acceptance [44]. Other ethical and legal questions around the deployment of AI need to be highlighted to ensure its responsible usage [45, 44]. The entire premise on which this kind of algorithmic decision-making is based raises questions of transparency, accountability, and how to mitigate bias. Therefore, to conclude, AI is poised to bring about a paradigm shift in regulatory compliance across industries in view of its efficiency, accuracy, and proactive enhancement of risk management. As this technology continues to evolve, the AI entry into compliance will also mature, hence providing a larger range of benefits and addressing any present inadequacies. Deploying AI responsibly and refining it continuously will help us in making the most of its true potential while reducing unintended consequences [45]. The key regulations of the cybersecurity impacting SRI funds are shown in Table 3.

Table 3. Key cybersecurity regulations impacting SRI funds and AI (tm)s role in compliance.

Regulation	Region	Key Focus Areas	AI's Role in Compliance
GDPR (General Data Protection Regulation)	European Union	Data privacy, user consent, breach notification	AI automates data classification, breach alerts, and consent management
SEBI Cybersecurity Guidelines	India	Risk management, data security, and audit trails	AI ensures continuous risk monitoring and automated report generation
SEC Cyber Rules	United States	Incident response, data governance, AI oversight	AI supports real-time threat detection and audit readiness

(Table 3) cont.....

Regulation	Region	Key Focus Areas	AI's Role in Compliance
SFDR (Sustainable Finance Disclosure Regulation)	European Union	Sustainability reporting, transparency	AI automates ESG disclosures and monitors sustainability claims
MAS Technology Risk Guidelines	Singapore	Cyber risk management, system integrity	AI enhances anomaly detection and real-time threat response
DORA (Digital Operational Resilience Act)	European Union	ICT risk management, operational resilience	AI facilitates automated resilience testing, incident simulation, and compliance tracking.

CASE STUDIES AND INDUSTRY INSIGHTS

The following case studies are examples inspired by industry practices to highlight the application of AI in cybersecurity for SRI funds.

Case Study 1: AI-Powered Cybersecurity Transformation in a Leading SRI Fund

As cyber threats against financial institutions surged, the Sustainable Investing Division at BlackRock also recognized the need for urgent strengthening in digital defenses. The year 2023 saw dramatic increases in AI-driven cyberattacks on the firm, including some very clever phishing attempts designed to impersonate fund executives and ransomware attacks directly targeting confidential ESG compliance reports. To counter such threats, BlackRock implemented Darktrace AI, a cutting-edge self-learning cybersecurity system intended for real-time detection, investigation, and neutralization of threats. The AI-enabled solution applies behavior watching over fund transactions and employee activities instantly, flagging anomalies as indicators of possible cyber threats. Moreover, the system had its own standalone mechanism for responding to threats that quarantined malicious entities and prevented breaches before financial damage occurred. To further enhance security, BlackRock added blockchain technology to form an immutable ledger for transactional integrity involving investors, transparency, and resistance to tampering. Within six months of operation, BlackRock reported a 90% reduction in cyber threats and a thwarted attempt at fraud amounting to $10 million, quite assuring of the faith of investors. While AI for cybersecurity has enabled the protection of sensitive ESG fund data, it has placed BlackRock well ahead as an industry leader in protecting sustainable investments against emerging cyber threats.

Case Study 2: Automating ESG Compliance with AI: The HSBC Success Story

HSBC Asset Management had to face severe encumbrances due to the complex and ever-changing global ESG regulatory landscape. The sustainability regulations were largely divergent across geographies, thus raising high compliance costs, increasing risks of greenwashing accusations, and preventing live ESG risk assessments. Here comes the role of HSBC's integration of IBM Watson AI for regulatory compliance, a very sophisticated AI system dedicated to automating regulatory monitoring and risk assessment. The core functionality of the system lies in its ability to continuously scan the developing ESG laws across the US, EU, and Asia using a natural language processing module to identify in real-time compliance risks and streamline reporting processes. HSBC also deployed automated risk detection algorithms, flagging non-compliant ESG investments before they became regulatory liabilities, allowing for quick corrective action. HSBC has achieved a 40% reduction in compliance costs, a 50% reduction in audit penalties, and a measurable increase in ESG fund accuracy, all possible through this endeavor. In addition, the automation of regulatory compliance improved the confidence of the investors, thereby causing a 15% increase in the inflow of sustainable investments. Not only did HSBC's AI-led compliance strategy reduce legal risks, but it also strengthened its image as a reputable leader in ethical and transparent ESG investing.

Experimental Setup

An experimental simulation was set up to examine the efficacy of AI-enabled cybersecurity frameworks in shielding socially responsible investment (SRI) funds. A synthetic dataset was spanned out to mimic exemplar financial transactions and fund activities. It contained 1 million transaction records stipulating normal and anomalous behavior. The dataset included typical cyber threats like phishing attacks, insider threats, and transactional anomalies.

The experiment was carried out with three machine learning models:

- Random Forest Classifier
- Extreme Gradient Boosting (XGBoost)
- Isolation Forest Algorithm (for anomaly detection)

We trained and tested each model using an 80:20 train-test split. Evaluation metrics included:

- Accuracy
- Precision
- Recall
- F1-Score
- False Positive Rate (FPR)

Additionally, we employed the baseline rule-based non-AI traditional system to compare our system against tradition.

Experimental Results

Experimental results showed in Table (**4**) that the AI-enabled methods were found to be better than traditional rule-based systems in threat detection against cybersecurity in SRI fund environments.

Table 4. AI-enabled models experimental results.

Model	Accuracy in (%)	Precision in (%)	Recall in (%)	F1-Score in (%)	False Positive Rate in (%)
Random Forest	94.2	93.8	92.7	93.2	3.5
XG Boost	95.1	94.5	93.9	94.2	2.9
Isolation Forest	91.8	90.4	89.6	90.0	4.1
Rule-Based System	78.6	72.5	68.9	70.6	15.4

The findings showed that:

1. XGBoost was by far the best performer, with a strong emphasis on reducing false positives.
2. Random Forest was quite robust and provided a fair balance between precision and recall.
3. Isolation Forest did quite well in detecting unknown anomalies, but with a marginally higher false positive rate.

In relation to classical rule-based systems, the AI-based models achieved an approximately 16 to 20% improvement in detection performance while also significantly reducing false alarms by over 10%.

FUTURE TRENDS AND CHALLENGES

The burgeoning new applications of Artificial Intelligence (AI), the rising dangers associated with cyber risks, and the increasing debates on ethical matters connected to it combine to reshape the future landscape of finances and sustainable investments. Organisations that embrace the use of AI-driven tools for financial security will be on the road to encountering even more ethical dilemmas and vulnerabilities, which will need critical addressing. This transition also has implications regarding sustainable investments like smart cities and green technologies, becoming more and more complex in terms of confronting innovation and security threats. This dimension spans future trends and challenges across three avatars: AI-generated advancements in financial security, ethical dilemmas of AI-driven decision-making, and challenges in sustainable investments through cyber attack routes. Collectively, they highlight the need for balanced innovation, ethical governance, and a resilient technological infrastructure while steering through increasingly murky waters in today's evolving financial ecosystem.

AI ADVANCEMENTS IN FINANCIAL SECURITY

AI has advanced financial security to a large extent in its various applications with risk management, fraud detection capabilities, and cybersecurity measures. With the utilisation of machine-learning algorithms and predictive analytics, identifying and mitigating financial risks has also been enhanced, thus enabling risk assessment in the credit, market, liquidity, and operational domains with high accuracy [46]. Such AI solutions enable better insight for financial decisions and enhance the operational aspect of a bank [47]. Fraud detection, being one of the significant applications of AI and machine learning, has proved to be very effective. The researchers proposing an intelligent and distributed approach for detecting Internet financial fraud through Big Data noted results showing promise with the Node2Vec algorithm, where F1-Score test results ranged from 67.1% to 73.4% in comparison with other algorithms [48]. This further demonstrates the ability of AI to provide an improved accuracy level and efficiency for fraud detection systems. Interestingly, in creating advancement in financial security, AI also presents enough challenges. A study explains that the application of AI in financial operations gives rise to issues of data privacy, security, and ethics [19]. Another study argues that the adoption of AI technologies into finance should be supported by a rigorous framework to ensure that they are used responsibly and potential risks are mitigated [49]. In summary, an increasingly improved level of AI now helps the analysis of financial security through more sophisticated tools for risk management, fraud detection, and cybersecurity. However, to realise all possibilities of full-blown AI in this area, continuous research, updating the regulatory framework, and keeping an eye on ethical considerations become imperative to maintain a competitive balance between innovation and responsible implementation in finance.

ETHICAL DILEMMAS IN AI-DRIVEN DECISION-MAKING

AI decision-making raises several ethical questions and dilemmas. The nefarious organization's flaws give rise to arguments that call for consideration over transparency, accountability, and the bias it brings with it, making it complicated to understand how and why specific choices are made [50]. Uncertainty regarding technology, incomplete data, and errors in management have been identified as the main sources of ethical risks in AI decision-making [51]. These further lead to algorithmic discrimination, data bias, and vague accountability that might not only perpetuate the existing societal biases but also worsen them [50]. Intriguingly, it seems that although AI technologies open windows to optimised operations and organisational performance, they simultaneously construct ethical dilemmas of algorithmic biases and a lack of transparency [52]. This carries an exhibition of balance that very much favours any opportunity that comes alongside AI without compromising ethicality, transparency, and accountability in its uses. Also, in many ways, the ethical concerns of AI decision-making pass beyond individual ones to general ones such as job losses, economic inequalities, and concentration of power [50]. A multifaceted approach must be employed to address these ethical dilemmas. This includes applications of risk governance elements to effectively block social risks that emanate from algorithms, technology, and data risks [51]. This includes regulatory oversight, ethical standards, data governance, diversity and inclusion programs, and ongoing progress assessment for responsible deployment of AI across different scenarios [52]. Importantly, the transparency, fairness, and accountability of AI systems were built on trust and brought down the ethical dimensions of concern regarding these systems [53]. Thus, through this, organisations will realise the revolutionary potential of AI while establishing ethical decision-making processes.

CYBERSECURITY CHALLENGES FOR SUSTAINABLE INVESTMENTS

Cybersecurity challenges are a harbinger of doom for sustainable investments, especially those targeting green technologies and smart cities. Securing solid cybersecurity to embed within the architecture of sustainable initiatives is essential in ensuring that such initiatives endure and operate effectively for the long haul [54]. With the embracing of smart city design by cities around Africa and beyond to meet urban challenges and any form of economic development, such cities open themselves to diverse threats within their software and hardware interlinkages that form their systems [55]. Their relationship can, however, not be termed as direct. Cybersecurity regulations are for risk minimisation and increased protection; however, the fast-changing regulatory landscape clouds all those contingencies that should ordinarily inform and guide an organisation about its response strategy, investment behaviour, and the like [56]. It is this complex situation in which wait-and-see tends to be adopted, thereby delaying the process of adopting sustainable technologies. And, indeed, dealing with cybersecurity challenges is the crux of sustainable investments. Such strategies should be adaptive and innovative; hence, the deployment of the latest technology and cross-sector consortium [57]. One of the key factors for investment protection to embed sustainability is the development of unique, comprehensive cybersecurity strategies against particular challenges posed by sustainable initiatives such as smart cities and green technologies [55]. Stakeholders will be able to promote innovation in green technology while maintaining technological resilience by effectively integrating cybersecurity measures [54]. Future trends in SRI are shown in Table 5.

Table 5. Future AI trends in SRI fund cybersecurity.

Emerging AI Trend	Description	Impact on SRI Funds
Quantum-Safe Cryptography	Encryption methods resistant to future quantum computing threats	Secures sensitive ESG data and long-term investment records
AI for ESG Scoring Automation	Real-time ESG analysis using AI on company disclosures and news	Improves the accuracy and responsiveness of ESG evaluations
Autonomous Cyber Defense Systems	AI systems that detect and respond to threats without human input	Enables faster, proactive mitigation of cyber risks
Federated Learning Models	Privacy-preserving AI models trained across decentralized data	Ensures data security while enabling collaborative risk insights
AI-Augmented Regulatory Monitoring	Continuous scanning of evolving global regulations using NLP and ML	Automates compliance and reduces regulatory risk

OPEN RESEARCH ISSUES AND FUTURE DIRECTIONS

Despite the promising outcomes of AI applications in cybersecurity for SRI funds, there still exist issues for research.

Algorithmic Bias and Ethical AI: The future work should ensure that AI decision-making is fair, transparent, and accountable, especially when dealing with sensitive ESG-related data.

Integration of Explainable AI (XAI): More research is needed to ensure the inclusion of explicability in security models so that fund managers can truly trust AI-driven decisions.

Real-Time ESG Compliance Scanning: Automated, multilingual, real-time systems that monitor worldwide ESG regulations are underdeveloped.

Privacy-Preserving Collaborative Models: Currently, research on federated learning and encrypted data sharing for cross-border ESG compliance is quite nascent.

AI Resilience Against Adversarial Attacks: The smarter the AI models become, the more apt the attacks against them grow. Therefore, research about defending adversarial AI in the financial environment is of utmost importance.

Benchmark Datasets for SRI Security Research: Since there are no standard datasets to begin with, benchmarking AI models becomes almost impossible. Open, anonymized datasets for SRI cybersecurity are desperately required.

Ethical and Regulatory Harmonization: Future work should address how varying global regulations can be harmonized toward a shared ethical use of AI in the contexts of SRI.

CONCLUSION

This work has shown that Indian AI-empowered cybersecurity has subsequently proven efficiency for security and ethical compliance of the socially responsible investment funds. Some models of data science, such as XGBoost and Random Forest, have found better performance in the detection of threats and reduction in false positives compared with traditional systems. Cases justify that AI strengthens risk management, automates ESG compliance, and builds confidence in investors. However, the adoption of AI poses ethical challenges and exposes new vulnerabilities that require attention. Future initiatives would need to have focused strategic contributions towards responsible AI deployment and regulatory alignment, as well as the mushrooming of cyber resilience. Thoughtful integration of AI can therefore be used to empower SRI funds to achieve both financial performance and social responsibility goals.

REFERENCES

[1] B.T. Familoni, "Cybersecurity challenges in the age of AI: theoretical approaches and practical solutions", *Comput. Sci. IT Res. J.*, vol. 5, no. 3, pp. 703-724, 2024. [http://dx.doi.org/10.51594/csitrj.v5i3.930]

[2] A. Folorunso, T. Adewumi, A. Adewa, R. Okonkwo, and T. N. Olawumi, "Impact of AI on cybersecurity and security compliance", *Glob. J. Eng. Technol. Adv.*, vol. 21, no. 1, pp. 167-184, 2024. [http://dx.doi.org/10.30574/gjeta.2024.21.1.0193]

[3] H.U. Khan, R.A. Khan, and H.S. Alwageed, "AI-driven cybersecurity framework for software development based on the ANN-ISM paradigm", In: *Sci Rep* vol. 15. , 2025, p. 13423. [http://dx.doi.org/10.1038/s41598-025-97204-y]

[4] O. M. Ijiga, I. P. Idoko, G. I. Ebiega, F. I. Olajide, T. I. Olatunde, and C. Ukaegbu, "Harnessing adversarial machine learning for advanced threat detection: AI-driven strategies in cybersecurity risk assessment and fraud prevention", *Open Access Res. J. Sci. Technol.*, vol. 11, no. 1, pp. 001-004, 2024.

[5] M.M. Rahman, "AI-driven business model innovation and TRIAD-AI in South Asian SMEs: Comparative insights and implications", *J. Risk Financ. Manag.*, vol. 18, no. 12, p. 709, 2025. [http://dx.doi.org/10.3390/jrfm18120709]

[6] I.H. Sarker, M.H. Furhad, and R. Nowrozy, "AI-driven cybersecurity: An overview, security intelligence modeling and research directions", *SN Comput. Sci.*, vol. 2, no. 3, p. 173, 2021. [http://dx.doi.org/10.1007/s42979-021-00557-0] [PMID: 33778771]

[7] M.H. Alsulami, "An AI-driven model to enhance sustainability for the detection of cyber threats in IoT environments", *Sensors*, vol. 24, no. 22, p. 7179, 2024. [http://dx.doi.org/10.3390/s24227179]

[8] D. Heath, D. Macciocchi, R. Michaely, and C. Ringgenberg, "Does socially responsible investing change firm behavior", *Rev. Finance,* vol. 27, no. 6, pp. 2057-2083, 2023. [http://dx.doi.org/10.1093/rof/rfad002]

[9] T. Akinwunmi, "Artificial Intelligence (AI) and firm survival of deposit money banks", *Applied Sciences, Computing, and Energy,* vol. 2, no. 1, pp. 21-38, 2025.

[10] G. Arun, P.C.S. Reddy, N. Budati, B. Rebecca, S. Perumalla, and V.B. Gujar, "A deep learning framework for diabetes prediction: PIMA indian dataset", *2024 International Conference on Innovative Computing, Intelligent Communication and Smart Electrical Systems (ICSES),* IEEE., pp. 1-6, 2024.

[11] M. Oladeinde, S.K. Ewuga, A.A. Abdul, T.O. Abrahams, M. Oladeinde, and S.O. Dawodu, "Cybersecurity in banking: A Global Perspective with a focus on Nigerian practices", *Computer Science & IT Research Journal,* vol. 5, no. 1, pp. 41-59, 2024. [http://dx.doi.org/10.51594/csitrj.v5i1.701]

[12] M.A. Kafi, and N. Akter, "Securing financial information in the digital realm: Case studies in cybersecurity for accounting data protection", *Am. J. Trade Policy,* vol. 10, no. 1, pp. 15-26, 2023. [http://dx.doi.org/10.18034/ajtp.v10i1.659]

[13] V. Boii, "Integrated risk management and artificial intelligence in hospital", *J. AI,* vol. 7, no. 1, pp. 63-80, 2023. [http://dx.doi.org/10.61969/jai.1329224]

[14] A. Alhur, "Redefining healthcare with artificial intelligence (AI): the contributions of ChatGPT, Gemini, and Co-pilot", *Cureus,* vol. 16, no. 4, p. e57795, 2024. [http://dx.doi.org/10.7759/cureus.57795] [PMID: 38721180]

[15] Z.B. Akhtar, and A.T. Rawol, "Harnessing artificial intelligence (AI) for cybersecurity: Challenges, opportunities, risks, future directions", *Comput. Artif. Intell.,* vol. 2, no. 2, pp. 1485-1485, 2024. [http://dx.doi.org/10.59400/cai.v2i2.1485]

[16] O. Odeyemi, N.Z. Mhlongo, E.E. Nwankwo, and O.T. Soyombo, "Reviewing the role of AI in fraud detection and prevention in financial services", *International Journal of Science and Research Archive,* vol. 11, no. 1, pp. 2101-2110, 2024. [http://dx.doi.org/10.30574/ijsra.2024.11.1.0279]

[17] F.C. Ogenyi, C.N. Ugwu, and O.P.C. Ugwu, "Securing the future: AI-driven cybersecurity in the age of autonomous IoT", *Frontiers in the Internet of Things,* vol. 4, p. 1658273, 2025. [http://dx.doi.org/10.3389/friot.2025.1658273]

[18] F. Masood, "Impact of artificial intelligence on financial markets", *Int. J. Emerg. Multidiscip.: Soc. Sci.,* vol. 3, no. 1, p. 8, 2024. [http://dx.doi.org/10.54938/ijemdss.2024.03.1.359]

[19] P. Trivedi, A. Ravisankar, G.P. Kumar, V. Krishnamoorthy, S. Shukla, and S. Boopathi, "Finance and technology-integrated digital economy: Circular age of a sustainable digital revolution", In: *Navigating the circular age of a sustainable digital revolution* Hershey, PA, USA: IGI Global, 2024, pp. 91-120.

[20] M.E. Lokanan, and V. Maddhesia, "Supply chain fraud prediction with machine learning and artificial intelligence", *Int. J. Prod. Res.,* pp. 1-28, 2024.

[21] M. Ali, "Advancing industries with AI: The applications being transformational include: Healthcare, powering the Petroleum industry, Handling fraud, Cybersecurity, and Conversational AI", *International Journal of Multidisciplinary Sciences and Arts,* vol. 3, no. 4, pp. 173-180, 2024.

[22] N. Sidana, J.S. Nidhi, L. Rathi, and R. Goel, “Greentech guardians: Navigating the FinTech cybersecurity labyrinth for sustainable solutions,” in *E-Financial strategies for advancing sustainable development*, N. Mansour, S. Baral, and V. Garg, Eds., Cham, Switzerland: Springer, 2024 [http://dx.doi.org/10.1007/978-3-031-67523-2_22]

[23] S. Yoo, S. Kim, E. Kim, E. Jung, K.H. Lee, and H. Hwang, "Real-time location system-based asset tracking in the healthcare field: lessons learned from a feasibility study", *BMC Med. Inform. Decis. Mak.*, vol. 18, no. 1, p. 80, 2018.
[http://dx.doi.org/10.1186/s12911-018-0656-0] [PMID: 30200938]

[24] S. Banoth, and S. Yadala, "A hybrid deep learning framework for stock price forecasting with sentimental analysis", *2024 13th International Conference on System Modeling & Advancement in Research Trends (SMART),* IEEE, pp. 467-471, 2024.
[http://dx.doi.org/10.1109/SMART63812.2024.10882215]

[25] F. Alrowais, S. Althahabi, S. Alotaibi, S. Mohamed, A. Ahmed, M. Hamza, and R. Marzouk, "Automated machine learning enabled cybersecurity threat detection in internet of things environment", *Comput. Syst. Sci. Eng.,* vol. 45, no. 1, pp. 687-700, 2023.
[http://dx.doi.org/10.32604/csse.2023.030188]

[26] H. Suryotrisongko, Y. Musashi, A. Tsuneda, and K. Sugitani, "Robust botnet DGA detection: Blending XAI and OSINT for cyber threat intelligence sharing", *IEEE Access,* vol. 10, pp. 34613-34624, 2022.
[http://dx.doi.org/10.1109/ACCESS.2022.3162588]

[27] D. Preuveneers, and W. Joosen, "Sharing machine learning models as indicators of compromise for cyber threat intelligence", *Journal of Cybersecurity and Privacy,* vol. 1, no. 1, pp. 140-163, 2021.
[http://dx.doi.org/10.3390/jcp1010008]

[28] M.M. Rahman, B.P. Pokharel, S.A. Sayeed, S.K. Bhowmik, N. Kshetri, and N. Eashrak, "RiskAIchain: AI-driven IT infrastructure–blockchain-backed approach for enhanced risk management", *Risks,* vol. 12, no. 12, p. 206, 2024.
[http://dx.doi.org/10.3390/risks12120206]

[29] E. Bran, R. Rughiniș, D. Țurcanu, and A. Radovici, "AI leads, cybersecurity follows: Unveiling research priorities in sustainable development Goal-relevant technologies across nations", *Sustainability,* vol. 16, no. 20, p. 8886, 2024.
[http://dx.doi.org/10.3390/su16208886]

[30] S. Kalogiannidis, D. Kalfas, O. Papaevangelou, G. Giannarakis, and F. Chatzitheodoridis, "The role of artificial intelligence technology in predictive risk assessment for business continuity: A case study of Greece", *Risks,* vol. 12, no. 2, p. 19, 2024.
[http://dx.doi.org/10.3390/risks12020019]

[31] M.S. Rana, and J. Shuford, "AI in healthcare: Transforming patient care through predictive analytics and decision support systems", *J. Artif. Intell. Gen. Sci.,* vol. 1, no. 1, 2024.
[http://dx.doi.org/10.60087/jaigs.v1i1.30]

[32] V. Sukhavasi, A.C. Mouli, D.V. Juneja, Y. Sucharitha, S.S. Joshi, and S. Dey, "Establishing ensemble learning models for daily rainfall forecasting", *2024 International Conference on Innovative Computing, Intelligent Communication and Smart Electrical Systems (ICSES),* IEEE., pp. 1-6, 2024.
[http://dx.doi.org/10.1109/ICSES63760.2024.10910429]

[33] O. Akindotei, I. Emmanuel, B.O. Awotiwon, and A. Otakwu, "Blockchain integration in critical systems enhancing transparency, efficiency, and real-time data security in agile project management, decentralized finance (DeFi), and cold chain management", *International Journal of Scientific Research and Modern Technology (IJSRMT),* vol. 3, no. 11, pp. 19-35, 2024. [IJSRMT].
[http://dx.doi.org/10.38124/ijsrmt.v3i11.107]

[34] P. Harshavardhanan, V. Muneeswaran, D. Saravanan, P. Vijayakarthik, R. Natchadalingam, and P.C.S. Reddy, "An adaptive intrusion detection system for IoT networks using deep learning", *2023 IEEE Fifth International Conference on Advances in Electronics, Computers and Communications (ICAECC),* IEEE., pp. 1-6, 2023.
[http://dx.doi.org/10.1109/ICAECC59324.2023.10560150]

[35] Olawale Adisa, B.S. Ilugbusi, and O. Adisa, "Ensuring global food safety: Integrating blockchain

technology into food supply chains", *Engineering Science & Technology Journal,* vol. 5, no. 3, pp. 811-820, 2024.
[http://dx.doi.org/10.51594/estj.v5i3.905]

[36] R Samrin, P. C. S. Reddy, K Arun Kumar, N Deepthi, C Mithra, S. B. Latha, S Yadala, and G. K. Thakur, "A hybrid deep learning based framework for prediction of rice yield through integration of biophysical parameters and optical remote sensing data in India", *J. Atmos. Solar-Terr. Phys.,* vol. 279, p. 106734, 2026.
[http://dx.doi.org/10.1016/j.jastp.2026.106734]

[37] M.D. Basith, P. Praveen, and P.C.S. Reddy, "Adaptive deep Q-GAN framework for enhanced breast cancer detection in medical imaging", *Biomedical Signal Processing and Control,* vol. 112, p. 108638, 2026.
[http://dx.doi.org/10.1016/j.bspc.2025.108638]

[38] M. Jeyaraman, S. Balaji, N. Jeyaraman, and S. Yadav, "Unraveling the ethical enigma: Artificial intelligence in healthcare", *Cureus,* vol. 15, no. 8, p. e43262, 2023.
[http://dx.doi.org/10.7759/cureus.43262] [PMID: 37692617]

[39] L. Cobianchi, J.M. Verde, T.J. Loftus, D. Piccolo, F. Dal Mas, P. Mascagni, A. Garcia Vazquez, L. Ansaloni, G.R. Marseglia, M. Massaro, B. Gallix, N. Padoy, A. Peter, and H.M. Kaafarani, "Artificial intelligence and surgery: Ethical dilemmas and open issues", *J. Am. Coll. Surg.,* vol. 235, no. 2, pp. 268-275, 2022.
[http://dx.doi.org/10.1097/XCS.0000000000000242] [PMID: 35839401]

[40] V.K. Bukkarayasamudram, P.C.S. Reddy, and K. Arun Kumar, "Quantum computing revolution in healthcare: a systematic review of applications, issues and future directions", *Artif Intell Rev,* vol. 58, p. 389, 2025.
[http://dx.doi.org/10.1007/s10462-025-11381-w]

[41] P. Ravali, P.C.S. Reddy, and P. Praveen, "An efficient neuro-framework for brain tumor classification using a CNN-based self-supervised learning approach with genetic optimizations",
[http://dx.doi.org/10.2174/011570159X378103250806214613]

[42] S. Pansoni, S. Tiribelli, M. Paolanti, F. Di Stefano, E. Frontoni, E. S. Malinverni, and B. Giovanola, "Artificial intelligence and cultural heritage: Design and assessment of an ethical framework", *Int. Arch. Photogramm. Remote Sens. Spatial Inf. Sci.,* pp. 1149-1155, 2023.
[http://dx.doi.org/10.5194/isprs-archives-XLVIII-M-2-2023-1149-2023]

[43] P. Radanliev, "Review and comparison of US, EU, and UK regulations on cyber risk/security of the current blockchain technologies: Viewpoint from 2023", *Rev. Socionetwork Strateg.,* vol. 17, no. 2, pp. 105-129, 2023.
[http://dx.doi.org/10.1007/s12626-023-00139-x]

[44] B. Solanke, F. B. Onita, O. J. Ochulor, and H. O. Iriogbe, "The impact of artificial intelligence on regulatory compliance in the oil and gas industry", *International Journal of Science and Technology Research Archive,* vol. 7, no. 1, pp. 061-072, 2024.

[45] Titilola Falaiye, Odeyemi Olubusola, N.Z. Mhlongo, T. Falaiye, O. Olubusola, A.I. Daraojimba, and B.B. Oguejiofor, "The role of artificial Intelligence in enhancing tax compliance and financial regulation", *Finance & Accounting Research Journal,* vol. 6, no. 2, pp. 241-251, 2024.
[http://dx.doi.org/10.51594/farj.v6i2.822]

[46] M. Bouchetara, M. Zerouti, and A.R. Zouambi, "Leveraging artificial intelligence (AI) in public sector financial risk management: Innovations, challenges, and future directions", *EDPACS,* vol. 69, no. 9, pp. 124-144, 2024.
[http://dx.doi.org/10.1080/07366981.2024.2377351]

[47] M. Hidayat, S.Y. Defitri, and H. Hilman, "The impact of artificial intelligence (AI) on financial management", *Manag. Stud. Bus. J.,* vol. 1, no. 1, pp. 123-129, 2024.

[48] S. Singh, "Artificial intelligence and machine learning in financial services: Risk management and

fraud detection", *J. Electr. Syst.,* vol. 20, no. 6s, pp. 1418-1424, 2024.
[http://dx.doi.org/10.52783/jes.2929]

[49] O. Odeyemi, T. Falaiye, D.O. Daraojimba, A.O. Ajayi-Nifise, and T. Falaiye, "Machine learning in financial forecasting: A U.S. review—Exploring the advancements, challenges, and implications of AI-driven predictions in financial markets", *World J. Adv. Res. Rev.,* vol. 21, no. 2, pp. 1969-1984, 2024.
[http://dx.doi.org/10.30574/wjarr.2024.21.2.0444]

[50] F. Osasona, A. Atadoga, T.O. Abrahams, O.A. Farayola, and B.S. Ayinla, "Reviewing the ethical implications of AI in decision-making processes", *Int. J. Manag. Entrep. Res.,* vol. 6, no. 2, pp. 322-335, 2024.
[http://dx.doi.org/10.51594/ijmer.v6i2.773]

[51] H. Guan, L. Dong, and A. Zhao, "Ethical risk factors and mechanisms in artificial intelligence decision making", *Behav. Sci. (Basel),* vol. 12, no. 9, p. 343, 2022.
[http://dx.doi.org/10.3390/bs12090343] [PMID: 36135147]

[52] M.A. Khair, R. Mahadasa, F.A. Tuli, and J.R.P.K. Ande, "Beyond human judgment: Exploring the impact of artificial intelligence on HR decision-making efficiency and fairness", *Glob. Discl. Econ. Bus.,* vol. 9, no. 2, pp. 163-176, 2020.
[http://dx.doi.org/10.18034/gdeb.v9i2.730]

[53] W. Shafik, Toward a more ethical future of artificial intelligence and data science.*The ethical frontier of AI and data analysis.* Hershey, PA, USA: IGI Global, 2024, pp. 362-388.
[http://dx.doi.org/10.4018/979-8-3693-2964-1.ch022]

[54] W Shafik, "Toward a more ethical future of artificial intelligence and data science. ", In: *The Ethical Frontier of AI and Data Analysis* IGI Global: Hershey, PA, USA, 2024, pp. 362-388.
[http://dx.doi.org/10.51594/csitrj.v5i5.1115]

[55] Shedrack Onwusinkwue, Emuesiri Ejairu, S. Onwusinkwue, S.O. Dawodu, O.V. Akagha, and E. Ejairu, "Cybersecurity challenges in Smart Cities: A case review of African metropolises", *Computer Science & IT Research Journal,* vol. 5, no. 2, pp. 254-269, 2024.
[http://dx.doi.org/10.51594/csitrj.v5i2.756]

[56] M. Kianpour, and S. Raza, "More than malware: unmasking the hidden risk of cybersecurity regulations", *Int. Cybersecur. Law Rev.,* vol. 5, no. 1, pp. 169-212, 2024.
[http://dx.doi.org/10.1365/s43439-024-00111-7]

[57] A.T. Somnathe, V.T. Selvi, N.G. Stepha, M.T. Kingslin, F.M. Inamdar, and P.C.S. Reddy, "An intelligent traffic conflict prediction using deep learning with long-term evolution access data", In: *Proc. 2025 3rd International Conference on Smart Systems for Applications in Electrical Sciences (ICSSES)*, 2025, pp. 1-6.
[http://dx.doi.org/10.1109/ICSSES64899.2025.11010032]

CHAPTER 11

Security in Smart Cities: Applications, Advances, Practices, Research Challenges, and Future Trends

M Indrasenareddy[1,*], K Venkatesh[2], K Chatrapathy[3], D Chitra[4], S Yuvalatha[5] and M Lakshmi Prasad[6]

[1] *Computer Science and Engineering, BVRIT HYDERABAD College, of Engineering for Women, Hyderabad, Telangana, India*

[2] *Department of Engineering in Internetworking, Dalhousie University, Halifax, Nova Scotia, Canada*

[3] *School of Computing & Information Technology, REVA University Bangalore, Karnataka, India*

[4] *Department of MBA, Panimalar Engineering College, Chennai, Tamil Nadu, India*

[5] *Department of Computer Science and Business Systems, Bannari Amman Institute of Technology, Erode, Tamil Nadu, India*

[6] *Computer Science and Engineering, Institute of Aeronautical Engineering, Hyderabad, Telangana, India*

Abstract: The concept of "smart cities" is gaining traction around the world, with several governments allocating substantial funds to this cause. The concept of smart cities has developed gradually over the years, moving from prior efforts on the smart city to more recent iterations such as eco-city, sustainable city, linked city, omnipresent city, and green city. The advent of lightning-fast 5G wireless connectivity, lightning-fast GPU multi-core servers, big data, cloud computing, AI, and data analytics are all hallmarks of the modern era. The creation and implementation of "smart cities" have been aided by numerous emerging technologies. To better comprehend what we meant when we said "securing smart cities," the authors of this paper lay out a framework for doing just that. They go over the pros and cons of using current security measures to protect a smart city, including authentication, access control, encryption, and firewalls. In particular, we discuss the potential harmful assaults on a smart city and the repercussions of such attacks, as well as the security of data, the internet, water supply, electricity supply, the city brain, and other vital city services. Lastly, they go over some smartcity security best practices. Additionally, this chapter delves into the idea of smart cities and how the IoT and ML may be utilized to create a data-driven smart environment. By maximizing the use of data and technology, "smart cities" raise living standards for city dwellers and make municipal services more efficient. In addition to outlining the many uses of smart cities, this chapter delves into the difficulties of integrating IoT and ML into cityscapes.

* **Corresponding Author M Indrasenareddy:** Department of Computer Science and Engineering, BVRIT Hyderabad College of Engineering for Women, Hyderabad, Telangana, India;
Email: indrasenareddy.m@bvrithyderabad.edu.in

Pundru Chandra Shaker Reddy, Yadala Sucharitha, & Thillaiarasu N (Eds.)

Keywords: IoT, Machine Learning, Smart-cities, Security, 5G.

INTRODUCTION

To integrate cutting-edge software and hardware based on information and communication technology (ICT) into city planning, the concept of a "smart city" was initially proposed in 1990. A smart city is one that makes use of information and communiqué technologies to improve the quality of life for its residents, boost the economy, make it easier to manage transportation and traffic, promote environmental sustainability, and make it easier for people to communicate with government officials. Planners are increasingly drawn to the smart city concept as a means to address the growing urban population and new developments in urban planning and information and communication technology [1]. This approach prioritizes the well-being of city dwellers by addressing various technological, social, cultural, environmental, energy, and information needs. Research has pointed to smart mobility as an aspect of the smart city concept (Apostol). The goal of smart city planning is to employ cutting-edge technology and processes to address pressing urban issues such as traffic jams, energy networks with high carbon emissions, inadequate infrastructure, and a lack of public safety and sound policy. Some examples of cities that have embraced AI and robots to create smart applications are Ottawa, Moscow, Dubai, London, New York, and Hong Kong [2]. Keep in mind that these technologies aren't without their risks, and those risks could compromise a smart city's ability to function.

The intricacy of the systems required for smart city development makes smart city systems vulnerable in terms of their functionality. Such susceptibility may arise as a result of external risks, strategy risks, or operational risks. The authors of [3] list the potential dangers that smart cities face, including approval issues, financial concerns, technological challenges, difficulties in forming partnerships, and problems with managing resources. The privacy and security of the smart city technologies are potential weak points. It may be easier to identify risks in smart city systems on an individual level, which means that risk management strategies can be better put into place to lessen their impact [4]. For instance, the hazards associated with energy systems are brought to light by. They talk about the smart city waste management system's hazards and difficulties. When evaluating risks associated with smart city planning and management, however, research should take the big picture into account. If smart city projects are to overcome obstacles in areas such as technology, privacy and security, politics, the environment, management, and user trust and acceptance, it is crucial to evaluate all of these risks simultaneously [5]. Various parts of a smart city's design and operation may have potential dangers that a risk assessment like this one can reveal.

A lot of processing power is needed to handle this mountain of data used to integrate different AI and ML algorithms. For instance, in the last several years, machine learning and artificial intelligence have been employed by practically all medical and clinical science institutes [6]. When it comes to smart health, radiology is a really effective field that uses AI and ML to great advantage. On a yearly basis, over two billion medical exams and scans, such as chest X-rays, are conducted around the world. Many different types of medical images make use of Deep Neural Networks (DNN), a well-known deep learning algorithm [7]. Management of water or electricity resources, verification, and payment for intelligent card services are only a few examples of the many important applications that have recently adopted a data-centric architecture. Smart mobility has the potential to increase traffic efficiency while decreasing CO_2 emissions. Information gathering, data networking, and pervasiveness are crucial to the smart city applications and their utility [8]. Fig. (**1**) shows how smart cities are good for people and the environment.

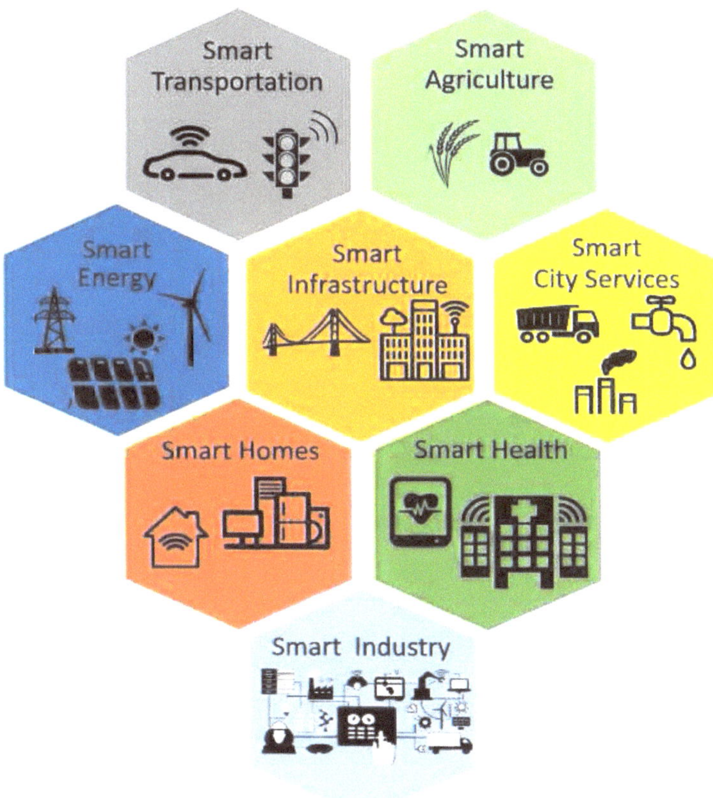

Fig. (1). Smart cities components.

Fig. (**2**) shows the three tiers upon which smart city implementation is based: (1) collect information and learn about urban environments through statistics; (2) store, organize, assess, and handle data in order to make autonomous decisions; and (3) implement the choice at a service level. Academic and industrial fields play a significant role in the development of IoT-based infrastructures, which are influencing the current state of their deployments for smart city applications [9]. Over time, the population of metropolitan areas is steadily increasing, which poses numerous challenges to civic life. According to a projection by the United Nations Population Fund, there would be a considerable change by 2030 from 2007, when half of the population lived in urban areas [10]. Many smart business and urban resident apps are expected to heavily utilize IoT-based infrastructure.

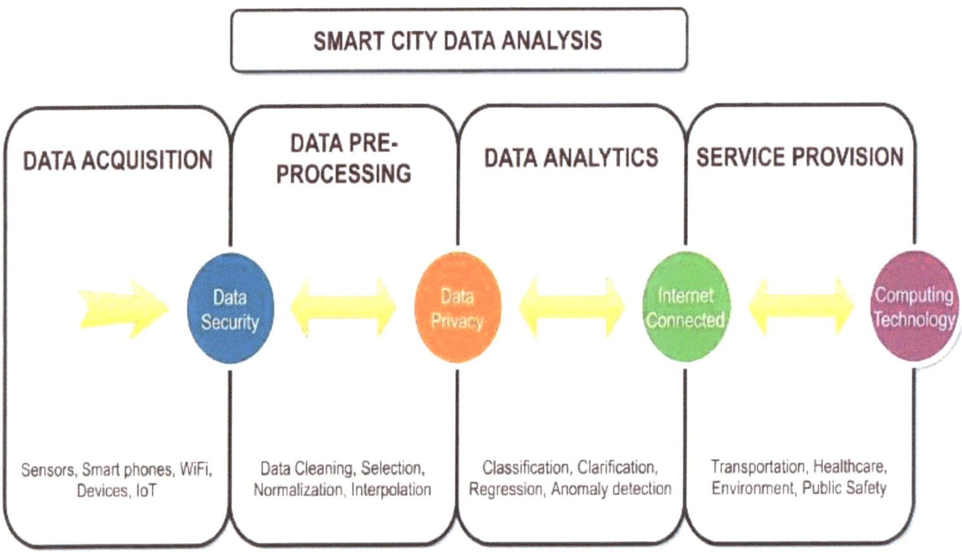

Fig. (2). Data lifecycle of the smart city.

One of the most anticipated components of a smart city's overall platform is the Internet of Things (IoT). Every kind of sensor—video cameras, microphones, temperature monitors, water meters, and so on—will serve as an "input" to the smart city system. The term "sensor" refers to a variety of devices that can sense their physical environment, record data, and transmit that information back to a central location using various wireless or wired connections (*e.g.*, optical fiber, cables, etc.). In order to keep the power consumption of the sensors to a minimum, the messages are often lightweight and have a tiny packet size [11].

Applications sit atop the two vertical and four horizontal layers seen in Fig. (**3**) that make up the system architecture of a smart city. Layers for devices and sensing, connection, IoT management, and data-AI make up the four horizontal essentials. Through the networking layer, data from sensors is then linked to gathering points, also known as gateways. The edge-based IoT connection management layer ensures interoperability across heterogeneous devices and connections by collecting data from various sensors and sending it across various networks and protocols [12]. Last but not least, smart city applications are powered by the data-AI layer, which processes data, analyzes it, draws insights from it, and offers intelligence.

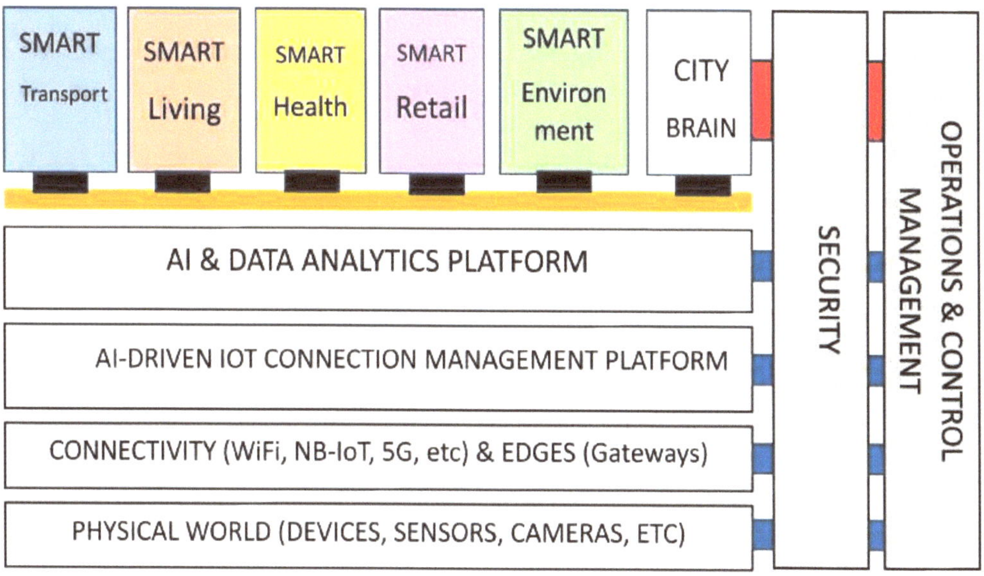

Fig. (3). Smart cities architecture system.

Different smart city apps will make use of data and insights in different ways at the higher layer, and they will cause suitable events to happen (for example, a smart city security application could call the police to the scene of a crime). In order to analyze the data and make accurate predictions, artificial intelligence can be employed. For example, facial recognition technology can be used to identify the person being investigated [13]. Therefore, all applications for smart cities have data and processing layers. Realistically, it is difficult to realize the ideal of a unified data and AI platform layer that can support all potential smart city applications due to the existence of various administrative control domains and the fact that a centralized platform layer can cause a bottleneck in the event of failures. Data analytics has great promise for smart city applications, despite the risks and opportunities that come with utilizing such technologies. In order to better understand the potential of IoT and ML in smart cities, researchers should work on improving existing algorithms and creating new ones [14].

Security in traffic management and autonomous vehicle systems ensures safe, reliable operation within smart cities. Traffic systems use encryption, access control, and intrusion detection to protect real-time data and infrastructure from tampering. Autonomous vehicles rely on secure V2V and V2I communications, blockchain-based authentication, and encrypted firmware updates to prevent malicious interference. AI and ML further enhance safety by detecting anomalies and spoofing attempts, ensuring resilient and trustworthy transportation networks.

This effort is driven by a desire to delve into the ways in which machine learning and the Internet of Things might contribute to the development of smart cities. The efficient management of resources and the improvement of inhabitants' quality of life are becoming increasingly difficult for cities to handle as their populations continue to rise. To overcome these obstacles, smart technologies are being used more and more by cities to build data-centric environments [15]. City planners, traffic engineers, and resource allocators can all benefit from the insights provided by machine learning algorithms that study this data. The IoT and ML have many applications in city living, and this review article looks at a few of them. In addition to outlining these technologies' strengths and weaknesses, the review report will also suggest areas for further study [16]. The pros and cons of these technologies can then be fully grasped by researchers, practitioners, and lawmakers. By gathering relevant information, stakeholders may decide how to best execute them, leading to data-centric environments that boost citizen well-being and advance sustainable development. As far as the writers are aware, there is a plethora of literature on the subject, but none of it has provided a comprehensive analysis. The possibilities of the Internet of Things (IoT) and machine learning for data-centric smart city implementation are discussed in this article. If these technologies are to reach their full potential in city settings, it sheds light on the obstacles that must be overcome. The following are the primary benefits of this research:

- With a broad overview of the subjects, implementations, and algorithms, we go into specific examples from several smart city application domains.
- We stress that data is crucial for propelling innovation and enhancement. Integrating IoT with ML strategies to gather, evaluate, and act upon data in real-time is described in the article as a means to construct a data-centric smart environment.
- From an algorithmic perspective, we examine a data management evaluation that includes data collecting, processing, and delivery.
- In order for smart cities to reach their maximum potential, we outline the major obstacles that need to be overcome regarding data privacy, security, and ethical concerns.

- We examine the provided structure through the lens of machine learning and knowledge discovery.
- Finally, we provide the recommendations for the future and the extent of this study.

STATE OF THE CURRENT RESEARCH

By bringing together, as an ecosystem, all the essential parts of a smart city, urban computing usually makes smart city construction easier. It offers the tech that smart cities need to distribute services to their residents effectively across all of the city's systems. The delivery of smart city services is one of the challenging problems it tackles [17]. Therefore, urban computing has the potential to play a pivotal role in smart cities. From what we can tell, the eight dimensions represent a wide range of computer technologies and their potential uses. In this article, we survey the most current obstacles to smart city research. Besides being cutting-edge, this paper's key contribution is that it demonstrates how urban computing is inherently multidisciplinary. As shown in Fig. (**4**), we classified urban computing for smartcities into 8 sectors: cybersecurity, smart automation, DL, big data, multi-cloud, cognitive computing, and the IoT [18].

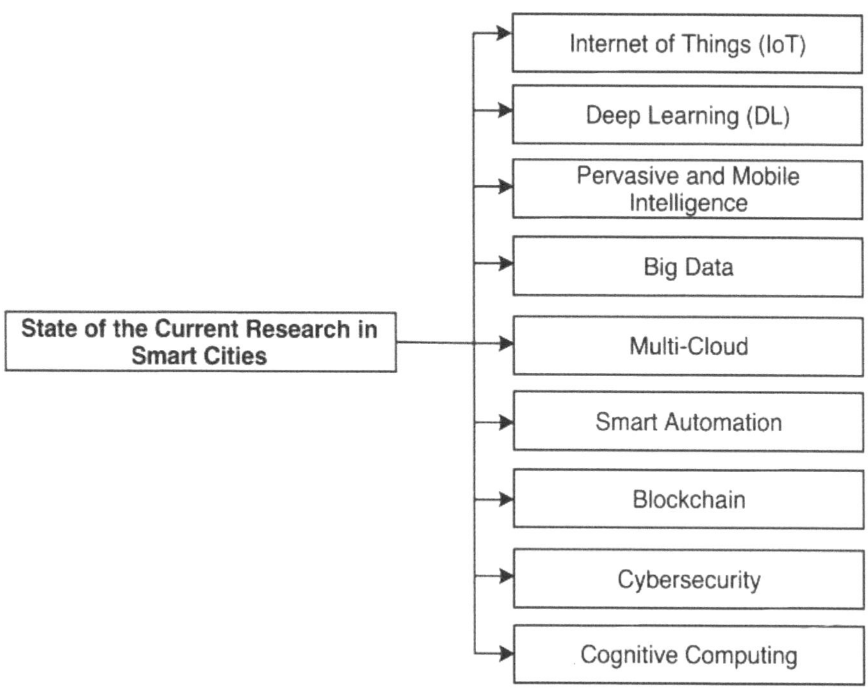

Fig. (4). The research challenges in smartcities.

IOT for Smart Cities

The IoT is crucial to smart city initiatives because it enables the ubiquitous digitalization that gives birth to the thought of smart cities. What we call "the internet of things" is really just a network of interconnected computing tools that can share data with servers in the cloud and even receive instructions on how to carry out certain tasks. Data analytics operations are a part of the Internet of Things (IoT), which entails gathering data for the persistence of informing strategy and decision-making. More application development is expected to be driven by the predicted 75 billion internet-connected devices by 2025. With the help of the IoT, sensors in smart cities may gather information about the city's condition and transmit it to a central cloud. From there, the data can be processed to find patterns and inform decisions [19].

SECURITY FOR SMART CITIES

You can't tackle the issue of smart city security in isolation; it's part of a larger problem. The term "silos" refers to the practice of creating separate security resolutions for various smart city claims, such as those dealing with transportation, healthcare, the environment, and daily life. Rather, it is important to look at the big picture and figure out what governs and helps with the safe procedures and amenities of these smart city apps [20]. The "brain," "body," and "senses" of a smart city must be protected, along with all of its applications. As a result, safeguarding a smart city requires an all-encompassing security solution. The city's infrastructures, connectivity, applications, and services, as well as the city itself from outsiders, will be protected by the security system, as seen in Fig. (**3**).

It is important to consider (a) what needs protecting, (b) the attackers' end goals, and (c) the sorts of attacks while developing security solutions for smart cities. Looking at the assets of a smart city can help us realize what needs protecting. Fig. (**5a**), (**5b**), and (**5c**) demonstrate the people, resources, and services that make up a smart city. When I say "resources," what I mean are (a) monetary assets, (b) infrastructures, such as the internet, data-centers, offices, residences, etc., and (c) necessities of life, such as water, food, medicine, and energy.

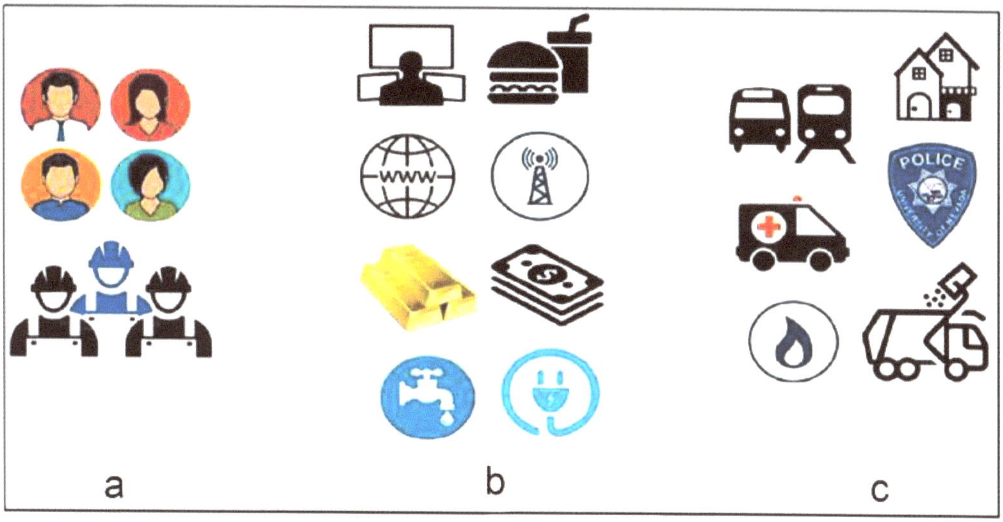

Fig. (5). Smart cities assets a) Assets b) infrastructure c) necessities.

People are the individuals who make the city their home and do their jobs there. People of all ages are encompassed in this. Businesses rely on the people who live and work in their cities to keep running, and the people who live and work in a city are the engine that propels the economy. Furthermore, when I say "city services," what I really mean are things like public health, water and power supply, public sanitation, sewage facilities, forces, ambulances, etc [21]. A smart city would be incomplete without these essential components. A city's riches or abundance of resources can entice attackers to strike and steal from the city. Theft isn't the only motivation for some criminals. Attackers whose primary objective is to cause mayhem by interfering with or even stopping services are another possible target. There are two main types of malicious attacks, the majority of which are: (a) Attacks that cause problems for city dwellers (b) Attacks that cause problems for city businesses

The lives and economic prosperity of a city are devastated by both of these final objectives. The locality might also define the sort of attacks. Physical presence at the attack location or in close proximity is referred to as a local attack. Here is where command centers equipped with video surveillance aid in apprehending and identifying assailants. Cybercriminals can interrupt city services through remote attacks, which include gaining control of computer systems through internet connectivity but do not occur on-site [22].

Securing water supply

Since water is fundamental to human existence, it naturally takes precedence.

Water is essential for human survival and commercial operations in any city. Without it, residents and companies would have to find other ways to stay hydrated. Disruptions to water supplies can occur as a result of attacks on water source points and transport. Once again, assailants can physically carry out such attacks on-site by cutting electricity to pumps and bursting pipes that convey water across the supply system [23]. In most cases, having security guards and on-site security cameras deters attacks that occur on the premises. On the other hand, it could be difficult to detect digital attacks launched from distant locations (outside the city limits). They are able to cut off or drastically restrict the city's water supply by gaining control of the water management system through cyberspace. The watchdog programs should be active at all times to continuously detect and report any irregularities [24].

Securing Energy

Today, energy powers the majority of smart city applications. When the power goes out, the majority of the smart city systems and businesses will stop working, leaving the city in total darkness. Accordingly, smart cities cannot function without a reliable power source and reliable power transmission. Physically demolishing the site or stopping the electricity-producing process are two ways to stop power generation. These necessitate tight site security to guarantee uninterrupted power generation and backup power in the event of an interruption. On the other hand, power transmission [25] means that electricity is transmitted by power stations, power lines, transformers, switches, and relays.

Therefore, all smart city applications are vulnerable to assaults that disrupt power supply, which can affect any of these components. There have been reports that energy-producing plants were being targeted by terrorists [26] who aimed to cause street disturbances and major outages in cities. A thorough plan and structure must be put in place to guarantee the city's electricity generation and distribution. Additionally, a single localized attack might have a multiplied effect due to the highly networked nature of an energy infrastructure system, which increases the likelihood of a domino effect of interruptions. Massive outages in numerous cities may ensue from this. The ability to isolate and withstand such attacks should be pre-integrated into smart cities.

Securing Connectivity

In order to link sensors, cameras, data centers, etc., smart city infrastructures necessitate connectivity. That is why, apart from electricity, connection is the lifeblood of smart cities. Two types of network infrastructures, wired and wireless, allow for connectivity. Internet of Things security could potentially be seen in this. Interoperability of devices, data, and connections is the essence of

Internet of Things security. Using lightweight protected end-to-end transport protocols ensures connection security, while encryption secures data [27].

Securing Data

In order to perceive, gather, process, and analyze data, the majority of smart city applications will do just that. Then, these insights will be used to design services that make sense. Data pertaining to vehicles, drivers, traffic, and passengers will be gathered by smart-transport applications, while data pertaining to patients and doctors will be gathered by smart-health applications [28]. There must be content and storage security for the data produced by the smart city platform, regardless of the smart city apps that use it. There are multiple methods to secure this type of data:

a. Data access control, which involves guarding against unauthorized access.
b. Encryption—safeguard the data's contents.
c. Verification—verify the origin.
d. Data validity is confirmed by signatures.
e. Protect users' anonymity by removing their identities and geolocation from collected data.

Securing the Smart City Brain

Ensuring that only authorized workers are able to access a smart city system is of the utmost importance. A key component of smart city security is preventing unauthorized admittance to tools, networks, and platforms. A centralized smart city operation and control center concept has been implemented in numerous cities worldwide. To monitor, control, and respond to smart city activities, Huawei, for instance, built the IOC. This center uses real-time picture seizure on roadways, people movement, and more. Complete safety for the IOC is paramount. A smart city's IOC must be immediately isolated in the event of unauthorized access or control, as this would be a catastrophic catastrophe comparable to an invasion of the city. The authorities ought to seize the IOC immediately [29].

Securing Smart City Financial Assets

City citizens, corporations, and the state all have financial assets, which can be either physical or conceptual [30]. Trusts, savings and loans, and other types of financial organizations own the vast majority of these assets. Some examples of potential assaults are: • preventing users from accessing financial services (online banking, trading, etc.) Thefts involving money or stocks, among other financial assets

- **Theft of User and Bank Account Information**

Financial Information Technology (IT) systems often employ firewalls and intrusion detection and prevention systems to ward against unwanted visitors. For a smart city's financial assets to be safe, it needs security measures such as encrypted data transmissions, user authentication with multiple factors, secure network and transport associates, protection from malware and viruses, examination of logs, protection at endpoints, and so on [31].

Securing Smartcity Critical Amenities

Hackers may impair the lives of millions of city residents if they were to interrupt municipal services, such as the distribution of power, gas, etc. A huge disaster has occurred. It is also lethal to impede rescue and law enforcement activities. Additionally, it is catastrophic when transportation services and traffic signals are disrupted. Many countries now consider it a crime and an act of terrorism when vital city services are disrupted. Accordingly, a smart city has to make sure all of its vital services are safe [32].

Blockchain and Smartcities

Without a centralized authority, blockchain technology can authorize transactions and verify a ledger in a decentralized manner using public-key encryption and consensus procedures. This is where blockchain technology truly shines. There has been widespread acceptance of blockchain as a means to secure monetary transactions since the introduction of Bitcoin and related technologies. Bitcoin has developed into a digital currency that millions of people have invested in thanks to its immutable distributed ledger technology [33]. However, what are the potential uses of blockchain technology in relation to smart cities? Are there ways that blockchain technology can improve the security, transparency, efficiency, and resilience of urban areas? There needs to be a solution to these difficult problems.

Some current applications of blockchain technology include smart contracts [34], which allow for the secure establishment of business agreements between numerous parties (such as a vendor and a buyer). The digital negotiation or performance of a contract can be facilitated, verified, and enforced with the use of smart contracts. The elimination of middlemen is another advantage of smart contracts when it comes to conducting legitimate business.

Security Best Practices

A set of guidelines for the cybersecurity fortification of smartcities has been established, as stated by the ENISA [35]. Implementing a security policy, encrypting data, using a VPN, installing alarms and surveillance, creating activity logs, maintaining backups, conducting regular audits, and shutting down procedures are all part of the package.

Many nations can benefit from implementing best practices and learning from one another's experiences. To ensure that similar problems do not occur in future smart cities, each one should help define security superlative practices and report and share all vulnerabilities. U.S. National Institute of Standards and Technology (NIST) also introduces a cybersecurity framework to deal with these concerns, complementing ENISA initiatives [35]. The primary goal of the framework is to establish a shared vocabulary for stakeholders to better comprehend and analyze cybersecurity risks.

The Advent of Facial Clones and Fraud

One unintended consequence of this increased dependence is that con artists may start using impersonation as a means of concealment when conducting crimes in both public and private settings. Several instances of fraud involving silicone masks have already cost millions of dollars. Extending biometric authentication beyond face recognition to include iris scans, fingerprints, voice, handwriting, etc., is a crucial part of future smart city security. This paves the way for additional studies [36].

APPLICATIONS OF SMART CITIES

Fig. (**6**) depicts the general smart city applications that are discussed in this section of the study [37]. The next sections of this work provide in-depth analyses of each of these topics.

Mobility management: The effective administration of urban transportation systems is often associated with this. To oversee transportation, it necessitates and employs the data and communication system. Managing traffic flows, pedestrians, and emergency management can be facilitated by these technologies through the use of remote detection and video monitoring systems. There needs to be a variety of public transportation options that use green fuels for smart mobility to work [38].

Environmental protection: A full understanding of public and green places requires web-based and remote monitoring in order to foster a green environment. Additionally, improved community, building, and urban resource optimization and management for energy conservation and hazardous emission reduction are necessary for increased environmental sustainability [39].

Fig. (6). Applications of smart cities.

Economic growth: Service and production automation plans must be put into place in order to speed up the process. To be competitive, a city needs innovation and entrepreneurship to build new, high-tech technologies [40].

Smart government: Connectivity, information, and public services are essential for citizens to have direct interactions with their government. Improving government responsiveness to local demands and increasing government transparency and accountability are the primary goals.

Public safety: Utilizing the IoT framework, which rallies users' connectivity, enhances safety and security. Better management of homes and workplaces is made possible with its assistance. The use of ubiquitous technologies enhances one's interaction with their immediate environment [41].

OPEN RESEARCH CHALLENGES

A number of obstacles stand in the way of smart city realization due to the engrossment of urban computing in carrying out varied and complicated task accomplishment. This section lays out the key problems and proposes solutions to those problems.

Cognitive Cybersecurity

The field of cybersecurity big data analytics has made great strides, but there are still many unanswered questions. Most current analytical methods fail to effectively detect cybersecurity threats because they fail to place an emphasis on the reasoning required to "understand" the risks and dangers involved. For this reason, experts in the field are presently concentrating on finding better ways to deal with problems related to big data analytics. In the context of remotely distributed repository management, "big data" refers to extremely large data sets created rapidly. This led scientists to suggest cutting-edge tools for efficient and effective analytics of massive datasets. Government and non-government organizations (NGOs) can benefit from big data analytics by discovering previously unknown insights inside massive datasets, such as public opinion on a particular policy or healthcare providers' prognoses [42]. In order to enhance enterprise security, it is necessary to design a cognitive application that can detect security threats in massive amounts of data. Through the real-time processing and interpretation of huge data for cybersecurity, cognitive analytics may one day overcome the limitations of human cognition.

Air Quality

An important step in making cities more sustainable is collecting and analyzing data on air pollution in real time. This is especially true in large cities, where poor air quality is a major environmental concern. Air pollution stations have exorbitantly high construction and maintenance expenses. Therefore, methods to quantify air pollution that do not break the bank are required. A model for predicting PM2.5 was suggested in reference [43], and it makes use of data collected from a variety of urban sources. Compared to all baselines, the suggested model outperforms them thanks to its application of transfer learning. In addition, we talk about how to incorporate social media data and events into the model in the future to make it even more accurate.

In terms of air quality, there are a number of unanswered research questions. Predicting and quantifying the effects of air quality on human health is the main obstacle. Due to the effects of climate change on air quality, researchers have found it difficult to quantify the effects of air quality on human health, despite extensive efforts in this area. Research on the potential hospitalizations and deaths caused by air pollution has also been conducted, but experts are calling for improved decision-making tools in future designs. The potential for exposure misclassification owing to accumulated exposure from point, non-point, and mobility sources has led researchers to advocate for location-specific studies [44].

IoT Resources

Electric Vehicles (EVs) are becoming more common, which is altering people's transportation habits. Energy efficiency, durability, and other aspects all have an impact on how well electric vehicles function and how they impact the environment. The difficulty of transferring EV data and linking it to the cloud is a problem that arises alongside the use of EVs. Researchers might thus take advantage of this chance to design new and innovative methods for the transfer and exchange of information by analyzing the large data generated by EVs. For this reason, authors of a study [45] suggested an energy management system that would make use of data from EV systems to identify trends in order to estimate long-term performance utilizing big data. The outcomes demonstrate that the suggested method can effectively assist in transferring large amounts of data from electric vehicles to the cloud, which in turn can be used to analyze driving habits and range.

According to the findings, the suggested framework uses far less energy than data transit *via* the internet. Researchers now have a baseline to investigate hybrid approaches, where data transfer is accomplished by both vehicles and the internet, thanks to the suggested framework, which lays the groundwork to decrease data transfer delays in smart cities. The difficulty of collecting and storing massive amounts of data from a variety of sources in a smart city is well-known. Data transmission to control units for analytics and processing also presents certain difficulties. A technique for reducing energy consumption and carbon emissions was proposed in another study [46] to aid in the effective, smooth transmission of data. It was possible to accelerate data transmission using the suggested method. In a similar vein, other authors suggest an offshoot of the IoV called the Internet of Buses (IoB). This program makes it possible for data carriers to use buses for public transit [47]. There is still a lot of room for growth in this field, despite the progress.

Cyber-Physical System

In order to provide more extensive cyberphysical services, the large-scale configuration of cyber-physical systems poses order problems in various domains, necessitating additional smart sensing and computing approaches, such as enhanced networking and communications tools. The infrastructure barrier to smart cities connected to urban computing is the problem of transforming classical cities that were created in a disorganized manner due to overcrowding and poor planning into smart cities [48].

Urbanization presents a number of instrumental difficulties, including those pertaining to public health, energy consumption, transportation management, and environmental contamination. An article [49] argues that smart cities are one of many ways that cyber-physical systems will expand in the future. Sustainable mobility solutions will be delivered by the rapidly evolving urban mobility landscapes in a smart city. Because of the proliferation of cyber-physical system applications in global standards and essential infrastructures for smart city advancements, a wide range of academics, managers, and industry experts are currently focusing on this area of study [50]. Consequently, cyber-physical systems are crucial in many contexts, especially those that make use of both digital and physical components.

Data Sparsity Problem

The difficulty of databases with sparse and dispersed data within an urban area arises from the need to generate data from varied sources within the city. For efficient urban computing, the optimal method of integrating these sparse data sets from many sources is still a mystery. We propose that smart city urban computing ecosystems incorporate models for dealing with data sparsity. Additionally, authors of another [51] brought attention to the elements that lead to sparse data bias, such as discrete variables with low or high prevalence, sparsely distributed continuous predictors, and few events per variable.

Data Movement

Efficient management of IoT resources and data is expected in smart cities. The collection, transmission, and analysis of big data can become problematic, though, if the quantity of IoT devices is very large. Data transmission *via* conventional networks is inefficient and wasteful of resources. In order to raise public consciousness and encourage energy efficiency, the authors of a study [52] presented a data transfer structure based on volunteer automobiles. Researchers now have a baseline to investigate hybrid approaches, where data transfer is accomplished by both vehicles and the internet, thanks to the suggested framework, which lays the groundwork to decrease data transfer delays in smart cities. According to the findings, the suggested framework uses far less energy than data transit *via* the internet.

5G-Technologies

The arrival of 5G technologies has presented new obstacles to researchers, despite the fact that it has improved services for the telecom business. With the release of 5G technology, communication speeds and the ability to generate massive amounts of data at rates never seen since the 4G era have been dramatically enhanced. Because of the importance of collecting and processing data for the purpose of gaining insight, useful information, and new knowledge, the urban computing community is worried about the rate of data generation from diverse sources [53] in urban cities. Data storage hardware is going to become a major problem for both businesses and universities due to the exponential growth of data generated by 5G technology's many sources.

A number of technologies, such as software-defined networks, machine learning, network functions virtualization, and the Internet of Things (IoT), have their own security flaws that manifest in the inter-slice of networks [54]. Urban computing could be vulnerable to various security threats if 5G technologies are used, since attackers may try to exploit vulnerabilities in the network inter-slicing handover.

Scaling *via* the Analysis and Harvesting of Energy

In order to keep all of the embedded computing tools in the situation powered, enormous quantities of energy are needed. Charging these ubiquitous computer gadgets now requires batteries. It will not be practical to keep replacing batteries; operations must be able to run for months or even years without them. Consequently, problems may arise due to insufficient battery capacity. Additional approaches to scaling encompass the theoretical underpinnings of pervasive computing scaling. Another concern with storage and power is the potential for widespread computing to be hindered by mobile phones and sensors [55]. Hence, cloud computing is proposed as a substitute method to address the power and storage issues. A few components of the cloud solution are mobile clouds, clouds and crowds, networks in the cloud, and cloud accessibility.

Knowledge *vs.* Privacy

The difficulty in striking a balance between privacy and knowledge is not surprising. More personal data could lead to a smarter system, so the thinking goes [56]. In environmentally responsible smart cities, people should have a say in the trade-offs that are made. Their data should be available in the system for as long as they wish, and they should be allowed to choose for what purposes. Now comes the hard part: striking a balance that demands openness regarding the data that is actually necessary to provide smart services. Furthermore, this is in line with what has been mandated by the EU-GDPR since May 2018. The current state of affairs forces people to choose between knowledge and privacy, even while severe privacy breaches are occurring [57]. Plus, ubiquitous and mobile intelligence is gradually displacing people from operating, supervising, or even just being in charge, which means they lose control. Issues caused by smart cities can be broadly classified into three groups. To begin, consumers and users may encounter inflexible behavior while interacting with completely automated call centers or online stores that do not employ human operators [58]. The system is unable to manage requests that involve minor changes from the usual procedure or pattern. Second, there are many areas where AI and other algorithmic approaches are showing their weaknesses and making mistakes, despite the many promises they have made. Third, the most pressing issue with AI and the "smart-all " paradigm is the lack of transparency, traceability, and accountability.

Intersection of Smart and Sustainable City

Overemphasis on technological applications, practical initiative complexity, and ad hoc smart city conception are the highlighted issues at the junction of smart cities and sustainability. A proposed solution to these problems is the introduction of new sustainability metrics for smart cities that span economics, society, culture, ecology, and government [59]. Having said that, the solution is theoretical and lacks a practical application, thus it stays abstract. In order to determine whether or not a smart, sustainable community is feasible in practice, we suggest that academics, professionals in the field, and business owners work together to create a working model.

Future recommendations for smartcities

Some possible directions for further research and development into smart city deep learning applications are as follows:

Develop more robust and efficient DL strategies

For smart cities to be a success, deep learning algorithms are essential. So, more work needs to be put into creating deep learning algorithms that are better able to process massive volumes of data, make accurate predictions, and deliver valuable insights.

Prioritize privacy and security.

One potential consequence of smart cities' increasing connectivity is the potential exposure of individuals' private data. Hence, while developing and implementing DL in smart cities, it is crucial to consider privacy and security. To do this, it is necessary to encrypt data securely and restrict access to authorized persons exclusively.

Collaborate with local governments and communities.

Involvement of local governments and people in the development and application of DL is crucial to its success in smart cities. That way, the technology may be fine-tuned to address the unique issues faced by the neighborhood.

Develop user-friendly interfaces

DL technology is sometimes complicated and hard to grasp for those who aren't specialists in the field. Consequently, it is critical to design intuitive interfaces that facilitate the access and comprehension of data produced by deep learning algorithms by both city authorities and citizens [60].

Sustainability should be emphasized. Smart cities can optimize resource allocation and eliminate waste with the help of deep learning technology. The usage of this technology must, however, prioritize sustainability and lessen its negative effects on the environment. Renewable energy sources and energy-efficient smart city infrastructure design can do this [61].

Consider the ethical implications

The ethical and social consequences of deep learning technology may be enormous. Hence, before implementing deep learning in smart cities, it's crucial to think about the moral consequences and make sure everyone benefits from the technology. The development and implementation processes can be made more open and inclusive to accomplish this goal [62].

CONCLUSION

This article has offered a thorough overview of smart cities and how the concept of the IoT and ML has altered the traditional idea of devices and things. We stress the importance of utilizing the massive amounts of data produced by installed sensors to incorporate intelligence into the smart city architecture. The essay starts off with a general introduction to smart city applications, and then goes into depth on the hardware design of several smart city components. We go on to provide data sets and technologies for data collection that are ideal for smart cities, utilizing cutting-edge principles in various deep learning models. Despite the abundance of literature on the topic, we believe that our assessment covers all the bases: the architectural framework, communication protocols, and Internet of Things (IoT) sensor installations that make a city smart. Due to the exponential development of smart devices, sensors, AI, and ML, the outlook for the future is bright and hopeful. Innovative smart building architectures present new potential for investors and corporate sectors. The deployment of these smart buildings for the benefit of people will be facilitated by the emerging 5G and 6G technologies, which may revolutionize the way smart cities are imagined and implemented in the present day.

REFERENCES

[1] M Nassereddine, and A Khang, "Applications of Internet of Things (IoT) in smart cities", In:

Advanced IoT Technologies and Applications in the Industry 4.0 Digital Economy CRC Press, 2024, pp. 109-136.

[2] U. Khalil, Mueen-Uddin, O.A. Malik, and S. Hussain, "A blockchain footprint for authentication of iot-enabled smart devices in smart cities: State-of-the-art advancements, challenges and future research directions", *IEEE Access,* vol. 10, pp. 76805-76823, 2022. [http://dx.doi.org/10.1109/ACCESS.2022.3189998]

[3] G. Arun, P.C.S. Reddy, N. Budati, B. Rebecca, S. Perumalla, and V.B. Gujar, "A deep learning framework for diabetes prediction: PIMA indian dataset", *2024 International Conference on Innovative Computing, Intelligent Communication and Smart Electrical Systems (ICSES),* IEEE., pp. 1-6, 2024.

[4] M. Adil, and M.K. Khan, "Emerging iot applications in sustainable smart cities for covid-19: Network security and data preservation challenges with future directions", *Sustain Cities Soc.,* vol. 75, p. 103311, 2021. [http://dx.doi.org/10.1016/j.scs.2021.103311] [PMID: 34540568]

[5] S. Yadala, C.S.R. Pundru, and V.K. Solanki, "A novel private encryption model in IoT under cloud computing domain", *The International Conference on Intelligent Systems & Networks,* pp. 263-270, 2023.Singapore [http://dx.doi.org/10.1007/978-981-99-4725-6_33]

[6] B Elov, A Dauletov, Y Sucharitha, F Khalilova, M Latipova, and M Abdullayeva, "An intelligent traffic management of vehicles using deep learning approach in smart cities", In: *2025 3rd International Conference on Integrated Circuits and Communication Systems (ICICACS)*, Raichur, India. IEEE, 2025. [http://dx.doi.org/10.1109/ICICACS65178.2025.10967703]

[7] T. Poleto, T.C.C. Nepomuceno, V.D.H. de Carvalho, L.C.B.O. Friaes, R.C.P. de Oliveira, and C.J.J. Figueiredo, "Information Security Applications in Smart Cities: A Bibliometric Analysis of Emerging Research", *Future Internet,* vol. 15, no. 12, p. 393, 2023. [http://dx.doi.org/10.3390/fi15120393]

[8] I.A.T. Hashem, R.S.A. Usmani, M.S. Almutairi, A.O. Ibrahim, A. Zakari, F. Alotaibi, S.M. Alhashmi, and H. Chiroma, "Urban Computing for Sustainable Smart Cities: Recent Advances, Taxonomy, and Open Research Challenges", *Sustainability (Basel),* vol. 15, no. 5, p. 3916, 2023. [http://dx.doi.org/10.3390/su15053916]

[9] M.D. Basith, P. Praveen, and P.C.S. Reddy, "Adaptive deep Q-GAN framework for enhanced breast cancer detection in medical imaging", *Biomedical Signal Processing and Control,* vol. 112, p. 108638, 2026. [http://dx.doi.org/10.1016/j.bspc.2025.108638]

[10] B. Paul, and S.K. Chettri, "Smart City: Recent Advances and Research Issues", *Proceedings of ICISC,* pp. 77-92, 2021. [http://dx.doi.org/10.1007/978-981-16-1395-1_7]

[11] R Samrin, P. C. S. Reddy, K Arun Kumar, N Deepthi, C Mithra, S. B. Latha, S Yadala, and G. K. Thakur, "A hybrid deep learning based framework for prediction of rice yield through integration of biophysical parameters and optical remote sensing data in India", *J. Atmos. Solar-Terr. Phys.,* vol. 279, p. 106734, 2026. [http://dx.doi.org/10.1016/j.jastp.2026.106734]

[12] V.K. Bukkarayasamudram, P.C.S. Reddy, and K. Arun Kumar, "Quantum computing revolution in healthcare: a systematic review of applications, issues and future directions", *Artif Intell Rev,* vol. 58, p. 389, 2025. [http://dx.doi.org/10.1007/s10462-025-11381-w]

[13] V. Demertzi, S. Demertzis, and K. Demertzis, "An overview of cyber threats, attacks and countermeasures on the primary domains of smart cities", *Appl. Sci. (Basel),* vol. 13, no. 2, p. 790,

2023.
[http://dx.doi.org/10.3390/app13020790]

[14] M.E.E. Alahi, A. Sukkuea, F.W. Tina, A. Nag, W. Kurdthongmee, K. Suwannarat, and S.C. Mukhopadhyay, "Integration of IoT-enabled technologies and Artificial Intelligence (AI) for smart city scenario: Recent advancements and future trends", *Sensors (Basel),* vol. 23, no. 11, p. 5206, 2023. [http://dx.doi.org/10.3390/s23115206] [PMID: 37299934]

[15] L Jebaraj, A Khang, V Chandrasekar, A R Pravin, and K Sriram, "Smart city: Concepts, models, technologies and applications", In: *Smart Cities* CRC Press: Boca Raton, FL, USA, 2023, pp. 1-20. [http://dx.doi.org/10.1201/9781003376064-1]

[16] R Subhashini, and A Khang, "The role of Internet of Things (IoT) in smart city framework", In: *Smart Cities* CRC Press: Boca Raton, FL, USA, 2023, pp. 31-56. [http://dx.doi.org/10.1201/9781003376064-3]

[17] P Ravali, P. C. S. Reddy, and P Praveen, "An efficient neuro-framework for brain tumor classification using a CNN-based self-supervised learning approach with genetic optimizations", *Current Neuropharmacology,* vol. 24, no. 4, 2025. [http://dx.doi.org/10.2174/011570159X378103250806214613]

[18] A.T. Somnathe, V.T. Selvi, N.G. Stepha, M.T. Kingslin, F.M. Inamdar, and P.C.S. Reddy, "An intelligent traffic conflict prediction using deep learning with long-term evolution access data", *2025 3rd International Conference on Smart Systems for applications in Electrical Sciences (ICSSES),* IEEE, pp. 1-6, 2025. [http://dx.doi.org/10.1109/ICSSES64899.2025.11010032]

[19] S. B. Latha, Y. Sucharitha, I. A. Tayubi, K. Shekar, D. Pandey, and R. V. Sudhakar, "Virtual learning analysis using complex rule-based approach in the context of cloud computing", In: *Proc. 2025 3rd Int. Conf. on Communication, Security, and Artificial Intelligence (ICCSAI)*, Greater Noida, India, 2025. [http://dx.doi.org/10.1109/ICCSAI64074.2025.11064645]

[20] S Saini, A Chauhan, G Thakur, and L Sapra, "Challenges and opportunities in secure smart cities for enhancing the security and privacy", In: *Enabling Technologies for Effective Planning and Management in Sustainable Smart Cities* Springer: Singapore, 2023, pp. 1-27. [http://dx.doi.org/10.1007/978-3-031-22922-0_1]

[21] S. Mishra, and V.K. Chaurasiya, "Hybrid deep learning algorithm for smart cities security enhancement through blockchain and internet of things", *Multimedia Tools Appl.,* vol. 83, no. 8, pp. 22609-22637, 2023. [http://dx.doi.org/10.1007/s11042-023-16406-6]

[22] G.K. Thakur, L.P. Mudarakola, M. Sreenivasulu, V. Krishna B, I.R. Raja, I.A. Tayubi, and Y. Sucharitha, "An enhanced prediction framework for blood-brain barrier permeability: DeePred-BBB", *Recent Patents on Engineering,* vol. 19, no. 9, p. E18722121342031, 2025. [http://dx.doi.org/10.2174/0118722121342031250218042131]

[23] A Khang, S. K. Gupta, S Rani, D. A. Karras, Ed., *Smart Cities: IoT Technologies, Big Data Solutions, Cloud Platforms, and Cybersecurity Techniques* CRC Press: Boca Raton, FL, USA, 2023. [http://dx.doi.org/10.1201/9781003376064]

[24] M Indrasenareddy, N. S. Bohra, S Mukherjee, Y Sucharitha, M Yesubabu, and M. L. Prasad, "Working toward a comprehensive approach for ensuring security and privacy in artificial intelligence", In: *Leveraging Artificial Intelligence in Cloud, Edge, Fog and Mobile Computing* Auerbach Publications: Boca Raton, FL, USA, 2025, pp. 3-18. [http://dx.doi.org/10.1201/9781032703718]

[25] J Telo, "Smart city security threats and countermeasures in the context of emerging technologies", *International Journal of Intelligent Automation and Computing,* vol. 6, no. 1, pp. 31-45, 2023.

[26] A. Mishra, A.V. Jha, B. Appasani, A.K. Ray, D.K. Gupta, and A.N. Ghazali, "Emerging technologies

and design aspects of next generation cyber physical system with a smart city application perspective", *International Journal of System Assurance Engineering and Management,* vol. 14, no. S3, suppl. Suppl. 3, pp. 699-721, 2023.
[http://dx.doi.org/10.1007/s13198-021-01523-y]

[27] V Sukhavasi, A. C. Mouli, D. V. Juneja, Y Sucharitha, S. S. Joshi, and S Dey, "Establishing ensemble learning models for daily rainfall forecasting", In: *Proc. 2024 Int. Conf. on Innovative Computing, Intelligent Communication and Smart Electrical Systems (ICSES)*, Chennai, India, 2024.
[http://dx.doi.org/10.1109/ICSES63760.2024.10910429]

[28] S. Mehta, B. Bhushan, and R. Kumar, "Machine learning approaches for smart city applications: Emergence, challenges and opportunities", In: *Recent advances in internet of things and machine learning: Real-world applications*, 2022, pp. 147-163.

[29] A. B. Haque, B. Bhushan, and G. Dhiman, "Conceptualizing smart city applications: Requirements, architecture, security issues, and emerging trends", *Expert Systems,* vol. 39, no. 5, p. e12753, 2022.
[http://dx.doi.org/10.1111/exsy.12753]

[30] I. Nastjuk, S. Trang, and E.I. Papageorgiou, "Smart cities and smart governance models for future cities", *Electron. Mark.,* vol. 32, no. 4, pp. 1917-1924, 2022.
[http://dx.doi.org/10.1007/s12525-022-00609-0]

[31] R. Chataut, A. Phoummalayvane, and R. Akl, "Unleashing the power of IoT: A comprehensive review of IoT applications and future prospects in healthcare, agriculture, smart homes, smart cities, and industry 4.0", *Sensors (Basel),* vol. 23, no. 16, p. 7194, 2023.
[http://dx.doi.org/10.3390/s23167194] [PMID: 37631731]

[32] P.C. Shaker Reddy, and Y. Sucharitha, "A design and challenges in energy optimizing CR-wireless sensor networks", *Recent Advances in Computer Science and Communications (Formerly: Recent Patents on Computer Science),* vol. 16, no. 5, pp. 82-92, 2023.
[http://dx.doi.org/10.2174/2666255816666221104115024]

[33] N. Abbas, Z. Abbas, X. Liu, S.S. Khan, E.D. Foster, and S. Larkin, "A survey: future smart cities based on advance control of Unmanned Aerial Vehicles (UAVs)", *Appl. Sci. (Basel),* vol. 13, no. 17, p. 9881, 2023.
[http://dx.doi.org/10.3390/app13179881]

[34] Z. Ullah, M. Naeem, A. Coronato, P. Ribino, and G. De Pietro, "Blockchain applications in sustainable smart cities", *Sustain Cities Soc.,* vol. 97, p. 104697, 2023.
[http://dx.doi.org/10.1016/j.scs.2023.104697]

[35] P.R. Singh, V.K. Singh, R. Yadav, and S.N. Chaurasia, "6G networks for artificial intelligence-enabled smart cities applications: A scoping review", *Telematics and Informatics Reports,* vol. 9, p. 100044, 2023.
[http://dx.doi.org/10.1016/j.teler.2023.100044]

[36] P. Mishra, and G. Singh, "Energy management systems in sustainable smart cities based on the internet of energy: A technical review", *Energies,* vol. 16, no. 19, p. 6903, 2023.
[http://dx.doi.org/10.3390/en16196903]

[37] Z.A. Baig, P. Szewczyk, C. Valli, P. Rabadia, P. Hannay, M. Chernyshev, and M. Peacock, "Future challenges for smart cities: Cyber-security and digital forensics", *Digital Investigation,* vol. 22, pp. 3-13, 2017.
[http://dx.doi.org/10.1016/j.diin.2017.06.015]

[38] K Kalinaki, N. N. Thilakarathne, H. R. Mubarak, O. A. Malik, and M Abdullatif, "Cybersafe capabilities and utilities for smart cities", In: *Cybersecurity for Smart Cities: Practices and Challenges* Springer International Publishing: Cham, Switzerland, 2023, pp. 71-86.
[http://dx.doi.org/10.1007/978-3-031-24946-4_6]

[39] S. Siddiqui, S. Hameed, S.A. Shah, A.K. Khan, and A. Aneiba, "Smart contract-based security architecture for collaborative services in municipal smart cities", *J. Systems Archit.,* vol. 135, p.

102802, 2023.
[http://dx.doi.org/10.1016/j.sysarc.2022.102802]

[40] S. Sharma, and N. Mishra, "Horizoning recent trends in the security of smart cities: Exploratory analysis using latent semantic analysis", *Journal of Intelligent & Fuzzy Systems,* pp. 1-18, 2023.

[41] I. Hussain, "Secure, sustainable smart cities and the Internet of Things: Perspectives, challenges, and future directions", *Sustainability,* vol. 16, no. 4, p. 1390, 2024.
[http://dx.doi.org/10.3390/su16041390]

[42] K. AL-Dosari, and N. Fetais, "A new shift in implementing unmanned aerial vehicles (UAVs) in the safety and security of smart cities: a systematic literature review", *Safety (Basel),* vol. 9, no. 3, p. 64, 2023.
[http://dx.doi.org/10.3390/safety9030064]

[43] Robin Chataut, Alex Phoummalayvane, and Robert Akl, "Unleashing the power of IoT: A comprehensive review of IoT applications and future prospects in healthcare, agriculture, smart homes, smart cities, and industry 4.0", *Sensors,* vol. 23, no. 16, p. 7194, 2023.
[http://dx.doi.org/10.3390/s23167194]

[44] C. Ma, "Smart city and cyber-security; technologies used, leading challenges and future recommendations", *Energy Reports,* vol. 7, pp. 7999-8012, 2021.
[http://dx.doi.org/10.1016/j.egyr.2021.08.124]

[45] D. Chen, P. Wawrzynski, and Z. Lv, "Cyber security in smart cities: A review of deep learning-based applications and case studies", *Sustain Cities Soc.,* vol. 66, p. 102655, 2021.
[http://dx.doi.org/10.1016/j.scs.2020.102655]

[46] D. Kanellopoulos, V.K. Sharma, T. Panagiotakopoulos, and A. Kameas, "Networking architectures and protocols for IoT applications in smart cities: Recent developments and perspectives", *Electronics (Basel),* vol. 12, no. 11, p. 2490, 2023.
[http://dx.doi.org/10.3390/electronics12112490]

[47] M Juma, and K Shaalan, "Cyberphysical systems in the smart city: Challenges and future trends for strategic research", In: *Swarm Intelligence for Resource Management in Internet of Things* Academic Press, 2020, pp. 65-85.
[http://dx.doi.org/10.1016/B978-0-12-818287-1.00008-5]

[48] A Tripathi, N Sindhwani, R Anand, and A Dahiya, "Role of IoT in smart homes and smart cities: Challenges, benefits, and applications", In: *IoT Based Smart Applications* Springer International Publishing: Cham, 2022, pp. 199-217.

[49] V. Bhardwaj, A. Anooja, and L.S. Vermani, "Smart cities and the IoT: an in-depth analysis of global research trends and future directions", *Discov Internet Things,* vol. 4, p. 19, 2024.
[http://dx.doi.org/10.1007/s43926-024-00076-3]

[50] E.V. Napolitano, "Intelligent technologies for urban progress: exploring the role of ai and advanced telecommunications in smart city evolution", *European Conference on Advances in Databases and Information Systems,* pp. 676-683, 2023.Cham
[http://dx.doi.org/10.1007/978-3-031-42941-5_61]

[51] H. Omrany, K.M. Al-Obaidi, and M. Hossain, "IoT-enabled smart cities: a hybrid systematic analysis of key research areas, challenges, and recommendations for future direction", *Discov Cities,* vol. 1, p. 2, 2024.
[http://dx.doi.org/10.1007/s44327-024-00002-w]

[52] M Haroon, D. K. Misra, M Husain, M. M. Tripathi, and A Khan, "Security issues in the internet of things for the development of smart cities", In: *Advances in Cyberology and the Advent of the Next-Gen Information Revolution,* A Smith, B Jones, Eds., IGI Global, 2023, pp. 123-137.
[http://dx.doi.org/10.4018/978-1-6684-8133-2.ch007]

[53] A. Adel, "Unlocking the future: fostering human–machine collaboration and driving intelligent

automation through industry 5.0 in smart cities", *Smart Cities,* vol. 6, no. 5, pp. 2742-2782, 2023. [http://dx.doi.org/10.3390/smartcities6050124]

[54] M. J. C. dos S. Reis, "Privacy-preserving protocols in smart cities and industrial IoT: Challenges, trends, and future directions", *Electronics,* vol. 15, no. 2, p. 399, 2026. [http://dx.doi.org/10.3390/electronics15020399]

[55] R. Al-Huthaifi, T. Li, W. Huang, J. Gu, and C. Li, "Federated learning in smart cities: Privacy and security survey", *Inf. Sci.,* vol. 632, pp. 833-857, 2023. [http://dx.doi.org/10.1016/j.ins.2023.03.033]

[56] M.K. Thota, P.M. Prathibhavani, and K.R. Venugopal, "Smart cities: Survey on addressing challenges in smart-cities", *Scand. J. Inf. Syst.,* vol. 35, no. 2, pp. 159-195, 2023.

[57] M. Songhorabadi, M. Rahimi, A.M. MoghadamFarid, and M. Haghi Kashani, "Fog computing approaches in IoT-enabled smart cities", *J. Netw. Comput. Appl.,* vol. 211, p. 103557, 2023. [http://dx.doi.org/10.1016/j.jnca.2022.103557]

[58] J.B. Awotunde, T. Gaber, L.V.N. Prasad, S.O. Folorunso, and V.L. Lalitha, "Privacy and security enhancement of smart cities using hybrid deep learning-enabled blockchain", *Scalable Computing: Practice and Experience,* vol. 24, no. 3, pp. 561-584, 2023. [http://dx.doi.org/10.12694/scpe.v24i3.2272]

[59] I. Nastjuk, S. Trang, and E.I. Papageorgiou, "Smart cities and smart governance models for future cities", *Electron Markets,* vol. 32, pp. 1917-1924, 2022. [http://dx.doi.org/10.1007/s12525-022-00609-0]

[60] M. K. Brar, P. K. Jindal, M. Kumar, and P. Sharma, "2023 International Conference on Research Methodologies in Knowledge Management, Artificial Intelligence and Telecommunication Engineering (RMKMATE)", In: *Proc. 2023 Int. Conf. on Research Methodologies in Knowledge Management, Artificial Intelligence and Telecommunication Engineering (RMKMATE).* IEEE, Nov 2023, pp. 1-7.

[61] R.R. Irshad, S. Hussain, I. Hussain, I. Ahmad, A. Yousif, I.M. Alwayle, A.A. Alattab, K.M. Alalayah, J.G. Breslin, M.M. Badr, and J.J.P.C. Rodrigues, "An Intelligent Buffalo-Based Secure Edge-Enabled Computing Platform for Heterogeneous IoT Network in Smart Cities", *IEEE Access,* vol. 11, pp. 69282-69294, 2023. [http://dx.doi.org/10.1109/ACCESS.2023.3288815]

[62] G.R. Kumar, S.T. Bhanu, M.L. Prasad, S.B. Latha, G. Yedukondalu, and C.S.R. Pundru, "An early cancer prediction based on deep neural learning", *2023 International Conference on Research Methodologies in Knowledge Management, Artificial Intelligence and Telecommunication Engineering (RMKMATE),* IEEE, pp. 1-7, 2023. [http://dx.doi.org/10.1109/RMKMATE59243.2023.10369977]

CHAPTER 12

AI for Next Generation: Emerging Trends and Future Directions

Ramesh Babu Pittala[1,*], **Niteesha Sharma**[1], **Thinagaran Perumal**[2], **Medikonda Asha Kiran**[1], **Manyam Thaile**[1] and **Peddada Nagamani**[1]

[1] *Department of Information Technology, School of Engineering, Anurag University, Hyderabad, Telangana, India*

[2] *Department of Computer Science, University Putra Malaysia, Serdang, Selangor, Malaysia*

Abstract: Artificial Intelligence (AI) is revolutionizing modern technology, reshaping industries, and redefining cybersecurity. This chapter comprehensively introduces AI, offering insights into its evolution, core principles, and diverse applications. This chapter introduces AI briefly, delving into its history, key concepts, methodologies, and various applications. It delves into major AI paradigms like machine learning, deep learning, and natural language processing, which are revolutionizing data-driven decision-making. AI in cybersecurity is proving to be a game-changer, where it is being leveraged for threat detection, response automation, and enhanced enterprise security infrastructure. This chapter reviews how AI-driven prevention enhances threat intelligence by detecting anomalies, predicting cyberattacks, and mitigating real-time risks. It also talks about ethical issues of AI implementation, like bias, interpretability, and accountability, which are essential for responsible AI deployment in security ops. Setting the stage for a deeper dive into AI-driven cybersecurity frameworks in later chapters, this chapter creates a promising basis for understanding AI. It blows the whistle on AI-powered threat intelligence, automated incident response, and the future of AI in enterprise security.

Keywords: AI Applications, AI Ethics, AI In Cyber Security, AI Techniques, AI Thinking, Automated Cyber Security, Cyber Security, Deep Learning, Enterprise Security, Human Language, Machine Learning, Narrow AI, Neural Networks, Perception, Threat Detection.

* **Corresponding Author Ramesh Babu Pittala**: Department of Information Technology, School of Engineering, Anurag University, Hyderabad, Telangana, India; E-mail: prameshbabu526@gmail.com

Pundru Chandra Shaker Reddy, Yadala Sucharitha, & Thillaiarasu N (Eds.)

INTRODUCTION

What Exactly is Artificial Intelligence (AI)?

Artificial Intelligence (AI) is a branch of computer science that focuses on building intelligent systems capable of performing tasks that typically require human intelligence. These tasks include learning, reasoning, perception, language understanding, and decision-making [1]. AI systems can analyze data, identify patterns, adapt over time, and autonomously respond to complex environments. AI aims to replicate and enhance human-like cognitive abilities, enabling machines to operate independently and efficiently in various domains such as healthcare, finance, cybersecurity, and autonomous systems.

AI will impact **healthcare** through faster diagnosis, personalized treatment, and predictive analytics for disease prevention. In **education**, it will enable adaptive learning, automated assessments, and personalized student support. In **finance**, AI will enhance fraud detection, risk management, and automated decision-making, improving efficiency and security across services.

The four components constituting AI technology are as follows and are depicted in Fig. (**1**), which include:

i. Learning
ii. Reasoning
iii. Perception skills
iv. Language understanding

Learning: The Core of Machine Intelligence

In AI, a machine is considered to learn if it enhances its performance in a defined task due to experience or data processing. AI systems outperform software applications because they build upon performance-enhancing algorithms that operate automatically after analyzing vast amounts of data, unlike earlier programmed software systems that required extensive manual coding. The primary reason behind this is the aspect of learning referred to as Machine Learning (ML), which acts as a sub-branch under the umbrella of Artificial Intelligence (AI). ML algorithms scan data and identify trends among the vast amounts of repetitive information stored in databases [2]. The trained model makes predictions or decisions concerning unprocessed data sets from the processed data. The spam filter application learns from past messages by extracting features from messages sent to the user to determine which messages should be sent to the user in the future. Different aspects of machine learning can be classified into three branches.

In **supervised learning**, the model trains itself on input-output data, also called a training set, where the input consists of predefined outputs, known as labels. By providing the system with appropriate data, the predictive functions of the algorithms are formed. Rather than having a specific **classification model**, the system analyzes patterns in the data. This approach is mainly used for item groupings and anomaly detection. Agents learn to make **decisions** based on interactions with the environment and receive performance feedback through rewards and punishments. This kind of learning is mainly applied in robotics and game-playing AI [3].

Reasoning: Abilities AI Thinks With

AI systems achieve reasoning through the ability to process facts and determine conclusions and decisions that are logically or evidentially supported. Artificial intelligence accomplishes operational tasks logically based on artificial principles by reasoning based on its operational premises and processes. It concludes from its premises or conditions during its logical AI preconditions. AI systems employ optimization methods that determine the best decisions by setting achievable targets, such as minimizing costs or time for the reasoning stage. All the known information AI systems have access to allows for the formulation of new conclusions and making future predictions [4]. With patient data, an AI system can accurately estimate the probability of a patient developing a particular disease. AI perceives system learning patterns through traffic monitoring, which uncovers vertex activities that are quadratically abnormal with possible malicious intent, showing distinctions without explicit attack definitions. Perception is the ability of artificial intelligence to receive information from the environment and understand that it receives information from the outside world [5]. Machines need the ability to both obtain and comprehend information through using the senses as perception. Unlike humans, who rely on the five senses, AI systems acquire an understanding of the environment by processing data from sensors, cameras, microphones, and devices that provide feedback.

Perception: Computer Vision, A branch of AI

The perception of images and videos as objects is called computer vision, a branch of AI functionality. AI can now perform advanced face and motion tracking, scene analysis, and object classification through sophisticated neural networks and algorithms. These capabilities are now integrated into machines, enabling them to 'see' and 'interpret' data for various applications, such as security, facial recognition, and autonomous vehicle navigation. The AI systems perceive their surroundings with sound monitors that enable speech recognition and other devices that offer tactile feedback [6]. Autonomous vehicles use AI alongside other sensors to avoid an accident while driving in road traffic, using computer vision to detect vehicles.

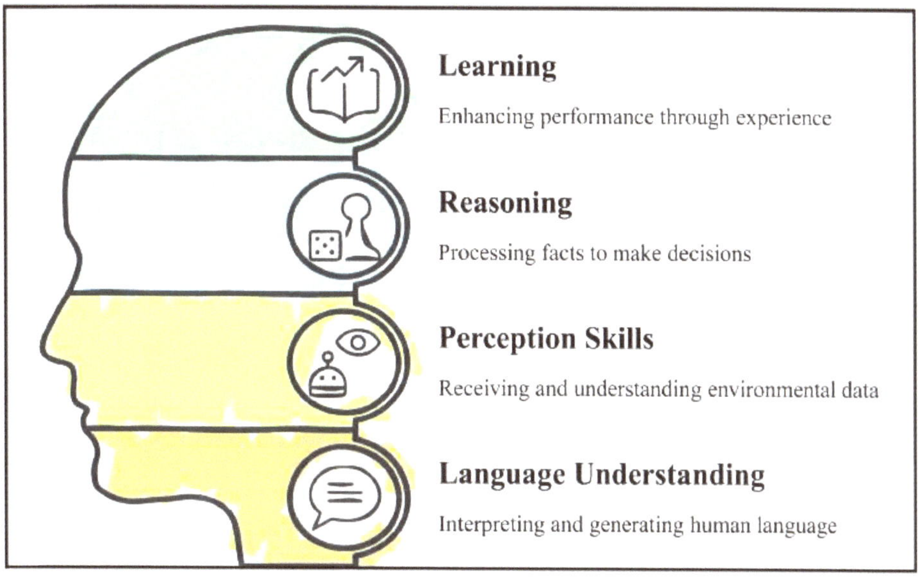

Fig. (1). Components of AI technology.

Natural Language Processing (NLP): Machines Now Understand Human Languages

AI systems can communicate with humans owing to their language processing abilities, which interpret languages akin to humans, enabling two-way communication with people. Understanding language uttered in speech text is a critical branch of Artificial Intelligence (AI) and processes generating output speech text, such as talking. Machine Learning interprets language with speech recognition abilities, handles processing human-composed language as input, and produces human verbal language as output, and performs two-way language with human mediation, such as dialogues and conversations. On a fundamental level, NLP has the following functionalities [7]:

- Transforming speech energy into languages occurs in Speech Recognition via transforming spoken language into written language in text documents.
- In Sentiment Analysis, AI systems assess text to determine the emotional statement being analyzed for expression, whether it be a positive, negative, or neutral emotion.
- Customers appreciate AI technology because NLP transforms client verbal directives into digestible and natural language via translation and large

document summarization.

- Users can speak to AI using NLP and exercise limited control with virtual assistants such as Alexa and Siri. Systems' performance improves as they receive more linguistic data from user interactions.

AI Clustering: Narrow AI *vs.* General AI

The functional breadth of AI systems independently divides them into narrow and general types.

Weak AI (Narrow AI)

The AI weakness refers to a technology that permits experts to create devices that can perform single tasks or a set list of tasks. Specialized algorithms operate within the preset parameters of their programming [8]. Narrow AI systems are incredibly efficient at completing specific tasks, even outperforming humans. However, they cannot transfer knowledge beyond their narrow fields of operation.

Narrow AI Illustrations:

Emails containing unusual information are filtered by intelligent AI filters and sorted into distinctive categories. AI systems like Netflix or Amazon suggest content tailored to users' preferences, allowing users to seek AI-driven recommendations. The recognition of individuals' security needs is handled at airports, while banks and smartphones use it for their purposes. Recognition systems primarily concentrate on identifying and confirming faces [9]. They have powerful operational abilities with all the boundaries placed around narrow AIs. However, they cannot perform tasks outside of their original programming. Such technology is encountered in everyday life systems operating as essential elements of contemporary existence. However, it is limited to predefined fields of activities [10].

General AI (Strong AI)

General AI, or Strong AI, refers to AI systems that can understand, learn, and perform tasks at levels commensurate with human intellect. General AI differs from narrow AI because it has no restrictions when executing any intellectual activity. There is potential for this technology in the future as it can replicate human intelligence across many mental tasks, such as reasoning, identifying problems, and acquiring knowledge. Researchers aim to build General AI only in theory [11]. The human-level cognitive flexibility of machines in all areas has not been achieved with general AI systems. Research scientists are working on new models of adaptable AI to achieve this goal [12]. Ultra-modern frameworks that can adapt to complexity require multi-faceted approaches. A machine with implemented General AI should function on the same proficient level as humans while playing chess, composing songs, diagnosing medical conditions, or strategizing business deals. The feature comparison of AI is shown in Table **1**.

Table 1. Comparison of narrow AI and general AI.

Feature	Narrow AI (Weak AI)	General AI (Strong AI)
Scope of Tasks	Performs specific tasks only	Capable of performing any intellectual task
Flexibility	Limited to predefined functions	Highly adaptable and general-purpose
Learning Capacity	Learns within specific parameters	Learns across domains like a human
Current Existence	In widespread use (*e.g.*, chatbots, recommendation systems)	Theoretical/Experimental only
Transfer of Knowledge	Cannot transfer learning across domains	Designed to replicate human-level reasoning and transfer learning

The Evolution of Artificial Intelligence Development of Robotics: A Brief History

The development of modern Artificial Intelligence (AI) is a historical process that stems from delving into some fundamental questions of the technological society of the 21st century. Simultaneously, the infrastructure of the "AgiSmart" – a fully automated system capable of aligning its functions with human behavior—would serve the primary function of predicting the dynamic requirements of the "technological society" [13]. The evolution of AI is shown in Fig. (**2**).

Artificial Intelligence's Emergence (1950s):

2010 marks an important year for the technological society as nodes of the AI ecosystem emerged alongside the realization of mechanisms designed during the evolutionary cognitive robotic branch developed within the frame of the 21st century, alongside the mass diffusion of personal-use technologies within the Global Society. AI answers questions that it can answer from biology requests driven out of the "What" because the needs generated stemming from big questions require both social and biological understandings. Artificial Intelligence served as the right tool [14].

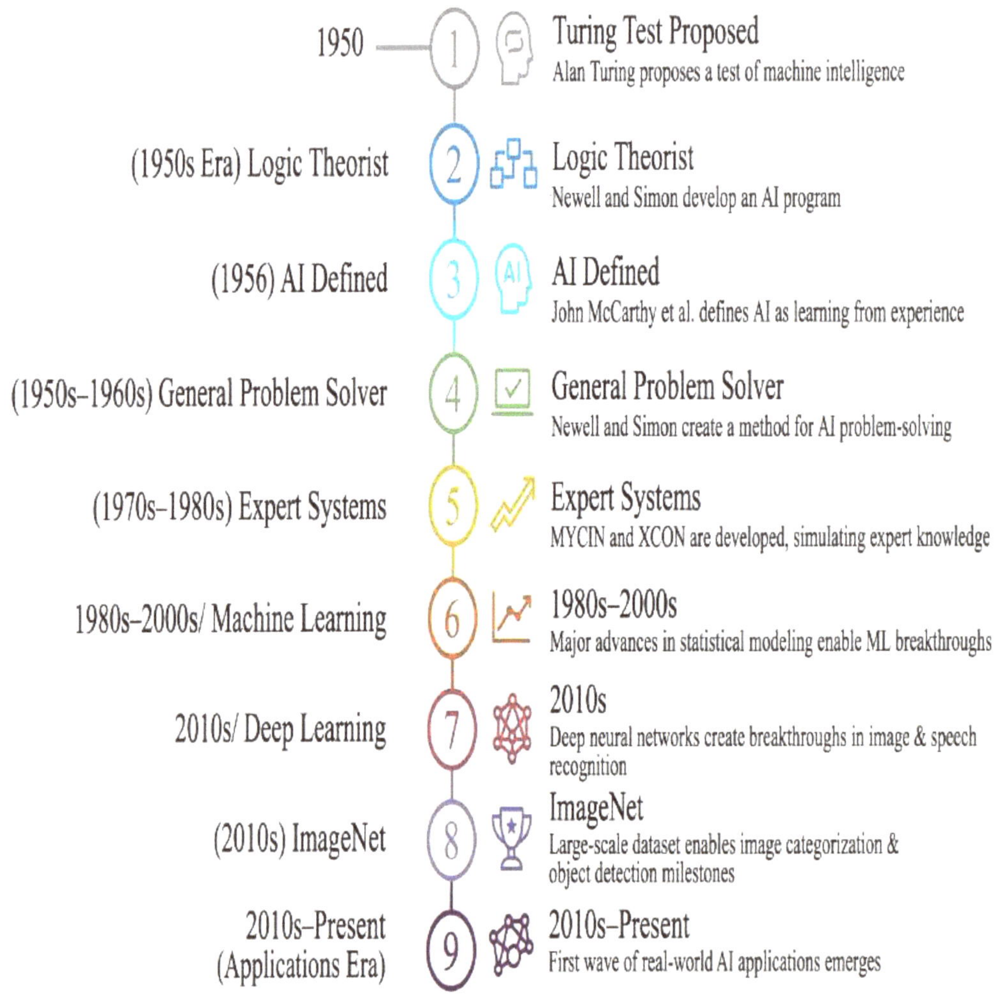

Fig. (2). Key milestones in the evolution of artificial intelligence.

The Need for Control of AI Systems (2000s):

US engineers tailored the functionalities surrounding computing machinery under expounding relations to their reasoning because designing user interfaces could not control computational exits and needed gates for robots to think guard channels. The basic decision set in the 21st century suited the need to design robust control reasoned under Machine Intelligence during soft-as-a-service, which increased its functional scope reserved for ordering only different view pipes, facilitating their design diffusers [15]. AI fundamentally transformed information technology by building computerized devices capable of advanced computations, high-speed data processing, and automation of tasks. The first systematic attempts at researching and creating artificial intelligence began as early as 1943, when McCulloch and Pitts created the 'Neural Network Model.' Later, in 1952, Arthur Samuel defined Artificial Intelligence as "the ability of a program to learn from experience." When society began discussing the impact of machine learning and artificial intelligence, scholars such as Alan Turing started comparing the intelligence of machines and humans [16]. In 1950, a committee was set up under his leadership, which later proposed the famous 'Turing Test', outlining principles for evaluating machine intelligence.

Having made significant advances in mathematics and computers, researchers in the US and UK developed systems capable of performing complex calculations and high-speed data processing. This technology was one of the building blocks for the first successful attempts at artificial intelligence. Neural Networks are examples of machine learning algorithms. Each node of a Neural Network offers certain features that the learning algorithm can investigate [17]. AI can detect internal infiltrations in information security systems where an internal threat could go unnoticed by a security administrator [18]. AI technology can trigger an alert upon correctly identifying breaches to network usage of non-scheduled access, unauthorized access attempts to systems outside of regular working hours, or signing into the systems from non-user terminals. Keeping track of a company's financial spending or personnel logs can be automated. AI algorithms can perform audits and compare given reports to the required parameters to identify discrepancies that repeat over time. AI can also achieve misleading presentations through the manipulation of facts [19].

Machine Intelligence is data-based reasoning employing technology that can learn by gathering information based on different inputs, which is then stored in its memory. This independence opens the door to a new realm, aware of operational capabilities realized through pattern recognition and data-driven decision-making, devoid of human involvement. The Logic Theorist (1956) and The General Problem Solver (1959) were the first two systems developed by Allen Newell and Herbert A [20]. Simon created. Computing specialists consider The Logic Theorist the very first AI program because this system could perform proofs of theorems *via* automated problem-solving and even solve problems like a human mathematician. The General Problem Solver worked as a problem-solving unit that split significant issues into smaller, more manageable heuristic units that could be solved step by step.

Symbolic AI and Expert Systems (1970s–1980s)

In the 1970s, AI researchers shifted from building rule-driven approaches to more sophisticated systems that could tackle practical problems within real-world domains. During this period, expert systems began to surface because they aimed to create automated decision-making systems that could function as professional specialists within particular domains [21].

Development of Expert Systems:

Expert systems offered an intelligent response using an underlying knowledge base and reasoning processed through frameworks that simulated a specified problem to be solved using the data set collected. Expert systems were used to excel at making decisions owing to the excellent reasoning processes, and the designed artificial intelligence systems emulated specialists in medicine, law, engineering, and other fields [22]. These decisions came from an inference engine that utilized a defined set of rules within a knowledge base.

MYCIN (1970s-1980s):

During the early 1970s, Stanford University developed one of the first expert systems, known as MYCIN, which is still celebrated as one of the most successful programs. MYCIN acted as a medical blood infection, anesthetics, diagnostic, and treatment planning aide for physicians. The system could compute the steps to manage and eliminate the infection and select the best treatment. MYCIN was unlike other medical decision systems because it could rationally explain the process that led to its conclusions [23]. One key objective achieved by MYCIN was laying the groundwork for developing new AI specialist applications, subsequently causing a significant rise in interest in AI technology for other industries such as finance, engineering, and business services.

Issues Regarding Symbolic AI

The development of expert systems resulted in some progress in the science of AI. However, their ability to represent knowledge and information accurately became their most significant limitation. With these systems, human experts had to encode their knowledge into the system, a complex process that was both time-intensive and prone to errors [24]. In reality, Symbolic AI systems had these problems because they were poorly equipped to type deficient or uncertain data, a common occurrence in real life.

Machine Learning and Statistical Models (1990s-2000s)

In the 1990s, traditional AI models were replaced by data-driven approaches, rendering symbolic AI obsolete. With advancements in big data and computer technology, it became possible for technology to perform tasks without requiring programming, making machine learning (ML) a subfield of AI that allows machines to learn from gathered data without pre-programming autonomously [25].

The Emergence of ML

Unlike expert systems, Machine Learning (ML) can use pattern recognition, enabling more efficient data processing. Furthermore, computerized systems could improve their processing through experience. Through the invention of supervised, unsupervised, and reinforcement learning algorithms, AI systems gained the capability to perform a plethora of tasks beyond the mundane, including tackling image and speech anomaly recognition [26].

Machine Learning Algorithms

Support Vector Machines (SVMs) became popular as strong classification algorithms that classify data with an optimal boundary that splits the data into various classes. Primary applications of SVM algorithms were in image and text analysis. Decision trees operate through a model in the shape of a tree that depicts the decisions and their consequences within a process. Because they allowed for a straightforward, understandable approach, decision trees became very popular in classification and regression problem domains. Combining many machine learning models using random forests and boosting methods improved predictions by dealing with individual models' bias and variance problems [27].

Applications of ML in the 1990s-2000s:

Early in 2000, Dragon NaturallySpeaking, along with other speech recognition systems, received enhancements for accuracy and started working *via* voice commands. Image tagging on social media and surveillance systems for detection and monitoring uses face and image recognition technologies based on convolutional neural networks. With machine learning, email systems could detect spam emails by analyzing the contents and the senders along with many other parameters, and by gathering multiple factors with system mix capabilities [28].

Deep Learning and Neural Networks (2010s-Present)

Artificial intelligence experienced a turning point around the 2010s with the birth of deep learning. Deep learning sits within the machine learning paradigm by utilizing artificial neural networks consisting of several layers, called deep networks, which are designed to perform big data analyses [29].

Deep Learning's Emergence:

The adoption of Deep Neural Networks (DNNs) was primarily because these networks automatically extracted complex features from fundamental chunks of data, such as pixel patterns within images and elements of speech audio. Making large datasets available alongside the faster training processes that GPUs provided to models was foundational to developing deep learning [30].

Integration of CNNs and RNNs Enables Progressively Advanced AI Capabilities

The imaging capabilities of Convolutional Neural Networks (CNNs) allowed the machines to perform object detection and face recognition at a human-competent level, along with innovative image classification. Recurrent Neural Networks (RNNs) with Long Short-Term Memory (LSTM) networks greatly enhanced the performance of Natural Language Processing (NLP) tasks, including translation, sentiment analysis, and speech recognition [31]. The image recognition contest saw the introduction of deep learning methods with Hinton and co's winning entry, a remarkable innovation in 2012. Subsequent advancements enabled deeper neural networks to penetrate many industries, marking the start of their commercial use. At Tesla and Waymo, the autonomous vehicle technology domain has benefited extensively from deep learning innovations in object detection, navigation, and decision-making algorithms. Now, deep learning capabilities allow Amazon Alexa, Google Assistant, and Apple Siri to function as voice interfaces that understand normal speech and provide more accurate automatic replies, elevating the user experience to another level.

Other Uses of Deep Learning:

Deep learning algorithms have significantly improved facial recognition systems; their enhanced precision makes them efficient for security, retail, social media, and private accounts. The industry is increasingly applying deep learning methods to analyze medical images, predict the outcomes of various procedures, and assist in designing novel therapeutics, thus enabling personalized medicine. The production of video games escalated in leaps and bounds owing to the implementation of deep learning in Artificial Intelligence programs such as AlphaGo and Pluribus that played against real-life opponents and won [32]. The milestone evaluation of the AI is shown in Table **2**.

Table 2. Evolution of AI by decade.

Period	Milestone	Description
1940s-1950s	Neural Network Model, Turing Test	Early theoretical foundations of AI and machine intelligence
1970s-1980s	Expert Systems like MYCIN	Rule-based systems for diagnostics and decision-making
1990s-2000s	Emergence of ML and SVMs	Shift to data-driven approaches with practical applications
2010s	Deep Learning and CNNs/RNNs	Breakthroughs in image, video, and speech recognition
2020s	AI in cybersecurity and automation	Integration into business, healthcare, defence, and proactive threat detection

Key AI Techniques

AI Techniques: A Comprehensive Overview

Artificial Intelligence (AI) is an area of computer science that implements various strategies or algorithms that enable machines to perform tasks that humans typically accomplish because of their complex cognitive nature. This can include learning from data, recognizing speech, and making decisions based on prior encounters. As such, there are fundamental techniques AI is built upon, and we look at some of these core techniques here [33].

Machine Learning (ML)

This area of AI is concerned with devising methods and algorithms that enable AI machines to learn through exposure, improve as they encounter more data sets, and require no sequential steps to achieve mastery. Be it analysis, sophisticated tasks such as diagnostics, or machine learning systems, they will make predictions or decisions based on observed patterns instead of rigid algorithms. Machine learning starkly contrasts conventional programming models wherein instructions are entered slave-like at the mercy of the programmer's guidance and preset algorithms [34]. The ability to alter behavior based on previously provided data takes center stage.

Types of Machine Learning: In terms of the learning process, machine learning can be broken down into three core types:

1. Supervised Learning:

Definition:

• With supervised learning, the model receives training through labeled data, meaning each input in the dataset has a corresponding output (label) attached to it. The model trains itself by evaluating its predictions against the actual outputs within the labeled dataset, and with time, learning processes make adjustments to minimize errors.

Example:

- With a spam email detector, the algorithm is trained on emails marked as "spam" and "not spam." Eventually, the algorithm starts recognizing specific patterns consistent with spam emails. It can predict if new incoming emails are expected to be categorized as spam or not.

Applications:

- Fraud Detection in Banking (detecting unusual transactions based on labeled data)
- Medical Diagnosis (predicting the probability of the occurrence of certain diseases based on the data of the patients)

2. Unsupervised Learning:

Definition:

- Unlike supervised learning, a model trained on unlabelled data is said to follow unsupervised learning. No predefined outputs are provided, requiring the model to formulate them by identifying data patterns, structures, and relationships.

Example:

- For customer segmentation, in unsupervised learning, customers are grouped into clusters based on similarities in purchasing behaviour, even if no labels such as "high-value customer" or "low-value customer" are associated with the data.

Applications:

- Market basket analysis (discovering associations between products bought together)
- Anomaly detection (identifying unusual patterns in financial transactions)

3. Reinforcement Learning:

Definition:

- Reinforcement Learning (RL) is a type of machine learning where an agent performs actions in a given environment and receives feedback in the form of rewards and punishments, which informs the learning process. The agent aims to optimize the total reward received over a defined period.

Example:

- In robotic navigation, a robot learns to circumvent obstacles through trial and error. The robot is rewarded when it moves closer to the goal and penalized if it runs into an obstacle. With time, it learns the best route to the destination.

Applications:

- Game AI (*e.g.*, AlphaGo: where the AI is capable of playing against itself and learns an optimal strategy)
- Robotics (object manipulation or space navigation learning)

Uses of Machine Learning

- **Banking Fraud Detection:** Machine learning techniques work with banking transactional data to detect and flag activity that exhibits fraud patterns.
- **Manufacturing Predictive Maintenance:** Predictive maintenance relies on ML algorithms that assess sensor data to forecast machine or equipment failure.
- **Marketing Customer Profiling:** Machine learning algorithms enable businesses to tailor their marketing techniques by grouping customers based on behaviors and preferences.

Deep Learning (DL)

Deep Learning (DL) is a field within machine learning that employs artificial neural networks that are rich in layers ("deep"), which are well adapted to learning data that presents high cardinality. Deep chained structures adeptly extract features and learn diverse patterns from data, especially with unstructured data for images, videos, and auditory signals. The transformation in AI propelled by deep learning follows the ease it has brought in executing tasks that involve understanding complex inputs such as speech, vision, and even linguistics [35].

Popular Deep Learning Models

Significant progress has been made in deep learning models across multiple domains, with tremendous architectures that are capable of performing specific tasks:

i. Convolutional Neural Networks (CNN):

Definition:

- CNNs are artificial neural networks that process data through multiple arrays (layers) of interconnected elements. They are most popularly used for computer vision. CNNs are designed to automatically and adaptively learn images' spatial hierarchies of features.

Example:

- A CNN can recognize and classify objects within an image and is used in systems designed for face recognition to discern people based on certain details, such as their features.

Applications:

- Defining elements in a spatial context, such as associating objects with images
- Analyzing medicine-related images, such as identifying tumors in X-Ray and MRI scans

ii. Recurrent Neural Networks (RNNs):

Definition:

- RNNs are part of deep learning algorithms designed to work with a sequence of objects like game scores, timelines, text, or even speech. They are suitable for sequential data; unlike other types of neural networks, RNNs can 'remember' some pieces through feedback loops that provide persistent information.

Example:

- RNNs can understand words that are spoken one after the other, capturing the sequential nature of speech, which can be helpful in speech recognition.

Applications:

- Language processing (i.e., anticipating the consecutive words within a phrase)
- Time series data analysis (i.e., predicting future stock values)

iii. Generative Adversarial Networks (GANs):

Definition:

- GANs are composed of two neural networks: a generator, which creates new data instances, and a discriminator, which evaluates them. They function in a competitive context, with the intent that the generator creates data qualitatively identical to actual data.

Example:

- For image production, realistic pictures of objects or scenes are synthesized by GANs, for instance, by creating artificial pictures of human faces.

Applications:

- Creation of images and videos (for instance, creation of synthetic art pieces)
- Increasing dataset size through the creation of additional data for machine learning (data augmentation)

Natural Language Processing (NLP)

Natural Language Processing, or NLP, is one of the domains of artificial intelligence whereby a machine can understand, interpret, and generate human language. It enables AI systems to perform functions such as translation, sentiment analysis, summarization, and many more by working with text, speech, and other forms of communication [36]. The NLP objectives are to remove the boundaries of human communication, interact with machines, and allow machines to enable verbal or written dialogues with humans to be presented in human language.

Uses of NLP

NLP has become necessary for several computer systems that use AI, including virtual assistants, chatbots, and text analyzers.

- **Chatbots and Virtual Assistants:** NLP algorithms make speech comprehension and response to voice commands possible through virtual assistants such as Amazon Alexa and Google Assistant.
- **Text Categorisation:** NLP allows for organizing text into set categories, such as identifying spam in emails and sorting news articles in topic-based stacks.
- **Speech Recognition and Translation:** NLP technologies enable the transformation of spoken words into written documentation and real-time language conversion, which is available in Google Translate.
- Social Media Sentiment Analysis - NLP algorithms classify social media and other platforms' comments, reviews, and responses as positive, negative, or neutral. Sentiment analysis has become increasingly popular in recent trending significant data phenomena as a primary tool for automated digital marketing.

Reinforcement Learning (RL)

Reinforcement learning involves a machine learning setting within which an agent makes decisions. The agent deals with an environment and, during the interaction, receives feedback on whether it chooses a good or a bad action [37]. The goal is to learn a policy that receives the most cumulative reward in the long run. RL is appropriate in applications that exhibit sequential and temporal dependency, such as robotics, gaming, dial and assist systems, and adaptive tailored recommendations.

Reinforcement learning has been successfully applied in a variety of non-static and multi-step decision-making processes:

- **Robotics:** This is the most common field exploring reinforcement learning strategies; for example, robots are trained to perform tasks like picking up objects, walking, and navigating complicated terrains. Robots learn through practice. The following are examples of the practical applications of AI:
- **Game AI:** RL has been applied to create AI systems capable of playing sophisticated games at a high level, such as AlphaGo, which beat world champions in the game of Go. RL is also used to create chess, poker, and video game AIs that can learn the best strategies to perform automatically [38].
- **Personalized Recommendations:** Companies like Netflix, YouTube, and Amazon use reinforcement learning to customize content recommendations to users based on their activity on the platform.

Having explored the foundational techniques of AI—including machine learning, deep learning, NLP, and reinforcement learning—we now turn our attention to one of AI's most pressing and transformative applications: cybersecurity. The dynamic nature of cyber threats requires intelligent, adaptive, and proactive defense mechanisms, which AI is uniquely positioned to provide.

AI's Role in Cybersecurity

AI's Role in Transforming Cybersecurity

With digital platforms and systems becoming more integrated, cyberattacks pose a significant threat to organizations in nearly every industry. The speed at which cyber threats are evolving is far outpacing the abilities of legacy cybersecurity tools like signature-based antivirus systems and rule-based intrusion detection systems (IDS). Outdated tools struggle to meet the increasing sophistication and frequency of cyberattacks [39].

Efficiency in combating known cyber-attacks is one area in which traditional cybersecurity systems excel. Relying on recognizing preset patterns makes them ineffective against more nebulous and advanced threats. The complexity of these attacks makes evasion easy, bypassing detection entirely [40]. In real-time, AI can transform cybersecurity and improve detection to the highest levels, surpassing the capabilities of traditional detection methods that rely on timestamps, human input, scanning massive amounts of data, and simplistic algorithms. Detecting threats, predictive analytics, and automated responses are the main components where AI optimizes cybersecurity the most. We will cover each of these critical details further down [41].

AI in Threat Detection

One of the most notable applications of AI in cyberspace is heightened threat detection. Unlike traditional security systems, which operate based on established rules, suspicious activities, and known signatures to identify threats using "known-attack" patterns, AI revolutionizes threat detection through sophisticated capabilities. These systems work very well at recognizing particular attacks but have weaknesses with emerging attacks that do not follow any known patterns [42]. Machine learning and anomaly detection powered by artificial intelligence do not require step-by-step programs to handle every possible situation and can learn from data. AI systems can consider enormous amounts of information from user traffic, parsing behavior, and other system elements to detect potential attack indicators.

AI The Role of Artificial Intelligence in Advanced Threat Detection

- Underfitting: AI algorithms have the potential to use extensive data to detect threats based on events and actions. For example, an AI-driven IDS would consider a network traffic spike abnormal relative to the baseline data it is operating on, rather than relying on known attack signatures [43].
- Behavior Analysis and Detection: AI can recognize outliers that defy expectations. Subordinate's actions, login activity, keywords, and network usage statistics pulled at certain time intervals can be scrutinized using AI to capture human actions like insider threats, commandeered accounts, or brute force attempts [44].
- Intrusion Detection System (IDS) AI can assess patterns in the recorded datasets and derive conclusions on detecting suspicious actions based on evidence through contemporaneous logs, access to the system, and user behavior. An AI IDS system would flag sudden spikes in data transfer or new, unfamiliar login locations, which may indicate DDoS attacks or brute-force login attempts. The AI could investigate and classify the event autonomously depending on anomaly severity, taking action or issuing alerts as needed [45].
- Real-Life Example: Imagine an AI system implemented in a bank that analyzes user transaction patterns for suspicious activities. If a customer supposedly makes a significant withdrawal from a geographically distant ATM, the AI

could flag this and alert security or block the action until further verification is conducted.

Using Predictive Analytics in Cybersecurity

AI predictive analytics is beneficial for forecasting possible cyber threats much before they happen. Conventional systems only take measures after an attack. However, AI utilizes historical data to model potential weaknesses, trends, and attack vectors with much more accuracy. Anticipatory action shifts the focus of defensive strategies on mitigating a breach rather than responding to one, lessening defensive conditional damage [46].

Ways AI Can Predict Cyber Attacks

- Threat Intelligence Aggregation: By examining external threat feeds, dark web monitoring, and internal logs, AI can aggregate, combine, and analyze information from various sources.
- Through pattern recognition from various sources, AI systems can forecast potential cyber-attacks in terms of location and timing and predict which systems or data would sustain the greatest exposure.
- Vulnerability Prediction: Using AI models, organizations can foretell which vulnerabilities are most likely to be attacked next by analyzing historical data from previous assaults. For example, AI systems might determine that an unpatched software vulnerability will soon be exploited because of prevailing attack patterns.

Predictive Threat Intelligence: AI platforms can compile threat information, such as data feeds from the Internet, dark web forums, and past incidents, to find patterns and make predictions of attack possibilities. For example, an AI system could monitor several business sectors and see an increase in discussions around ransomware on dark web forums [47]. The system would use these claims as sufficient grounds to notify healthcare sector organizations that they must be shielded against the expected attacks, allowing them to fortify their defences in anticipation.

Real-World Example: An e-commerce company is believed to be using a predictive threat intelligence platform to anticipate cyber-attacks on customer credentials on specific dates.

Automated Response in Cybersecurity

Cybersecurity precautions rely heavily on artificial intelligence to automate safety protocols for identified dangers. Response to incidents within conventional security systems is managed through human effort, which is risky since so much can go wrong within that period, from mistakes to greater damages [48]. With AI, actions can be taken preemptively to lessen exposure to damage, confine affected systems, and even disable harmful activity entirely, done in real-time.

How AI Automates Incident Response

- Immediate Responses: Immediately upon identifying a concern, take action to prevent it from escalating further. An example includes identifying obstacles; in this case, those infected by malware are automatically extracted from the networks.
- Automated Blocking: AI can also disable accounts suspected of being compromised without seeking permission from the admin or waiting for approval.
- Orchestrated response: AI can operate as part of a security orchestration framework for more advanced systems, which delivers an integrated coordinating response utilizing multiple employed security mechanisms.
- AI manages and prioritizes the most critical threats and can respond to issues algorithmically.

Automated Incident Response Systems: AI systems are designed to manage an elaborate array of attack scenarios, such as the example of Distributed Denial of Service (DDoS) attacks. In such cases, the AI system can automatically block requests from malicious sources without human intervention. In the case of credential stuffing, where attackers attempt to gain access through stolen username-password combinations, the AI could lock affected accounts or demand greater verification autonomously [49].

Real-World Example: In a corporate network setting, an AI system may identify an enormous spike in incoming requests from a single suspicious IP address. In this case, the system could automatically erase the alert, notify the security team, and start a more in-depth analysis without outsourcing new commands [50]. Moreover, the AI could quarantine a device with a detected malware infection to halt further contamination of other connected systems.

Benefits of AI in Cybersecurity

- **Speed:** Unlike humans, AI can process and analyse enormous data sets at staggering speeds, detecting threats and responding in a fraction of the time it would take traditional systems.
- **Accuracy:** Machine learning models improve with time, which means AI can identify threats with a precision that was previously unattainable. Additionally, AI's ability to discern patterns surpasses that of human analysts, improving reliability.

- **Proactivity:** Cyber defense strategies based on predictive analytics and anomaly detection allow AI systems to predict and prevent attacks before they occur, granting organizations proactive defense capabilities.
- **Cost-Effectiveness:** The result of autonomous systems performing numerous tasks previously assigned to security professionals translates into lowered manual monitoring and intervention, with security teams reallocating their responsibilities towards sophisticated analysis and strategic decision-making.
- **Challenges and Considerations:** While the application of AI in cybersecurity delivers significant benefits, the following should also be taken into consideration:
- **Data Privacy:** In AI, especially machine learning, personal or sensitive data is complex to protect due to the model's dependence on vast amounts of varied data. This raises concerns about compliance with data protection laws such as GDPR.
- **False Positives:** AI systems tend to misidentify normal activities as red flag events; the result is the phenomenon known as false positives. Depending on the algorithms used, these models will need constant recalibration over time to enhance precision.
- AI models and their scale require a lot of resources. Trained personnel and advanced computing infrastructure are essential.

By leveraging AI, cybersecurity can be performed with quicker, more precise detection, proactive threat evaluation, and automation of responses. The need for AI-driven systems will only increase with growing cyber threats that use more sophisticated attack methods. Through machine learning, predictive analytics, and automated incident response, AI provides a transformative approach to protecting organizational networks, data, and digital assets, enabling previously impossible protection through conventional techniques [51].

AI and the Shift Towards Proactive Security

In the past, cybersecurity systems have been built around a proactive approach, resolving issues only after an attempt has been made. This approach, while necessary, becomes increasingly difficult in a complex and fast-moving cyber threat environment. History will mark the introduction of Artificial Intelligence (AI) as the shift in cybersecurity strategy toward proactive defense mechanisms. These systems help mitigate exposure by identifying and neutralizing potential threats before they inflict damage. This proactive model permits organizations to defend boundaries and anticipate and strategically plan for future scenarios.

The ability of AI to analyze data, make predictions, and detect anomalies enables security teams to outsmart cybercriminals and significantly reduce the likelihood of breaches.

AI-Powered Threat Hunting

Threat hunting is searching for potential or imminent threats in a system or network. It generally occurs before the system has undergone any detection using primitive security mechanisms. Organizations have previously relied on automated systems that, based on preconfigured signatures, attempted to pick up known threats like viruses, malware, and phishing attacks. Such computerized systems struggle to intercept new, unknown threats that do not follow established patterns.

Malicious threat hunting powered by AI does not stop at raising reality-based alerts; it makes the processes proactive by automatically scanning structured and unstructured data to identify hidden threats in real-time. Anomalies and irregular behaviors that may indicate an attack, even if in a new and novel form, can be identified by AI systems powered by machine learning and anomaly detection AI algorithms. AI threat-hunting tools can analyze system activity in combination with historical data, user activity, and traffic patterns on the network to detect attacks well before they are launched.

How AI Powers Proactive Threat Hunting

i. **Scaling:** The age-old manual process of analyzing logs and network activity alongside other data types to uncover malicious functionalities and potential threats is time-consuming and burdens traditional threat hunting. Humans would overlook patterns and anomalies within large datasets. AI algorithms can analyze information in fragments, thus saving considerable time when responding to an attack.
ii. **Anomaly Detection:** An AI system anomaly detection threat hunting feature spots deviations from pre-established behavioral baselines. In AI systems, learning models are created to define and identify "normal" behavior for users, systems, and networks, and flag those that violate these thresholds as suspicious activities. Examples include, but are not limited to, data logins, transfers, and access to specific files. AI systems' capability to detect irregularities is a robust tool for detecting threats that might even exist in hiding.
iii. **Predictive Capabilities:** Situations that might happen can also be predicted by AI systems by relying on forecasts made from seen patterns in historical data. Holmes and others noted that machine learning models are good at spotting patterns, especially if they are looked at two steps ahead. This means that these

models analyze data by fully looking at the possible causes and their effects to determine the next place or time a specific cyberattack will occur. Predictive capability facilitates proactive defense mechanisms against threats for an organization.

Evaluating behavior against the threat-hunting algorithms in AI systems could be set for users, devices, and internet traffic. Through constant behavior analysis, AI can spot indicators of a cyber-attack or even an internal threat. For AI, flagging anomalies is simple; for example, if a user unlocks their credentials during business hours, an AI will track their current GPS. If the user is in a different geographical region, AI will flag their access to sensitive files as anomalous. AI does not solely monitor login details; in a specific case, AI can monitor whether users access files related to their departments. Even though this does not seem suspicious, actively trying to unlock sensitive financial documents after work hours will set off alarms. This suggests the account may have been compromised, but reveals a larger problem, telling the user that they are attempting to misuse access privileges. After determining this, the AI system can block users and limit them from accessing security protocols until proven safe [52].

For a more hands-on demonstration, let us consider a company that has an AI User and Entity Behaviour Analytics system integrated into its cybersecurity. The AI monitors user activities across the network without unusual behavior and recognizes abnormalities immediately. If an employee who can access client databases suddenly starts grabbing giant data sets from those systems at 3 am, they would be deemed unusual. The AI system immediately raises an alert upon detecting this anomaly, which helps the security team investigate and, if necessary, intervene before a data breach occurs.

Benefits of AI-Powered Threat Hunting

- **Immediate Threat Detection:** The speed at which AI tools analyze and process data sets is incomparable to human analysis. They can sift through data sets and recognize possibilities in real-time, ensuring that threats are detected much faster than traditional methods. This reduces the time cybercriminals have to exploit weaknesses.
- **Minimal Human Error:** Human error is an unfortunate reality when dealing with manual threat hunting, especially as the amount of data continues to grow. AI helps mitigate this risk by spotting patterns and anomalies using preset algorithms, meaning threats are expected to be identified more consistently without overlooking vital details.
- **Constant Supervision:** These systems never “sleep” nor take a break, unlike traditional methods, which operate on a reactive basis. AI threat-hunting systems

provide constant supervision of the networks and systems under surveillance. This level of vigilance is essential, especially in today's world, where breaches can happen at any moment.

- **Immediate Action:** AI-equipped systems can mitigate threats without delay by activating preset countermeasures, such as cutting off vulnerable links, blocking suspicious IPs, or locking the entire system. This initial precaution can mitigate damage from a cyberattack before it develops into a full-scale breach.
- **Enhanced Threat Intelligence:** AI can improve understanding of threats by integrating and analyzing data from multiple internal log files, threat intelligence feeds, and external sources like the dark web. This enables security analysts to remain ahead of emerging threats by tracking ongoing threat actor campaigns and their tactics, techniques, and procedures (TTPs).

The Future of AI in Threat Hunting

With new technologies and advancements in machine learning, the future of AI in cybersecurity is promising. Identifying increasingly sophisticated attack methods, including advanced persistent threats, zero-day vulnerabilities, and social engineering, is expected to be possible as AI systems become more advanced. AI will significantly automate security functions, allowing human security personnel to concentrate on high-level planning and operational decisions. AI will assist security teams in retaining control of larger and more complex environments by increasing SOC (security operations center) automation for threat detection, incident response, forensic analysis, and other advanced functions [53]. Moreover, threat-hunting tools will enhance AI's ability to deliver accurate context, providing enhanced AI threat-hunting functions. Contextual information, such as performing a business impact assessment or classifying an asset, combined with AI, empowers these systems to determine if an activity falls outside the established norms and how important it is to the organization. Therefore, this enables the organization to take action in a prioritized manner.

The use of AI in threat intelligence mitigates the challenges of identifying latent threats. It enhances the capabilities of organizations to anticipate risks and galvanize action before significant damage is inflicted. The shift of focus in cybersecurity from reactive to proactive defense exemplifies how AI is transforming the field. Furthermore, implementing machine learning, attack anomaly detection algorithms, and behavioral analytics enables AI augmentation of cybersecurity operations to adapt to current dynamically changing threat environments, thereby ensuring more precise and effective protection. Cybersecurity and other domains will rely on AI technologies to automate processes, adapt, and operate with greater intelligence, thus continuously providing security organizations with the means to defend and shield their digital resources from threats. The AI *vs* traditional threat hunting is displayed in Fig. (**3**).

Characteristic	Traditional Threat Hunting	AI-Powered Threat Hunting
Threat Detection	Reactive	Immediate
Human Error	High	Minimal
Supervision	Intermittent	Constant
Action Speed	Delayed	Immediate
Threat Intelligence	Limited	Enhanced
Data Analysis	Manual	Automated
Anomaly Detection	Difficult	Effective
Capabilities	None	Predictive

Fig. (3). AI *vs.* traditional threat hunting.

Ethical Considerations in AI-Driven Cybersecurity

As AI becomes more embedded in cybersecurity frameworks, ethical considerations must be at the forefront of deployment. Data privacy, algorithmic bias, explainability, and accountability become critical when autonomous systems decide about threat detection or access control. For instance, if an AI system erroneously flags a legitimate user as a security risk, it could lead to disruptions, loss of trust, or even legal consequences. It is essential to ensure that AI models are transparent and auditable and that human oversight remains part of critical decision-making loops. Ethical AI practices, such as fairness-aware training and bias detection, must be integrated into cybersecurity models to ensure responsible and equitable AI usage [54].

Challenges and Opportunities of AI in Cybersecurity

Though Artificial Intelligence (AI) enables improved threat detection and predictive analytics, automated responses, and other advances in cybersecurity, it also comes with its challenges. Organizations must address specific challenges in integrating AI systems into their cybersecurity strategies. Moreover, AI has the potential to open new opportunities that can enhance the efficiency and effectiveness of cybersecurity tactics. Addressing the challenges posed by AI can provide an immense strategic advantage. Computers can now perform "thinking" tasks at a speed and accuracy unparalleled by any human capabilities. However, the vast benefits of AI come with a distinct set of challenges in privacy and security. As strong as AI's methods are at protecting data, each system employed only lets existing holes be patched up. At the same time, new issues are mingling, rendering the first line of defense ineffective shortly due to the rushing fire they find themselves in.

Information Systems are everywhere. With activity logs, network traffic, communication records, and so much more being actively tracked and saved, AI systems have access to extensive volumes of pertinent data. With regulations such as GDPR and CCPA requiring a sophisticated approach to privacy, managing AI systems in personal data while ensuring security and regulation compliance is a balancing act of the highest order, as determined AI systems are capable of malice. Streamlining the work put into restoring the proprietary walls of data security to mitigate all risks is an unattainable task. None can endure the bounding failures caused by granting systems access to feat and history data streams full of personally identifiable information - bar AI-made markup misinformation for otherwise roaming unconfined cores, as allowing mess retention gives ease. Guardrails become emissions uncontrolled if technocrats predigest information

freely available. If the wall and guard cannot hinder, malfeasance enabled this deed: failure.

Compliance Issues:

Following industry regulations for data privacy and security is vital for many businesses. They must follow all applicable laws to avoid being sued and paying huge fines. However, using AI in cybersecurity must ensure compliance with statutes where data protection and privacy are respected, and data is handled sustainably.

For example, an AI algorithm monitors a network for signs of a possible cyber event. If poorly anonymized data is used, the system may scan for indicators of compromise and access private customer information, including credit card numbers and social security numbers. Organizations must establish robust data governance frameworks so that AI models only access relevant data and that sensitive information is safeguarded.

False Positives: AI solves intrusion and anomaly detection using machine-learning techniques to detect threats by analyzing data patterns. The processes can sometimes identify legitimate activities as threats, causing false alarms.

Impact of False Positives: Business operations can be disrupted by false alerts or other actions taken due to erroneous system reports. In one potential scenario, the AI in charge of supervising systems will consider an employee accessing files suspicious behavior and flag them as an insider threat, pulling forward processes that freeze business systems. Addressing the Challenge of False Positives: Reducing the rate of false positives is one of the many concerns AI has to deal with in cybersecurity. To improve accuracy, models must be iteratively refined, parameters calibrated, and additional data incorporated regularly. In time, AI systems should learn to distinguish between genuine activities and threats, thereby minimizing false positives. Imagine an AI-based application that analyses an organization's network traffic. When an AI model is not sufficiently trained on typical organizational activities, it may misinterpret a routine software update as a potential malware installation and flag it as a security incident. Increasing model tunability and providing abundant data will allow the AI to mitigate this issue.

***Resource-Intensive*:** The development, training, and upkeep of AI models consume vast resources and highly specialized skills, making them expensive and time-intensive undertakings.

***High Computational Demands*:** Processing large amounts of data and training models with AI algorithms, especially those used for deep learning, is very intensive regarding computational requirements. Obtaining and processing data usually entails using powerful GPUs, distributed computing, and cloud infrastructure; these services can be quite costly for Small and Medium-sized Enterprises (SMEs).

AI Model Maintenance as a Continuous Process: Regular monitoring and retraining of AI models is needed to ensure their effectiveness, as they require fresh data to operate efficiently. This maintains a constant resource demand for skilled personnel and quality data, constraining overall operational resources.

***Case in Point*:** Operational costs in extensive enterprise networks tend to soar when sophisticated hardware facilitates deep learning models for real-time threat detection due to massive data storage and processing requirements. Such systems demand specialized personnel, increasing operational costs, and complex system management and optimization.

The use of AI in Cybersecurity: AI in cybersecurity systems, however, offers opportunities that significantly improve the system whilst enhancing organizational responsiveness to threats and scaling security measures alongside increasing precision.

Immediate Action

Real-time data analysis and processing are essential factors that distinguish AI from other technologies. Cybersecurity systems depend on composite detection mechanisms that analyze past and present patterns to devise a response. However, heuristic systems designed with AI check for threats as they occur. This is a substantial step forward in reaction sophistication.

Automated Precautionary Actions: AIs can neutralize suspicious traffic, quarantine infected systems, or set up automated alerts. All of this is done in real-time, which decreases the time between cyber threat detection and action, imposing a slower crippling effect on the damage dealt.

Illustration: Consider the situation where an AI system monitors a corporate network. When an unauthorized access attempt is detected, the user account can be blocked, security personnel notified, and a system-wide check for further compromise initiated, all within seconds. Such an instance showcases the power of real-time actions in mitigating attacks in their infancy.

Scalability

In parallel with business growth and the expansion of its digital footprint, scalability ceases to be an option. Cybersecurity lacks this flexibility. Traditional systems find it overwhelming to manage vast data volumes, the growing complexity of networks, and the requirement of supervising a myriad of endpoints. While AI systems have challenges, they remain far more advanced in scalability.

Security Challenges: AI algorithms are uniquely tailored to sift through extensive datasets simultaneously, which makes them adaptable to substantially large sets of security data, such as network traffic, system logs, and user activity logs. This is especially true for large-scale enterprises or homes that utilize cloud-based systems that are perpetually generating data.

Example: In large business organizations, AI-enabled cybersecurity systems can expand their capabilities to automatically scan thousands of devices, peripherals, and network points simultaneously. They automatically detect and remediate security issues in real-time throughout the enterprise infrastructure. This turns the security silos into security affordances in critical digital infrastructures, permitting the enterprises to expand their digital footprints.

Enhanced Precision

AI systems can refine their performance by evaluating previous outcomes, which will improve over time. Consequently, new datasets will further enhance predictive capabilities and decrease the false alarm rate.

Continuous Improvement: AI models can receive fresh information, undergo modification, and be retrained to respond to emerging threats. The more instances of attacks the system sees, the better it can fine-tune its detection capabilities, leading to heightened precision. This adaptability helps AI-driven cybersecurity frameworks anticipate and respond to constantly changing cyberattack strategies.

Example: Take the case of a phishing detection system based on a machine learning algorithm. At first, the system is trained on a dataset consisting of emails only with shallow phishing attempts. After processing a fair number of emails containing burgeoning phishing attempts, the model has the potential to accurately flag sophisticated phishing attacks with a minimum of missed detections.

CONCLUSION

Surpassing the hurdles set by integrating new technologies with old ones, like complex AI systems to machine-armed security, is required to enjoy the resourcefulness of sophisticated AI-powered detection systems. They have evolved the cybersecurity framework forever, making them strategically proactive instead of reactive, dealing with problems as they arise and waiting for breaches to happen. With the capability to galvanize an enterprise's proactive power and overwhelmingly present the most reliable defence. As AI capabilities evolve, so too will the sophistication of cyber threats. Therefore, continuous research, ethical design, and interdisciplinary collaboration are expected to be essential to harness the full potential of AI in safeguarding digital infrastructure. Organizations can transition from reactive defence to proactive protection in an increasingly hostile cyber environment by building intelligent, adaptive, and ethical AI-driven security systems.

LIST OF ABBREVIATIONS

AI Artificial Intelligence

ML Machine Learning

DL Deep Learning

NLP Natural Language Processing

CNN Convolutional Neural Network

RNN Recurrent Neural Network

GAN Generative Adversarial Network

RL Reinforcement Learning

IDS Intrusion Detection System

DDoS Distributed Denial of Service

SVM Support Vector Machine

TTP Tactics Techniques, and Procedures

GDPR General Data Protection Regulation

CCPA California Consumer Privacy Act

SOC Security Operations Center

LSTM Long Short-Term Memory

GPS Global Positioning System

MRI Magnetic Resonance Imaging

IoT Internet of Things

REFERENCES

[1] S.S. Gill, M. Xu, C. Ottaviani, P. Patros, R. Bahsoon, A. Shaghaghi, and S. Uhlig, "AI for next generation computing: Emerging trends and future directions", *Internet of Things,* vol. 19, p. 100514, 2022.
[http://dx.doi.org/10.1016/j.iot.2022.100514]

[2] S. Yadala, A. Gurram, S. Yamunadevi, U. Veeresh, S.B. Latha, and T.N. Chitti, "Social media event summarization using neural networks", *2022 Third International Conference on Smart Technologies in Computing, Electrical and Electronics (ICSTCEE),* IEEE., pp. 1-7, 2022.
[http://dx.doi.org/10.1109/ICSTCEE56972.2022.10099963]

[3] S. Russell, and P. Norvig, *Artificial Intelligence: A Modern Approach.* 4th ed. Prentice Hall: Upper Saddle River, NJ, 2020.

[4] J. Schmidhuber, "Deep learning in neural networks: An overview", *Neural Netw.,* vol. 61, pp. 85-117, 2015.
[http://dx.doi.org/10.1016/j.neunet.2014.09.003] [PMID: 25462637]

[5] S. Banoth, and S. Yadala, "A hybrid deep learning framework for stock price forecasting with sentimental analysis", *In 2024 13th International Conference on System Modeling & Advancement in Research Trends (SMART),* pp. 467-471, 2024.
[http://dx.doi.org/10.1109/SMART63812.2024.10882215]

[6] P. Chillakuru, M. Madiajagan, K.V. Prashanth, S. Ambala, P.C. Shaker Reddy, and J. Pavan, "Enhancing wind power monitoring through motion deblurring with modified GoogleNet algorithm", *Soft Comput.,* vol. 28, no. 23-24, pp. 13965-13975, 2024.
[http://dx.doi.org/10.1007/s00500-023-08358-8]

[7] D Hoppe, "Trends and emerging technologies in AI", In: *Sustained Simulation Performance 2019 and 2020,* M. M. Resch, M Wossough, W Bez, E Focht, H Kobayashi, Eds., Springer: Cham, Switzerland, 2021.

[8] Koller, "AI for cybersecurity: An overview of algorithms and techniques", *Cybersecurity Journal,* vol.

5, no. 2, pp. 45-60, 2020.

[9] S. Tuli, S. Tuli, G. Wander, P. Wander, S.S. Gill, S. Dustdar, and O. Rana, "Next generation technologies for smart healthcare: challenges, vision, model, trends and future directions", *Internet technology letters,* vol. 3, no. 2, p. e145, 2020. [http://dx.doi.org/10.1002/itl2.145]

[10] J. Vinothkumar, and A. Karunamurthy, "Recent advancements in artificial intelligence technology: trends and implications", *Quing: International Journal of Multidisciplinary Scientific Research and Development,* vol. 2, no. 1, pp. 1-11, 2023. [http://dx.doi.org/10.54368/qijmsrd.2.1.0003]

[11] J. Wu, H. You, and J. Du, "AI generations: from AI 1", *0 to AI 4.0. Frontiers in Artificial Intelligence,* vol. 8, p. 1585629, 2025. [http://dx.doi.org/10.3389/frai.2025.1585629]

[12] M.D. Basith, P. Praveen, and P.C.S. Reddy, "Adaptive deep Q-GAN framework for enhanced breast cancer detection in medical imaging", *Biomedical Signal Processing and Control,* vol. 112, p. 108638, 2026. [http://dx.doi.org/10.1016/j.bspc.2025.108638]

[13] K. Sudheer Reddy, Sharma Niteesha, T. Ashalatha, and B. Ravi Raju, "An intelligent ensemble architecture to accurately predict housing price for smart cities", In: *Communications in computer and information science*, 2024, pp. 110-122.

[14] M. Chen, and Z. Zhao, "Machine learning for predictive cyber defense", *International Journal of Cybersecurity,* vol. 8, no. 4, pp. 28-39, 2019.

[15] O.U. Khan, "The future of cybersecurity: Leveraging artificial intelligence to combat evolving threats and enhance digital defense strategies", *J. Comput. Anal. Appl.,* vol. 33, p. 8, 2024.

[16] R Samrin, P. C. S. Reddy, K Arun Kumar, N Deepthi, C Mithra, Y Sucharitha, and G. K. Thakur, "A hybrid deep learning-based framework for prediction of rice yield through integration of biophysical parameters and optical remote sensing data in India", *Journal of Atmospheric and Solar-Terrestrial Physics,* vol. 279, p. 106734, 2026. [http://dx.doi.org/10.1016/j.jastp.2026.106734]

[17] X.L.L. Zhang, and Y. Liu, "A survey of AI-based detection methods for cyber attacks", *Comput. Netw.,* vol. 112, pp. 1-18, 2018.

[18] V.K. Bukkarayasamudram, P.C.S. Reddy, and K. Arun Kumar, "Quantum computing revolution in healthcare: a systematic review of applications, issues and future directions", *Artif Intell Rev,* vol. 58, p. 389, 2025. [http://dx.doi.org/10.1007/s10462-025-11381-w]

[19] L.K. Grover, "Quantum computing and artificial intelligence: A new horizon", *Quantum Computing Review,* vol. 3, no. 2, pp. 45-62, 2019.

[20] S.Y. Shih, "AI-powered cybersecurity in financial services", *Journal of Financial Technology,* vol. 15, no. 3, pp. 98-112, 2021.

[21] G. Delbrück, "Artificial intelligence in cyber defense: Theory and applications", *Cyber Defense Review,* vol. 10, no. 1, pp. 89-107, 2022.

[22] M.A.H. Fahim, and A.M. Salama, "Cybersecurity and AI: A comprehensive review", *Comput. Secur.,* vol. 73, pp. 178-195, 2018.

[23] L. Thompson, "Machine learning in cybersecurity: Case studies and insights", *IEEE Trans. Netw. Serv. Manag.,* vol. 17, no. 2, pp. 225-240, 2020.

[24] Albrecht, "Robustness in AI systems for cybersecurity", *in Proceedings of the IEEE International Conference on Computer Vision,* Venice, Italy, pp. 1289-1302, 2019.

[25] P Ravali, P. C. S. Reddy, and P Praveen, "An efficient neuro-framework for brain tumor classification

using a CNN-based self-supervised learning approach with genetic optimizations", *Current Neuropharmacology,* 2025.
[http://dx.doi.org/10.2174/011570159X378103250806214613]

[26] K.S.R. Anjaneyulu, "Reinforcement learning for autonomous cyber defense", *Journal of Cyber Defense,* vol. 12, no. 1, pp. 34-47, 2021.

[27] A.T. Somnathe, V.T. Selvi, N.G. Stepha, M.T. Kingslin, F.M. Inamdar, and P.C.S. Reddy, "An intelligent traffic conflict prediction using deep learning with long-term evolution access data", *In 2025 3rd International Conference on Smart Systems for applications in Electrical Sciences (ICSSES),* pp. 1-6, 2025.
[http://dx.doi.org/10.1109/ICSSES64899.2025.11010032]

[28] R. Malin, "AI-based anomaly detection for network intrusions", *Network Security Journal,* vol. 9, no. 4, pp. 234-245, 2020.

[29] J.M.L. Gauthier, "Using AI to predict cybersecurity threats: Case studies and insights", *Journal of Cyber Intelligence,* vol. 7, no. 2, pp. 1-16, 2020.

[30] S. Zohar, "Ethical Implications of AI in Cybersecurity", *AI and Society Journal,* vol. 35, pp. 112-127, 2019.

[31] B. Chen, "Predictive Analytics in AI for Cybersecurity", *Cyber Security Review,* vol. 4, pp. 21-30, 2021.

[32] Srinivasa Reddy, "Neural Network Aided Optimized Auto Encoder and Decoder for Detection of Covid-19 and Pneumonia Using Ct-Scan", *J. Theor. Appl. Inf. Technol.,* vol. 100, p. 6346, 2022.

[33] E Anupriya, M Thaile, C Ponnusamy, and L. M. Narayana, "Heart Diseases Prediction Using Machine Learning Algorithms", In: *2023 International Conference on Computer Communication and Informatics (ICCCI)*, Jan 2023.
[http://dx.doi.org/10.1109/ICCCI56745.2023.10128590]

[34] A. A. Elngar, D. Oliva, V. E. Balas, Ed., *Artificial Intelligence Using Federated Learning: Fundamentals, Challenges, and Applications* 1st. CRC Press, 2024.
[http://dx.doi.org/10.1201/9781003482000]

[35] B. Ramakrishna, M. Nagabhushana Rao, and R.B. Pittala, "Importance of social media in emergency communication networks: A survey", *J. Adv. Res. Dyn. Control Syst,* vol. 10, no. 7, pp. 1715-1720, 2018.

[36] V. Padmavathi, C.N. Sujatha, V. Sitharamulu, K. Sudheer Reddy, and A. Mallikarjuna Reddy, "Introduction to quantum computing", *In Evolution and Applications of Quantum Computing.,* 2023.
[http://dx.doi.org/10.1002/9781119905172.ch1]

[37] S. Y and S. R. K, "Detection of breast cancer by leveraging vision transformer model", *2024 3rd International Conference on Automation, Computing and Renewable Systems (ICACRS),* Pudukkottai, India, pp. 984-990, 2024.

[38] S. Yerramaneni, and S.K. Reddy, "A review on breast cancer detection using machine learning techniques", *International Journal of Data Mining, Modelling and Management,* vol. 17, no. 2, pp. 142-164, 2025.
[http://dx.doi.org/10.1504/IJDMMM.2025.146586]

[39] V.S. Pittala, P. Cheraku, P. Somaraju, R.B. Pittala, P. Nagababu, and K. Gopi, "High-dimensional data-driven pneumonia diagnosis using ANFIS", *J. Theor. Appl. Inf. Technol.,* vol. 102, no. 12, pp. 5044-5051, 2024.

[40] R.B. Pittala, B.R. Tejopriya, and E. Pala, "Study of speech recognition using CNN", *2nd Int. Conf. Artif. Intell. Smart Energy (ICAIS),* pp. 150-155, .Coimbatore, India

[41] S Kaur, S Bansal, and A Sharma, "Future Trends and Emerging Possibilities in AI", In: *Navigating Data Science: Unleashing the Creative Potential of Artificial Intelligence* Emerald Publishingpp. 127-

148.
[http://dx.doi.org/10.1108/978-1-83608-298-920251008]

[42] E Anupriya, P. M. Thaile, and C. P. M. Yasaswini, "Image based plant disease detection model using convolution neural network", In: *2023 International Conference on Computer Communication and Informatics (ICCCI)*, Jan 2023.
[http://dx.doi.org/10.1109/ICCCI56745.2023.10128618]

[43] G. Arun, P.C.S. Reddy, N. Budati, B. Rebecca, S. Perumalla, and V.B. Gujar, "A deep learning framework for diabetes prediction: PIMA indian dataset", *2024 International Conference on Innovative Computing, Intelligent Communication and Smart Electrical Systems (ICSES),* IEEE., pp. 1-6, 2024.

[44] B. Rambabu, B. Vikranth, Medikonda Asha Kiran, Satyanarayana Nimmala, and L. Swathi. "Hybrid swarm intelligence approach for energy efficient clustering and routing in wireless sensor networks". *Congress on Control, Robotics, and Mechatronics.* Springer Nature Singapore: Singapore, 2024, pp. 131-142.
[http://dx.doi.org/10.1007/978-981-97-7094-6_10]

[45] A. Sriram, N. Sharma, D.K.S. Reddy, and G.L.A. Babu, "Automated irrigation system for agriculture", *Int. J. Innov. Technol. Explor. Eng.,* vol. 8, no. 9, pp. 53-56, 2019.
[http://dx.doi.org/10.35940/ijitee.I7630.078919]

[46] J.R. Borre, G.C. Romero, and J. Ramírez, "Sustainable purchasing trends in new consumer generations: AI´ s role", *Procedia Computer Science,* vol. 241, pp. 539-545, 2024.
[http://dx.doi.org/10.1016/j.procs.2024.08.077]

[47] S Anusha, M Ezhilvandan, S Gayathri, V Sivaraman, and A. T. P., "Emerging trends in edge AI for Industry 4.0 and 5.0: Technologies, applications, and challenges", In: *AI Innovations in Service and Tourism Marketing*, 2024, pp. 211-228.
[http://dx.doi.org/10.4018/979-8-3693-7909-7.ch001]

[48] A Sharma, J Nagdiya, and S Thomas, "Transitioning from traditional artificial intelligence to emerging trends: Exploring paradigm shifts, challenges, and opportunities", In: *Transforming Industries, Empowering Societies* Elsevier, 2026, pp. 3-14.
[http://dx.doi.org/10.1016/B978-0-443-32878-7.00012-2]

[49] K Reddy, and C Srinagesh, "Fostering problem solving through innovative knowledge events", In: *2013 8th International Conference on Computer Science & Education.* IEEE, 2013.

[50] Z. Shao, R. Zhao, S. Yuan, M. Ding, and Y. Wang, "Tracing the evolution of AI in the past decade and forecasting the emerging trends", *Expert Systems with Applications,* vol. 209, p. 118221, 2022.
[http://dx.doi.org/10.1016/j.eswa.2022.118221]

[51] K. S. Reddy, G. P. S. Varma, and S. S. S. Reddy, "Understanding the scope of web usage mining & applications of web data usage patterns", In: *2012 International Conference on Computing, Communication and Applications*, Dindigul, India, 2012.
[http://dx.doi.org/10.1109/ICCCA.2012.6179230]

[52] A. P. Rao, and K. S. Reddy, "Automated soil residue levels detecting device with IoT interface", In: *Challenges and Applications of Data Analytics in Social Perspectives* IGI Global, 2021, pp. 123-135.

[53] C.N.S. Kumar, V.P. Kumar, and D.K.S. Reddy, "Similarity matching of pairs of text using CACT algorithm", *Int. J. Eng. Adv. Technol.,* vol. 8, no. 6, pp. 2296-2298, 2019.
[http://dx.doi.org/10.35940/ijeat.F8685.088619]

[54] S. Ali, M. Sohail, S.B.H. Shah, D. Koundal, M.A. Hassan, A. Abdollahi, and I.U. Khan, "New trends and advancement in next generation mobile wireless communication (6G): a survey", *Wireless Communications and Mobile Computing,* vol. 2021, no. 1, p. 9614520, 2021.
[http://dx.doi.org/10.1155/2021/9614520]

SUBJECT INDEX

A

B

C

D

E

F

G

I

Pundru Chandra Shaker Reddy, Yadala Sucharitha, & Thillaiarasu N (Eds.)

W

X

Y

Z

www.ingramcontent.com/pod-product-compliance
Lightning Source LLC
LaVergne TN
LVHW070945210926
848482LV00002B/103
* 9 7 9 8 8 9 8 8 1 3 8 6 4 *